THE
EUROPEAN ARREST WARRANT
IN
IRELAND

THE
EUROPEAN ARREST WARRANT
IN
IRELAND

REMY FARRELL
Barrister-at-Law

ANTHONY HANRAHAN
Barrister-at-Law

Published by
Clarus Press Ltd,
Griffith Campus,
South Circular Road,
Dublin 8.

Typeset by
Amnet International,
30 Pembroke Street,
Dublin 2.

Printed by
MPG Books Ltd
Victoria Square, Bodmin, Cornwall.

ISBN
978-1-905536-34-4

Quae dum in Asia geruntur, accidit casu, ut legati Prusiae Romae apud L. Quintium Flamininum consularem cenarent atque ibi de Hannibale mentione facta ex his unus diceret eum in Prusiae regno esse. Id postero die Flamininus senatui detulit. Patres conscripti, qui Hannibale vivo numquam se sine insidiis futuros existimarent, legatos in Bithyniam miserunt, in his Flamininum, qui ab rege peterent, ne inimicissimum suum secum haberet sibique dederet. His Prusia negare ausus non est: illud recusavit, ne id a se fieri postularent, quod adversus ius hospitii esset: ipsi, si possent, comprehenderent; locum ubi esset, facile inventuros. Hannibal enim uno loco se tenebat, in castello, quod ei a rege datum erat muneri, idque sic aedificarat, ut in omnibus partibus aedificii exitus haberet, scilicet verens, ne usu veniret, quod accidit. Huc cum legati Romanorum venissent ac multitudine domum eius circumdedissent, puer ab ianua prospiciens Hannibali dixit plures praeter consuetudinem armatos apparere. Qui imperavit ei, ut omnes fores aedificii circumiret ac propere sibi nuntiaret, num eodem modo undique obsideretur. Puer cum celeriter, quid esset, renuntiasset omnisque exitus occupatos ostendisset, sensit id non fortuito factum, sed se peti neque sibi diutius vitam esse retinendam. Quam ne alieno arbitrio dimitteret, memor pristinarum virtutum venenum, quod semper secum habere consuerat, sumpsit.

Nepos, Liber de excellentibus ducibus exterarum gentium: Hannibal XII

FOREWORD

The authors are to be congratulated in providing judges and practitioners in this ever-developing area of law with a textbook of such quality both in terms of its content, style and readability. It will undoubtedly become an indispensable aid for those whose professional practice forces them to grapple with the undoubted difficulties frequently encountered in applications for surrender on foot of a European arrest warrant.

As the authors themselves refer to in their Preface, a stated objective of the Council Framework Decision of 13 June 2002 (2002/584/JHA) was *"the introduction of a new simplified system of surrender of sentenced or suspected persons for the purposes of execution or prosecution of criminal sentences [which] makes it possible to remove the complexity and potential for delay inherent in the present extradition procedures"*.

The Framework Decision does not have direct effect, and in this jurisdiction required the enactment of the European Arrest Warrant Act 2003 in order to give effect to its provisions, some of which are mandatory and others of which are optional. The manner in which the Oireachtas chose to enact the Act of 2003 has been described judicially as "idiosyncratic", and the large number of judgments both of the High Court and the Supreme Court since 1 January 2004 is itself testament to the fact that this stated objective has not been achieved, and that fresh complexities have been born, which, together with the sheer volume of warrants which are transmitted to this State, make it inevitable that delays persist despite the best efforts of the courts to process them expeditiously and efficiently.

It was the tragic events of 11 September 2001 at the World Trade Centre in New York which swiftly provided an impetus at the European Council to introduce the European arrest warrant. However, it was in October 1999 at a European Council Summit meeting at Tampere under the Finnish Presidency, in the context of creating an area of freedom, security and justice in the European Union, that a number of measures were first considered, including the abolition of existing extradition procedures and their replacement by a simple and fast-tracked system for the transfer of fugitives between Member States in compliance with Article 6 of the Treaty on European Union. Other measures considered included a European Evidence Warrant and enhanced mutual recognition of judicial decisions and judgments. Some progress was made but without any perceivable urgency. That sense of urgency came following 9/11. In fact nine days later on the 20 September 2001 the Justice and Home Affairs Council met and discussed, inter alia, a proposal for Framework Decision on the approximation of Member States' criminal laws with a view to establishing a common definition of a terrorist act and laying down common criminal sanctions and a Framework Decision on the creation of the European arrest warrant. A strict timetable for these measures was agreed. By the time the European Council met again at Laeken in December 2001, the Framework Decision had been drafted, and with commendable speed, all Member States adopted Framework Decision on the European arrest warrant on 13 June 2001 to be implemented nationally by 1 January 2004.

Given the political context in which these new surrender arrangements came into existence, one would be forgiven for believing that the principal focus of Member States was on the prevention of terrorism and ensuring that within the European Union there would be no hiding place for those involved in terrorism. Having been the judge assigned to hear applications for surrender since 1 January 2001 I can say with confidence that of the many hundreds of such applications which I have heard since that date, scarcely more than one handful have involved any act of terrorism or even an element of serious organised crime. While many warrants disclose serious crimes such as murder, rape, sexual assault, assault causing harm, and a myriad of different drugs offences, many on the other hand disclose offences at the lower end of seriousness, the most memorable being the theft of three chickens and one bicycle!

While it is obviously a worthy and desirable objective that criminals should not be able to avoid justice by fleeing to another jurisdiction, and that there should be surrender arrangements in place to facilitate the speedy and efficient return of such persons to the state who wishes to prosecute or punish them, there must be a question over the manner in which minimum gravity has been defined in the Framework Decision for the purpose of a European arrest warrant. Currently, the volume of warrants arriving in this State in respect of relatively minor offences is causing unavoidable delays in the hearing of applications, and of course imposes a considerable expense upon the State which is obliged to provide legal advice and representation to the person sought as well as interpretation. There are other significant expenses in terms of An Garda Siochána, the Prison Service and the Courts Service, which in the majority of cases are out of all proportion to the offence for which surrender is sought by the issuing state.

While the Framework Decision provides a list of 32 categories of offence for which double criminality/correspondence is not required to be verified, I can see no reason why that list could not be added to by the inclusion of commonplace and easily understood offences, which are common in all jurisdictions, such as theft, robbery, burglary and assault. That would add greatly to the stated objective of simplifying and expediting applications for surrender.

There are many shortcomings in the Framework Decision and in the legislation which gives effect to it. The original Act has been amended on two occasions in an effort to improve it. More work undoubtedly needs to be done. The authors of this volume refer to many of these difficulties, and admirably and concisely refer to and discuss the many judgments delivered both in the High Court and Supreme Court, who have spared no effort in trying to resolve them and make sense of the Act in the light of the Framework Decision in order to achieve its objectives. We are all in their debt.

Michael D. Peart
The High Court
Dublin
14th December, 2010

PREFACE

For most practitioners who specialise in the area of criminal law it had long been the case the European Law was an obscure topic best left to practitioners of a civil bent who were concerned with the habitats of rare snails and the relative curvature of imported bananas. However, the creation of the "third pillar" of EU law by the Maastricht Treaty and the more recent innovations of the Lisbon Treaty have meant that justice and home affairs issues are now deeply embedded within the law making structures of the Union.

The European Arrest Warrant Act 2003 was the first piece of domestic legislation promulgated on foot of a Framework Decision. Given the constraints of Title VI of the EU Treaty which were then applicable the Oireachtas did not, indeed could not, concern itself unduly with the underlying objectives of the Act it passed. Its sole legislative function was to give effect to those objectives rather than consider their merits or demerits. It is perhaps unsurprising that there would seem to have been a lack of engagement on the part of the Oireachtas in the legislative process which resulted in the 2003 Act.

As originally passed the European Arrest Warrant Act 2003 was essentially unworkable. Rather than simplifying the process of surrender it rendered it impossibly complicated – the case of *Minister for Justice, Equality and Law Reform v Gokano*[1] demonstrates the bewildering complexity of the system that replaced the procedure under the Extradition Act 1965. Whilst matters have improved considerably in the interim this has been largely as a result of wholesale legislative emergency surgery in the form of the Criminal Justice (Terrorist Offences) Act 2005 and the Criminal Justice (Miscellaneous Provisions) Act 2009.

However, significant problems remain. The comments of Murray CJ in the recent case of *Rimsa v Governor of Cloverhill Prison*[2] in relation to the apparent incorporation of, at least parts of, the Framework Decision in a directly effective manner into the 2003 Act ring true:

> In *Altaravicius* … I referred to this manner of legislating, in restrained language, as "idiosyncratic". It is a most unsatisfactory way of legislating and I still consider that I am expressing myself in restrained terms.

That case neatly demonstrated the difficulties that inevitably arise from such an approach. In that regard it is somewhat dispiriting to note that a similar approach, albeit to a lesser extent, has been taken with the Criminal Justice (Mutual Assistance) Act, 2008. In *Rimsa* the Chief Justice predicted that the manner in which the Framework Decision has been incorporated will inevitably lead to further litigation.

Quite apart from concerns as to the manner in which the Framework Decision has been invoked in a directly effective fashion in the Act one might also wonder when the penny will drop with our European neighbours that that Act has apparently repealed entirely the rule of specialty in relation to those surrendered into the State.

---

[1] [2004] 3 IR 216.

[2] [2010] IESC 47.

Such criticisms are made not in a spirit of frustration but rather in an attempt to be constructive. The flood of litigation predicted by the Chief Justice is not likely to be a source of anxiety to any right thinking member of the Irish Bar. Indeed the *corpus iuris* which has already developed in relation to the European arrest warrant over the last seven years is of itself impressive, although this is perhaps attributable to the conspicuous dedication of certain members of the judiciary rather than the ingenuity of lawyers.

At a time when criminal justice legislation is frequently criticised as being imposed by government with little debate or opportunity for comment or amendment by the legislature it might well be said that such concerns apply with even greater force to measures emanating from Europe. The law of extradition and surrender is, at times, exquisitely complex and difficult. It contains exotic sounding concepts of international criminal law such as *ne bis in idem* and the rule of specialty. The same is likely to be true of other instruments of EU law which will require implementation by way of domestic legislation in the future many of which will relate to substantive as opposed to procedural criminal law. It remains to be seen whether the lessons so readily apparent from the experience of the courts with the European Arrest Warrant Act 2003 will be learned.

The task of writing any legal textbook is ultimately thankless, joyless and, we are assured by our publisher, David McCartney, entirely unprofitable. Nevertheless that task has been rendered immeasurably less difficult by the assistance of a great many colleagues who have passed on obscure judgments, allowed their submissions to be plagiarised by the authors (knowingly or otherwise) and provided advice and assistance along the way. Particular thanks are due to James Dwyer , Anne Marie Lawlor, Ronan Kennedy, Catherine Almond, Ronan Munro, Patrick Gageby SC, John Fitzgerald, Robert Barron SC, John Byrne, Rebecca Smith, Shane Murphy SC, Katherine McGillicuddy, Brian Gageby, Garnett Orange, Aisling Dunne, Michael Bowman, Lisa Dempsey, Aileen Donnelly SC, Elva Duffy, Hugh Hartnett SC (who insightfully described extradition law as being just like drunk driving with airplanes), Paddy McGrath, Tony McGillicuddy, Kathleen Noctor, Tom O'Connell SC and Maurice Collins SC (who the authors note with surprise and a little sadness has never been acknowledged in any textbook heretofore).

Thanks are also due those in the Office of the Chief State Solicitor who provided various hard to find and ex tempore judgements: Jevon Alcock, Karl Gordon, Hugh Dockry, Eamon Wilson, Joseph Maguire, Jean Murray and Roy Pearson. Special thanks are due to Ken Ruane who was pestered relentlessly over a period of two years for the most obscure judgments and papers and came up with the goods on each and every occasion. We are also grateful to the anonymous souls in the Office of the Attorney General who compiled and kept updated the list of cases circulated to counsel for the Minister without which this book would be much less comprehensive than it hopefully is.

We are also indebted to friends and family for ongoing support and encouragement over the last two years.

Finally, special thanks are due to our publisher David McCartney of Clarus Press who knew when to push us and much more importantly when not to.

12th December 2010

Siem Reap.

CONTENTS

CONTENTS

TABLE OF CASES

TABLE OF LEGISLATION

Part I
The European Arrest Warrant

CHAPTER 1

The Nature of the European Arrest Warrant

INTRODUCTION

The European arrest warrant is generally regarded as a significant innovation when compared with the system of extradition which operated heretofore between Member States of the European Union. In a strict sense the new system is not one of extradition as such but rather one of rendition. Whilst the distinction between the two may seem somewhat technical the practical implications are potentially far-reaching. **1–01**

THE NATURE OF EXTRADITION

The general idea of extradition is easily defined as the handing over of a person who either stands convicted or accused of a crime for the purpose of being tried or punished for it. The practical application of the idea is considerably more complex largely due to the differences between various legal systems and the idea that an obligation on one state to hand over a fugitive (who may be a citizen of that state) somehow offends against the principle of state sovereignty. Add to this the frequently arising political concerns that may surround a particular case and it is not difficult to understand why it is that the law of extradition is extremely **1–02** complex. In order to understand and appreciate the innovation that the European arrest warrant represents it is first necessary to have some understanding of the process that it is in large part intended to replace.

1-03 Historically the question of extradition has been a matter for the executive branch of government rather than the judicial branch. After all the nature of a request for extradition is a request between the executive branches of two sovereign governments rather than as between their respective judiciaries. This has, perhaps, been less apparent in this jurisdiction where the judiciary have played a much greater role in traditional extradition proceedings than in other jurisdictions where the role of the judiciary has been to do little more than confirm that the request for extradition satisfies the relevant formal requirements. Indeed on occasion the judiciary here have intimated that it is their function rather than that of the executive to exercise the appropriate discretion in relation to extradition requests. In *Aamand v Smithwick*[1] the court briefly considered the discretion given by the European Convention on Extradition 1957 in relation to extra-territorial offences and made the assumption that it was for the court to exercise that discretion in whatever way seemed appropriate:

> "There are no grounds on which it is possible in the provisions of this sub-Article of the Convention to ascertain any basis consistent with justice in which a court would have as it were a discretion to refuse extradition under the circumstances provided for in Article 7.2 in one case and to grant it in another."

1-04 It appears not to have occurred to the court that the discretion provided for in the treaty in question was left over to the executive rather than the judiciary. Indeed when one considers the scheme of the 1965 Act which still governs extradition to non-EU states it is reasonably clear that the function of the court is simply to confirm that the various conditions laid down in the legislation and treaty have been complied with. There is no question of the court exercising any discretion as to whether or not the person sought should be extradited.

1-05 The 1965 Act requires the Minister for Justice and Law Reform to certify the extradition request before it is presented to the High Court which will then issue an arrest warrant. Insofar as the underlying extradition treaty will allow for any discretion to be exercised this will occur before the Minister certifies the request and as such is a purely executive function. At first glance it is surprising that the manner in which the courts here have involved themselves so centrally in the extradition process has not lead to some tension as between them and the executive. However, when one considers the frequently highly politically charged nature of many extradition requests in the 1970s and 1980s it is difficult to avoid the conclusion that the executive branch of government was by and large content to leave such matters to the courts.

1-06 In many other jurisdictions the question of extradition was almost purely one of executive discretion in respect of which there was little or no review provided for by the courts. Extradition was seen as being an almost entirely diplomatic (and by extension political) issue. In such instances the only function of the courts was a purely formal one to certify the request as being in order.

1-07 One of the effects of an extensive involvement by the judiciary in the extradition process has been a significant increase in the time it takes to process requests. The procedure envisaged by the 1965 Act provides for a two stage process. The first

---

[1] [1995] 1 ILRM 61.

stage is the presentation of the request by the requesting state to the Minister. This will frequently result in a request for further information or clarification and is often the subject of considerable delay given the need to obtain translations of documents or legal advice at both ends of the process. A weakness of this process is that it is difficult to set out either in legislation or in the underlying treaties the extent of the information that will be required in a given case. Whilst the treaty will set out the documentation that must be presented to the Minister[2] the requirements are generic rather than specific. Where issues arise in relation to substantive issues such as correspondence of offences it is frequently necessary to seek further information in order to show that the offence in question would also be a crime in this jurisdiction. As such the 1965 Act does not stipulate a standard format for requests which may be adopted by requesting state.

Once the request is in order and duly certified an application[3] is then made to the High Court for an arrest warrant on foot of which the requested person is ultimately brought before the court. At that stage the substantive issues of extradition law will be litigated and quite possibly appealed. It is not unusual for this process to take months or even years.　　　　　　　　　　　　　　　　　　　　　　　　　**1–08**

THE EUROPEAN ARREST WARRANT — AN INNOVATION

It is primarily these two issues of complexity of procedure and delay which the　**1–09** European arrest warrant seeks to address. The Framework Decision which underlies the 2003 Act is explicit in this aim which it recites as being:

> "…the introduction of a new simplified system of surrender of sentenced or suspected persons for the purposes of execution or prosecution of criminal sentences makes it possible to remove the complexity and potential for delay inherent in the present extradition procedures. Traditional cooperation relations which have prevailed up till now between Member States should be replaced by a system of free movement of judicial decisions in criminal matters, covering both pre-sentence and final decisions, within an area of freedom, security and justice."[4]

In other words the Framework Decision envisages no less than the total abolition　**1–10** of the pre-existing extradition procedures as between Member States in favour of a system of mutual recognition of "judicial decisions on criminal matters" i.e. convictions, sentences, arrest warrants and other orders having equivalent effect. It achieves this by putting in place a system whereby "judicial authorities" are allowed to communicate with each other for the purpose of implementing judicial decisions. In effect what the Framework Decision seeks to do is to cut out the middle man in the form of the executive and remove decisions in relation to extradition (or more properly "surrender") from a political and diplomatic context into a purely judicial context. Necessarily this means that questions of political or diplomatic expedience no longer feature in relation to surrender requests which are now dealt with purely on the basis of whether or not there is an obligation as between Member States to

---

[2] This will generally be in the same terms as the information set out in s 25 of the Extradition Act 1965.

[3] s 26, Extradition Act 1965.

[4] Recital 5 of the Framework Decision.

surrender the requested person. The role of the executive (which is described as the "Central Authority" in the terminology of the Framework Decision) is specifically relegated to an administrative one:

> "The role of central authorities in the execution of a European arrest warrant *must be limited* to practical and administrative assistance."[5]

1–11 It is clear form this and the rest of the Framework Decision that the executive is no longer in a position to refuse a request for surrender on foot of a European arrest warrant. That function is reserved exclusively to the judiciary:

> "Decisions on the execution of the European arrest warrant must be subject to sufficient controls, which means that a judicial authority of the Member State where the requested person has been arrested will have to take the decision on his or her surrender."[6]

1–12 As noted previously the traditional role which the judiciary played in relation to extradition requests in this jurisdiction coupled with a reluctance on the part of government to be seen to be intimately involved in the process may render the change effected by the European arrest warrant somewhat less obvious. However, in other jurisdictions, particularly where the judiciary had little or no decision making function in relation to extradition, it represents a major new departure.

RENDITION

1–13 The Framework Decision is quite explicit in its requirement that pre-existing extradition procedures be abolished in favour of the new system of surrender as between Member States. It goes on to specifically avoid using the expression "extradition" in relation to the system envisaged by the European arrest warrant. As such it is incorrect to describe it as a form of extradition. Rather it is a form of rendition[7] i.e. the execution of a judicial order by third parties. In this regard it has certain similarities with the rendition procedure provided for by way of backing of warrants as between Ireland and the United Kingdom under Part III of the Extradition Act 1965 which has since been repealed.

1–14 The significance of the distinction between extradition in the traditional sense and the form of rendition provided for under the 2003 Act was considered by McKechnie J in *O'Sullivan v Governor of Cloverhil Prison*[8]:

> "...it cannot be accurate to assimilate, ideologically or practically, the case law or mind-set of extradition into those *of intra*-Union surrender: *Minister for Justice, Equality and Law Reform v. Altaravicius* [2006] 3 IR 148 and *Minister for Justice, Equality and Law Reform v. Stapleton* [2008] 1 IR 669 are ample support for this conclusion. I am satisfied that this represents an entirely new

---

[5] Recital 9 of the Framework Decision.
[6] Recital 8 of the Framework Decision.
[7] In *MJELR v Altaravicius* [2006] 3 IR 148 at p 171 Denham J described the European arrest warrant as "a new scheme introduced with the intent of simplifying the procedures of rendition between the member states".
[8] Unreported, High Court, 25 May 2010, McKechnie J.

system. Surrender is not extradition. There is no hearing into the merits of the prosecution, pending or anticipated in the requesting jurisdiction; nor should there be; and the Executive no longer has a role. There is a special relationship between the Member States of the Union. By virtue of this unity there is increased judicial co-operation between Members. However there is necessarily a great level of trust that the other Member State will act in accordance with the highest and fundamental principles of the Union; namely rule of law, peace, freedom and democracy. Nonetheless, there may be circumstances where certain Member States may be lacking in this regard. It is for this reason that procedural safeguards are placed within the Framework Decision.

The movement of persons accused or convicted of crimes in another Member State of the Union is fundamentally different from the movement of such a person to a non-Member State. Surrender within the Union must be seen as more akin to the transfer of persons from one federal jurisdiction to another within a federal state, rather than between independent states. There is a significant level of integration and reciprocity within the Union. How could an area of freedom and security be maintained if national measures imposed serious restriction on the surrender of suspects or convicts from one Member State to another? The criminal would merely move to another Member State; as indeed many Irish criminals did in the 1980s and 1990s. With citizenship of the Union there comes both benefits and obligations. Those who use the freedoms afforded to move between the States of the Union, should not be surprised if, when they commit a crime in another State, they are easily and swiftly returned there to face charges. As stated, such is a necessary corollary of the creation of an area of freedom and security.

In my opinion therefore there is a fundamental difference in the nature of proceedings for surrender and those for extradition. They are founded upon very different relationships between the States in question. Persons being extradited are therefore in a different situation to those being surrendered. It is therefore not the case that there is discrimination between persons in a similar position, and in any event I am satisfied that any differences which do exist between the two systems are entirely justified given the ultimate objectives of the EAW scheme under the Framework Decision."

This is not, however, to say that case-law arising under the 1965 Act has no application. Rather it should be approached with some degree of circumspection.   **1–15**

THE FRAMEWORK DECISION – EUROPEAN LAW CONTEXT

The Framework Decision upon which the 2003 Act is based and which is to some extent incorporated into that Act in a somewhat ungainly fashion is, in the first instance, an instrument of European law. It has its origins in Title VI of the Treaty on European Union[9] which concerned police and judicial co-operation in criminal matters. Article 29 set out the goals to be achieved under this heading: **1–16**

"Without prejudice to the powers of the European Community, the Union's objective shall be to provide citizens with a high level of safety within an area of freedom, security and justice by developing common action among

---

[9] This has now been superseded by the provisions of the Lisbon Treaty.

the Member States in the fields of police and judicial cooperation in criminal matters and by preventing and combating racism and xenophobia.

That objective shall be achieved by preventing and combating crime, organised or otherwise, in particular terrorism, trafficking in persons and offences against children, illicit drug trafficking and illicit arms trafficking, corruption and fraud, through:

- closer cooperation between police forces, customs authorities and other competent authorities in the Member States, both directly and through the European Police Office (Europol), in accordance with the provisions of Articles 30 and 32;

- closer cooperation between judicial and other competent authorities of the Member States in accordance with the provisions of Articles 31(a) to (d) and 32;

- approximation, where necessary, of rules on criminal matters in the Member States, in accordance with the provisions of Article 31 (e)."

1–17 The creation of what was described as an "area of freedom, security and justice" has to be seen in the context not only of combating crime at a trans-national level but also in the context of the free movement of citizens within the EU. The ability to travel freely necessarily brings with it the ability to commit criminal offences freely in the various Member States. The aim of Article 29 was to allow an equivalent freedom of movement to police forces and judicial decisions in the criminal sphere. Article 31 expressly defined common action on judicial cooperation in criminal matters as including extradition.

FRAMEWORK DECISIONS

1–18 Article 34(2)(b) of the Treaty on European Union provided for the use of Framework Decisions as an instrument of EU law. These are expressly not directly effective.[10] Framework Decisions are binding on Member States as regards the result to be achieved but it is left to the Member State to decide the best means by which to achieve the requisite result. The Framework Decision procedure is a more straightforward and attractive proposition than a convention or treaty as it does not need to be ratified as such. Also its application is (in theory) more homogenous as regards the various Member States as it is less easy to implement subject to reservations.

1–19   In purely colloquial terms it might be said that a Framework Decision is a recipe for a domestic statute which implements the various requirements set out therein. This becomes particularly apparent when one considers that the

---

[10] "34(2) The Council shall take measures and promote cooperation, using the appropriate form and procedures as set out in this title, contributing to the pursuit of the objectives of the Union. To that end, acting unanimously on the initiative of any Member State or of the Commission, the Council may:

…(b) adopt framework decisions for the purpose of approximation of the laws and regulations of the Member States. Framework decisions shall be binding upon the Member States as to the result to be achieved but shall leave to the national authorities the choice of form and methods. They shall not entail direct effect."

Framework Decision itself not only presumes that the different Member States will implement it in whatever manner they see fit but also grants various options and alternatives to Member States which they can include, or not, on a purely discretionary basis. For example Art 4 sets out various grounds for refusing to surrender which the Member State may incorporate into its domestic legislation i.e. non-correspondence, *ne bis in idem*, extra-territoriality. It is an unhappy incident of the drafting of the European Arrest Warrant Act 2003 that it purports to preclude surrender where to do so would be contrary to the Framework Decision[11] – such a prohibition would seem to take little or no account of the fact that many of the grounds for refusing surrender are optional as opposed to mandatory. In *Minister for Justice, Equality and Law Reform v Ó Fallúin*[12] it was argued that the surrender of the respondent could be refused by the High Court on a discretionary basis by virtue of Art 4.7 of the Framework Decision which concerned offences committed within the territory of the executing state. Finnegan P drew a distinction between the those parts of the Framework Decision that granted to a Member State an entitlement to avail of an opt out when implementing the Framework Decision on the one hand and an absolute bar to surrender on the other:

> "The Framework Decision was given effect in Irish law by the European Arrest Warrant Act 2003. Article 4.7 of the Framework Decision confers upon Members States a discretion in implementing the Framework Decision in domestic legislation to provide in the circumstances therein set out that there shall be no surrender. It is left to the Member States to decide whether they want to implement Article 4.7 and, if so, as an optional or as a mandatory ground of non-execution. In relation to Article 4.7 the Oireachtas enacted section 42 of the 2003 Act as amended by the 2005 Act. In these circumstances Article 4.7 has no application outside the circumstances expressly provided for in section 42 as amended."

Similarly Art 5 of the Framework Decision sets out various conditions precedent **1–20** to surrender which the Member State can insist on being satisfied of by way of guarantee prior to surrender. Again it is up to the Member State to decide whether or not to incorporate such conditions precedent into its domestic legislation. Quite apart from the terms of Art 34(2)(b) which make it clear that the Framework Decision does not have direct effect the discretionary nature of many of the provisions mean that it would be entirely meaningless to talk of it in terms of having direct effect *per se* as an option cannot by its nature be directly effective.

A further consequence of the very broad margin given to Member States in relation **1–21** to the manner in which they implement the Framework Decision and the various opt outs which they can choose to include or ignore is that little of the 2003 Act which implements the Framework Decision could, strictly speaking, be said to be "necessitated by the obligations of membership of the European Union". As such it is unlikely to attract the immunity from constitutional challenge provided for in Art 29.4.10 of the Constitution.[13]

---

[11] See ss 10 and 38.

[12] [2010] IESC 37.

[13] See also *Greene v Minister for Agriculture* [1990] 2 IR 17 and *Meagher v Minister for Agriculture* [1994] 1 IR 329.

JURISDICTION OF THE EUROPEAN COURT OF JUSTICE

1–22   As an instrument of European law it is possible for the European Court of Justice
to exercise some jurisdiction in relation to the validity of the Framework Decision
itself in the context of EU law. Article 35 contemplates the possibility of the Court of
Justice exercising jurisdiction in relation to the operation of the Framework Decision
by way of reference from the domestic courts of the Member States. However, such
jurisdiction is in effect optional and is dependent upon a Member State having made
a declaration to the effect that the Court of Justice can exercise such jurisdiction.
Ireland has not made such a declaration. Therefore it is not possible to ask any of
the domestic courts to refer any question to the European Court of Justice. Article
35[14] would have given the Court of Justice jurisdiction to give rulings not only on
the interpretation of the Framework Decision but also its validity. This was noted by
Fennelly J in *Dundon v Governor of Cloverhill Prison*[15]:

> "The court, on this appeal, has to consider an Act of the Oireachtas which
> implements a framework decision adopted pursuant to the provisions of Title VI
> of the Treaty on European Union. However, Ireland has not made the declaration
> which is necessary under Article 35 of the Treaty on European Union before the
> Court of Justice can exercise the interpretative jurisdiction envisaged by that
> Article. Hence, this court decides this question without any guidance from that
> court. The Court of Justice may, of course, be asked, on a reference from another
> member state, to rule on the interpretation of the 60 day period."[16]

1–23   By virtue of the fact that Ireland has not made a declaration allowing the Court of
Justice to exercise jurisdiction the practical upshot is that the courts here will have
to leave it to the courts of other Member States to refer issues that may arise before
them to the Court of Justice before receiving any guidance from it.

1–24   The failure by the State to make the relevant declaration was the subject of
constitutional challenge in *O'Sullivan v Governor of Cloverhill Prison*[17] where
it was suggested that it amounted to a fettering of access to the courts and was
discriminatory having regard to the fact that the facility was available in the majority
of other Member States. McKechnie J rejected this argument:

> "The applicant finally drew attention to the fact that the State has failed to make
> any Declaration under Article 35(2) allowing preliminary references to the Court
> of Justice: this putting him in a worse position when compared to persons in other
> Member States (see para 40 *supra*). I am again satisfied that the applicant can
> have no legitimate complaint in this regard. The making of such a Declaration is

---

[14] "35(1). The Court of Justice of the European Communities shall have jurisdiction, subject
to the conditions laid down in this article, to give preliminary rulings on the validity and
interpretation of framework decisions and decisions, on the interpretation of conventions
established under this title and on the validity and interpretation of the measures
implementing them.
(2) By a declaration made at the time of signature of the Treaty of Amsterdam or at any time
thereafter, any Member State shall be able to accept the jurisdiction of the Court of Justice
to give preliminary rulings as specified in paragraph 1".

[15] [2006] 1 IR 518.

[16] p 545.

[17] Unreported, High Court, 25 May 2010, McKechnie J.

a function purely for each Member State. Where specific provision is made for the opting out of certain provisions there can be no complaint where the State chooses to so do. If the provision was meant to be compulsory it would have stated so. To hold as a form of discrimination the fact that a Member State had not made a voluntary Declaration would wholly undermine its voluntary nature. This fact cannot therefore be said to assist the applicant in this regard. In any event, as stated, the Court has no role in investigating why no Declaration has been made, nor has it a role in commenting thereupon."

The position has, however, changed somewhat since the entry into force of the Lisbon Treaty. Article 267 provides for jurisdiction in relation to what had previously been described as "third pillar" matters including the operation and implementation of the Framework Decision. Whilst Ireland continues to opt out of the ECJ exercising such jurisdiction by means of the 36th Protocol to the Treaty this opt out will only last for five years from the entry into force of the Lisbon Treaty. Thereafter it will be possible to seek a reference in the ordinary way.   **1–25**

THE SCOPE OF THE FRAMEWORK DECISION

The genesis and scope of the Framework Decision was considered by the European Court of Justice in *Advocaten voor de Wereld v Leden van de Ministerrad*[18]. In that case it was suggested that the list of offences created by Art 2.2 of the Framework Decision, in respect of which the requirement to show dual criminality was dispensed with, offended against the principle of legal certainty in that the offences comprising the list were overly vague and poorly defined. The Court rejected this argument on the basis that the purpose of the Framework Decision was to bring about harmonisation of procedural measures rather than substantive criminal measures and as such concerns with regard to the level of certainty normally required in relation to the definition of substantive criminal offences did not apply: **1–26**

> "With regard, second, to the fact that the lack of precision in the definition of the categories of offences in question risks giving rise to disparate implementation of the Framework Decision within the various national legal orders, suffice it to point out that it is not the objective of the Framework Decision to harmonise the substantive criminal law of the member states and that nothing in Title VI of the EU Treaty, arts 34 and 31 of which were indicated as forming the legal basis of the Framework Decision, makes the application of the European arrest warrant conditional on harmonisation of the criminal laws of the member states within the area of the offences in question (see by way of analogy, inter alia, *Criminal proceedings against Gözütok* Joined cases C-187/01 and C-385/01 [2003] ECR I-1345 (para 32) and *Criminal proceedings against Gasparini* Case C-467/04 [2006] ECR I-9199 (para 29)).
>
> It follows that, in so far as it dispenses with verification of double criminality in respect of the offences listed therein, art 2(2) of the Framework Decision is not invalid inasmuch as it does not breach art 6(2) EU or, more specifically, the principle of legality of criminal offences and penalties and the principle of equality and non-discrimination."[19]

---

[18] Case C-303/05 (3 May 2007).
[19] Paras 59 and 60.

1–27   In effect the ECJ took the view that Art 2.2 was not a provision which affected the substantive criminal law – i.e. it was not a measure aimed at approximation of laws, rather it was aimed at the approximation of certain surrender procedures. Therefore the requirement that the offences be fully defined in a consistent and universal fashion was of considerably less importance. Given that the only use to which the list was put was in relation to waiving the requirement that double criminality be established it was of little real significance that it was drawn in wide terms.

1–28   The Framework Decision and the subsequent implementing measures such as the 2003 Act are, therefore, best regarded as procedural rather than substantive measures by virtue of their origins under Title VI of the EU Treaty.

CRITICISM OF THE FRAMEWORK DECISION

1–29   It is no secret that the process of attempting to simplify and streamline the various extradition procedures of the Member States was a project which had been ongoing in a somewhat desultory fashion for a number of years prior to 2001. The events of 11 September of that year changed matters radically. Within a matter of months the Framework Decision which had previously seemed an impossibility was in place. Whilst such speed may be commendable it has necessarily resulted in a number of errors within the Framework Decision itself and a degree of vagueness which might be considered surprising in a formal legal instrument. As much has been acknowledged by the courts:

> "It has to be acknowledged, at once, that the legislation presents unusual problems of interpretation. The European arrest warrant is itself a novel instrument. It was adopted in the wake of the devastatingly tragic events of the 11th September, 2001. The drafting is extraordinarily loose and vague, particularly in the manner in which offences are defined."[20]

1–30   Murray CJ was similarly critical in *Minister for Justice, Equality and Law Reform v Ferenca*[21] when he made reference to the "somewhat vague language and curious construction" of the Framework Decision.

INCORPORATION OF THE FRAMEWORK DECISION IN THE 2003 ACT

1–31   Whatever the criticisms that might be made of the Framework Decision itself the manner in which it has been incorporated in a partially directly effective manner in the 2003 Act is at best peculiar and in truth all but incomprehensible. For reasons that are unclear it was decided to not only append the Framework Decision to the 2003 Act but also to refer to it in the body of the Act and incorporate parts of it in an operative fashion. This approach has, not surprisingly, been the subject of some judicial criticism. In *Dundon v Governor of Cloverhill Prison*[22] Geoghegan J exercised restraint in observing that the "Act is not happily drafted"[23]. Specifically

---

[20] As per Fennelly J in *Dundon v Governor of Cloverhill Prison* [2006] 1 IR 518 at 545.
[21] [2008] 4 IR 480.
[22] [2006] 1 IR 518.
[23] At p 536.

the mode of drafting muddies the waters to a considerable extent in relation to the issue of direct effect. These difficulties were noted by Murray CJ in *Minister for Justice, Equality and Law Reform v Altaravicius*[24]:

> "Although the framework decision cannot, in terms of community law, have direct effect (since Article 34.2(b) of the Treaty on European Union expressly excludes such effect) the Oireachtas has chosen to give it, at least as regards a significant number of its provisions, such effect and make it directly applicable within the State. This is achieved, *inter alia*, by s. 10 of the Act of 2003 which provides that where a European arrest warrant has been duly issued in respect of a person "that person shall, subject to and in accordance with the *provisions of this Act and the Framework Decision*, be arrested and surrendered to the issuing state". The Act of 2003 does not confine itself to including the framework decision in a schedule for reference purposes. There are other provisions of the Act of 2003 which require the courts to interpret and apply the framework decision directly but it is sufficient for present purposes to note that s. 10 means that in deciding on an application for a surrender pursuant to the terms of the Act of 2003 the court must apply both the provisions of the Act and the framework decision. It is, to say the least, an idiosyncratic method of legislating and likely to create ambiguity."[25]

Murray CJ went on to note that the incorporation of the Framework Decision within the terms of a domestic statute which referenced its terms in an operative and directly effective manner gave rise to somewhat bizarre situation whereby the Oireachtas had made a Framework Decision directly effective: **1–32**

> "Thus this court is in the unusual position of having to interpret and apply article 8 of the framework decision directly because of the effect given to it in national law by the Oireachtas and not by Community law."[26]

This was all the more unsatisfactory given that it is not possible for the domestic courts to seek a reference to the Court of Justice in relation to the interpretation of the Framework Decision due to the terms of Art 35 of the Treaty on European Union. In effect the courts are left in a situation whereby they are obliged to give rulings on the meaning and effect of provisions of the Framework Decision notwithstanding their inability to refer any such issues to the Court of Justice: **1–33**

> "A reference of a question concerning the interpretation or application of the framework decision to the Court of Justice for a preliminary ruling pursuant to Article 35.1 of the Treaty on European Union cannot be made since Ireland has not made a declaration accepting the jurisdiction of the Court of Justice to give such a preliminary ruling which Article 35.2 makes a precondition to any such jurisdiction. It is a matter for this court to determine, in final instance, the interpretation of the framework decision…"[27]

---

[24] [2006] 3 IR 148.
[25] p 155.
[26] p 156.
[27] p 156.

1-34   However, the difficulties created by the manner in which parts of the Framework Decision had been directly incorporated into the Act are most apparent in the decision of the Supreme Court in *Rimsa v Governor of Cloverhill Prison*[28] where the provisions of s 16(5)(b) of the Act clearly conflicted with Art 23.3 of the Framework Decision. Murray CJ considered that the provisions of s 10 of the Act required that surrender be effected in accordance with the provisions of the Framework Decision. In turn this meant that some of the provisions of the Framework Decision would come into play in a directly effective fashion in that a respondent would be entitled to expressly invoke and rely on them:

> "So far as this case is concerned s. 10 expressly requires that the surrender of the appellant in this case be done not only and in accordance with the Act but, additionally, in accordance with the Framework Decision. An individual must be able to rely on such provisions of the Framework Decision at least so far as that measure is made applicable in Irish law by the Act itself. If it were otherwise it would render the express reference to the Framework Decision in s. 10 meaningless.

> Accordingly the appellant was entitled to place reliance, pursuant to s. 10, on the provisions of the Framework Decision which applied to his surrender to the issuing State, Latvia.

> In my view Article 23.3 is clearly an article which governs the surrender of a person on foot of a European arrest warrant. Accordingly by virtue of s. 10 of the Act of 2003 the Central Authority, in assisting and giving effect to the Order of the Court for surrender, was under a duty to do so in accordance with the provisions of the Framework Decision as s. 10 expressly provides."

1-35   It follows, therefore, that there will be many parts of the Framework Decision which are in practical terms directly effective by reason of having been invoked in ss 10 and 38 of the Act. It remains to be seen precisely which parts of the Framework Decision will be so regarded.

1-36   In the course of the same judgment Murray CJ recalled the comments he had made in *Minister for Justice, Equality and Law Reform v Altaravicius*[29] and questioned the prudence of incorporating a Framework Decision as part of the domestic legislation:

> "In *Altaravicius* the two applicable norms were s. 11 of the Act and Article 8 of the Framework Decision. In the latter case I referred to this manner of legislating, in restrained language, as "idiosyncratic". It is a most unsatisfactory way of legislating and I still consider that I am expressing myself in restrained terms. Framework Decisions, as their name suggests, are legislative measures drafted in terms which range from the general to the specific intended to be effectively implemented in each Member State through its own national legislative measures as Article 34(2)(b) of the Treaty makes clear. In principle therefore it is national legislation which must give effect to the Framework Decision and achieve its objectives. That will usually mean that the provisions of the Acts of the Oireachtas themselves contain all the elements necessary to

---

[28] [2010] IESC 47.
[29] [2006] 3 IR 148.

give effect to a Framework Decision. That would not preclude, however, an Act expressly requiring something to be done in accordance with a specific provision of a Framework Decision particularly, where such a provision is sufficiently clear and defined so as to be capable of being enforced or applied by a Court.

That might be done provided a section of the Act itself does not at the same time, and in parallel with the particular provision of the Framework Decision, purport to give effect to the latter provision so as to ensure that there is only one legal norm or provision applying to a particular matter.

What is unsatisfactory and which has given rise to litigation, and likely to do so in the future, is to have a provision of a Framework Decision made applicable to a particular matter at the same time or in parallel with a specific section or part of an Act governing the same matter."

It is difficult to disagree with the description of the comments made in the course of the judgment in Altaravicius as "restrained".   **1–37**

OTHER CRITICISMS OF THE ACT

Leaving aside the manner in which the 2003 Act seeks to implement the Framework Decision it would appear that as initially enacted it was replete with obvious errors. The Act as it currently stands was very substantially amended by the Criminal Justice (Terrorist Offences) Act 2005 largely due to it being practically unworkable in its original form. Even a brief perusal of some of the earlier decisions[30] suggest that far from simplifying the pre-existing extradition procedures the 2003 Act in its un-amended form succeeded only in complicating matters to a quite spectacular degree with its apparent requirement that multiple undertakings and guarantees be supplied in addition to the warrant itself. The effect of the 2005 Act was largely to insert presumptions in respect of such matters which thereby rendered the supplying of the various guarantees and undertakings unnecessary. Notwithstanding such amendments the drafting of the Act has still been characterised as not being in "optimum terms".[31]   **1–38**

Further fundamental amendments were made by the Criminal Justice (Miscellaneous Provisions) Act 2009. Most notably the requirement that the respondent be shown to have fled the issuing state in sentence cases was finally excised as was the apparent *invitation to treat* in relation to the law of the issuing state deriving from the requirement in s 10 that the warrant have been "duly issued".   **1–39**

INTERPRETATION OF THE 2003 ACT

One of the most significant practical consequences of the 2003 Act's European law underpinnings is that the courts here are obliged to have regard to the Framework Decision upon which it is based when any issue of interpretation arises. Whilst this is not necessarily a novel principle it is one which has been cast into particularly sharp relief in the context of the 2003 Act.   **1–40**

---

[30] See for example *Minister for Justice, Equality and Law Reform v Gokano* [2004] 3 IR 216.
[31] *Minister for Justice, Equality and Law Reform v Gotszlik* 2009 [IESC] 13.

INTERPRETATION OF THE EXTRADITION ACT 1965

1–41   Prior to the introduction of the European Arrest Warrant Act 2003 the conventional wisdom dictated that extradition statutes such as the Extradition Act 1965 ought to be interpreted strictly as they were properly regarded as penal statutes affecting the rights and liberties of those who were subject to their provisions. This approach was most clearly set out in *Aamand v Smithwick*[32]:

> "It is clear and of importance in this case that the Act of 1965 and the Statutory Instrument made pursuant to it incorporating the convention is a penal statutory code involving penal sanctions on an individual and must therefore be construed strictly as is contended in the sense that not by anything other than unambiguous provision should a person be subjected to detention and extradition."

1–42   The briefest perusal of the various judgments arising subsequent to the introduction of the 2003 Act reveals that the strict interpretative approach has been all but abandoned in favour of the principle of conforming interpretation. In *Minister for Justice, Equality and Law Reform v Biggins*[33] the court acknowledged that whilst a strict interpretation had been applied to extradition statutes in the past the provisions underlying the European Arrest Warrant Act 2003 gave rise to a different approach in that the guarantees in respect of fundamental rights were contained in the relevant provisions and they were in any event informed by an explicit mutual trust and understanding:

> "...the obligation to strictly construe penal statutes or statutory provisions which have the capacity to deprive a person of his or her liberty must be kept in context. While I appreciate that some of the decisions refer specifically to an extradition context, it must be recalled that such context was at a time prior to 1st January 2004, when the European Arrest Warrant Act, 2003 came into law giving effect to the new surrender arrangements set forth in the Framework Decision. That Framework Decision has introduced a fundamental change in the nature of the process undertaken when one Member State seeks the surrender of a person resident in another Member State. Those arrangements have replaced former extradition procedures with a process of surrender for the purpose of the mutual recognition of arrest warrants issued in the requesting Member State. In so doing, fundamental rights are respected, and certain safeguards have been included in order to protect the constitutional and Convention rights of persons whose surrender is sought. But it is expressly stated in the Preamble to the Framework Decision at Recital (10) that *"the mechanism of the European arrest warrant is based on a high level of confidence between Member States"*, and *"that its implementation may be suspended only in the event of a serious and persistent breach by one of the Member States of the principles of Article 6(1) of the Treaty on European Union....."*. This cannot be simply regarded as an empty formula. The Framework Decision is to be referred to when interpreting and construing the legislation."

1–43   As such it would appear that the approach as previously outlined in *Aamand v Smithwick* is no longer of general applicability.

---

[32]   [1995] 1 ILRM 61.
[33]   [2006] IEHC 351.

PRINCIPLE OF CONFORMING INTERPRETATION

Whilst the Framework Decision leaves it up to each Member State to decide how best to give effect to it, the domestic courts are under a positive duty to interpret the domestic legislation in such a manner so as to give effect to the underlying purpose of the Framework Decision. This principle was clearly enunciated by the European Court of Justice in *Case of Pupino*[34]: **1–44**

> "...the court concludes that the principle of interpretation in conformity with Community law is binding in relation to framework decisions adopted in the context of Title VI of the Treaty on European Union. When applying national law, the national court that is called upon to interpret it must do so as far as possible in the light of the wording of the purpose of the framework decision in order to attain the result which it pursues and thus comply with article 34(2)(b)EU."[35]

However such an obligation is to some extent limited by the actual terms of the domestic enactment and the court is not required to interpret the legislation in a manner which would run contrary to the express terms of the relevant enactment. **1–45**

> "The obligation on the national court to refer to the content of a Framework Decision when interpreting the relevant rules of its national law ceases when the latter cannot receive an application which would lead to a result compatible with that envisaged by that Framework Decision. In other words, the principle of interpretation in conformity with Community law cannot serve as the basis for an interpretation of national law *contra legem*. That principle does, however, require that, where necessary, the national court consider the whole of national law in order to assess how far it can be applied in such a way as not to produce a result contrary to that envisaged by the framework decision."[36]

The principle of conforming interpretation has been applied by the courts here on a number of occasions. Its effect was summarised by Denham J in *Dundon v Governor of Cloverhill Prison*[37]: **1–46**

> "Thus, the national court when applying the national law should do so as far as possible in light of the Council framework decision, to attain the result sought. This can not be done if it is contrary to the national law, but the national court should consider the whole of the national law to see if it can be applied so as not to produce a result contrary to the council framework decision."[38]

The principle was similarly summarised by Murray CJ in a frequently cited passage in the case of *Minister for Justice, Equality and Law Reform v Altaravicius*[39]: **1–47**

---

[34] (Case C-105/03) *Pupino* [2005] ECR 1-05285.

[35] At para 43.

[36] At para 45.

[37] [2006] 1 IR 518.

[38] p 531.

[39] [2006] 3 IR 148.

> "When applying and interpreting national provisions giving effect to a Framework Decision the Courts "... must do so as far as possible in this light of the wording and purpose of the Framework Decision in order to attain the result which it pursues ..." (C-105/03 Pupino ECJ 16th June, 2005). The principle of conforming interpretation is limited, as the Court of Justice has pointed out in Pupino and other cases, to the extent that it is possible to give such an interpretation. It does not require a national court to interpret national legislation contra legem. If national legislation, having been interpreted as far as possible in conformity with community legislation to which it purports to give effect, but still falls short of what is required by the latter, a national Court must, as a general principle, apply that legislation as interpreted although there may be other consequences for a Member State which has failed to fully implement a Directive or Framework Decision".[40]

1–48   Given the somewhat unhappy manner in which much of the 2003 Act has been drafted the courts have had occasion to consider various ambiguities and difficulties on more than one occasion. In such cases the principle of conforming interpretation has been applied.

CONSISTENCY OF APPROACH

1–49   The approach of the courts in relation to the manner in which the Act ought to be interpreted has, however, not been entirely consistent. In *Butenas v Governor of Cloverhill*[41] the applicant sought to challenge his remand in custody pending surrender on the grounds that s 16 of the Act must be unconstitutional as it made no provision for the possibility of bail in such circumstances. The Supreme Court avoided having to determine that the provision was repugnant by adopting a strict interpretation of the provision and holding that the Oireachtas would have used much clearer terminology had they intended to oust the jurisdiction of the High Court in relation to bail:

> "The Court is of the view that if the Oireachtas had intended to oust the inherent jurisdiction of the High Court to grant bail in all cases where an order for surrender has been made, irrespective of the circumstances, it would have explicitly and unambiguously done so. To interpret the subsection otherwise would be to assume that the Oireachtas intended that persons should be detained for the purpose of their surrender even in cases where such detention was not necessary for such a purpose. Again the Court does not consider that the section discloses any grounds for such an assumption."[42]

1–50   It is of particular note that the High Court had concluded that the relevant provision which, on the face of it, appeared to preclude an application for bail by a person whose surrender had been ordered was permissible in light of the provisions of the Framework Decision and had expressly interpreted it in that context. Whilst the decision of the Supreme Court makes reference to the Framework Decision it is clear that the manner in which it interpreted s 16 was not in any real sense informed by it. Rather there appears to have been an appreciation that the only constitutionally

---

[40] p 156.
[41] [2008] 4 IR 189.
[42] p 201.

permissible interpretation of the provision was one which to an extent, at least, ignored the requirements of the Framework Decision.

Whilst the Supreme Court judgment has an obvious pragmatic appeal in that **1–51** the court was faced with the rather unpalatable alternative of deeming the relevant provisions to be unconstitutional it is difficult to discern a consistent approach to the issue of interpretation. Whilst the courts would appear to have rejected the strict penal approach outlined in *Aamand v Smithwick* in favour of the principle of conforming interpretation predicated on the State's obligations under European Law, they have on at least one occasion reverted to a more traditional approach in order to avoid having to declare a part of the Act unconstitutional. Although not explicitly described as such in the judgment in *Butenas*, this might legitimately be regarded as a manifestation of the double construction test.

THE TRADITIONAL CANONS OF INTERPRETATION

Whilst the traditional cannons of interpretation will be of some use in construing the **1–52** provisions of the Act, it is reference to the principles and goals of the Framework Decision which will be of greatest assistance. At best, other rules take a back seat. In *Minister for Justice, Equality and Law Reform v Altaravicius (No. 2)*[43] McMenamin J declined to apply the *ejusdem generis* rule in circumstances where it would have resulted in a construction not in accordance with the provisions of the Framework Decision:

> "In the course of submissions counsel for the respondent has relied on a number of authorities which relate to the e*jusdem generis* rule. ... While such an interpretative tool is undoubtedly of *secondary assistance* in the interpretation of words and phrases, its application in the instant case diminishes to the point of insignificance when seen in the context of the terms of the Act itself and the Framework Decision to which this court, as was pointed out by the Supreme Court in *Minister for Justice v. Alatravicius* [2006] IESC 23, [2006] 3 I.R. 148 must have close regard in the process of interpretation. As observed by Lord Scarman in his speech in *Quazi v. Quazi (Fam. D.)* [1980] A.C. 744, the rule is at best 'a very secondary guide to the meaning of a statute'".[44]

It seems reasonable to assume that where the application of any of the traditional **1–53** cannons of interpretation conflict with the more purposive interpretation dictated by the decision in *Pupino* the latter approach will prevail.

INTERPRETING THE FRAMEWORK DECISION

The rather peculiar manner in which the Framework Decision has been incorporated **1–54** in a partially directly effective manner into the 2003 Act potentially throws up a rather complex issue of statutory interpretation. On the one hand there is no definitive version of the Framework Decision as it has been published in each of the working languages of the EU. As such it is not immediately clear as to how ambiguities or discrepancies which may arise as between different versions might

---

[43] [2007] 2 IR 265.
[44] p 277.

be reconciled. On the other hand it might be observed that because the Framework Decision is appended to the 2003 Act in both the Irish and English language versions it would seem to follow from a purely domestic point of view that in the event of an ambiguity arising the Irish language version should be favoured[45]. Such an approach rather obviously raises issues in circumstances where the courts may seek to give effect to a particular phrase or meaning in the context of the Irish language version of the Framework Decision in circumstances where it is reasonable to assume that none of the other Member States would necessarily have addressed their minds to the nuance or distinction in question. Suffice it to note that the courts have yet to address this issue.

1–55   The courts have, however, had some regard to some of the other official language versions of the Framework Decision. In the course of his judgment in *Minister for Justice, Equality and Law Reform v MM*[46], Peart J made reference to the use of the indefinite article in the French, German and Italian versions of the Framework Decision for the purpose of underlining the distinction drawn between sentences of imprisonment and detention orders. Such an approach is possibly problematic in circumstances where only some of the various versions of the Framework Decision are referred to.

1–56   On appeal to the Supreme Court[47] Denham J considered some of the *travaux preparatoires* to the Framework Decision in order to determine whether detention in a psychiatric hospital subsequent to conviction came within the meaning of detention as set out in Art 5 of the Framework Decision. The Court also considered a decision of the Supreme Court of Finland on the same topic:

> "Article 5 of the Framework Decision has been set out earlier in this judgment, where the reference to "custodial life sentence or lifetime detention order" is underlined. Counsel for the Minister referred the Court to "Proposals for a Council Framework Decision on the European Arrest Warrant and Surrender Procedures between Member States" presented by the European Commission on the 25th day of September 2001 where the Commission set out an explanation of what was proposed to be introduced in the Framework Decision, together with a commentary. The Commission stated that the definition of detention order is taken from the 1957 Convention, being the European Extradition Convention of the 13th December, 1957. Article 25 of that Convention provided:-
>
>> "For the purpose of this Convention, the expression 'detention order' means any order involving deprivation of liberty which has been made by a criminal court in addition to or instead of a prison sentence."
>
> This is not, of course, a binding authority on the Court in relation to s.10(d) of the Act of 2003, but it is helpful. Indeed, in a case of the Supreme Court of Finland, on an EAW, counsel for the government in that case referred also to Article 25 of the 1957 Convention on Extradition."

1–57   Whilst such an approach would appear to be at odds with other dicta of the Supreme Court, i.e. *Controller of Patents, Designs & Trade Marks v Ireland*[48], there must,

---

[45] See Dodd, *Statutory Interpretation in Ireland* (2008 Tottel Publishing) at para [5.112].

[46] [2007] IEHC 443.

[47] Unreported, 19 March 2010.

[48] [2001] 4 IR 229.

nonetheless, be some merit in seeking to interpret the Framework Decision in a consistent manner on a pan-European basis. In relation to the citing of a decision of the Supreme Court of Finland Denham J made the following observation:

> "While this case is, of course, not a binding precedent, it illustrates an analysis of the Framework Decision similar to that which I have made and applied in this case. It also illustrates the benefit which would be obtained for the Member States if there was a centralised site where judgments of the courts of Members States on European arrest warrants would be available. Similar issues must arise constantly before the courts of the Member States and it would be of assistance to see the interpretation of the Framework Decision given by the courts of other Member States."

Undoubtedly such a resource would go some considerable way to ensuring a more consistent interpretation of the Framework Decision across the EU.   **1–58**

MUTUAL TRUST

Paragraph 10 of the recitals to the Framework Decision expressly indicates that the   **1–59**
operation of the operation of the European arrest warrant system is necessarily based on the principle of mutual trust or confidence by Member States in each other:

> "The mechanism of the European arrest warrant is based on a high level of confidence between Member States."

Whilst the European arrest warrant represents a radical departure from pre-existing   **1–60**
extradition arrangements it would be incorrect to assume that the principle of mutual trust and confidence underlying the implementation of the Framework Decision is entirely novel. Such a principle has, in the past, been applied, albeit in a significantly more watered down version, to extradition arrangements:

> "I am satisfied that I am entitled to have regard to the fact that an extradition Act is necessarily the consequence, ... of an agreement between two sovereign states reposing confidence in each other, and I should not, in the first instance, suppose that the court and other authorities of the country by which extradition is sought are using a deceit so as to secure the apprehension of the plaintiff."[49]

This principle has found a more pronounced expression in relation to the European   **1–61**
arrest warrant particularly where the courts have had occasion to consider the position of the issuing judicial authority. Specifically the courts have applied the principal of mutual trust to a broad range of issues principally in relation to what might be characterised as the formalities which need to be included in a given warrant. However, whilst the courts have not been slow to point out that the manner in which the Framework Decision is operated between Member States is predicated on mutual trust they have also been careful to point out the limitations of the principal. In *Minister for Justice, Equality and Law Reform v Ferenca*[50] Murray CJ appeared to disagree with the sentiments of the High Court which had ordered

---

[49] As per Finlay J in *Wyatt v McLoughlin* [1974] IR 378 at p 390.
[50] [2008] 4 IR 480.

surrender *inter alia* on the grounds that the respondent had been convicted in the requesting state and, as such, on the basis of mutual trust there was a prima facie obligation to surrender:

> "Apart from other considerations referred to later in this judgment, the learned trial judge, having referred to the purposes of the Framework Decision and the basis of mutual trust on which it is to be operated concluded: *"That would suggest that if one member state has convicted a requested person for conduct which is an offence in that state then this State should respect the law and allow the requesting state to recover the fugitive offender".* That is in effect to say that once a person is convicted in one member state that is sufficient for his or her surrender without the correspondence of offences being required for any offence. But this is not what the Act of 2003 says or envisages. Section 38(1) of the Act prohibits the surrender to an issuing state in respect of any offence unless the conditions set out in paragraphs (a) or (b) are fulfilled. If the Act had the meaning inferred by the High Court there would be no need for a provision in the terms of s. 38 as a whole nor any need for a reference to Article 2.2 of the Decision which only gives dispensation from the correspondence test for a limited number of offences."

1–62   So whilst mutual trust will inform the manner in which the various judicial authorities may interact it will not have the effect of somehow reinforcing the obligation to surrender. That obligation is spelled out in the Act in reasonably simple terms. Whilst the principle of mutual trust may well give rise to what are practically speaking best viewed as implicit evidential burdens against the respondent in relation to issues such as the bona fides of the prosecuting authorities in the requesting state and due process rights, it will not water down the prohibitions on surrender in relation to matters of minimum gravity, correspondence and so on.

1–63   It would also seem that the principle of mutual trust may be limited in its application to emanations of judicial authorities. In *Minister for Justice, Equality and Law Reform v Ficzere*[51] Peart J considered that he could not afford the same weight to an undertaking provided by a Central Authority as he might to one given by a judicial authority:

> "In so far as it may be considered that the principle of mutual recognition and the underpinning concepts of a high level of trust and confidence between Member States might imply that if a Central Authority, as in the present case, guarantees a retrial to the respondent such should simply be accepted without question, I would say that mutual recognition applies only in respect of judicial decisions, and that the non-existence of an undertaking from the judicial authority because it has no power to give one is not a matter intended to be covered by the undoubted trust and confidence which exists between this State and the Republic of Hungary. What is at issue in this case is simply whether a provision of Irish law is complied with or not. It does not speak at all to the trust and confidence in the Republic of Hungary."[52]

1–64   As such the principle of mutual trust is something that is peculiar to the European arrest warrant system by virtue of the fact that it allows for direct judicial co-operation

---

[51] [2009] 1 IR 486.
[52] p 500. See also *Minister for Justice, Equality and Law Reform v Rimsa* [2010] IESC 47.

in circumstances where the role of the executive in the form of the Central Authority is relegated to the provision of administrative and technical assistance.

At a practical level it will mean that the courts will be very reluctant to entertain **1–65** any objection to surrender which calls into question to propriety of either the issuing of the European arrest warrant or whatever events may transpire subsequent to surrender. Notwithstanding this s 10 of the 2003 Act as originally enacted contained something of an invitation to litigate the circumstances surrounding the issuing of the warrant in the requesting state in that it seemed to suggest that the court must first be satisfied that the warrant was "duly issued"[53]. The courts, however, displayed a marked reluctance to entertain such arguments[54].

In *Minister for Justice, Equality and Law Reform v Iqbal, Sulej & Puta*[55] the **1–66** respondents sought to argue that the warrants in their cases had not been "duly issued" in the Czech Republic, as they were unlawful under Czech law. This was in circumstances where the offences to which they related predated the introduction of the European Arrest Warrant system and there was consequently a lack of reciprocity, in that the Czech Republic did not surrender its own citizens in respect of such offences. This lack of reciprocity, the respondents argued, amounted to discrimination contrary to Czech constitutional principles, although no relevant judgments of the Czech courts were presented to support this. It was argued that in the circumstances the warrants could not have been said to have been "duly issued". The respondents argued that since s 10 provided that the obligation to surrender only arose in relation to "duly issued" European arrest warrants, the question of whether a warrant had been duly issued in the issuing state was justiciable in this jurisdiction. Giving judgment for the Supreme Court, Fennelly J roundly rejected such a contention:

> "The appellants wish this Court to rule that the provisions of Czech law which implement the European arrest warrant are contrary to Czech constitutional principles. This Court could not conceivably pass judgment on the validity of existing Czech legal provisions. That is patently exclusively a matter for the domestic legal system".

The word "duly" has more recently been excised from the phrase "duly issued" in **1–67** s 10 by s 6 of the Criminal Justice (Miscellaneous Provisions) Act 2009. As such the grounds for inviting the courts to examine the circumstances in which the warrant was issued in the requesting state would appear to be all but non-existent.

---

[53] The word "duly" was subsequently excised by s 6 of the Criminal Justice (Miscellaneous Provisions) Act 2009.

[54] See *Minister for Justice, Equality and Law Reform v Michael Gerard Ward* (Unreported, High Court 4 July 2006).

[55] [2008] IESC 30.

CHAPTER 2

Overview of the European Arrest Warrant

In this chapter it is proposed to describe in broad terms the manner in which the European arrest warrant system is intended to work, the roles of the various players and explain the purpose of each of the various parts of the standard form of the warrant. **2–01**

OVERVIEW

As previously discussed one of the principal innovations of the European arrest warrant is that it allows judicial authorities to transmit warrants to each other for the purpose of execution. In effect it greatly curtails the role of the executive which had previously enjoyed a significant degree of discretion in relation to whether or not a particular extradition request would be granted. Instead a series of binding obligations has been created which are policed by the relevant judicial authorities, with role of the executive having been reduced that that of merely providing administrative assistance and support. **2–02**

2–03   Typically a request for surrender pursuant to a European arrest warrant will have its genesis in the issuing of a domestic warrant, or some similar measure, in the issuing state for the requested person. The domestic warrant may be regarded as being broadly similar to an arrest warrant issued for the purpose of commencing proceedings[1] or in the case of a person who fails to appear having been summonsed, charged or otherwise compelled to appear, a bench warrant. It is the domestic warrant which the European arrest warrant seeks to give effect to. Once the domestic warrant has been issued and it becomes apparent that the individual who is its subject is no longer within the jurisdiction, the prosecuting authorities in the requesting state will cause an application to be made to the appropriate judicial authority for a European arrest warrant. This will then be transmitted to the Central Authority, i.e. the Minister for Justice and Law Reform here who will cause an application to be made to the High Court pursuant to s 13 of the 2003 Act to have it endorsed for the purpose of execution. Thereafter the person named in the warrant is found, arrested and brought before the High Court.

THE ROLES OF THE VARIOUS PLAYERS

Designated State

2–04   By virtue of the provisions of Title VI of the EU Treaty Member States are obliged to implement the provisions of the Framework Decision. Once they have done so they may be designated by the Minister for Foreign Affairs as having done so.[2] They are then "designated states". For the purposes of the 2003 Act these are:

Country	Statutory Instrument	Designation Date
Austria	SI 206/2004	5th May, 2004
Belgium	SI 4/2004	1st January, 2004
Bulgaria	SI 59/2007	13th February, 2007
Cyprus	SI 206/2004	5th May, 2004
Czech Republic	SI 27/2005	25th January, 2005
Denmark	SI 4/2004	1st January, 2004
Estonia	SI 449/2004	21st July, 2004
Finland	SI 4/2004	1st January, 2004
France	SI 130/2004	2nd April, 2004
Germany	SI 532/2004	31st August, 2004
Greece	SI 449/2004	21st July, 2004
Hungary	SI 206/2004	5th May, 2004
Italy	SI 240/2005	15th May, 2005
Latvia	SI 449/2004	21st July, 2004
Lithuania	SI 206/2004	5th May, 2004

---

[1] E.g. pursuant to s 10 of the Petty Sessions Act 1851.

[2] s 3(1) of the European Arrest Warrant Act 2003 allows the Minister to designate Member States by way of Statutory Instrument.

Luxembourg	SI 130/2004	2nd April, 2004
Malta	SI 400/2004	24th June, 2004
Netherlands	SI 400/2004	24th June, 2004
Poland	SI 206/2004	5th May, 2004
Portugal	SI 4/2004	1st January, 2004
Romania	SI 59/2007	13th February, 2007
Slovakia	SI 532/2004	31st August, 2004
Slovenia	SI 206/2004	5th May, 2004
Spain	SI 4/2004	1st January, 2004
Sweden	SI 4/2004	1st January, 2004
United Kingdom	SI 4/2004	1st January, 2004

Judicial Authority

The Framework Decision requires each Member State to designate a judicial authority   **2–05**
for the purpose of issuing European arrest warrants, the "issuing judicial authority",
and a judicial authority for the purpose of executing them, the "executing judicial
authority". In this jurisdiction the executing judicial authority is the High Court[3]
whilst the issuing judicial authority is either the court which issued the domestic
warrant on which the European arrest warrant is based or the High Court.[4]

In the case of other Member States the identity and nature of the person or   **2–06**
body appointed as the issuing judicial authority will vary widely. The Framework
Decision does not provide any definition for the term "judicial authority" and as
such it would appear that Member States have a free hand in this regard. In common
law jurisdictions the distinction between the role of the prosecutor and the judiciary
has always been clear. Such distinctions are much less clear in continental systems
where the role of prosecutor has frequently evolved from what was originally a
judicial role in the form of an investigating magistrate. As such it is not unusual
for the issuing judicial authority to effectively be a prosecutor. In Sweden the
relevant issuing judicial authority is in fact the "Director General of the National
Police". Whilst such designations may seem unusual or even inappropriate from a
common law perspective, given the implicit requirement that the designated body
exercise a "judicial" function of some kind, it must equally be borne in mind that
the function of the issuing judicial authority is quite limited in that it simply issues
the European arrest warrant. In effect it makes the request. In the context of pre-
existing extradition procedures this was, in any event, a role fulfilled by and large
by the executive.

In a number of cases surrender has been resisted on the grounds that the European   **2–07**
arrest warrant is defective as the issuing judicial authority cannot be regarded as
being a judicial body in the sense contemplated by s 2 of the 2003 Act which defines
a "judicial authority" as being:

---

[3] s 9, European Arrest Warrant Act 2003.
[4] s 33(5) of the 2003 Act defines the "court" which is entitled to act as the issuing judicial
authority as "(a) the court that issued the domestic warrant to which subparagraph (i) of
Section 33(1)(a) applies, or (b) the High Court".

> "...the judge, magistrate or other person authorised under the law of the Member State concerned to perform functions the same as or similar to those performed under Section 33 by a court in the State".

2–08 In *Minister for Justice, Equality and Law Reform v Altaravicius (No.2)*[5] the respondent had contended that some form of extrinsic evidence was required to prove the identity and entitlement of the judicial authority who had purportedly issued the warrant. McMenamin J rejected this contention relying upon the principle of mutual trust and confidence as between judicial authorities. In that case the request had emanated from Lithuania and the warrant indicated the designated judicial authority there as being the "Prosecutor General of the Republic of Lithuania". The respondent went on to contend that the designation of the Prosecutor General as a judicial authority was something which was not contemplated by the 2003 Act.

2–09 McMenamin J declined to conclude that the Prosecutor General was not a judicial authority within the meaning of the Act, noting the different roles played by various players in the criminal justice systems of Member States and the fact that it would require cogent and material evidence to rebut the evidence as to the identity of the judicial authority contained in the warrant:

> "This court concludes, therefore, that the fact that the warrant in suit has been issued by the prosecuting authority in Lithuania in no way raises sufficient doubt as to the compliance by that state with the provisions of the framework decision. Judicial notice must be taken of the fact that most European member states operate within a civil law system. Direct comparisons between functions and roles of institutions within the administration of justice may not be apposite. No evidential material has been placed before this court which displaces the presumption that the prosecutor general in Lithuania is a competent judicial authority for the purposes of the framework decision and Act of 2003."[6]

2–10 A similar argument was raised in *Minister for Justice, Equality and Law Reform v Ferenca*[7] where the respondent sought to object to his surrender on the basis that the warrant had been issued by the "Lithuanian Minister for Justice"[8] who had been designated as the appropriate judicial authority. The respondent suggested that the designation of an apparently non-judicial person flew in the face of the underlying rationale of the Framework Decision. Peart J rejected this objection and noted that Lithuania had been duly designated under the 2003 Act and that it was not for the respondent to question whether the Lithuanian Minister for Justice should or should not be designated as the relevant judicial authority.

2–11 Whilst it is not immediately clear as to how the Irish courts could exercise any jurisdiction in relation to the question of who is designated as an issuing judicial authority by another Member State, it would seem that the criticisms raised by

---

[5] [2007] 2 IR 265.

[6] p 279.

[7] [2007] IEHC 199 – the decision was subsequently successfully appealed to the Supreme Court on unrelated grounds.

[8] The domestic provisions in Lithuania designated the Prosecutor General as the issuing judicial authority in the case of requested persons who had not yet been convicted and sentenced and the Ministry of Justice in the case of requested persons who had.

the respondents in such cases may not have been unduly wide of the mark. In a Commission Staff Working Document annexed to the Commission's report[9] on the implementation of the Framework Decision the Commission was expressly critical of Lithuania and the manner in which it had purported to designate what were clearly exclusively executive bodies as the relevant issuing judicial authorities:

> "The Ministry of Justice is not a judicial authority, but rather part of the executive. In particular, in the case the issuing of a EAW is asked by the prison department, there is no involvement at all of the judiciary. As to the Office of the Prosecutor General, it is considered as judicial authority in [Lithuania] because the related provision is inserted in Chapter 9 of its Constitution entitled "The Court" of the judicial Procedure. Hence, there is no strong support to the argument that the Office of the Prosecutor General is a judicial authority in [Lithuania]. Again, the Framework Decision states that an EAW must be issued or executed by a judicial authority and as a consequence [Lithuania]'s implementation of Article 6 is contrary to the Framework Decision."

Notwithstanding the somewhat impenetrable nature of the official translation of the working document the conclusion seems reasonably clear: it may not be permissible to designate bodies which are purely executive in nature as judicial authorities. What is considerably less clear is what the courts here can or should do when presented with such a situation. **2–12**

More controversial will be the designation of a purely executive body as the executing judicial authority. A case in point is Denmark which has designated its Ministry of Justice as both the issuing and executing judicial authorities. Although the exercise of its functions is subject to a form of judicial review this designation has been criticised by the Commission.[10] **2–13**

Designations of executing judicial authorities are obviously very unlikely to be a feature of litigation in this jurisdiction as the issue will only be of relevance to inward surrender cases. **2–14**

Central Authority

Section 6 of the 2003 Act designates the Minister for Justice and Law Reform as the Central Authority within the State. In practical terms this means that the Minister must provide the necessary administrative assistance for the purpose of responding to requests for surrender made by other Member States. As previously noted the role of the Central Authority is contemplated by the Framework Decision as being quite limited: **2–15**

> "The role of central authorities in the execution of a European arrest warrant must be limited to practical and administrative assistance."[11]

Whilst this may be strictly true, the reality is that the Minister is in effect the moving party in all surrender applications and is the party entitled to move an application for endorsement of a warrant for the purpose of execution pursuant to s 13. Section 20(2) **2–16**

---

[9] 11 July 2007 [Com(2007)407].

[10] The same Commission Staff Working Document commented that "…it is difficult to view such a designation as being in the spirit of the Framework Decision".

[11] Recital 9 of the Framework Decision.

also envisages that the Minister may seek additional information from the issuing state where the information provided is deemed to be inadequate. However, whilst s 20(2) makes reference to the Central Authority being entitled to "require" the issuing state to provide additional information it would seem that by virtue of the broader scheme of the Act and the Framework Decision it cannot effectively refuse to give effect to a European arrest warrant by refusing to make an application to endorse same because of some perceived defect. To do so would be tantamount to the Central Authority refusing surrender in circumstances where that is a matter which has been left to the executing judicial authority.

2–17　　The Supreme Court in *Rimsa v Goverer of Cloverhill Prison*[12] considered that the role of the Minister as Central Authority must be limited, as the backbone of the European arrest warrant system, namely the concept of mutual trust, arose by virtue of the more limited role played by the executive branch of government in the system of mutual surrender:

> It may be seen therefore that the Framework Decision intends that the role of any Central Authority, which, in contrast to a Judicial Authority referred to in the Framework Decision, belongs to the executive arm of a state, is confined to assisting the competent judicial authority and may also, if necessary, have responsibility for the administrative transmission and reception of European arrest warrants and related official correspondence.

> This limitation placed on the role of the central authorities of the member states, in contrast to that of a judicial authority, is of importance when one considers an objective of the Framework Decision, as set out at Recital (5) of the Preamble, is the establishment of an area, within the Union, of freedom, security and justice which would lead to the abolition of extradition between member states and replace it "by a *system of surrender between judicial authorities*."

2–18　　In *Rimsa* the Central Authority had purported to agree to the extension of time within which a person could be surrendered even though this was a function reserved to the judicial authority under Art 23.3. The court considered that the Central Authority was not entitled to do so given the limited role it played.

THE WARRANT

2–19　　Whilst previously under extradition arrangements the courts would have to consider a number of distinct documents comprising of warrants, undertakings, certified translations and so on, one of the main innovations of the European arrest warrant has been to streamline the procedure to the extent that the court now (by and large) only has to consider the warrant itself. The Framework Decision explicitly states as one of the goals of the new dispensation the simplification of the pre-existing procedures:

> "...the introduction of a new simplified system of surrender of sentenced or suspected persons for the purposes of execution or prosecution of criminal sentences makes it possible to remove the complexity and potential for delay inherent in the present extradition procedure."[13]

---

[12] [2010] IESC 47.
[13] Recital (5) of the Framework Decision.

The significance of this as an innovation cannot be understated. In traditional **2–20** extradition cases it is not uncommon for a straightforward request for extradition to comprise the original domestic arrest warrant or committal order, a detailed statement of the offence, a copy of all of the relevant legislation, a description of the person and various certificates authenticating each of the various documents.

The European arrest warrant essentially contains all of the information required **2–21** in one standardised document. The challenge of so doing is not insignificant when it is considered that the standard form of the warrant must take account of the vagaries and peccadilloes of criminal justice systems from common law, civil and former socialist traditions. Necessarily the result is not perfect and from time to time the inherent incompatibilities between these various systems become apparent.

From the requested person's point of view, the purpose of the warrant is not to **2–22** provide him with sufficient information to defend the case against him in the issuing state, but rather to enable him to deal with the surrender proceedings. As Peart J noted in *Minster for Justice, Equality and Law Reform v Dimitrovas*,[14] the purpose of the warrant is:

> "...to ensure that a person arrested has the necessary basic information upon arrest as to the offences for which his surrender is sought. It is not a document designed or intended to provide him with every piece of information which he might wish to have for the purpose of his trial..."

Thus an analogy may be drawn with a domestic arrest warrant. In the seminal House **2–23** of Lords decision in *Christie v Leachinsky*,[15] which has been approved in this jurisdiction[16], Viscount Simon explained the purpose of such a warrant:

> "...when an arrest is made on warrant, the warrant in normal cases has to be read to the person arrested. All this is for the obvious purpose of securing that a citizen who is prima facie entitled to personal freedom should know why for the time being his personal freedom is interfered with."

Like a domestic arrest warrant, a European arrest warrant is not required to go **2–24** further than to make the requested person aware of why he is being arrested.[17] In the case of a European arrest warrant, this obviously necessitates providing him with information as to why his surrender is sought by the issuing State, but this does not mean that he must be put in the position of being able to defend any charges which may be brought against him in that State. It follows that the warrant need not disclose a prima facie case against the requested person.

---

[14] [2007] IEHC 26.

[15] [1947] AC 573, at 585.

[16] See *In re Ó Laighléis* [1960] IR 93, *People (DPP) v Walsh* [1980] IR 294.

[17] However, the 2003 Act does not appear to give a requested person an automatic entitlement to be informed of the reasons for his or her arrest: s 13(3) of the Act allows for the warrant to be shown to a requested person at any time within 24 hours of his or her arrest, should the arresting member not be in possession of the warrant at the time of arrest. In such circumstances however it is possible that the requested person retains a common law entitlement to be told at least that he or she is being arrested because a European arrest warrant has been issued in respect of him or her.

Defects in the Warrant

2–25   As already noted the purpose of the standard form of the warrant in the Framework Decision is not necessarily to provide the respondent with information in relation to the prosecution against him in the requesting state but rather to provide him with sufficient information to deal with the proceedings under the European Arrest Warrant Act 2003. Any complaint to the effect that the warrant contains inadequate particulars must be considered in that context.

2–26   The courts have, on a number of occasions, considered various difficulties and defects which have arisen in respect of European arrest warrants. The critical issue when such problems arise will be whether or not the defect actually goes to any of the substantive issues with which the court is concerned. In *Minister for Justice, Equality and Law Reform v Rodnov*[18] the court noted that there were substantial defects in the warrant but that nonetheless, its purpose and meaning was still clear in that the defects did not give rise to a "…want of formality which affected in any way the substance or effect of the European arrest warrant." The Supreme Court did, however, suggest that it might not adopt such an understanding approach in future cases. In this regard the court noted that the responsibility in relation to ensuring that the formalities of the warrant were in order rested with the Minister:

> "I would add that there is nonetheless a duty on the applicant in these proceedings to examine requests for surrender and all documents which may be associated with a request in order to ensure that they are complete and correct. It would be wholly unsatisfactory if such an obligation on an applicant was disregarded on the basis that the court could be asked to look for further information pursuant to Section 20 of the Act…"

2–27   Whilst the concerns expressed by the courts in relation to some warrants are understandable there is, perhaps, a failure to fully appreciate that European arrest warrants are not necessarily directed or targeted at the executing state in the same way that extradition requests are. Frequently the warrant will be issued prior to the issuing state being aware of where the proposed respondent is. In this regard the whole purpose of the Framework Decision is that the same warrant should be capable of being executed across the entirety of the European Union. Such considerations were adverted to by Baroness Hale in the House of Lords Decision of *Regina (Hilali) v Governor of Whitemoor Prison*[19]:

> "A European Arrest Warrant may be executed in any of the Member States. The issuing judicial authority will not always know where the person concerned will be found. It cannot tailor the warrant to any particular or idiosyncratic requirements of another Member State. So, while I agree that every issuing State should do its best to comply with the requirements of the Framework Decision, it seems equally important that every requested State should approach the matter on the basis that this has been done: in other words, in a spirit of mutual trust and respect and not in a spirit of suspicion and disrespect."[20]

---

[18] Unreported, Supreme Court, 1 June 2006.

[19] [2008] 2 WLR 299.

[20] pp 309–310.

Insofar as issues arise in relation to particular warrants it may be as important to consider whether these arise by virtue of idiosyncrasies in relation the their issue or idiosyncrasies arising from the legislative scheme in the country of execution.   **2–28**

In *Minister for Justice, Equality and Law Reform v Stelmahs*[21] the quality of the translation of the warrant was extremely poor but it was, nonetheless, possible to glean is meaning and effect. In the circumstances the court was prepared to act upon it.   **2–29**

As with defects in form the existence of factual errors in the warrant will only be of relevance if they go to some substantive issue in the context of the surrender proceedings. In *Minister for Justice, Equality and Law Reform v Power*[22] the court noted that serious factual errors in a warrant might lead to a refusal to surrender. However, in a given case it remained to be determined as to whether the factual errors contained on the face of the warrant were actually material. In *Power* an error in relation to some of the facts recited on the face of the warrant was not held to be fatal as it did not affect any of the various issues which the court had to deal with in the course of the s 16 hearing. From a purely practical perspective it might be observed that very few factual errors will be patent. By and large the errors will be brought to light by the respondent who will indicate what the correct situation actually is. On the assumption that the correction of the error does not materially alter the nature of the court's inquiry, it is unlikely to be of any great significance.   **2–30**

A similar approach has been taken in the United Kingdom. In *Pietrzak v Regional Court in Wloclawek, Poland*,[23] the requested person had already served part of the sentence of imprisonment for which he was sought. The warrant in relation to this sentence incorrectly stated that the requested person had two years and four months left to serve, whereas it was clear from a second warrant received (seeking his surrender for prosecution in respect of his escape from custody) that the correct figure left to serve was in fact seven months. Latham LJ in the Queen's Bench Division felt that this error was of no significance: as long as the warrant disclosed a remaining sentence of more than four months, it was immaterial whether this sentence was in fact two years and four months or seven months.   **2–31**

THE VARIOUS PARTS OF THE WARRANT

The standard form of the European arrest warrant is annexed to the Framework Decision and Member States are obliged to adhere to this form when making requests. Section 11 of the Act provides: **2–32**

> "A European arrest warrant shall, in so far as practicable, be in the form set out in the Annex to the Framework Decision".

When duly completed the European arrest warrant contains a significant amount of information – in truth considerably more than will be required in the context of a given case. From a practitioners point of view it can sometimes be difficult to distinguish the relevant information from the irrelevant and even to identify which part of the warrant deals with the various issues which may arise. What follows is a description of each of the various parts of the warrant, the function that each part serves and a discussion of the various issues which may arise in respect of each part.   **2–33**

---

[21] [2006] IEHC 293.

[22] [2007] IEHC 285.

[23] [2009] 1 WLR 866.

Heading

> *This warrant has been issued by a competent judicial authority. I request that the person mentioned below be arrested and surrendered for the purposes of conducting a criminal prosecution or executing a custodial sentence or detention order.*

2–34 The standard form of the European arrest warrant annexed to the Framework Decision contains a heading in the terms set out above. At first glance the recital to the effect that the warrant has been issued for the purpose of either prosecuting the respondent or enforcing a sentence may seem to be little more than surplusage. However, it establishes an important proof in the context of any application for surrender. Whilst s 21A of the 2003 Act provides for a presumption to the effect that a decision has been made to charge the respondent, the courts have on occasion expressly relied upon the terms of the heading of the warrant in support of such a presumption.[24] In a given case this may be of significance as s 10 of the Act implements Art 1.1 of the Framework Decision which requires surrender to be made "for the purposes of conducting a criminal prosecution or executing a custodial sentence or detention order". By implication, therefore, surrender will not be granted where the arrest of the respondent is sought for some other purpose, most notably, for investigative purposes.

Paragraph (a) – Information Regarding the Identity of the Requested Person

> *Name:*
>
> *Forename(s):*
>
> *Maiden name, where applicable:*
>
> *Aliases, where applicable:*
>
> *Sex:*
>
> *Nationality:*
>
> *Date of birth:*
>
> *Place of birth:*
>
> *Residence and/or known address:*
>
> *Language(s) which the requested person understands (if known):*
>
> *Distinctive marks/description of the requested person:*
>
> *Photo and fingerprints of the requested person, if they are available and can be transmitted, or contact details of the person to be contacted in order to obtain such information or a DNA profile (where this evidence can be supplied but has not been included).*

2–35 The content of this part of the warrant is largely self explanatory. The information to be provided under this heading is specifically designed to allow some degree of compatibility with the Schengen Information System and broadly follows the same template.

---

[24] E.g. *Minister for Justice, Equality and Law Reform v Balciunas* [2007] 1 ILRM 516.

Given the significant amount of information that is usually contained in a European 2–36
arrest warrant, issues in respect of identification tend to arise only infrequently. That
said the court needs to be satisfied that the respondent is the person named in the
warrant not only for the purpose of the s 16 hearing[25] but also when the respondent
is first brought before the High Court after the warrant has been executed.[26] Indeed
it would seem that in relation to the first appearance before the High Court it is a
condition precedent to any remand or other step in the proceedings that the court be
satisfied that the person arrested is one and the same as the person described in the
warrant.

The issue of the identity of the respondent is ultimately a matter of fact and the 2–37
extent of any contest will largely be dependent upon the extent of the detail provided
by para (a) in relation to identity. The purpose of details set out in para (a) is to allow
the court to determine the question of identity rather than an exercise in formalism.
The fact that there is some discrepancy or even error in relation to the name of the
respondent or any of the other details recited is simply a matter to be considered in
the overall context of the issue of the respondent's identity.[27]

Whilst the standard form of the warrant envisages that information under a 2–38
number of different headings (including potentially fingerprints and DNA profiles)
be provided, both Art 8 of the Framework Decision and s 11(a) of the Act only
require that the name and nationality of the requested person be provided. Although
the requirement that a name be provided is obvious, the insistence on the nationality
also being furnished is perhaps less so. Presumably the obligation to furnish the
nationality stems from the possibility of one or more of the optional grounds for
non-surrender or conditional surrender outlined in the Framework Decision arising
by virtue of the nationality of the respondent. Given that civil law systems tend
to exercise such jurisdiction on the grounds of nationality, it may be of potential
significance particularly in the context of extraterritorial offence.

As a result of amendments effected by the Criminal Justice (Miscellaneous 2–39
Provisions) Act 2009 there are now extensive powers available to an Garda Síochána
to take fingerprints and other bodily samples from arrested persons for the purpose
of proving identity for the purposes of the 2003 Act. Section 45A empowers a
member of an Garda Síochána to use reasonable force if necessary to obtain such
samples and allows the court to accept at face value the accuracy of any fingerprint
or photograph received from the issuing State.

Paragraph (b) – Decision on which the Warrant is Based

1. Arrest warrant or judicial decision having the same effect:

Type:

2. Enforceable judgment:

Reference:

---

[25] s 16(1)(a).

[26] s 13(5).

[27] In *Minister for Justice, Equality and Law Reform v TMC* [2006] IEHC 372 there was some
minor discrepancy in relation to the respondent's name which was not such as to cause the
court any great difficulty in relation to the issue of identification.

2–40   This is the part of the warrant which indicates the basis upon which the respondent is sought. As a general rule details in relation to an "enforceable judgment" will only be given in circumstances where the respondent has been sentenced to a period of imprisonment or detention as it is essentially an alternative to the "arrest warrant or judicial decision" referred to at para (b)1. There will, however, be cases where an individual is sought in respect of offences for which he has been sentenced and offences for which he has not – in such circumstances details of both will be given.

2–41   In the case of *Minister for Justice, Equality and Law Reform v Kavanagh*[28] the court considered this part of the standard form. Under this heading the warrant simply noted that the respondent was suspected of having contravened various statutory provisions of the Dutch Narcotics Act. It made no reference to any arrest warrant having been issued nor a judicial decision which had the same effect as an arrest warrant. The High Court had taken the view that the omission was not a particularly serious one when viewed in the context of the other information available in the warrant. In particular it relied on the provisions of s 21A of the Act which provides for a presumption in favour of the requesting state that it made a decision to charge or try the respondent for the offence in question. The Supreme Court disagreed and expressed the view that the European arrest warrant ought not even have been endorsed in the absence of an express reference to an underlying warrant.

2–42   In the subsequent case of *Minister for Justice, Equality and Law Reform v Ostrowski*[29] the High Court considered a European arrest warrant that contained incorrect details in relation to the underlying domestic warrant as being fatally flawed even though the authorities in the issuing state had provided additional information explaining the error and providing the correct details in respect of the domestic warrant. The decision is to be contrasted with that in the case of *Minister for Justice, Equality and Law Reform v Spencer*[30] where the European arrest warrant cited itself as the basis for its issue. The issuing judicial authority subsequently clarified matters by providing details of a domestic warrant. In that case the High Court did not consider the defect to be fatal.

2–43   In *SMR v Governor of Cloverhill Prison*[31] the underlying domestic warrant was accidentally withdrawn in the issuing state between the making of the s 16 order and the hearing of an appeal in relation to same. There was conflicting expert evidence as to the legal significance of the withdrawal of the warrant in the issuing state. There was, however, evidence before the court to the effect that the issuing state nonetheless intended to prosecute the respondent if returned. Ultimately the High Court concluded that it was not permissible nor desirable to engage in any detailed analysis as to the validity of the warrant under the law of the issuing state as this would offend against the principle of mutual trust. It was sufficient that the underlying domestic warrant had been in existence at the time of endorsement and its subsequent withdrawal did not affect the proceedings in the executing state.

2–44   There can be no difficulty where it is reasonably clear that a warrant or some equivalent issued in the issuing state. In *Minister for Justice, Equality and Law Reform v Stelmahs*[32] the rather poor translation of the warrant described the underlying arrest warrant or equivalent as having been a decision by the relevant

---

[28] Ex tempore, Supreme Court, 23 October 2009.
[29] Unreported, High Court, 19 March 2010.
[30] Ex tempore, High Court, 19 February 2010.
[31] [2009] IEHC 442.
[32] [2006] IEHC 293.

criminal court to "change of security measures" in respect of the respondent and "proclaim of his quest". The court held that in the context of the case this ought to be understood to be the equivalent of the issue of a judicial arrest warrant.

Paragraph (c) – Indications on the Length of the Sentence

> *1. Maximum length of the custodial sentence or detention order which may be imposed for the offence(s):*
>
> *2. Length of the custodial sentence or detention order imposed:*
>
> *Remaining sentence to be served:*

The principle purpose of the information under this heading is to allow the court to determine that there is compliance with the minimum gravity requirements. Obviously in relation to pre-conviction cases the information at para (c)2 is not applicable. **2–45**

A difficulty may arise from time to time where the warrant relates to a number of different offences in respect of which penalties have been imposed but no distinction is drawn as to the actual penalty imposed in respect of each separate offence. Such composite sentences can frequently give rise to difficulties in circumstances where one or more of the offences does not correspond. **2–46**

Frequently the sentence imposed will have been suspended or part suspended or subjected to some equivalent form of non-execution. Whilst the warrant may contain details of the circumstances in which the suspension or its equivalent came to be lifted this is not strictly necessary.[33] **2–47**

Paragraph (d) – Decision Rendered in Absentia

> - *the person concerned has been summoned in person or otherwise informed of the date and place of the hearing which led to the decision rendered in absentia,*
>
> *Or*
>
> - *the person concerned has not been summoned in person or otherwise informed of the date and place of the hearing which led to the decision rendered in absentia but has the following legal guarantees after surrender (such guarantees can be given in advance).*

This part of the warrant only needs to be filled out in the event that the respondent has been convicted in absentia. Where there has been a conviction in absentia it is necessary for para (d) to indicate which of the alternative scenarios outlined actually arises. If the respondent had been summonsed in person or otherwise informed then surrender can take place irrespective of whether or not the legal guarantees referred to in the second paragraph are present. Where the person has not been so summonsed or otherwise informed surrender can only take place where an appropriate guarantee as to a retrial is given. **2–48**

---

[33] *Minister for Justice, Equality and Law Reform v Adach* (Ex tempore, Peart J, 20 October 2009).

2–49   Whilst it is not necessarily mandated by the standard form of the warrant, it is frequently the case that details as to the manner in which the respondent was personally summonsed or otherwise made aware of the proceedings will be set out in this part of the warrant. Given the relatively strict terms of s 45 and the requirement that the respondent has been given actual rather than constructive notice of the place and date of trial, it is often the case that additional information will have to be sought in this regard.

2–50   Similarly, although s 12(3) allows an undertaking to be included in a European arrest warrant, it will frequently be necessary to obtain a separate written undertaking that complies strictly with the terms of s 45 should one be required.

Paragraph (e) – Offences

This warrant relates to in total: ....offences.

Description of the circumstances in which the offence(s) was (were) committed, including the time, place and degree of participation in the offence(s) by the requested person:

Nature and legal classification of the offence(s) and the applicable statutory provision/code:

2–51   This is perhaps the most significant part of the warrant from a practitioner's point of view as it will generally contain the information on foot of which an assessment is made in relation to correspondence. The extent of the information provided varies greatly. Generally a summary will be given of the offence in question and the involvement, alleged or otherwise, of the respondent. Frequently some detail will also be given in relation to procedural matters such as the circumstances of conviction of the respondent where appropriate or perhaps the issuing of a bench warrant.

2–52   The number of offences to which the warrant relates can be of significance particularly in the context of severability where one or more of the offences is found not to correspond. Moreover it is sometimes less than obvious from the narrative of events as to precisely how many offences the warrant relates to.

2–53   The principal purpose of this part of the warrant is to provide a description of the circumstances of the offence which might allow the court to determine the issue of correspondence should that be necessary. One of the immediate differences between the European arrest warrant and the more minimalist "dressed up warrants"[34] which were common under the 1965 Act is that the European arrest warrant will generally contain much more information in respect of the offence than warrants under the old regime. At a practical level this means that the warrant is much less likely to encounter a difficulty in respect of correspondence due to a lack of detail or a failure to make reference to a particular element of the offence.[35]

2–54   This is not to say that the format of the European arrest warrant is without difficulties. It is frequently the case that where an excess of detail is given in respect

---

[34] See *Trimbole v Governor of Mountjoy* [1985] ILRM 449 at p 476.
[35] For example in the case of *AG v Dyer* [2004] 1 IR 40 the failure on the face of the warrant to allege a fraudulent intent was held to be fatal on the issue of correspondence.

of the offences to which the warrant relates it becomes very difficult to assess what conduct on the part of the respondent is said to amount to the offending conduct and what is included simply by way of background or incidental detail.

Whilst para (e) of the warrant and s 11(1)(f) of the Act require that the relevant **2–55** degree of involvement on the part of the respondent in the offence be set out, this requirement must be viewed in context. The principal purpose of a detailed narrative of the offence being set out in the warrant including a description of the respondent's role (i.e. that of principal, aider or abettor or some other involvement in the nature of a joint enterprise) is to allow the court to determine the question of correspondence. It necessarily follows that a failure to set out explicitly the extent of the respondent's involvement will only become an issue where it gives rise to a specific difficulty. In *Minister for Justice, Equality and Law Reform v Hamilton*[36] the court expressed itself to be largely unconcerned as to the failure of the warrant to describe the respondent's role in the offence in circumstances where the offence was one of murder, which in any event was not only a corresponding offence but also a listed offence:

> "It is hard to imagine what further information is necessary in order to indicate a degree of involvement, apart from somebody being actually in the bathroom when injury was inflicted and who could then say whether this respondent inflicted the blows, or whether he was simply an onlooker to what was happening, or whether he was an accessory and so forth. These are matters which will no doubt be ventilated at any trial which will take place. But there is detail sufficient to show a degree of involvement, and this Court is not required to pass any judgment upon the level or amount of that involvement. I am satisfied that the form of the warrant complies with the prescribed form as provided for in the Framework Decision."[37]

Similarly in *Minister for Justice, Equality and Law Reform v Martin Stafford*,[38] **2–56** the European arrest warrant contained a mixture of ticked offences and ordinary offences. The offences for which the respondent was sought included murder and "sexual touching without consent", in circumstances where the respondent's semen had been found in the car of a missing person, along with that person's blood. The respondent had been identified in CCTV footage driving the car on the morning of the victim's disappearance, and he had been staying at the same guest house as her. The respondent unsuccessfully argued that there was insufficient detail given in the warrant linking him with the commission of the offences in question. The court relied on the principle of mutual recognition to find that, as long as *some* degree of participation is shown, the strength or weakness of the case against the requested person is of no relevance to the issue of surrender:

> "The question which arises for determination is whether the acts alleged on the warrant show a link with the requested person. It is not necessary to show a *prima facie* case. It is not necessary to show a "strong" case. The issue of guilt or innocence is for the jury in the requesting state.

---

[36] [2008] 1 IR 60.

[37] p 65.

[38] [2009] IESC 83.

> This case is one of circumstantial evidence. There is no reason why an accusation of a crime based upon circumstantial evidence could not be the basis for a European arrest warrant. It is necessary to look at the facts alleged in each warrant."

In the same case the heading "degree of participation in the offence by the requested person" was omitted from the warrant. This was held not to be fatal in the circumstances.

Obviously some degree of participation must be alleged. Surrender was refused in relation to an offence in *Minister for Justice, Equality and Law Reform v Kasprowicz*[39] where persons other than the respondent were alleged to have committed it and there was no mention of the respondent's name in the warrant in relation to that particular offence.

2-57   The information provided at para (e) of the warrant was central to the decision in the Northern Ireland case of *In the Matter of Arturo Villanueva Arteaga*.[40] In that case, the offence for which surrender was sought was *"membership of an illegal terrorist organisation"*. The warrant gave what appeared to be very vague particulars of acts which were said to connect the requested person with the JARRAI organisation in Spain, which was a subdivision of ETA. These particulars were:

> "...he carried out violent and coercive actions from 1994 to 2000, such as a course of conduct directed to disturb the public peace through the use of violent means in the streets, he set street furniture and buses on fire, made arson attacks against courts and government facilities, carried out attacks against private individuals and police, organised campaigns to discredit judges and police, he encouraged that institutions be persecuted by citizens, Basque businesses be coerced and forced to pay money if they do not want to suffer damages".

2-58   The case was complicated somewhat by the fact that the acts were alleged to have been committed before JARRAI was declared a terrorist organisation in 2007, although this ultimately did not have a bearing on the outcome. Burgess J carried out an examination of the authorities on the issue of the level of specificity which is required at paragraph (e) of the warrant. Although it was clear that each case had to be decided on its own particular facts, the decisions considered by Burgess J all concerned warrants which contained details of the offence above and beyond what he now had to consider. He concluded that the particulars given in the warrant before him were insufficient in that, for example, no location was given for the burning of street furniture and buses, nor was it specified on whom the requested person carried out attacks. Essentially, Burgess J was of the view that the particulars given did not provide sufficient connection to the offence alleged:

> "I have therefore concluded that the particulars given are general and lack any specificity as to the actions of the Requested Person which evidences his alleged membership of the organisation such as attending meetings; giving interviews; being involved in the organisation of the Group (and if so, how) and other outward manifestations that might allow the court to come to a view that the element of membership of the Group is particularised with proper specificity".

---

[39] [2010] IEHC 207.
[40] [2009] NI Cty 7.

Although *Arteaga* is instructive as to what level of detail might be required at para   **2–59**
(e), it must be said that membership of an illegal organisation is an offence in respect
of which the particular conduct required to prove its commission is quite broad and
uncertain, when compared with, for example, assault or possession of drugs. As
such, it may be a case which would be seen to turn on its own particular facts, and an
attempt to transpose the requirements imposed by Burgess J onto the facts of another
case could lead to a judge effectively requiring that the warrant disclose a prima
facie case which, as noted above, would not be a permissible requirement.

In general the omission of detail that is not required for the purpose of determining   **2–60**
whether an order under s 16 will be made will not of itself represent a bar to surrender.
In *Minister for Justice, Equality and Law Reform v Jordan*[41] the omission of the
complainant's name in relation to a sexual offence was considered to be immaterial.

The information provided under the heading *"Nature and Legal Classification of*   **2–61**
the Offence" will generally make it clear what relevant law or statutory provision the
offence is contrary to. At a practical level this may well provide useful information
as the provision cited should obviously correspond to the relevant penalty cited
elsewhere in the warrant. Similarly it may be of assistance in attempting to identify
which parts of the factual narrative relate to which offences – this may be an important
exercise in the context of determining whether or not the offence corresponds.

The failure to cite the relevant statutory provision will not necessarily be fatal   **2–62**
to the warrant. In *Minister for Justice, Equality and Law Reform v Dimitrovas*[42] the
warrant did not set out all of the statutory provisions which applied to the offences
in respect of which it had issued. Peart J concluded that this did not give rise to any
particular difficulty:

> "The Framework Decision itself and the Act provide a specimen of the form
> of warrant to be used for a European arrest warrant. Its purpose is to ensure
> that the person arrested has the necessary basic information upon arrest as to
> the offences for which his surrender is sought. It is not a document designed
> or intended to provide him with every piece of information which he might
> wish to have but he is entitled to know in a general way what offence is alleged
> and the provision of the law of the issuing state he is said to have infringed,
> and of course the potential penalty he might face if convicted. This court also
> requires a certain minimum of detail if it is required to determine the question
> of correspondence and minimum gravity. That is another purpose filled by a
> correct completion of the warrant."

A similar conclusion was reached by the House of Lords in *Dabas v High Court*   **2–63**
of Justice Madrid[43] where Hope LJ observed:

> "Any scheme which retained scrutiny of the text of the foreign law as a
> requirement would be bound to give rise to delay and complexity – the very
> things that in dealings between Member States the Framework Decision was
> designed to eliminate…There is no requirement here that the text of the law
> which gives rise to that punishment must be made available."[44]

---

[41] [2009] IEHC 469.
[42] [2007] IEHC 26.
[43] [2007] 2 AC 31.
[44] pp 53–54.

2–64   The foregoing is also in accordance with decisions of the Supreme Court of the Netherlands[45] and the Oberlandesgericht, Stuttgart.[46] It has, however been suggested[47] that it may not be sufficient to simply provide the article or section numbers of the relevant statute or penal code and that the requested person is at a minimum entitled to be made aware of the essence of the offence for which he is arrested.

Paragraph (e) I: The list of Offences

> I. If applicable, tick one or more of the following offences punishable in the issuing Member State by a custodial sentence or detention order of a maximum of at least 3 years as defined by the laws of the issuing Member State:
>
> (List of offences as per Article 2.2 of the Framework Decision)

2–65   This is the part of the warrant that allows the requesting state to certify that one or more of the offences in respect of which surrender is sought come within the Art 2.2 list and, as such, it is not necessary to show correspondence. It is for the requesting state alone to certify and even though the description of a given offence may suggest that it ought to come within one of the categories, it will not be regarded as coming within the Art 2.2 list unless the relevant box is ticked.[48]

2–66   The list of offences prescribed by Art 2.2 of the Framework Decision is reproduced in the standard form of the warrant. However, some Member States have from time to time included additional elements within the list as it appears in the warrant not envisaged by the Framework Decision. In particular Italy has, in the past, disregarded the Art 2.2 list and effectively replaced it with its own list of equivalent domestic offences. It is inevitable that where the requesting state deviates from the prescribed list the courts will simply regard the certification as ineffective and it will be necessary to show correspondence in the ordinary way.

Paragraph (e) II: Offences Not Included in the List

> II. Full descriptions of offence(s) not covered by section I above:

2–67   Because para (e)I of the warrant does not make it clear which offences come within the Art 2.2 list and which do not, it is frequently necessary to have regard to this part of the warrant for the purpose of ascertaining which offences are not covered by the Art 2.2 certification. Any offences which are included here will be subject to the normal requirement that correspondence be established. In *Minister for Justice, Equality and Law Reform v Paulauskas*[49] the offence in question had been included in both the Art 2.2 list at para (e)I and at para (e)II. This was obviously somewhat self contradictory. In the circumstances the court concluded that it would be necessary to establish correspondence in the ordinary way.

---

[45] Case LJN BD2447, 8 July 2008.

[46] Case 3 Ausl 52/06 para. II.5, 26 October 2006.

[47] *The European Arrest Warrant in Practice* (2009) Keijzer & Van Sliedregt, p 9.

[48] *Minister for Justice, Equality and Law Reform v Ferenca* [2008] 4 IR 480.

[49] [2009] IEHC 32.

Paragraph (f): Other Circumstances

> *Other circumstances relevant to the case (optional information):*
>
> *(NB: This could cover remarks on extraterritoriality, interruption of periods of time limitation and other consequences of the offence)*

Various different types of information may be provided here. It is important to note   **2–68** that the information provided under this heading is entirely optional and as such the omission of information in relation to, for example, extraterritoriality should not be regarded as an indication that an issue does not arise in relation to same. Frequently the requesting state will take the opportunity to give an account of the manner in which it is said the requested person was notified where a conviction or sentence has been imposed in absentia.

Paragraph (g): Seizure of Property and Evidence

> *This warrant pertains also to the seizure and handing over of property which may be required as evidence:*
>
> *This warrant pertains also to the seizure and handing over of property acquired by the requested person as a result of the offence:*
>
> *Description of the property (and location) (if known):*

This part of the warrant is rarely completed in practice. Paragraph (g) differentiates   **2–69** between property which may be required as evidence on the one hand and property acquired as a result of the offence, i.e. proceeds of crime. The distinction between the two types of property is not of any great significance as far as the European Arrest Warrant Act 2003 is concerned as s 25 which allows for the seizure of such property does not draw any distinction between the two.

Paragraph (h): Undertakings in Relation to Life Sentences

> *The offence(s) on the basis of which this warrant has been issued is(are) punishable by/has(have) led to a custodial life sentence or lifetime detention order:*
>
> - *the legal system of the issuing Member State allows for a review of the penalty or measure imposed — on request or at least after 20 years — aiming at a non-execution of such penalty or measure,*
>
> *and/or*
>
> - *the legal system of the issuing Member State allows for the application of measures of clemency to which the person is entitled under the law or practice of the issuing Member State, aiming at non-execution of such penalty or measure.*

2–70   Article 5(2) of the Framework Decision[50] provides an optional ground upon which surrender may be refused in the event of the imposition, or possible imposition, of a life sentence. In such circumstances surrender can be subject to the existence under the law of the requesting state of an entitlement on the part of the requested person to seek clemency, parole or some other form of suspension or non-execution of the sentence after a given period of time. As this optional ground for surrender has not been implemented by the 2003 Act it would not seem to be of any great relevance even though this part of the warrant is routinely completed in the case of requests to this jurisdiction. The contents of para (h) are, therefore, unlikely to arise in practice. Article 5(2) was briefly considered by the Supreme Court in *Minister for Justice, Equality and Law Reform v Brennan*[51] where the respondent unsuccessfully argued that the information provided at para (h) of the warrant amounted to an indication that a mandatory life sentence would be imposed in that particular case. The court rejected this argument.

Paragraph (i): Details of the Judicial and Central Authorities

> *The judicial authority which issued the warrant:*
>
> *Official name:*
>
> *Name of its representative:*
>
> *Post held (title/grade):*
>
> *File reference:*
>
> *Address:*
>
> *Tel:*
>
> *Contact details of the person to contact to make necessary practical arrangements for the surrender.*

2–71   The information required under this part of the warrant is directed towards enabling ease of communication as between the judicial/central authorities in the issuing and executing States.

---

[50] "5. The execution of the European arrest warrant by the executing judicial authority may, by the law of the executing Member State, be subject to the following conditions:
…2. if the offence on the basis of which the European arrest warrant has been issued is punishable by custodial life sentence or life-time detention order, the execution of the said arrest warrant may be subject to the condition that the issuing Member State has provisions in its legal system for a review of the penalty or measure imposed, on request or at the latest after 20 years, or for the application of measures of clemency to which the person is entitled to apply for under the law or practice of the issuing Member State, aiming at non-execution of such penalty or measure;".

[51] [2007] 3 IR 732.

Signature of the Judicial Authority

> *The judicial authority which issued the warrant[52]:*
>
> *Official name:*
>
> *Name of its representative:*
>
> *Post held (title/grade):*
>
> *File reference:*
>
> *Address:*
>
> *Tel:*
>
> *Contact details of the person to contact to make necessary practical arrangements for the surrender:*

This is, essentially, the operative part of the warrant in that it is the fact that the warrant emanates from a judicial authority that allows the executing state to extend the appropriate degree of mutual trust. By reason of s 12(8)(a) of the 2003 Act the signature of the judicial authority effectively proves itself and the courts will not, in general, go behind it. In *Minister for Justice, Equality and Law Reform v Ostrovskij*[53] the warrant indicated that the appropriate issuing judicial authority was the "Prosecutor General's Office of the Republic of Lithuania" whilst the warrant was actually signed by the "acting prosecutor general". The respondent argued that this amounted to a discrepancy of a serious nature. Not surprisingly this argument was rejected by the court.

2–72

---

[52] For States where a central authority has been made responsible for the transmission and administration of warrants the information provided in this part of the warrant will relate to the relevant person in the central authority as opposed to the judicial authority.

[53] [2006] IEHC 242.

The Obligation to Surrender

Whilst any system of extradition is generally understood to concern itself with making those who are the subject of either prosecution or sentence answerable to the system, the actual scope of what is covered in any specific system is ultimately a matter of definition. The European Arrest Warrant Act 2003 is no different in this regard in that it, at various points, sets out the circumstances in which it is intended to apply. **3–01**

SCOPE OF THE FRAMEWORK DECISION

The Framework Decision sets out quite clearly and concisely the scope of the European arrest warrant at Art 1(1): **3–02**

> "The European arrest warrant is a judicial decision issued by a Member State with a view to the arrest and surrender by another Member State of a requested person, for the purposes of conducting a criminal prosecution or executing a custodial sentence or detention order."

Essentially the Framework Decision envisages that the European arrest warrant will only apply in cases where the requested person is sought in order that he or she may be prosecuted or alternatively for the purpose of enforcing a custodial penalty of some type. In cases where the person has been convicted and sentenced the warrant will only apply where a "custodial sentence or detention order" has been imposed. In all other cases surrender will be confined to situations where it is sought for the express purpose of conducting a criminal prosecution as opposed, for example, for the purpose of investigation. **3–03**

CIRCUMSTANCES GIVING RISE TO AN OBLIGATION TO SURRENDER

Section 10 of the 2003 Act

3–04 Article 1(1) of the Framework Decision is given effect by means of s 10 of the European Arrest Warrant Act 2003 which sets out the scope of application of the Act itself. As noted previously one of the major distinctions between a system of extradition and a system of rendition is that the latter imposes a mandatory obligation on the requested state whereas requests received in relation to the former can be dealt with on a discretionary basis to a greater or lesser degree. As such s 10 seeks to set out the scope of these obligations and attempts to describe in an exhaustive fashion the circumstances in which there is an obligation on the State to surrender:

> "10.—Where a judicial authority in an issuing state issues a European arrest warrant in respect of a person—
>
> (a) against whom that state intends to bring proceedings for an offence to which the European arrest warrant relates,
>
> (b) who is the subject of proceedings in that state for an offence to which the European arrest warrant relates,
>
> (c) who has been convicted of, but not yet sentenced in respect of, an offence in that state to which the European arrest warrant relates, or
>
> (d) on whom a sentence of imprisonment or detention has been imposed in that state in respect of an offence to which the European arrest warrant relates,
>
> that person shall, subject to and in accordance with the provisions of this Act and the Framework Decision, be arrested and surrendered to the issuing state."

3–05 The section attempts to describe in a comprehensive fashion each of the circumstances in which an obligation to surrender arises on the part of the State. These might be summarised in terms of equivalent domestic criminal procedure as follows:

(i) A person who has not been charged but who it is intended to prosecute;

(ii) A person who has already been charged but has presumably left the jurisdiction of the requesting state;

(iii) A person who left the requesting state subsequent to conviction but prior to sentence;

(iv) A person who has had a sentence of imprisonment imposed.

3–06 The current form of s 10 represents the third attempt by the legislature to define the scope of the Act. When initially enacted the section failed to provide for surrender in circumstances where a person had absconded subsequent to charge and a person who had been convicted but not yet sentenced. Experience would tend to suggest that it is the first of these categories which tends to give rise to the majority of requests for surrender which makes it all the more surprising that it was omitted in its entirety from the Act as initially passed.

Subsequent amendments effected by the Criminal Justice (Terrorist Offences) Act 2005 improved matters somewhat but imposed a requirement that a person who had been convicted and sentenced in the issuing state would have to be shown to have "fled" from the issuing state. This gave rise to considerable difficulties and amounted to the imposition of a proof that was not mandated by the Framework Decision. The difficulties which have arisen in relation to the manner in which s 10 has been promulgated arise principally from the fact that an attempt has been made to seek to describe in detail all of the circumstances in which surrender must be ordered when it was in all probability unnecessary to do so. The somewhat clearer and more straightforward template provided by Art 1.1 of the Framework Decision might be said to have had much to recommend it in this regard.   **3–07**

In reality the only meaningful distinction drawn by the Framework Decision in terms of the scope of the European arrest warrant is in relation to those sought for prosecution and those sought for execution of sentence. Paragraph 5 of the Preamble refers to "the introduction of a new simplified system of surrender of sentenced or suspected persons for the purposes of execution or prosecution of criminal sentences…". It goes on to envisage that the European Arrest Warrant will cover "both pre-sentence and final decisions…". As such it is difficult to understand why it was considered necessary for s 10 of the 2003 Act to seek to further sub-divide, refine and exhaustively define the circumstances which would give rise to an obligation to surrender.   **3–08**

The form of the European Arrest Warrant appended to the Framework Decision is also instructive in that it distinguishes between two distinct types of order namely an "arrest warrant or judicial decision having the same effect"[1] on the one hand and an "enforceable judgment"[2] on the other. That the concept of an enforceable judgment includes a conviction in absentia is implicit in the provisions of the Framework Decision which, whilst not expressly authorising surrender in such circumstances, provides for certain assurances to be given in such cases.[3]   **3–09**

It is difficult to avoid the conclusion that s 10 of the Act as initially drafted unnecessarily complicated what was otherwise a relatively straightforward concept which had been set out clearly in the Framework Decision. This did no more than seek to require surrender firstly where it was desired to conduct a criminal prosecution and secondly for the purposes of executing a sentence or detention order. Section 10 sought to further define and sub-divide the various situations which might arise and rather inexplicably sought to impose a further requirement in cases where sentence had been imposed in absentia, namely, the requirement that the respondent had "fled" the requesting state. Given the wide variation   **3–10**

---

[1] para (a)1 of the standard form of the European arrest warrant.

[2] para (a)2.

[3] Art 5.1 of the Framework Decision.

between criminal procedures in Member States it is a more or less impossible task to seek to define, on a pan-European basis, the various circumstances which might arise. Indeed the divergence of procedure renders the definition of even the most elementary concepts and terms at best slippery. For example it is often very difficult to even identify the point at which a person may become a suspect in some jurisdictions let alone adopt a common understanding as to what might constitute the commencement of proceedings.

MJELR v Tobin

3–11   The frailties of s 10(d) and in particular the requirement that the respondent be shown to have fled were cast into stark relief in the case of *Minister for Justice, Equality and Law Reform v Tobin*.[4] The respondent in that case had been the subject of a prosecution in Hungary in relation to an offence that arose out of a road traffic accident in April 2000. An investigation into the offence commenced more or less in the immediate aftermath of the accident. This was ongoing in August 2000 when the respondent was allowed to return to Ireland for a period of time. He returned to Hungary in October 2000 and ultimately left that jurisdiction permanently in November 2000. This latter departure was with the full knowledge and consent of the Hungarian prosecuting authorities in circumstances where the respondent had effectively opted for trial in absentia. He was in due course convicted and sentenced to a period of imprisonment in his absence which was sought to be executed by way of a European arrest warrant.

3–12   The principal issue which arose before the Supreme Court was whether surrender in such circumstances was contemplated by the provisions of s 10 and specifically whether it was a condition precedent to surrender that the respondent had "fled" the jurisdiction of the requesting state. Having considered various definitions of the word the Supreme Court concluded that fleeing necessarily entailed the leaving of the jurisdiction of the requesting state for the purpose of avoiding arrest or the consequences of one's actions and as such implied an unauthorised absence. In the particular circumstances of the case the actions of the respondent did not amount to him having fled and as such the court refused to surrender him.

Post-Tobin

3–13   Subsequent to the decision in *Tobin* the same point was raised in a significant number of cases without success.[5] Given that the "fleeing" requirement has been removed

---

[4] [2008] 4 IR 42.

[5] *Minister for Justice, Equality and Law Reform v Horvath* [2007] IEHC 202, *Minister for Justice, Equality and Law Reform v Sliczynski* 2008 IESC 73, *Minister for Justice, Equality and Law Reform v Snela* [2008] IEHC 202, *Minister for Justice, Equality and Law Reform v Ciobanica* [2008] IEHC 61, *Minister for Justice, Equality and Law Reform v Gheorghe* [2009] IESC 76. One of the very few cases where a respondent succeeded on such a point is *Minister for Justice, Equality and Law Reform v Slonski* [2010] IESC 19.

from s 10(d) of the Act by the Criminal Justice (Miscellaneous Provisions) Act 2009 these cases are now somewhat less significant. One of the more peculiar aspects of the case-law in relation to what came to be referred to as the "Tobin Point" was the suggestion that a "heavy onus" of proof lay on a respondent who wished to assert that he had not fled from the issuing State. The imposition of differentiated burdens of proof on applicants and respondents depending on the nature of the matter of fact in issue clearly had little or no forensic basis and if anything was at odds with the more inquisitorial nature of proceedings under the European Arrest Warrant Act 2003. Ultimately in the case of *Minister for Justice, Equality and Law Reform v Sliczynski*[6] the Supreme Court eschewed such an approach.

One issue, however, which remains somewhat uncertain is the extent to which the **3–14** provisions of the 2009 Act operate retrospectively. This was considered in *Minister for Justice Equality and Law Reform v Jastrzebski*[7] where Peart J considered that the amendment did operate retrospectively:

> "Section 1 of the 1999 Act provides in the usual way that the Act shall come into operation on such day or days as the Minister may by order or orders appoint. By Statutory Instrument 330 of 2009 signed by the Minister for Justice, Equality and Law Reform on the 20th August 2009, he ordered that the 25th August 2009 is appointed as the day on which a number of provisions of the Act, including s. 6 thereof *"shall come into operation"*. Neither Section 6 of the 2009 Act nor any other provision thereof provides that the amendment to s. 10 of the principal Act shall operate only in respect of applications for surrender made, or warrants dated or endorsed, after the commencement date.
>
> In my view it is clear that the amendment to s. 10 of the Principal Act achieved by s. 6 of the 2009 Act operates in respect of any application for an order for surrender which comes before the court for hearing on any date subsequent to the 25th August 2009, regardless of the date of the warrant, the date of endorsement thereof or the date on which the respondent was arrested on foot of such warrant."

This conclusion was not surprising in circumstances where there was no specific **3–15** legislative saver or transitional provision as there had been in relation to the amendments brought about by the Criminal Justice (Terrorist Offences) Act 2005. In a peculiar twist, however, the applicant, who had contended for the conclusion ultimately reached by the Court consented to the certification of a point of law of

---

[6] [2008] IESC 73.
[7] [2010] IEHC 201.

exceptional public importance for the purposes of appeal apparently on the basis that the point had been incorrectly decided.[8]

3–16   Pending the determination of the appeal on this issue it would seem that notwithstanding the decision of the High Court in *Jastrzebski* the common view is that the amendments to s 10 do not apply retrospectively. As such a "Tobin Point" may still arise in certain cases.

CUSTODIAL SENTENCE OR DETENTION ORDER

3–17   Section 10(d) does not confine itself to sentences of imprisonment only – it also contemplates surrender where an order by way of detention has been made in the requesting state. "Detention" is not at any point defined in the Act. However, it seems clear from the context that it is not a reference to detention in the sense that that word is used under the domestic Criminal Justice Acts, namely detention of young offenders at an appropriately designated institution. Whilst the Act refers to the execution of a "sentence of imprisonment or detention" the Framework Decision draws some slight distinction between the two insofar as it refers to execution of a "custodial sentence or detention order".[9] The distinction between a custodial sentence and a detention order would appear to be deliberate and necessarily seeks to encompass a broader category of situations than would be encompassed by reference to a custodial sentence alone.

---

[8] See *Minister for Justice, Equality and Law Reform v Jastrzebski* [2010] IEHC 2 where Peart J gave his reasons for certifying the point of law pursuant to s 16(12) as follows:

"The question now is whether that amendment operates only in respect of applications for surrender on foot of European arrest warrants which issue in the requesting state after the 25th August 2009 (being the date of commencement prescribed by S.I. 330 of 2009), and not to applications for surrender on foot of warrants which, though issued prior to that date, come on for hearing after that that commencement date.

I should perhaps record that in the present case the warrant issued and endorsed prior to the 25th August 2009, and the respondent was also arrested and brought before the court as required, well before that date. In fact his Points of Objection had been filed and delivered before the 25th August 2009. The 2009 Act contains no transitional provisions such as was contained in s. 50 of the 2003 Act, and is therefore silent as to the warrants to which the amendments shall apply, save that s. 1 thereof provides that the Act shall come into operation on such day or days as the Minister may by order appoint. That date for commencement is the 25th August 2009.

I feel it is appropriate to state that on the application for surrender before me, the applicant argued that the amendment operated in respect of the hearing of the application for surrender in respect of the present warrant. In my judgment I agreed for the reasons appearing. But the applicant has now reconsidered the question, and no longer stands over the arguments put forward on that occasion, and is consenting to this Court certifying a point of exceptional importance for determination by the Supreme Court".

[9] Art 1.1.

As to what may be contemplated by "detention" was considered in the case **3–18** of *Minister for Justice, Equality and Law Reform v M*[10] where the respondent was sought on foot of a "Hospital Order" which was a type of therapeutic mental treatment order imposed by a criminal court subsequent to his conviction in relation to rape offences in England. The issue which arose was whether or not such an order was contemplated by the expression "detention" order. Denham J concluded that it was:

> "I would define a detention order under s.10(d) as any order involving deprivation of liberty which has been made by a criminal court in addition to or instead of a prison sentence. In this case the detention order was made by a criminal court after conviction, for the extraditable offences of rape and assault occasioning bodily harm, instead of a prison sentence. Thus I am satisfied that s.10(d) of the Act of 2003 applies to the detention order in this case."

It would appear, therefore, that a rather broad interpretation is given to the concept **3–19** of a detention order. It includes orders that are not necessarily punitive in nature. However, whatever the purpose of such an order it must have been made in the context of criminal proceedings.

PURPOSE FOR WHICH THE WARRANT IS ISSUED

It is implicit from the terms of Art 1.1 that where the requested person has not yet been **3–20** convicted and sentenced the obligation to surrender only arises where the intention of the requesting state is to prosecute the requested person. It is not permissible to seek the surrender of a person for the purpose of having him or her questioned or otherwise examined as part of a purely investigative process. This does not preclude such questioning or examination taking place subsequent to surrender in the context of a trial however. The prohibition on surrender for an ulterior purpose is given express effect by the provisions of s 21A(1) of the Act:

> "Where a European arrest warrant is issued in the issuing state in respect of a person who has not been convicted of an offence specified therein, the High Court shall refuse to surrender the person if it is satisfied that a decision has not been made to charge the person with, and try him or her for the offence in the issuing state."

This is of significance as s 16(1)(d) requires that the High Court be satisfied that no **3–21** issue arises under s 21A(1) prior to surrendering a respondent. Necessarily an issue will only arise as a matter of practice in relation to warrants concerning offences where the respondent has not been convicted as in any other case the clear purpose of the warrant will be in relation to the execution of a sentence or detention order. In a number of cases the respondent has sought to challenge surrender on the grounds that there is insufficient evidence to show that surrender is sought for the purpose of criminal prosecution.

---

[10] [2010] IESC 17.

3–22   Most of these challenges have been predicated on the basis that the surrender is sought for the purpose of questioning the respondent. That such a basis for surrender is impermissible is reasonably clear:

> "The mere fact that an arrest warrant is issued by a judge in a foreign jurisdiction may not of itself necessarily imply that it is issued only for the purpose of charging the person concerned and putting him or her on trial for an offence or offences. In some jurisdictions, particularly in what may be termed civil law jurisdictions, criminal investigations are often conducted by or under the supervision of a judge. Such a judge may require a suspected person to appear before him or attend in his chamber in connection with the conduct of the criminal investigation rather than for the purpose of charging that person with a view to putting him or her on trial. Warrants issued for the purpose of such investigations could not be considered as requiring the surrender of a person for the purpose of being tried for an offence. The surrender of a person for the purpose of prosecution and trying him or her on a criminal offence means that the decision taken by the relevant authority to prosecute and try that person is not contingent on the outcome of further factual investigation. That requirement does not of course preclude the pursuit of any continuing or parallel investigation into the circumstances of the offence. It means that the decision to prosecute is not dependant on such further investigation producing sufficient evidence to justify putting a person on trial."[11]

3–23   Whilst it is true that surrender is not permissible simply for the purpose of questioning a person it is frequently a feature of continental criminal processes that the accused will at some point be questioned in the course of his trial. In other words the two ideas are not mutually exclusive. Moreover our concept of what amounts to a "trial" is quite different to that which applies elsewhere. The inquisitorial trial may necessarily be a significantly longer and more punctuated process than the unitary affair that trial by jury necessitates.

3–24   Typically arguments against surrender under this heading will be grounded upon the content of the warrant which will disclose some ambiguity in relation to precisely what will happen to the respondent when and if he is returned. The courts have been slow to entertain such objections as they frequently arise not from any real concern that the respondent will not be prosecuted but rather from differences between the legal systems of various Member States some of which require judicial intervention before a formal decision is made to "charge" the respondent. In such cases the warrant will typically disclose that once returned the respondent will be brought before a judge or magistrate who will then formally decide whether or not to prosecute the respondent.

Presumption of Intention to Prosecute

3–25   The difficulty with mounting an objection to surrender on such a basis is that there are essentially two evidential presumptions operating against the respondent. In the first instance s 21A(2) of the Act provides:

---

[11]   As per Murray CJ in *Minister for Justice, Equality and Law Reform v McArdle* [2005] 4 IR 260 at pp 266–267.

> "Where a European arrest warrant is issued in respect of a person who has not been convicted of an offence specified therein, it shall be presumed that a decision has been made to charge the person with, and try him or her for that offence in the issuing state unless the contrary is proved."

Secondly the recital appearing at the top of the standard form of the European arrest warrant to the effect that the warrant has been issued for the purpose of procuring the arrest of the respondent in order that he might be prosecuted is something that the courts have taken account of. They have looked on it as more than mere boilerplate text – rather it is regarded as an express assurance by the issuing judicial authority.   **3–26**

Perhaps the large number of cases in which it has been sought to suggest that the presumption under s 21A has been rebutted stems from the earlier decisions of *Minister for Justice, Equality and Law Reform v LG*[12] where an ambiguity in relation to what would happen once the respondent was returned caused Peart J to consider that the presumption had been rebutted and consequently surrender was refused. In later judgments Peart J expressed the view that in hindsight his decision in *LG* may have been incorrect given subsequent pronouncements by the courts in relation to the strong interpretative obligation and the principle of mutual trust and understanding as between judicial authorities. In fact it would seem that few, if any, of the challenges to surrender which were mounted subsequent to *LG* have been successful.   **3–27**

In *Minister for Justice, Equality and Law Reform v Balcianus*[13] Peart J made express reference to the earlier case of *Minister for Justice, Equality and Law Reform v LG*. In *Balcianus* the same formula of words appeared on the warrant which indicated that within 48 hours of surrender to Lithuania[14] the respondent would be brought before a judge for the purpose of ascertaining whether there were grounds for his arrest. In effect the relevant provisions of the Lithuanian Penal Code required such a procedural step prior to the institution of proceedings. The respondent argued that the effect of this uncertainty as to whether he would be prosecuted rebutted the presumption created by s 21A.   **3–28**

Peart J cited the recital at the start of the warrant to the effect that it had been issued "for the purpose of a criminal prosecution".[15] As such the court was entitled to rely upon this assertion which, coupled with the presumption contained in s 21A, entitled it to come to the view that there had been no rebuttal of the presumption of an intention to prosecute. The position in relation to the Lithuanian Penal Code, which itself is not uncommon, serves to highlight the many different considerations that will arise in differing jurisdictions in relation to the commencement of proceedings. Specifically it casts into sharp relief the difficulties created by the use of domestic terms of art in s 21A which refers to the "charging" of the respondent. The use of this expression does not derive from the provisions of the Framework Decision which more prudently simply refers to surrender for the purpose of "conducting a criminal prosecution". The differences in terminology and procedure between   **3–29**

---

[12] [2005] IEHC 310.

[13] [2007] IEHC 34.

[14] The respondent in *LG* had also been sought by the Lithuanian authorities.

[15] See also *Minister for Justice, Equality and Law Reform v Butenas* [2006] IEHC 378.

various jurisdictions in this regard were acknowledged to some degree by the courts in *Minister for Justice, Equality and Law Reform v Ostrovskij*[16]:

> "It will not be possible to examine minutely the procedures applicable in each requesting State. It may well be that differences in such procedures will mean that, as understood in this State, a prosecution may not have actually commenced by the time the respondent has fled the jurisdiction of the requesting state, but that the requesting state will regard the prosecution process as having commenced under its own procedures...Nevertheless the prosecution process can be seen to have got under way by the investigations having been carried out subsequent to the alleged events giving rise to the alleged offence, by the prosecutor's office determining that there is among the material examined sufficient to regard the respondent as having committed a criminal offence, and by the prosecutor obtaining a warrant from the District Court in Vilnius for the arrest of the respondent who was known to have fled. It has to be borne in mind that in many Member States the relationship of the Prosecutor to the criminal court is of a different nature to that which pertains in this State. Again, that is something which the new European arrest procedures are designed to overcome."

3–30   In jurisdictions where the decision whether to prosecute or not reposes to a significant degree in an investigating judge who will not make any formal decision until the accused is present, there is no analogy to the "charging" of the respondent. This leads to the rather unsatisfactory situation whereby s 21A seems to require that there be an intention to "charge" the respondent in the requesting state where this is frequently a procedural impossibility, whilst at the same time creating a presumption which is shored up by the recital at the start of every European arrest warrant.

3–31   The case of *Minister for Justice, Equality and Law Reform v Ollsen*[17] is instructive in that it highlights the frequently diverse criminal processes applicable in the various Member States. The respondent had made the point that under Swedish law no formal decision to prosecute him could be made until he was actually brought before a Swedish court. Whilst on the face of it this seemed to preclude the Swedish authorities from stating that a decision had been made to prosecute, the court was satisfied on the basis of the presumption contained in s 21A and the recital on the warrant that it was intended to prosecute the respondent once he was surrendered. In addition there was evidence from a Swedish prosecutor explaining the procedure and making it clear that the surrender of the respondent and his subsequent production before the Swedish court that would make the decision whether or not to prosecute was the first step in the process of bringing criminal proceedings.

3–32   It is clear from the various authorities that any respondent who seeks to suggest that his surrender is sought for a purpose other than prosecution faces an uphill struggle. In *Minister for Justice, Equality and Law Reform v Stuina*[18] the court drew attention to the unambiguous terms of s 21A insofar as it created an evidential presumption. The court went on to note that where a respondent is seeking to contradict the assertion or presumption that a decision has been taken to prosecute the respondent, this should be done by way of a lawyer from the requesting jurisdiction swearing an

---

[16]   [2006] IEHC 242.
[17]   [2008] IEHC 37.
[18]   [2007] IEHC 220.

affidavit setting out the basis for such a claim. In *Ostrovskij*[19] it was said that there was a "heavy onus"[20] on a respondent who wished to rebut the presumption.

Even where the respondent can show that the "injured party" to the substantive   **3–33** proceedings in the requesting state has effectively withdrawn the underlying complaint, the presumption will not have been deemed to be rebutted particularly if there is an indication from the prosecuting authorities in the requesting state that they desire to proceed with the prosecution in any event.[21]

DIFFERENCES BETWEEN VARIOUS LEGAL SYSTEMS

Difficulties in assessing when a person is being sought for the purpose of criminal   **3–34** prosecution as opposed to other purposes are not unique to this jurisdiction. In *Bhoudiba v Central Examining Court No. 5*[22] the English courts considered the difficulties that arise from seeking to impose domestic terms of art on foreign judicial systems:

> "Both counsel agreed that the correct approach had been set out in *Re Ismail* [1999] 1 AC 320, where, on an application for habeas corpus in extradition proceedings under the Extradition Act 1989, the question arose as to whether the applicant was an accused person or a mere suspect. Lord Steyn said, at p 326h , that the word "accused" is not a term of art. It was a question of fact in each case whether the person passed the threshold test of being an accused person as opposed to a suspect. He said, at p 327a, that there was a transnational interest in bringing to justice those accused of serious crimes. It followed that extradition statutes ought to be accorded a broad and generous construction, so far as the text permitted. Then he said, at p 327:
>
>> "It is not always easy for an English court to decide when in a civil law jurisdiction a suspect becomes an 'accused' person. All one can say with confidence is that a purposive interpretation of 'accused' ought to be adopted in order to accommodate the differences between legal systems. In other words, it is necessary for our courts to adopt a cosmopolitan approach to the question whether as a matter of substance rather than form the requirement of there being an 'accused' person is satisfied."
>
> A little later he continued:
>
>> "For my part I am satisfied that the Divisional Court in this case posed the right test by addressing the broad question whether the competent authorities in the foreign jurisdiction had taken a step which can fairly be described as the commencement of a prosecution."

The foregoing passage has been cited with approval in this jurisdiction.[23]   **3–35**

---

[19] [2006] IEHC 242.

[20] The reference to a "heavy onus" may have to be reconsidered in light of the decision of the Supreme Court in *Minister for Justice, Equality and Law Reform v Sliczynski* [2008] IESC 73.

[21] See *Minister for Justice, Equality and Law Reform v Dubikatlis* [2006] IEHC 332.

[22] [2007] 1 WLR 124.

[23] *Minister for Justice, Equality and Law Reform v Butenas* [2006] IEHC 378.

TEMPORAL LIMITATION

3–36 Prior to the Criminal Justice (Miscellaneous Provisions) Act 2009 the general rule in relation to the European Arrest Warrant Act 2003 was that it applied both to offences committed before and after the commencement of the Act subject to certain exceptions in relation to Austria, Italy and France. However, the amendments to s 4 of the 2003 Act effectively removed these exceptions:

> "4.—This Act shall apply in relation to an offence, whether committed or alleged
> to have been committed before or after the commencement of this Act."

3–37 As matters stand there is no temporal limitation in relation to offences for which surrender is sought.

TRANSFERRED PRISONERS

3–38 Whilst it is not made explicit in either the 2003 Act or the Framework Decision it is not possible, in practical terms, to seek to surrender prisoners who are serving sentences within the State on foot of the provisions of the Transfer of Sentenced Persons Act 1995. Necessarily the surrender of a person serving a sentence can only be given effect by either postponing such surrender under s 18 or surrendering the person mid-sentence under s 19. However both of these sections require as a condition precedent that the sentence which necessitates the postponement under s 18 or the sentence which is interrupted under s 19 be one that was imposed in respect of "an offence of which he or she was convicted in the State". *A fortiori* this excludes sentences which have been the subject of transfer and as such it would seem to follow that transferred prisoners fall outside the ambit of the European Arrest Warrant Act 2003 for practical reasons.

Part II
Procedure

CHAPTER 4

Receipt and Endorsement

All proceedings in relation to outward surrender take place in the High Court and as **4–01** such the Rules of the Superior Courts are generally applicable. Specific rules in relation to the European Arrest Warrant have also been promulgated.[1] These rules by and large mirror the terms of the Act which, in any event, provide for the general procedure to be employed on such applications. The provisions of Ord 98 have not tended to feature in any significant way in litigation to date. To a very considerable extent the practice and procedure now applicable has developed by way of trial and error and some of the provisions of Ord 98 (specifically those relating to discovery) appear to be redundant given the pronouncements in various judgments since the promulgation of the rules.

TRANSMISSION AND RECEIPT OF THE EUROPEAN ARREST WARRANT

The transmission and receipt of a European Arrest Warrant in any given case is **4–02** obviously a part of the process that remains largely opaque to practitioners as it necessarily occurs as between the judicial or Central Authority in the issuing state and the Central Authority here, i.e. the Minister for Justice and Law Reform. Section 12[2] of the European Arrest Warrant Act 2003 governs the procedure to be observed in relation to this aspect of the process.

The wording of s 12 would appear to suggest the somewhat unlikely assumption **4–03** that the warrant might be transmitted in the Irish language. In the event that it is not it provides that it may be in English or such other language as the Minister may prescribe by order.[3] Where it is in a language other than English or Irish a

---

[1] SI 23 of 2005 substitutes a new Ord 98 which covers both proceedings under the European Arrest Warrant Act 2003 and proceedings under Part II of the Extradition Act 1965.

[2] s 12 had initially provided for the rather limited means of transmission of warrant by way of post and secure facsimile. However, since the amendments effected by the Criminal Justice (Miscellaneous Provisions) Act 2009 a European arrest warrant or any other information may be transmitted "by any means capable of producing a written record under conditions allowing the Central Authority in the State to establish its authenticity". In other words instantaneous transmission by way of email is now possible.

[3] The Minister has not, to date, prescribed any such languages. It is worth noting that a number of other member states allow surrender of foot of European Arrest Warrants that are not in their own official language. Belgium and the Netherlands both accept warrants in English whilst Sweden accepts warrants in English, Danish and Norwegian.

translation is also required to be transmitted with the original version of the warrant. The quality of these translations is variable and frequently gives rise to considerable difficulties in establishing whether even the most basic formal requirements have been complied with. Notwithstanding these difficulties s 12(8)(c) provides that any such translation shall be received in evidence without the requirement for any further proof. It remains to be seen whether the courts will entertain arguments arising from differences in interpretation or translation of the original European Arrest Warrant.

4-04   Both ss 11 and 12 presuppose that documentation other than the European Arrest Warrant may be transmitted to the Central Authority. Section 11(2) allows the inclusion of additional information other than in the body of the warrant itself whilst s 12 makes provision in relation to the transmission and translation of undertakings and any other additional information or documentation in the same manner as applies to the transmission of the warrant. This information will frequently have been sought by the Central Authority for the purpose of clarifying some issue of form or substance. Whilst the requirement for undertakings in relation to many of the formal requirements has largely been dispensed with by the numerous evidential presumptions inserted by the Criminal Justice (Terrorist Offences) Act 2005, undertakings are still frequently required in relation to the question of re-trial in cases where a conviction has been recorded in absentia.[4] In addition it is not unusual for additional information to be furnished in order to more fully describe the circumstances of the offence which is the subject of the European arrest warrant in order to allow the Central Authority in the first instance, and in due course the court, to take a view in relation to the issue of correspondence.

ENDORSEMENT

4-05   The European arrest warrant is ineffective and incapable of execution until such time as it has been endorsed for the purposes of execution by the High Court. Necessarily it is up to the Central Authority to make the application. The procedure in relation to such applications is provided for by s 13 of the 2003 Act.

Delay in Making the Endorsement Application

4-06   One difficulty which has arisen in relation to the terms of s 13(1) is the apparent requirement that the application for endorsement is made as soon as possible:

> "The Central Authority in the State shall, as soon as may be after it receives a European arrest warrant transmitted to it in accordance with *section 12*, apply, or cause an application to be made, to the High Court for the endorsement by it of the European arrest warrant, or a true copy thereof, for execution of the European arrest warrant concerned."

4-07   The requirement contained in s 13(1) that the endorsement application be made "as soon as may be" after its receipt reflects the provisions of Art 17.1 of the Framework Decision which requires the requested Member State to deal with and execute European arrest warrants "as a matter of urgency".

---

[4] See s 45 of the European Arrest Warrant Act 2003.

Notwithstanding the express terms of s 13(1) there is no indication as to the **4–08** consequences of non-compliance with this requirement. The obligation imposed would appear to be one which arises as a matter between Member States and their operation of the Framework Decision as opposed to an obligation imposed for the purpose of granting any specific protection or actionable right to the prospective respondent. Given that it is clear that s 13(1) has its genesis in Art 17.1 of the Framework Decision it would appear that the observations of the courts in relation to the rationale behind such provisions applies with equal force to s 13(1):

> "While the Framework Decision in Article 17.1 provides that a European arrest warrant shall be dealt with as a matter of urgency it is clear from the decision in *Dundon v Governor of Clover Hill* [2006] 1 I.L.R.M. 321 that this requirement is directed to internal discipline within the Member States and is not intended to confer individual rights."[5]

In this regard the requirement that the endorsement application be made as soon as **4–09** possible ought to be regarded as applying in a similar fashion to the time limits set out in the Framework Decision i.e. a delay on the part of the Central Authority in making the endorsement application will not be fatal to the proceedings and does not give rise to any actionable basis for objecting to surrender on the part of the respondent.

Any attempts which have been made in the past to raise the issue of delay, **4–10** specifically as they relate to the period of time between the issuing of the European arrest warrant by the requesting state and its endorsement here as a basis for objection, have failed. In *Minister for Justice, Equality and Law Reform v LG*[6] there had been a delay of some six months between the date of issue of the warrant and the application for its endorsement. No explanation was given to the court in relation to this period. Peart J took the view that whilst the court might well canvass the question of delay in the course of the endorsement application, the absence of any strict time limit which might be breached would not subsequently give rise to any objection:

> "I am of the view that the requirement contained in section 16(1) of the Act that the Court be satisfied that the warrant was endorsed in accordance with section 13 of the Act means that this Court must ensure that the warrant was endorsed for execution prior to the arrest and bringing before the Court of the respondent. While that section states that the application should be made as soon as may be, I am not satisfied that the Court prior to endorsing the warrant must at all times enquire as to whether the application might not have been made earlier, except in very clear cases of what I will loosely term significant or extreme delay. No strict time limit has been inserted in the Act or in the Framework Decision itself. The phrase "as soon as may be" permits of some passage of time clearly. In the present case I am satisfied that the warrant has been endorsed for execution in accordance with section 13 of the Act."

---

[5] As per Finnegan J in *Minister for Justice, Equality and Law Reform v SMR* [2008] 2 IR 242 at 258; the idea that the requirements as to speedy operation of the surrender provisions contained in the Framework Decision was not intended to confer individual rights was reiterated in *Minister for Justice, Equality and Law Reform v Peciukenas* [2006] IEHC 374.
[6] [2005] IEHC 310.

4-11   In *Minister for Justice, Equality and Law Reform v Fallon*[7] there had been a delay of in excess of a year between the issue of the warrant and the endorsement application. This arose in circumstances where there had been a considerable degree of uncertainty in relation to the operation of the 2003 Act pending the decision of the Supreme Court in *Dundon v Governor of Cloverhill Prison*.[8] The court took the view that where the High Court had seen fit to endorse the warrant pursuant to the provisions of s 13 it had necessarily taken the view that such an endorsement was in compliance with the terms of the 2003 Act. As such it was not open to a respondent to seek to re-open the issue of whether or not the delay was permissible in light of the terms of s 13(1). This sentiment was subsequently echoed in *Minister for Justice, Equality and Law Reform v Koncis*[9] where the court in essence suggested that the fact that the court had endorsed the warrant pursuant to s 13 created a presumption that the terms of s 13(1) had been complied with.

4-12   The question of delay was again considered by Peart J in *Minister for Justice, Equality and Law Reform v JBF*[10] in some detail. Specifically the court adverted to the practical realities of the operation of the European arrest warrant system. Necessarily the process of transmitting warrants from the requesting state to the requested state involves the input of the Central Authority who may well have observations to make in relation to the content and formalities of the warrant itself. In *JBF* the warrant had been transmitted to the Central Authority who had raised certain queries which the requesting state had taken a considerable period of time to answer. The court considered that it would be an absurdity to read s 13(1) as giving rise to a situation whereby an application to endorse the warrant had to be made even in circumstances where it was manifestly apparent that there were defects of both form and substance in the warrant. In such circumstances it was to be expected that there would be some delay as it would be necessary to revert to the requesting state in order that such issues might be clarified.

4-13   Whilst it is clear from the various examples cited above that s 13(1) cannot be regarded as giving rise to a ground of objection on the part of a respondent, there is perhaps some slight degree of confusion on the part of the courts as to what the consequences of a delay in seeking an endorsement might be. The decision in *LG* expressly suggests that in cases of extreme delay the application for endorsement might be refused. Given that the purpose of the obligation to endorse the warrant "as soon as may be" after it is received is directed towards the more general objective of Member States acting promptly in relation to the processing of requests, it would be peculiar for the High Court to seek to give effect to a statutory obligation on the part of the Central Authority to act promptly in processing the request of the issuing state by means of making an order which had the effect of permanently frustrating that same request.

The Endorsement Application

4-14   Section 13(2) simply allows the High Court to endorse the European arrest warrant where it is satisfied that "there has been compliance with the provisions of this Act...".

---

[7] [2005] IEHC 321.

[8] [2006] 1 IR 518.

[9] [2006] IEHC 379.

[10] [2006] 3 IR 411.

Whilst the application of such a broad criterion potentially suggests a wide ranging examination of the warrant, the practice has tended to be that the court confines itself to a brief consideration of the formalities of the warrant and possibly some consideration of any obvious difficulties that might arise in relation to correspondence, extra-territoriality, minimum gravity, etc. If there has been an obvious delay between the date of issue of the warrant and the endorsement application the court may also seek an explanation for this although, as noted above, even an egregious delay should, arguably, not of itself be a ground for refusing the application to endorse the warrant. By and large the approach adopted by the courts has been to regard any substantive difficulties which arise at this stage, i.e. issues in relation to correspondence, trial in absentia etc, as being issues which can more properly be canvassed in the course of the s 16 hearing. Insofar as applications for endorsement are refused, this tends to be on the grounds of some manifest defect in the warrant such as a failure on the part of the issuing judicial authority to sign the warrant or some part of the warrant being absent or incomplete. Occasionally the court may decline to endorse where it is clear that an undertaking as to a re-trial will be required under s 45 but where none has been given or where it is clear that correspondence cannot be established. The courts have also declined to endorse warrants in circumstances where the issuing state has included offences in the list at para (e)I which are not listed offences for the purposes of Art 2.2 of the Framework Decision.

Order 98, r 2(2) requires that the endorsement application be made ex parte. **4–15** This is hardly surprising given that the nature of the application is in essence one for the issue of an arrest warrant for the putative respondent. One related practical consideration which is neither covered by the Act nor the rules concerns the implicit requirement that endorsement applications be moved in open court. The reporting or disclosing of the fact that an endorsement application has been made in relation to a particular named individual may well have the effect of providing the respondent with an opportunity to flee the jurisdiction, thereby defeating the entire purpose of the application. In response to this concern a practice has developed whereby the application will be moved in open court but no reference will be made by either the moving party or the judge to the identity of the respondent nor will specific reference be made to the offences which are the subject matter of the warrant to the extent that the prospective respondent might be capable of being identified. As such the procedure adopted is similar to that which is frequently observed in relation to applications for search warrants.

If the court grants the application the registrar will then endorse it for execution. **4–16** The specific terms of the endorsement are set out in Ord 98, r 2(3):

"This warrant is endorsed for execution pursuant to Order of the High Court."

This endorsement is then signed and dated by the registrar. The endorsed warrant **4–17** is then returned to the solicitor for the applicant and passed to the Gardaí for the purpose of execution.

CHAPTER 5

Arrest and Execution

Whilst proceedings under the European Arrest Warrant Act 2003 commence at the **5–01** point when an application is made to endorse a warrant for the purposes of execution within the State, the first that the respondent will know of the institution of the proceedings will be at the point of arrest. It is noteworthy that irrespective of the manner in which the underlying domestic proceedings were commenced (i.e. by way of summons or some equivalent procedure), once the 2003 Act is invoked it necessarily requires that the respondent be subject to arrest.

DUE PROCESS

As proceedings under the 2003 Act do not involve any determination of guilt or **5–02** innocence in relation to underlying substantive charges the full panoply of rights guaranteed by Art 38 of the Constitution in relation to the domestic criminal process does not apply. However, the guarantee contained in Art 40.4.1 that no-one shall be deprived of personal liberty save in accordance with law is of relevance. As stated by Fennelly J in *O'Falluin v Governor of Cloverhill Prison*[1]:

> "...arrest and detention are essential steps in any form of extradition or surrender, but they depend for their validity on clear legal rules."

---
[1] [2007] 3 IR 414 at 418.

5-03   As such a reasonably strict adherence to both form and procedure in the context of the provisions of the 2003 Act which govern both arrest and detention is necessary.

5-04   The right to due process has been held to apply in cases of arrest for the purposes of extradition proceedings under the 1965 Act in *State (McFadden) v Governor of Mountjoy Prison*,[2] where Barrington J concluded that the order for extradition made in respect of the prosecutor in that case was invalid, as the prosecutor had not been given a copy of the warrant, and had not been asked whether he wished to obtain legal advice prior to the making of the order. In *McFadden*, Barrington J confirmed the application of due process rights to extradition proceedings, acknowledging the far-reaching effects such proceedings have on the person extradited, and further noting that "in a sense, extradition proceedings are ancillary to criminal proceedings".

5-05   These comments apply equally to an arrest for the purposes of surrender under the 2003 Act, and a person arrested pursuant to a European arrest warrant has, in effect, the same substantive entitlements as a person arrested on domestic criminal charges in relation to being cautioned, informed of the reasons for the arrest, and informed of the right to obtain legal advice and access to an interpreter. Indeed, s 13(4) of the 2003 Act expressly provides that a person arrested pursuant to a European arrest warrant shall, on arrest, be informed of the right to legal advice and representation and to an interpreter, as well as being informed of the right to consent to surrender.

ARREST

Arrest Pursuant to Section 13

5-06   Before a European arrest warrant can be executed (i.e. before the person named therein can be arrested), an application must be made to the court to have it endorsed for execution.[3] The court will grant such an application where it is satisfied that the warrant is in compliance with the 2003 Act. After the warrant has been endorsed, any member of An Garda Síochána may arrest the requested person in any part of the State.

5-07   It is not strictly necessary for that member to have a copy of the European arrest warrant in his or her possession when effecting the arrest, although the requested person must be shown a copy of the European arrest warrant no later than 24 hours after arrest.[4]

5-08   Once a respondent has been arrested he or she must be informed of a number of entitlements in accordance with s 13(4):

> "(4) A person arrested under a European arrest warrant shall, upon his or her arrest, be informed of his or her right to—
>
> (a)   consent to his or her being surrendered to the issuing state under *section 15*,
>
> (b)   obtain, or be provided with, professional legal advice and representation, and

---

[2] [1981] ILRM 113.

[3] s 13(1).

[4] s 13(3).

(c)   where appropriate, obtain, or be provided with, the services of an interpreter."

The obligation on the arresting Garda to inform the respondent of these entitlements is mirrored by a similar obligation on the High Court to effectively reiterate these entitlements to the respondent at the conclusion of the execution hearing. In other words, by the conclusion of the execution hearing the respondent will have been told twice of his or her entitlements.   **5–09**

It is noteworthy that the respondent is not explicitly entitled to be told of the reason for his or her arrest at the point of arrest. The only express entitlement in this regard is to be given a copy of the European arrest warrant within 24 hours of the time of arrest. To date this has not arisen as an issue given that European arrest warrants have tended to be executed on a targeted basis by specifically assigned Gardaí who are already in possession of the endorsed warrant. This is likely to change as the Schengen Information System becomes more integrated and widely used and European arrest warrants are executed by the Gardaí not on a targeted basis but rather as and when respondents come to Garda attention. At that point it is entirely probable that respondents will, for a period of time at least, be unaware as to the reason for their arrest. Such an eventuality sits uneasily with the conventional position as set out by the Supreme Court in *Re O Laighleis*[5]:   **5–10**

> "We accept it as settled law that in the case of an arrest without the production of a warrant the arrest will not be lawful unless the person being arrested is told why he is being arrested or unless he otherwise knows: see *Christie v Leachinsky* [1947] AC 573 at 587. The reason for the rule is not far to seek. Arrest must be for a lawful purpose; and since no one is obliged to submit to an unlawful arrest the citizen has a right before acquiescing in his arrest to know why he is being arrested."[6]

It is difficult to see how a prospective respondent can make any judgment as to whether or not to submit to arrest in circumstances where he or she may not see the warrant on foot of which the arrest has taken place until the following day.   **5–11**

Once arrested s 13(5) requires that the respondent be brought before the High Court "as soon as may be after his arrest" for the purposes of the execution application.   **5–12**

Delay in Arresting

The 2003 Act does not set a time limit within which an endorsed warrant must be executed. However, the 2003 Act is to be interpreted in light of the Framework Decision, Art 17 of which provides that "a European Arrest Warrant shall be dealt with and executed as a matter of urgency". One of the points of objection raised by the respondent in *Minister for Justice, Equality and Law Reform v Saldugei*[7] was in relation to the fact that the European arrest warrant had been endorsed for execution on 6th April 2005, but the arrest was not actually made until the 10th June 2005. The respondent contended that such a delay was contrary to the spirit of the 2003 Act.   **5–13**

---

[5]   [1960] IR 93.

[6]   p 129.

[7]   [2005] IEHC 259.

The point was not pursued at hearing, but the court did comment on the issue taken with the delay of just over two months, stating:

> "I would be satisfied in any event that such a short period of time could not possibly constitute a culpable lapse of time, short of some extraordinary and exceptional circumstance which I cannot at the moment imagine."

5–14   It is unlikely that any delay on the part of the State in executing a European arrest warrant would in practice ever contribute to oppressive pre-trial incarceration. Similarly anxiety is unlikely to be an issue as the prospective respondent will, in all likelihood, be entirely unaware of his or her impending arrest and probable surrender. In relation to the possibility of impairment of defence it would seem that in light of the Supreme Court decision in *Minister for Justice, Equality and Law Reform v Stapleton*[8] the court is likely to take the view that the criminal justice system in the issuing state will be capable of adequately protecting the rights of the requested person, and prohibiting the trial if necessary.

5–15   Any objection to surrender based on a delay between the date of endorsement and the date of arrest is in large part predicated upon the assumption that the respondent enjoys some form of actionable right in relation to such a delay. As we have seen the Framework Decision grants no entitlements directly to prospective respondents and as such it is doubtful that the provisions of Art 17 give rise to, or were ever intended to give rise to, any such entitlements. If anything the provisions of Art 17 would appear to be directed towards the mutual obligation on Member States to act in a timely fashion and as such the same considerations as arise in relation to delays in endorsing European arrest warrants subsequent to their receipt would appear to apply here.

Arrest where the Respondent is in Custody

5–16   As Denham J commented in *Clarke v Governor of Portlaoise Prison*,[9] "it is well settled jurisprudence that a person who is already in custody may be arrested by another". In that case, the applicant had been serving a sentence in Portlaoise prison. Less than a week before he was due to be released, he was produced at the Four Courts in Dublin on foot of a ministerial production order for the purposes of executing a European arrest warrant. The Supreme Court affirmed the High Court's refusal to order the release of the applicant, Denham J finding that his arrest had been lawful and noting that:

> "The Minister, on being informed that a prisoner is the subject of a European arrest warrant, has the power by way of a production order to bring a prisoner to court for the purpose of the European Arrest Warrant Act, 2003, as amended. It is an entirely appropriate use of the production order system."

5–17   The court also rejected the contention that the arrest was ineffective or otherwise amounted to a colourable device on the grounds that it amounted to an arrest upon an arrest.

---

[8] [2008] 1 IR 669.
[9] [2006] IESC 32.

PRODUCTION BEFORE THE HIGH COURT

Subsequent to arrest s 13(5) requires that the respondent be brought before the High **5–18** Court "as soon as may be after his arrest". It is perhaps unfortunate that the same expression as appears in s 13(1) is used in this regard. Whilst the courts interpreted the expression "as soon as may be" in the context of s 13(1) to be a somewhat diffuse obligation, there would appear to be little room for such an interpretation in relation to a respondent who is in custody subsequent to arrest. Obviously the context of this expression is entirely different in s 13(5) and the same degree of latitude would, presumably, not be allowed.

The only matter of which the High Court need be satisfied when a respondent is **5–19** brought before it on such an application is that the person arrested is the person in respect of whom the European arrest warrant was issued. In other words the only question for the court at this stage is that of identification.

Identification

Given that the European arrest warrant allows for the inclusion of photographs, **5–20** fingerprints and even the transmission of the requested person's DNA profile, there are numerous means of establishing identification. Section 45A of the European Arrest Warrant Act 2003 allows the Gardaí to take fingerprints or other bodily samples from the arrested person in order to allow the necessary process of comparison to take place in cases of contested identity. Prior to the introduction of this provision[10] the Gardaí had on occasion used fingerprints to identify respondents[11]; however s 45A now allows the Gardaí to use reasonable force to take fingerprints or photographs for the purpose of identification.

Paragraph (a) of the warrant requires that the name, address, gender, nationality, **5–21** date of birth, place of birth, language and description of the person be included. In addition to such means of identification there is obviously also the more straightforward expedient whereby the executing Garda will simply ask of the arrested person whether or not he or she is the person described in the warrant.

As a matter of practice the issue of identification of the respondent at this stage of **5–22** the proceedings is generally expressed by the court to be without prejudice to such an issue being raised in the course of the s 16 hearing. In reality such issues tend to arise only rarely in any meaningful fashion. In cases where they have arisen in the context of a s 16 hearing the applicant is obliged to once more prove the identity of the respondent notwithstanding the fact that it may have already been determined for the purposes of the execution application.

Whilst s 13 requires the court to be satisfied on the issue of identification, this **5–23** does not preclude a different finding in the context of a s 16 hearing. The issue of identification is one that is determined in the normal way on the evidence. A bald denial by the respondent in *Minister for Justice, Equality and Law Reform v Gokano*[12] that he was the person in respect of whom the warrant had been issued was deemed insufficient to contradict the evidence given by the arresting Garda, in circumstances where the respondent had accepted at the time of his arrest that

---

[10] It was introduced by s 20 of the Criminal Justice (Miscellaneous Provisions) Act 2009.
[11] See *Minister for Justice, Equality and Law Reform v Betancourt* [2006] IEHC 423.
[12] [2004] 3 IR 216.

one of the names given in the warrant was his and that the date of birth therein corresponded to his own. In addition the respondent had not given any evidence regarding his identity. Somewhat unusually however, although the court was satisfied that the respondent was the person in respect of whom the warrant had been issued, surrender was refused on the basis, inter alia, that the court was not satisfied that the respondent was the person referred to in the undertakings given pursuant to ss 22 to 24 of the 2003 Act, as those undertakings referred to "Gokano Landi" rather than the "Landi Gokano" named in the warrant. This confusion was sufficient to invalidate the undertakings. The court noted:

> "I have stressed on other occasions the extent to which the greatest possible care must be taken by all concerned to ensure that all documentation relied upon in these matters is correct."

5–24   Where the court refuses to surrender on the grounds that it is not satisfied that the respondent is the person named in the warrant, a further European arrest warrant may be issued, containing additional information as to the identity of the requested person. In such circumstances the issue of identity will not be regarded as *res judicata*.[13]

5–25   Whilst, in theory at least, the issue of identification may well become of central importance either at the execution application or on the substantive hearing, it would appear that the privilege against self incrimination does not extend to allowing a respondent to effectively exclude evidence as to his or her identity. In *Minister for Justice, Equality and Law Reform v Saldugei*,[14] the arresting officer had asked the respondent a number of questions to establish his identity before arresting and cautioning him. The respondent claimed that proper procedure had not been followed, as he should have been cautioned before he was asked any questions. Peart J rejected this submission, finding that it was entirely proper that the arresting officer, before arresting the respondent, would ask questions of him with a view to establishing that he was the person named in the European arrest warrant.

Execution Hearing

5–26   Once it has been established that the respondent is the same as the person referred to in the European arrest warrant the court is obliged to inform him or her of the right to:

1.   consent to surrender pursuant to s 15;
2.   be provided with legal advice and representation;
3.   be provided with the services of an interpreter.

5–27   It will almost invariably be the case that by this stage the respondent will already have procured the services of both a lawyer and interpreter. Nonetheless the terms of s 13(5) would appear to be mandatory and as a matter of practice the court will inform the respondent of these rights even where they have already been availed of.

5–28   Unless the respondent indicates a clear wish to consent to surrender at this stage the court will remand him or her either in custody or on bail. Section 13(5)(b) requires the court at this stage to fix a hearing date not more than 21 days from the date of

---

[13] *Minister for Justice, Equality and Law Reform v McG* [2007] IEHC 47.
[14] [2005] IEHC 259.

the respondent's arrest.[15] Presumably this requirement was included in the Act in the context of the other time limits set out in the Framework Decision. Whilst it is observed in a formal sense the "hearing date" is generally of the purely notional variety.

BAIL

Once an arrested person has been brought before the High Court and the formalities   **5–29** of s 13(4) have been observed the court will either "remand the person in custody or on bail". At this point in proceedings the respondent will necessarily be in custody having been arrested on foot of the endorsed warrant. In practice the question of bail will frequently be deferred for a brief period of time.

State's Obligation to the Issuing State

The granting of bail has long been a feature of extradition cases and the system of   **5–30** mutual surrender introduced by the European arrest warrant also provides for the granting of bail. Article 12 of the Framework Decision makes it clear that whilst bail can be granted it must be done in the context of the state's overriding obligation to ensure that the respondent is ultimately made available for surrender:

> "When a person is arrested on the basis of a European arrest warrant, the executing judicial authority shall take a decision on whether the requested person should remain in detention, in accordance with the law of the executing Member State. The person may be released provisionally at any time in conformity with the domestic law of the executing Member State, provided that the competent authority of the said Member State takes all the measures it deems necessary to prevent the person absconding."

In *Minister for Justice, Equality and Law Reform v Ostrovskij*[16] the court expressly   **5–31** acknowledged the state's obligation to take all necessary measures to prevent the respondent absconding to the extent that it considered it necessary for the respondent to satisfy the court on the balance of probabilities that bail was appropriate:

> "The Court's duty and obligation is to ensure as far as is reasonably possible that in accordance with the State's obligations under the Framework Decision dated 13th June 2002 to which the 2003 Act, as amended by the 2005 Act gives effect, that in the event that the Court grants an application for the applicant's surrender, the State will be in a position to so surrender the applicant on foot thereof. The Court would have to be satisfied as a matter of probability, having regard to all the circumstances of the case, that the terms and conditions of any bail which may be granted will be sufficient to ensure that the applicant will appear in Court for the application under s. 16 of the Act."

The obligation on the part of the State to ensure that a person requested for the   **5–32** purposes of onward extradition remains amenable to the processes of the courts existed prior to the introduction of the European arrest warrant. In *The People*

---

[15] It should be noted that this date may be different from the date upon which the respondent is brought before the High Court.

[16] [2005] IEHC 427.

(Attorney General) v Gilliland[17] the nature of the obligation was described as follows:

> "For my part I consider that there is no reason for applying the absconding test any differently in extradition cases as compared with ordinary criminal cases. In an extradition case the State's duty is to take all reasonable steps to ensure that the prisoner will ultimately be available for extradition. In an ordinary criminal case the State's duty is to ensure that the prisoner will be available for his trial. In either case the State's duty must operate in a way that will not conflict with the fundamental right to personal liberty of a person who stands unconvicted of an offence under the law of the State. That right to personal liberty should not be lost save where the loss is necessary for the effectuation of the duty of the State as the guardian of the common good - in the extradition cases the duty normally being to fulfill treaty obligations and in ordinary criminal cases normally to enable the criminal process to advance to a proper trial."[18]

Applicable Criteria

5–33   The application of the statement in *Gilliland* to European arrest warrant proceedings was confirmed by Peart J in *Minister for Justice, Equality and Law Reform v Vojik*[19] who observed in the circumstances of that case:

> "There is no reason why a foreign national should be at any greater disadvantage, simply by being here, being arrested on an extradition warrant, but there is no reason why he should be in a different position as far as bail is concerned. That is not to say that the reality of his status here and his presence here cannot be taken into account, just as particular circumstances of any other ordinary criminal case, domestic criminal case, can be taken into account.
>
> Each applicant for bail has particular circumstances which the court must have regard to. Simply because the court has regard to particular circumstances existing in relation to somebody who is not of Irish nationality and has no ties here does not mean that those are not circumstances that can at least be taken into account. Of course there is no question about bail being refused simply because somebody is not of Irish nationality. That is obvious and clear."

5–34   Whilst the decision in *Ostrovskij* seems to suggest that it is up to the respondent to satisfy the court in relation to the issue of bail it would appear from the decision in *Gilliland*, which actually addressed the issue of where the burden of proof lay, that this is not so:

> "I would particularly reject the submission that the onus in regard to this test should rest on the prisoner. Apart from the inherent unfairness in requiring proof of a negative, it is plain that in many cases it would be grossly unfair to expect a prisoner awaiting extradition in a jail in a foreign country to be in a position to adduce evidence to rebut the likelihood of his absconding. Where an application for bail is made by a prisoner, it is for the party resisting that application to put forward such evidence as will enable the court to hold

---

[17] [1985] IR 643.

[18] p 646.

[19] High Court, ex tempore, 28 February 2007.

that there is a probability that the prisoner will abscond if granted bail. The discretion of the court hearing the application must necessarily be wide."[20]

Given that the obligation created by Art 12 of the Framework Decision expresses itself to be subject to the law of the executing Member State, it is difficult to see how the position could have changed so radically without express intervention by the Oireachtas.   **5–35**

Because of the nature of such proceedings, where it is frequently alleged that the requested person absconded from the issuing state, the Minister may have an easier task in convincing the Court that there is a risk of the requested person absconding than would be the case in normal criminal proceedings. However, as noted by Henchy J, this fact does not put any burden on the requested person to prove that he will not abscond. Rather it is a matter that must be addressed on a substantive basis in the course of any application for bail. In *Ostrovskij* the court noted the practical consequences arising from the fact that the respondent was a foreign national: **5–36**

> "It is relevant that this application has as its background an application for the surrender of the applicant to his home country on foot of a European arrest warrant. [Counsel] has submitted that this Court must not make any distinction between a national and a non-national as far as the granting or refusal of bail is concerned. He is certainly correct that a non-national must not be discriminated against on the ground that he is a non-national. But that does not mean that the Court must not have regard to the fact that the applicant's ties here are bound to be less than those of a national who has lived here and put down roots here and so forth. That is simply a reality to which the Court must have regard, and to take it into account is not to discriminate in any unfair way as between a national or non-national."

Bail Act 1997

Whilst as a general proposition it is true that the general principles which apply to the granting of bail in domestic proceedings also apply in European arrest warrant and extradition cases, there are specific provisions which apply to domestic proceedings which have no application elsewhere. Specifically it would appear that the provisions of the Bail Act 1997 and Art 40.4.7 of the Constitution have no application. This Article of the Constitution allows for the refusal of bail in respect of a person "charged with a serious offence" on the grounds that there is an apprehension that the person may commit further serious offences. The Bail Act 1997 provided the legislative machinery to give effect to this provision which had been the subject of a constitutional amendment. Whilst it might conceivably have been possible to suggest that a person who is the subject of a European arrest warrant ought to be regarded as a person "charged" with an offence, the provisions of s 1 of the Bail Act 1997 limit its applicability to courts which are exercising criminal jurisdiction. As the High Court is not exercising criminal jurisdiction in the case of proceedings under the European Arrest Warrant Act 2003 it follows that the provisions of s 2 of the Bail Act 1997 have no application. Quite apart from such jurisdictional considerations it would, in any event, be more or less impossible to regard an offence described in a   **5–37**

---

[20] p 646.

European arrest warrant as being a scheduled offence for the purpose of the Bail Act 1997 as all such scheduled offences are necessarily domestic offences.

5–38   In theory at least, therefore, it should be easier for a respondent to obtain bail in proceedings under the 2003 Act than in domestic criminal proceedings, as the former are not subject to the restrictions on bail introduced on foot of the Bail Act 1997. As such the general situation which pertained prior to the introduction of that Act continues to apply in the case of European arrest warrant and extradition proceedings. The relevant criteria to be applied were set out in *The People (Attorney General) v O'Callaghan*.[21] Significantly that decision is authority for the proposition that bail ought not to be refused on the basis of an apprehension of the commission of further offences. Moreover it clearly places the entitlement to bail in the context of the constitutional right to liberty and predicates an approach on the part of the court which ought to be informed by a presumption in favour of bail being granted on the grounds that bail is properly regarded as an entitlement rather than a privilege.

5–39   That said, the courts have yet to address an important distinction which arises in the context of many extradition cases. Frequently the surrender of an individual will be sought in circumstances where that person has been convicted and possibly sentenced for an offence. Given that much of the domestic jurisprudence in relation to the entitlement to bail is rooted in the presumption of innocence it remains to be seen whether the courts will draw a distinction between those respondents who stand convicted and those who simply stand accused in the context of an application for bail.

Remand

5–40   Section 27 of the 2003 Act provides that a requested person remanded in custody for the purposes of proceedings under the Act may be detained in a prison, remand institution (if not more than 21 years of age), or, for a period not exceeding 48 hours, in a Garda Station. Section 27 further provides that a requested person may not be remanded on bail or otherwise released from custody where he is serving a sentence in the State or has been remanded in custody in relation to domestic charges.

5–41   Where a person is remanded in custody the provisions of ss 10 and 11 of the Criminal Justice Act 1960, which simply provide the legal machinery for the transfer of prisoners between different prisons, will apply mutatis mutandis.

ARREST ON FOOT OF SCHENGEN ALERT – SECTION 14

5–42   Prior to the Criminal Justice (Miscellaneous Provisions) Act 2009 the 2003 Act had provided for a rarely (if ever) used procedure whereby a member of an Garda Síochána could arrest a person without a warrant in circumstances where a Schengen Alert had been issued in a Member State for the person and there was an apprehension that the person would leave the State before a European arrest warrant would be made available for the purposes of execution. Given the fact that the Gardaí did not fully participate in the operation of the Schengen Information System (SIS), the provision was perhaps somewhat previous.

---

[21] [1966] IR 501.

The 2009 Act now provides for the active participation of both the Gardaí and customs officers in the SIS.[22] It is to be anticipated, therefore, that there may well be a shift away from the execution of European arrest warrants on an exclusively targeted basis to the execution of warrants and "alerts" on a more opportunistic basis as the subjects of such warrants and alerts come to the attention of law enforcement agencies in the ordinary way.

5–43

The SIS

The Schengen Information System is a radial database to which the law enforcement databases of the various participating countries are connected. The creation of such a database is as much a significant technical achievement as it is a political or legal one in that it must necessarily accommodate the differing computer systems used by police forces across Europe. The database holds information on over 10 million individuals and vehicles allowing checks to be made across Europe for the purpose of border checks and law enforcement. Significantly the information contained on the database is updated constantly and in real time by means of the automatic interaction of the SIS with domestic police and customs databases.

5–44

Ireland's participation in the SIS is limited as it takes the form of the more truncated degree of access provided for by the Schengen Acquis rather than the Schengen Convention. However, one of the categories of alert that is available relates to alerts entered in the SIS in respect of persons who are the subject of European arrest warrants. Given that the Schengen Convention requires participating countries to undertake to keep all relevant alerts updated and current the theory behind the system is that an executing state can take the information provided by the SIS at face value.

5–45

"Alert"

The amended s 14 now provides the Gardaí with a power of arrest where they have reasonable grounds for believing that a person is named in an "alert". For the purposes of the Act an "alert" is defined as:

5–46

> "…an alert entered in the SIS for the arrest and surrender, on foot of a European arrest warrant, of the person named therein;"[23]

Whilst the SIS allows for alerts to be entered on the system for all manner of reasons, the definition provided for by s 2 clearly only relates to an alert entered on foot of a European arrest warrant. It is, therefore, not possible to invoke s 14 in circumstances where the alert relates to, for example, a domestic arrest warrant issued in another Member State.

5–47

The use of such alerts is expressly contemplated by the Framework Decision Art 9 of which provides:

5–48

---

[22] s 22(1) of the Criminal Justice (Miscellaneous Provisions) Act 2009 now provides: "A member of the Garda Síochána, an officer of customs and excise or any other person or category of persons of a description specified in an order made by the Minister under this section may provide and receive information for the purposes of the operation of the Council Decision or Schengen Convention".

[23] s 2.

"(2) The issuing judicial authority may, in any event, decide to issue an alert for the requested person in the Schengen Information System (SIS).

(3) Such an alert shall be effected in accordance with the provisions of Article 95 of the Convention...An alert in the Schengen Information System shall be equivalent to a European arrest warrant accompanied by the information set out in Article 8.1."[24]

5–49　Therefore, where an alert is issued in the SIS the information contained in it will be more or less equivalent to the information contained in a European arrest warrant.

Arrest

5–50　Section 14(3) provides for a similar procedure, mutatis mutandis, in terms of arrest and production before the High Court as applies in the case of arrest on foot of a European arrest warrant pursuant to s 13. The arrested person has an entitlement to be furnished with a copy of the alert upon arrest.

5–51　The only matter on which the High Court needs to be satisfied once the person is produced before it is that the person is the individual named in the alert. In that regard it should be noted that the Schengen Convention requires that much the same information that is needed for identification purposes in a European arrest warrant is included in an alert for the purposes of the SIS. In addition the powers to take fingerprints and photographs for identification purposes provided for by s 45A of the Act also apply in relation to arrest pursuant to s 14.

Bail following Arrest under Section 14

5–52　Once the issue of identification has been dealt with the High Court can remand the person in custody or on bail pending the production of the European arrest warrant underlying the alert. The express power to grant bail provided for in s 14(3) represents a shift from the position under the original provision as enacted in the 2003 Act, which seemed to presuppose that a person arrested on grounds of urgency would automatically be remanded in custody.[25] The Act provides little by way of guidance to the court in terms of the criteria to be applied upon such an application. Moreover, it is unclear what evidential status, if any, the alert will have. It would not appear to enjoy any of the evidential presumptions provided for by s 12 of the Act and given the emergency nature of the s 14 procedure it is probably unlikely that an Garda Síochána will have much by way of information in respect of the arrested person. It very much remains to be seen how the courts will approach the question of bail in such situations, particularly bearing in mind the somewhat speculative nature of any arrest pursuant to s 14.

PRODUCTION OF THE EUROPEAN ARREST WARRANT

5–53　The purpose of the remand, whether on bail or in custody, is to allow time for the production of the European arrest warrant underlying the alert. Necessarily the court

---

[24] i.e. the information required to be included in a European arrest warrant.

[25] s 14(3) had previously provided that "...the High Court shall...remand the person in custody...".

must remand the arrested person to a particular date to allow this to be done. Section 14(4) provides that where the warrant is transmitted to the Central Authority prior to that date the person shall be brought back before the High Court. The mechanism of such production is not specified although presumably in the case of a person in custody a production order will suffice. At that point the warrant will be produced to the court which will engage in a consideration of its terms analogous to an endorsement application. If the High Court is satisfied that the warrant is in order, it will proceed to deal with the respondent in a manner similar to the execution procedure under s 13. At that point the respondent may consent to surrender[26] or a hearing date must be fixed within 21 days.[27]

Section 14(5) provides that where the warrant has not been produced by the remand date then the respondent "shall be released from custody". Quite what is meant by this is not entirely clear given that the subsection expressly presupposes that the respondent may have been granted bail at an earlier point. Given the purpose and rationale of s 14 it is doubtful that the court has jurisdiction to further remand the respondent at this stage unless the warrant in produced. **5–54**

---

[26] s 15(2).
[27] s 14(4)(d)(ii)(II).

Post-Arrest Procedure

FIXING THE HEARING DATE

Once the formalities of arrest and bail have been dealt with the High Court is obliged **6–01** to fix a hearing date within 21 days of the date of arrest[1] unless the respondent consents to surrender on a voluntary basis. The date to be fixed for the purposes of s 16 should in theory be the hearing date on which the Minister applies for an order for surrender under s 16(1) and such order is granted or refused by the court. In practice, however, a number of remands often take place before the hearing of the application takes place. This reality was acknowledged by the insertion of s 16(2A) by s 76(c) of the Criminal Justice (Terrorist Offences) Act 2005, which provides that, where the Court does not order the surrender of the requested person on a date fixed for the purposes of s 16, it may remand him or her in custody or on bail to a further date. In practice the 21 day time limit is entirely notional and largely aspirational. The provisions of s 13(5) do, however, require that the initial remand of the respondent be within 21 days even though subsequent remands may well be considerably longer.

VOLUNTARY SURRENDER

By the time a respondent has been brought before the High Court and dealt with **6–02** under s 13 he or she will have been informed at least twice of the entitlement to consent to surrender pursuant to s 15. Firstly he or she will have been informed of the right to consent by the arresting Garda and secondly by the High Court. Whilst the respondent may now be regarded as being fully aware of the right to consent to surrender he or she may not have any great appreciation of the consequences of surrendering. It is clear from the terms of the Framework Decision that the function

---

[1] s 13(5).

of explaining the consequences of surrender to a respondent in order that he or she can make an informed decision falls to "legal counsel":

> "Each Member State shall adopt the measures to ensure that consent and, where appropriate, renunciation, as referred to in paragraph 1, are established in such a way as to show that the person concerned has expressed them voluntarily and in full awareness of the consequences. To that end, the requested person shall have the right to legal counsel."[2]

6–03   It is, therefore, up to the legal representatives, whether assigned by the court or otherwise, to explain to the respondent what the consequences of surrendering voluntarily may be. Such an explanation may well be far from straightforward and will involve considerably more than just the trite observation that voluntary surrender precludes the possibility of contesting the proceedings. Matters such as the operation of the rule of specialty in the requesting state, the possibility of contesting surrender in respect of some offences but not others, and the possibility of deducting time spent in custody in the State once returned are but a few of the issues which may arise. Frequently there may well also be issues in relation to the interaction of any surrender order with ongoing domestic proceedings or a sentence of imprisonment that the respondent is currently serving. Informed consent in relation to such issues will obviously require full information. It is rarely possible for a respondent to make an informed choice in the immediate aftermath of arrest.

Consent Procedure

6–04   The consent procedure is set out in s 15 of the 2003 which provides that the High Court must be satisfied of the following matters:

(i)   Firstly that the European arrest warrant has been endorsed in accordance with s 13 for execution.[3] In practice this tends not to present any great difficulty as the fact of the endorsement will generally be apparent from the original warrant itself.

(ii) The court must be satisfied that the person consents to surrender and is aware of the consequences of this.[4] In large part the High Court will rely upon the fact that the respondent has been provided with legal representation for the purpose of satisfying itself that the respondent understands the consequences of surrender.

(iii) The court must also be satisfied that the person has been afforded the opportunity of obtaining legal advice prior to consenting.[5] The terms of s 15(1)(b)(ii) obviously allow a respondent to dispense with the obtaining of legal advice and to consent to voluntary surrender in its absence. At a practical level this will necessarily impose upon the High Court a significantly heavier burden in terms of satisfying itself that the respondent fully understands the consequences of surrender.

---

[2]   Art 13.4 of the Framework Decision.
[3]   s 15(1)(a).
[4]   s 15(1)(b)(i).
[5]   s 15(1)(b)(ii).

(iv) That surrender is not precluded by the terms of ss 21A, 22, 23 or 24 of the Act. These provisions require the court to refuse surrender where there has not been a decision to prosecute in the requesting state, where the rule of specialty may be breached and where the respondent might be subject to onward surrender either to another Member State or a third party state. Each of the sections providing for refusal of surrender in such circumstances also provides for a presumption that such circumstances will not arise. As such the court can be automatically satisfied that the relevant conditions are satisfied, unless there is something in the warrant or otherwise before the court that has the effect of upsetting any of these presumptions.

(v) Finally the High Court must be satisfied that surrender is not precluded by virtue of Part 3 of the Act or the Framework Decision. In essence the court must be satisfied that the offences in the warrant correspond, that they meet the relevant minimum gravity requirements, that surrender is not precluded on the basis of double jeopardy, extraterritoriality or age and that surrender will not amount to a breach of fundamental rights under s 37. Additionally the court will have to consider whether an undertaking in accordance with s 45 is required in the circumstances of the particular case. Whilst the courts have spoken in terms of the existence of a *de facto* presumption in favour of surrender in the context of anticipated breach of fundamental rights,[6] no such presumptions arise in respect of the other prospective bars to surrender. Once more, the court will rely on the assistance of the respondent's legal advisers for the purpose of being assured that no such issues arise. In the absence of such representation the court will be obliged to conduct a very much more detailed review of the warrant prior to ordering the surrender of the respondent.

It should be clear from the foregoing that the making of an order under s 15 is not simply a formality but rather presupposes a reasonably detailed enquiry by the court. In practice much of this enquiry has been, in effect, delegated to the respondent's legal representatives who will draw the court's attention to any issue which they perceive as arising. **6-05**

Once made the court is obliged to inform the respondent that he has the right to make a complaint under Art 40.4.2 of the Constitution at any time prior to his surrender. The respondent will also be informed that the order will take effect in 10 days time. Thereafter surrender will generally have to be effected within a further period of 10 days. This is of some practical significance to the respondent as he or she is entitled to waive the initial 10 day period and thus reduce the period of time during which he or she may be required to be held in custody in this jurisdiction.[7] **6-06**

The court is also obliged to record in writing that the respondent consented to surrender.[8] In this regard a form of consent is prescribed by Order 98 of the Rules of the Superior Courts which the respondent is required to sign. **6-07**

---

[6] *Minister for Justice, Equality and Law Reform v Brennan* [2007] 3 IR 732.

[7] s 15(3).

[8] s 15(4)(c).

Irrevocability

6–08   Prior to the Criminal Justice (Miscellaneous Provisions) Act 2009 it was possible for a respondent to revoke his or her consent after it had been given.[9] This situation has been changed by virtue of s 11 of the 2009 Act which substitutes a limited right of appeal subject to certification by the High Court that the order or decision involves a point of law of exceptional public importance and that it is desirable in the public interest that an appeal should be taken to the Supreme Court. Whilst it is difficult to envisage circumstances in which an appeal may be certified where the respondent has previously consented to surrender, such an approach would seem to be in line with Art 13.4 of the Framework Decision which states that "[i]n principle, consent may not be revoked…".

6–09   The amendment effected by s 11 of the 2009 Act is a significant one in the context of voluntary surrender. Given that consent to surrender is now, in practical terms at least, irrevocable, the obligation of the court and the respondent's legal representatives to ensure the consent is fully informed is underlined in stark terms.

POINTS OF OBJECTION

6–10   Where the respondent does not consent to surrender pursuant to s 15 the court must proceed to deal with the matter pursuant to the provisions of s 16 of the Act. Order 98, r 5(1) of the Rules of the Superior Courts makes express provision for the service of Points of Objection in such circumstances:

> "Where a person does not consent to his or her surrender to the issuing State, or withdraws his or her consent under Section 15(9) of the 2003 Act, he shall be at liberty, not later than 4 days before the date fixed for the purposes of Section 16 of the 2003 Act, to deliver to the solicitor for the Central Authority in the State and file in the Central Office, Points of Objection to his or her surrender."

6–11   The rules do not append or specify any particular format or template to be adopted. The content of the Points of Objection is, however, set out in brief in Ord 98, r 5(2):

> "Points of Objection shall contain a statement in summary form of the grounds and of the material facts on which the person relies to resist the execution of the European Arrest Warrant but not the evidence by which such material facts are to be proved."

6–12   In other words it would seem that the Points of Objection are contemplated as being a traditional form of pleading, the purpose of which is to identify and put in issue the contested issues of fact and law without necessarily requiring the respondent to set out specifically the evidence, if any, which will be relied upon.

6–13   The nature of proceedings under the European Arrest Warrant Act 2003 are, like extradition proceedings, best regarded as *sui generis*. In *Minister for Justice, Equality and Law Reform v McGrath*[10] Macken J made reference to the expressly

---

[9] s 15(9) had provided: "A person who has consented under this section to his or her being surrendered may, at any time thereafter but before his or her surrender in accordance with an order under this section, withdraw his or her consent…".

[10] [2006] 1 IR 321.

inquisitorial nature of the proceedings. One of the consequences of this approach is that a respondent who wishes to object to surrender must clearly state the basis for such objection in advance of the s 16 hearing rather than simply raise a generic objection or seek to put the applicant on proof with a view to raising a technical deficiency in the proofs at the conclusion of the hearing.

On a number of occasions the courts have criticised the filing of generic or formulaic points of objection[11]. In *Minister for Justice, Equality and Law Reform v Skowronski*[12] the court noted that the purpose of points of objection was to allow the issues which formed the basis for the objection to be identified by both parties:

    6–14

> "This Court has said on previous occasions that the purpose of Points of Objection is to put the applicant on notice in a sufficiently precise and clear manner of just what points of objection will be relied upon at the hearing of the application, and that it is not appropriate or sufficient to simply file a document called Points of Objection but which contains to a large extent merely unspecific allegations of non-compliance with various requirements of the European Arrest Warrant Act, 2003 as amended or the Framework Decision. I have noted before that the application for an order under s. 16 of the Act is not to be treated in the same manner as a civil action where very frequently fairly meaningless pleadings are exchanged, on the basis that eventually in replies to particulars some meat is put on the flesh and the other party at last knows what case it has to meet. In such applications, Points of Objection serve the purpose only to put the applicant on notice in a meaningful way of what case is being made to oppose the application. Fair procedures require this, and it must always be remembered that these are not criminal proceedings where the accused is under no obligation to disclose in advance of the trial what his or her defence might be. Rules of procedure have been provided for."

The court went on to suggest that where formulaic points of objection were served in circumstances which served to frustrate this aim the court might consider it appropriate to withdraw its recommendation under the Attorney General's Scheme. More frequently, however, where the applicant considers that the Points of Objection as served are unduly vague or generic a Notice for Particulars will be served in respect of them.

    6–15

DISCOVERY

The terms of Ord 98, r 8 of the Rules of the Superior Courts[13] seem to suggest that discovery would feature as a major element of litigation under the 2003 Act. Notwithstanding the elaborate provisions in relation to discovery the reality has been otherwise. Insofar as respondents have sought to invoke an entitlement to discovery or disclosure in the context of European arrest warrant proceedings such applications have more often than not failed.

    6–16

In *Minister for Justice, Equality and Law Reform v Altaravicius (No. 1)*[14] the respondent had sought, by way of discovery, a copy of the underlying domestic

    6–17

---

[11] *Minister for Justice, Equality and Law Reform v Draisey* [2006] IEHC 375.

[12] [2006] IEHC 321.

[13] As amended by SI No 23 of 2005.

[14] [2006] 3 IR 148.

warrant issued in the requesting state on foot of which the European arrest warrant had been issued. An order for discovery had been granted in the High Court. In granting the order, the court stated that it was likely that a similar application would be warranted in most cases under the Act given the requirement in s 10 that the court be satisfied that the warrant was "duly issued" in the issuing state. This approach was rejected by the Supreme Court. In the course of his judgment Murray CJ considered in detail the provisions of the Framework Decision and in particular the purpose underlying it, namely the introduction of simplified procedures between the judicial authorities of Member States based on mutual trust and understanding. In this context it made little sense to require production of the underlying domestic warrant as a matter of course given that the whole idea behind the European arrest warrant is that it would be an entirely self contained procedure reduced to one document, the European arrest warrant, wherever possible.

6–18 The Court considered that the production of the underlying domestic warrant was not envisaged by the Framework Decision and was not, in any event, necessary for the purpose of the High Court discharging its functions under the Act:

> "The respondent in these proceedings has asserted that he wishes to look at the underlying domestic warrant in order to check whether there might be any inconsistency between the charge or charges in that warrant and the European arrest warrant. The issue raised is purely speculative. No material or evidential basis has been raised from which it could be inferred that any such inconsistency exists. Speculation or assertion as to what procedures might or might not have been followed in the issuing state is not sufficient to raise an issue to be tried in these proceedings.
>
> The operative document in an application for surrender pursuant to the Act is the European arrest warrant issued by a judicial authority of the issuing state within the meaning of the framework decision. That is the essential basis on which the High Court is required to act in an application pursuant to s. 16 of the Act of 2003."[15]

6–19 Given that the production of the domestic warrant was not necessary or germane in the context of an application pursuant to s 16 it could not be said that the respondent had not been accorded fair procedures.

6–20 A similar approach was adopted in *Minister for Justice, Equality and Law Reform v Stapleton*[16] where the respondent had filed Points of Objection which indicated an objection to surrender on the grounds of delay and an apprehension of inhumane and degrading treatment. The respondent's wife had been convicted of related charges and the respondent sought to make various comparisons in relation to her treatment at the hands of the prosecuting authorities both during and subsequent to her trial. Discovery was sought in relation to a wide range of documentation relating to her treatment. Peart J noted that in order for an application for discovery to succeed, the party seeking discovery would be obliged to show that it was not just relevant but also necessary. In the context of proceedings under the European Arrest Warrant Act 2003 there was a limit to the breadth and scope of issues which might arise. Ultimately the court took the view that whilst the respondent had to some degree

---

[15] At pp 162–163.
[16] [2005] IEHC 386.

established relevance in the context of the Points of Objection which had been filed, the application for discovery was essentially a "fishing expedition" and as such the respondent had not satisfied the court on the grounds of necessity.

Whilst *Altaravicius* can be regarded as authority for the general proposition   **6–21** that production of the domestic warrant will not be required, there have been cases where the courts have requested the production of the underlying domestic warrant. Considerable attention was given in the course of the judgment in *Altaravicius* to an earlier decision of the High Court in *Minister for Justice, Equality and Law Reform v Fallon*[17] where an order for the production of the domestic warrant had been made. It should be noted that this was not by way of a discovery application but rather the court acceded to the respondent's request that the domestic warrant be examined by the Court on foot of objections which had been canvassed in the course of the s 16 hearing. The court adjourned the hearing in order that the warrant could be produced (presumably pursuant to the provisions of s 20). In that case, however, there had been evidence put before the court which raised a serious issue in relation to the manner in which the domestic warrant had been issued. The High Court had concluded in that case that:

> "…if a respondent puts before the court evidence which, if accepted, establishes as a matter of probability that the European arrest warrant was not issued in accordance with the requirements of the Framework Decision or the requirements of the Framework Decision as implemented in the issuing state then this court is bound to inquire whether such a European arrest warrant has been duly issued. The averments made by [the witness] raise such an issue in this application."

The distinction between *Fallon* and *Altaravicius* would appear to be that in the   **6–22** former case there was an amount of evidence to displace the presumption that the warrant was duly issued whilst in the latter the suggestion that there may have been a defect in relation to it was purely speculative. It would seem to follow that the court will require to be convinced on some concrete basis that there is a difficulty in relation to the manner in which the warrant was issued in the requesting state before it will order production of the underlying domestic warrant or presumably discovery of other documentation.

The respondent in *Altaravicius* had also suggested that the existence of an   **6–23** evidential presumption against him meant that he should be entitled to discovery for the purpose of rebutting it. Such an argument was rejected on the grounds that a presumption could not as a matter of principle be invoked for the purpose of seeking discovery. In other words the respondent could not claim to be entitled to certain documentation merely by virtue of the fact that it might represent a means of upsetting the evidential presumption in question:

> "In effect the applicant seeks to turn this presumption on its head and, rather than the court proceeding on the European arrest warrant and the presumption, requires that this document be furnished in addition from the requesting state. The submission on behalf of the respondent, that while the presumption exists he bears the burden of rebutting it and so should be furnished with the documentation from the requesting State, is ingenious, but contrary to both the framework decision and the Act of 2003."[18]

---

[17] [2005] IEHC 321.
[18] p 169.

6–24   Were it otherwise the very act of creating an evidential presumption in respect of any of the matters with which the court is concerned in relation to a hearing under s 16 would give rise to a concomitant obligation to make discovery of documentation for the purpose of enabling the respondent to rebut the presumption. This would be unlikely to be regarded as a simplification or streamlining of the pre-existing procedures as is required by the Framework Decision.

6–25   The case-law in relation to the production of the underlying domestic warrant is unlikely to continue to be of great significance given the amendment to s 10 of the 2003 Act brought about by s 6(a) of the Criminal Justice (Miscellaneous Provisions) Act 2009 which excises the word "duly". As such the court no longer has to be satisfied that the warrant was "duly issued". This would seem to further limit the scope of the matters which can be agitated by a respondent in relation to the underlying domestic warrant to the extent that it may be extremely difficult to establish the relevance of such a document even where there is an issue in relation to the circumstances in which it came to be issued.

Seeking Information Pursuant to Section 20

6–26   It may be the case that a respondent who believes that additional documentation from the requesting state would be of assistance would be better advised to invoke the terms of s 20(1) of the European Arrest Warrant Act 2003 which provides:

> "In proceedings to which this Act applies the High Court may, if of the opinion that the documentation or information provided to it is not sufficient to enable it to perform its functions under this Act, require the issuing judicial authority or the issuing state, as may be appropriate, to provide it with such additional documentation or information as it may specify, within such period as it may specify."

6–27   Whilst s 20(1) empowers the court rather than the respondent to seek additional information, there is no reason why a respondent cannot apply to the court to exercise its entitlement to seek additional information. This is particularly the case if an issue arises in relation to any question of correspondence, minimum gravity, extraterritoriality etc. The provision of additional information may well resolve an ambiguity in the respondent's favour.

ATTORNEY GENERAL'S SCHEME

6–28   The majority of cases coming before the courts are dealt with under the provisions of the Attorney General's Scheme. Whilst the terms of the scheme are published by the Office of the Attorney General the manner in which it is operated and the amount payable in respect of a given case remain somewhat opaque.[19] The scheme requires that application for payment must be made at the outset of proceedings:

> "…a person wishing to obtain from the court a recommendation to the Attorney General that the Scheme be applied must make his or her application (personally

---

[19] Rather ominously the Scheme as published by the AGO concludes as follows: "These are the main conditions relating to the Attorney General's Scheme." What other conditions may apply is unclear.

or through his or her lawyer) at the commencement of the proceedings and must obtain the recommendation at the commencement of the proceedings."

Whilst the court can grant a recommendation under the Scheme on foot of such **6–29** an application if satisfied as to the respondent's lack of means it is clear that any such recommendation is not binding and ultimately falls to be decided as a matter of discretion by the Attorney General. For some time there have been considerable misgivings as to the entirely discretionary nature of the scheme and the fact that those who represent respondents have no real recourse in the event of non-payment. This arises by virtue of the fact that it is necessary to make an application at the outset of the proceedings in circumstances where, as a matter of practice, the court will not make a formal recommendation under the Scheme until the conclusion of the proceedings. In effect the legal representatives are expected to represent respondents in hope more than expectation.

In the case of *Minister for Justice, Equality and Law Reform v Ollsen*[20] the respondent **6–30** mounted a broad challenge to the Attorney General's Scheme on the grounds that it did not satisfy the requirements of the Constitution or of the Framework Decision.[21] Whilst acknowledging the difficulties surrounding the manner in which the scheme had been operated, the Court concluded that it complied with the requirements of the Framework Decision and s 13(4) of the Act if for no other reason than there were lawyers prepared to represent respondents on a daily basis:

> "The Court cannot blind itself to the fact that for many years now lawyers have found the scheme unsatisfactory both in terms of the level of remuneration thereunder, its discretionary and non-statutory nature, and the speed or perhaps more correctly, the lack of it, by which payment is actually received. But while there may be disquiet in relation to the way in which the scheme operates, the fact is that every day of the week lawyers appear before the High Court on applications such as Habeas Corpus, Bail, EAW applications and Judicial Review and those counsel are always instructed by solicitors. In other words there appears to be no shortage of lawyers in both branches of the profession who are prepared to act for clients on the basis of the remuneration available under the scheme, in spite of what they perceive as its shortcomings. Until that situation ceases it appears to me that the Scheme works in the sense that it ensures that persons who have an entitlement to legal representation before a Court, whether in a criminal matter or otherwise, and a matter such as the present case are professionally represented."

The Court went on to acknowledge that the deficiencies of the Scheme might **6–31** well be canvassed in other ways but by virtue of the simple fact that professional representation was facilitated by the Scheme any challenge to surrender which was predicated upon its failure to ensure representation must fail.[22]

---

[20] [2008] IEHC 37.

[21] Art 11.2 provides: "A requested person who is arrested for the purpose of the execution of a European arrest warrant shall have a right to be assisted by a legal counsel and by an interpreter in accordance with the law of the executing member state". This is given effect by s 13(4) of the Act which provides that the respondent will have legal advice and representation made available.

[22] A similar conclusion was reached in *Minister for Justice, Equality and Law Reform v O'Connor*, ex tempore, Peart J, 19 January 2010.

CHAPTER 7

The Hearing

THE NATURE OF THE HEARING

There is an ample amount of authority to support the proposition that proceedings **7–01**
under the European Arrest Warrant Act 2003 are better regarded as inquisitorial in
nature rather than adversarial:

> "...this is not an enquiry in which there is an onus on the applicant to prove
> beyond reasonable doubt that the respondent is the person sought to be
> surrendered. Nor is it appropriate, as was stated by Denham J. in the above case,
> to adopt the civil standard of proof "on the balance of probabilities", although
> this might be closer to what is apt. In my view the obligation on the court is to
> take full account of the warrant and the accompanying materials and affidavits
> filed and make all appropriate enquiries which I consider necessary, including,
> pursuant to the Framework decision requesting further information from the
> issuing authority..."[1]

A similar view had been expressed earlier by Murray CJ in the case of *AG v Parke*[2] **7–02**
which concerned an application for extradition under the Extradition Act 1965:

> "The burden of proof of facts which may rest on the applicant in these
> proceedings is not that of a criminal trial. I hasten to add that the learned
> High Court Judge did not approach this matter on such a basis and it is just
> that I consider it appropriate at this point to distinguish between extradition
> proceedings and other forms of proceedings, criminal and civil. An extradition
> proceeding pursuant to the relevant Acts has its own special features which in a
> certain sense makes it sui generis."[3]

---

[1] As per Macken J in *Minister for Justice, Equality and Law Reform v McGrath* [2006] 1 IR
321 at p 334
[2] [2004] IESC 100.
[3] p 587.

7–03 Later in the judgment it was stated

> "The role of the requested State, indeed its duty, is to give effect to a lawful request from a requesting State once it is determined that the request fulfils the criteria laid down by the relevant legislation .... The responsibility for bringing a person named in a warrant before the High Court clearly rests with authorities in the State. Once that is done the task in determining whether all legal requirements for the making of an Order pursuant to s. 47 are fulfilled rests with the High Court Judge. That is an inherently inquisitorial function."[4]

7–04 Like extradition proceedings, litigation under the 2003 Act is not solely concerned with assessing rights and entitlements as between an individual and the State but is also concerned with the State's obligations under EU law to other Member States. As such a purely adversarial approach is not appropriate. Most recently the Supreme Court considered the nature of proceedings in respect of the European arrest warrant in *Minister for Justice, Equality and Law Reform v Sliczynski*[5]:

> "As regards the onus of proof, Counsel for the appellant properly acknowledged that extradition proceedings are neither strictly criminal nor civil in nature but the ordinary rules of evidence apply. It was submitted, citing *Minister for Justice, Equality & Law Reform v Abimbola* [2006 IEHC 325] which in turn relied on *R (Levin) v Governor of Brixton Prison* 1997 AC that while not strictly criminal proceedings, in extradition matters criminal procedure and rules of evidence should apply. Suffice it to say that the latter case, the United Kingdom case, referred to a particular form of extradition proceedings in the context of arrangements for extradition between the United Kingdom and the United States which involved a wholly different procedure for extradition than that which arises under the system of surrender provided for in the Act of 2003 as amended. Section 10 of the Act of 2003 provides *"Where a Judicial Authority in an issuing State duly issues a European Arrest Warrant in respect of a person ... that person shall, subject to and in accordance with the provisions of this Act and the Framework Decision be arrested and surrendered to the issuing State."* For the purpose of making an Order pursuant to s. 10 the trial Judge has to be satisfied that the requirements of the Act, and where specified, the Framework Decision, have been complied with. Once so satisfied he or she is bound to make the Order for surrender."

7–05 However, the courts have, on occasion, adopted a somewhat more adversarial approach particularly insofar as assertions made by a respondent are concerned. If one contrasts the approach taken to information emanating from the authorities in the issuing State with information and assertion emanating from the respondent a clear difference of approach is apparent. On the one hand the courts have been prepared to accept such material emanating from the issuing State at face value on the basis of mutual trust and confidence between Member States and also by virtue of the special nature of the proceedings. In *Minister for Justice, Equality and Law Reform v Sliczynski* Peart J noted that:

---

[4] pp 588–589.
[5] [2008] IESC 73.

"...under the European arrest warrant arrangements, a system of surrender has been put in place that is what has been described as sui generis. The application for surrender is not one which is the subject of adversarial proceedings in the normal sense of that word, even though there are points of objection which can be filed and the points of objection argued as to why surrender ought not be made. But it is made clear in the Framework Decision that the arrangements under the European arrest warrant are arrangements between one judicial authority and another judicial authority, and it is the case and does in fact occur that a requesting judicial authority will communicate and may communicate directly with the judicial authority in the requested state and information can be transmitted directly from one judicial authority to another under other arrangements, and it is not the case that every document that might emanate from such communication must be proven in evidence in the way one would be accustomed to expect in normal if you like, adversarial proceedings."[6]

He went on to suggest that there was a "heavy onus" on the respondent to establish **7–06** the relevant facts in order to argue that he had not fled the issuing State. In the course of the same judgment he also considered that the court could not rely on the averment on affidavit of the respondent in relation to his reasons for leaving the requesting State on the basis that "[t]he personal motivation of the respondent in this case is not something that is capable of being examined in any way by the Applicant". Whilst the Supreme Court[7] took a somewhat more nuanced approach and appeared to eschew the imposition of a "heavy onus" the conclusion reached was ultimately the same:

"I do not consider that the learned High Court judge altered the onus of proof required of an applicant in s.10 of the Act of 2003. Rather his judgment, while perhaps slightly infelicitously worded, must be understood in the sense that, having had all of the information from the issuing judicial authority which enabled him to find that the appellant had, on the basis of that information when viewed objectively, fled Poland, the appellant had not himself chosen to do any of the several things he might have done to counter that inevitable conclusion, which flowed from an examination of the information provided. When speaking of the heavy onus, I think it fairer to say that this concerned, not a legal onus on the appellant to establish in law something he was not obliged to establish, but rather an onus on him having regard to the information and material furnished in Mr. Doyle's affidavit, the veracity of which was not challenged in any way by the appellant, to establish that the material furnished did not support its natural conclusion that he had fled."[8]

Whilst the principle of mutual trust and the inquisitorial nature of the proceedings **7–07** provide a basis for relaxing the rules of evidence to a significant degree it would appear from the authorities that this operates by and large only in ease of the requesting State and rarely in ease of the respondent. In *Minister for Justice, Equality and Law Reform v Stankiewicz*[9] the issue before the court was whether or not the respondent had fled the requesting State prior to the activation of a

---

[6] High Court, *ex tempore,* 11 October 2007.

[7] [2008] IESC 73.

[8] As per Macken J at p 20.

[9] [2008] IEHC 129.

suspended sentence thereby coming within the ambit of s 10. A very similar issue had arisen in *Sliczynski* where the judicial authority had supplied the court with details of the terms of the suspension which had been breached by the respondent leaving the requesting State. In *Stankiewicz*, however, the details of the terms of the suspension were not before the court and the respondent asserted on affidavit that he had not breached any such terms by leaving the requesting State. This assertion was effectively unchallenged on the evidence. However, the court declined to act on the basis of such evidence:

> "...this Court can safely assume that an issuing state acts in good faith in these matters, and it follows that there is a heavy onus upon any respondent who raises a point of objection, to support that objection by cogent evidence. *Mere assertion cannot be sufficient*. To conclude otherwise would lead to a situation where the aims and objectives of the Framework Decision would be undermined and set at nought simply by unsubstantiated assertions made on affidavit by a respondent."[10]

> [*emphasis added*]

7–08   The contrast between the manner in which the courts deal with the evidence adduced by the applicant on the one hand and that adduced by the respondent on the other is indeed stark. Whilst s 4A of the Act and the principle of mutual trust allow the court to presume compliance on the part of the requesting State with the requirements of the Framework Decision it is difficult to see why they should give rise to a "heavy onus" as opposed to the normal onus of proof. Moreover it might well be said that it is problematic to characterise the establishing of facts by way of affidavit evidence as "mere assertion" which as a general rule is incapable of overcoming what might as easily be characterised as a "mere presumption". Whilst the proceedings are in theory inquisitorial in nature a respondent who wishes to assert matters of fact in controversy is well advised to approach their proof on a more adversarial footing.

EVIDENCE

7–09   During the course of a s 16 hearing the court is entitled to take the warrant and much of the other supporting documentation at face value. As such it is not necessary that such material be exhibited by way of affidavit. Whilst this is an innovation of the 2003 Act it does not represent a radical departure from the situation which existed under the Extradition Act 1965. In *Wyatt v McLoughlin*[11] Walsh J indicated a willingness to effectively regard the content of arrest warrants issued for the purpose of extradition as evidence:

> "Until there is some reason to believe to the contrary, it is to be assumed that a statement of facts such as the one appearing on the warrant executed in this case, or any warrant sent here for execution, is a truthful statement of the facts of the case in respect of which the arrest is sought."

---

[10] This reasoning and the subsequent conclusion was endorsed by the Supreme Court on appeal – see [2009] IESC 79.

[11] [1974] IR 378 at 395.

Section 12(8) of the 2003 now allows the court to receive in evidence without further proof any of the following documents: **7–10**

> "(a) a European arrest warrant issued by a judicial authority in the issuing state,
>
> (b) an undertaking required under this Act of an issuing judicial authority or the issuing state, as may be appropriate,
>
> (c) a translation[12] of a European arrest warrant or undertaking under this Act, or
>
> (d) a document referred to in section 11(2A) (inserted by *section 72(b)* of the *Criminal Justice (Terrorist Offences) Act 2005*),[13]
>
> (e) a true copy of such a document,"

The question of what amounts to a "true copy" was considered in *Minister for Justice, Equality and Law Reform v Kavanagh*[14] where the warrant before the court did not contain the signature of the issuing judicial authority. It seemed that the document that had been transmitted was a copy in the sense that there was a signed copy in existence somewhere but what had been sent was an unsigned copy. Peart J considered the provisions of s 12 in detail and ultimately concluded that this was a "true copy" within the meaning of s 12(8)(e): **7–11**

> "In the present case, the document received here by the Central Authority and which was endorsed by the High Court for execution can be seen to be a "true copy" of the original European arrest warrant. It is not a photostatic copy of the original warrant since it is not a photograph of the original warrant as signed. But it is a copy in the sense that it contains everything that is contained in the original warrant. In my view there is no provision in the Act which prevents the Respondent from being arrested on foot of a "true copy" of the original European arrest warrant issued in the issuing state provided that the true copy has been endorsed by the High Court for execution here. On the contrary, the receipt of the true copy of the warrant is expressly envisaged as one possibility."

This decision was, however, overturned on appeal by the Supreme Court in an ex tempore decision.[15] That court considered that the document which had been presented for endorsement could not in any meaningful sense be regarded as a European arrest warrant. **7–12**

Evidence on Affidavit

Order 98, r 7 of the Rules of the Superior Courts presupposes that the default mode of proof in proceedings under the Act is by way of affidavit: **7–13**

---

[12] Perhaps somewhat surprisingly s 12 does not provide for a similar presumption in respect of the translation of other documents such as additional information provided under s 20 although it is unlikely that any point would be taken in relation to same.

[13] There appears to be a minor formatting error in the amendment effected by s 73(g) of the Criminal Justice (Terrorist Offences) Act 2005 which purports to insert a "new paragraph" rather than substitute the existing s 11(8)(c) resulting in the creation of two s 11(8)(c)s.

[14] [2008] IEHC 81.

[15] 23 October 2009.

> "Evidence at the hearing fixed for the purposes of section 16 of the 2003 Act shall be adduced on affidavit save where the Court, in urgent cases or if the interests of justice so require, otherwise directs."

7–14 These rules predate the amendments brought about by the Criminal Justice (Terrorist Offences) Act 2005 and the Criminal Justice (Miscellaneous Provisions) Act 2009 and are presumably without prejudice to the provisions of the 2003 Act which allow most documents to be received by the court without the necessity of proof by affidavit.

7–15 Section 20(3) makes explicit provision for the use of affidavit evidence and allows the court to receive in addition to affidavit evidence sworn documents in the form of declarations, affirmations or attestations:

> "In proceedings under this Act, evidence as to any matter to which such proceedings relate may be given by affidavit, declaration, affirmation, attestation or by a statement in writing that purports to have been sworn—
>
> (a) by the deponent in a place other than the State, and
>
> (b) in the presence of a person duly authorised under the law of the place concerned to attest to the swearing of such a statement by a deponent, howsoever such a statement is described under the law of that place."

7–16 The only matter which is routinely dealt with by way of affidavit evidence is the question of identification which rarely enough arises in practice. This is normally dealt with by way of the simple expedient of the arresting member of an Garda Síochána swearing a brief affidavit setting out the circumstances of the arrest of the respondent. Invariably this will contain sufficient evidence by way of the response of the respondent to the various questions concerning his or her identity to allow the court to be satisfied as to it. It is questionable as to whether such evidence is formally necessary in circumstances where no issue in relation to identity is raised on the Points of Objection.

7–17 Where the respondent wishes to raise some issue of fact in aid of the Points of Objection it would appear necessary that the respondent swear the affidavit personally rather than through his solicitor. In *Minister for Justice, Equality and Law Reform v Horvath*[16] an affidavit sworn by the respondent's solicitor was filed in support of the contention that he had not fled the requesting State. Little or no weight was attached to the averments contained in the affidavit on the basis that they were essentially hearsay:

> "The fact is that the respondent has chosen not to swear any affidavit is support of his objections. His solicitor has sworn an affidavit on his instructions. Everything in that affidavit is therefore hearsay and incapable of being tested by any cross-examination."

7–18 Whilst the swearing and filing of an affidavit on behalf of the respondent necessarily invites the possibility of cross-examination this rarely occurs in practice.

---

[16] [2007] IEHC 202.

PRESUMPTIONS

Section 4A: Future Compliance with the Framework Decision

The European Arrest Warrant Act 2003 is replete with presumptions of various types **7–19** which have the effect of shifting the evidential burden in respect of various matters to the respondent. The most far reaching of these is the presumption provided for in s 4A:

> "It shall be presumed that an issuing state will comply with the requirements of the Framework Decision, unless the contrary is shown."

The use of the future tense in s 4A is significant in that it means that the presumption **7–20** only operates prospectively in that it only concerns events that may occur subsequent to the surrender of the respondent. This provision was considered in *Minister for Justice, Equality and Law Reform v Altaravicius*[17]:

> "That section only arises for consideration when an application for surrender is made. The section is couched in the future tense and plainly speaks of future compliance by the issuing state with the requirements of the framework decision subsequent to the making of an order for a person's surrender. This is quite logical since the framework decision imposes duties and obligations on the issuing state concerning the manner in which they deal with the person surrendered after surrender has taken place."[18]

Consequently it is of little use in relation to issues concerning events that have **7–21** already transpired in the issuing State. It does, however, allow the court to presume compliance in relation to the operation of the more generalised recitals of the Framework Decision that relate to the observation of fundamental rights and due process. It is doubtful as to whether the presumption has any practical application in relation to the other specific grounds for refusal of surrender under the 2003 Act except insofar as the provisions regarding specialty, onward surrender and onward extradition are concerned.

In the context of s 45 the High Court in the case of *Minister for Justice, Equality* **7–22** *and Law Reform v Sliczynski*[19] had concluded that a somewhat bare reference to the possibility of applying for a retrial satisfied the obligation on the requesting State to provide an undertaking as to a retrial on the basis that s 4A allowed the court to presume future compliance with the terms of the Framework Decision. The Supreme Court, however disagreed with such an approach. Murray CJ noted that s 45 of the Act, and indeed the relevant part of the Framework Decision, imposed an obligation upon the requested State rather than the requesting State and as such it was not logical to consider that the presumption in s 4A was of application at all:

> "I do not think that s. 4(A) has any pertinence to this particular point. That section refers to a presumption that an issuing State will comply with *the requirements* of the Framework Decision. But Article 5.1 does not impose any

---

[17] [2006] 3 IR 148.
[18] pp 158–159.
[19] [2008] IESC 73.

obligation or make any requirement of a requesting State to provide for a retrial even should the person surrendered apply for one. It is merely a permissive provision which allows a requested Member State to make it a pre-condition to the surrender of a person in relation to an offence for which that person has been tried in absentia that a guarantee is given that the person will have an opportunity of a retrial if surrendered."

7–23   It would seem to follow that before s 4A applies the relevant part of the Framework Decision will have to give rise to an obligation upon the requesting Member State rather than the requested Member State.

Section 21A(2): Presumption of Intention to Prosecute

7–24   The court is also entitled to assume that a decision has been taken in the requesting State to bring proceedings against the respondent. This is a condition precedent to surrender. Section 21A(2) provides:

"Where a European arrest warrant is issued in respect of a person who has not been convicted of an offence specified therein, it shall be presumed that a decision has been made to charge the person with, and try him or her for, that offence in the issuing state, unless the contrary is proved."

7–25   The courts have made frequent use of this presumption in a series of cases where the respondent has sought to argue that surrender is sought for the purpose of investigation rather than prosecution.

Specialty and Onward Surrender Presumptions

7–26   Sections 22, 23 and 24 preclude surrender in circumstances where there is an apprehension that the rule of specialty might be breached or that the respondent will be surrendered to either another Member State or a third party State without the consent of the State. Each of these sections, however, also creates an evidential presumption to the effect that the anticipated breach of the specialty rule or onward surrender provisions will not arise.[20]

SEEKING ADDITIONAL INFORMATION

7–27   Section 20(1) of the European Arrest Warrant Act 2003 allows the court at any time to seek additional information from the requesting State:

"In proceedings to which this Act applies the High Court may, if of the opinion that the documentation or information provided to it is not sufficient to enable it to perform its functions under this Act, require the issuing judicial authority or the issuing state, as may be appropriate, to provide it with such additional documentation or information as it may specify, within such period as it may specify."

7–28   The terms of s 20 would seem to suggest that the court must be of the view that it is not capable of performing its functions under the Act in the absence of the additional

---

[20] See Chapter 14.

information. This ought not mean that such information will only be sought where it might result in a refusal of surrender were it not available. The functions of the court include conducting an enquiry into the warrant for the purpose of ascertaining whether or not any of the bars to surrender arise or whether undertakings are required. It would, therefore, seem to be permissible for the court to seek additional information for the purpose of clarifying an ambiguity or putting a particular issue to rest. Indeed, the purpose of the information appearing at para (i) of the warrant is to allow for quick and convenient communication between judicial authorities to this end.

Section 20 contemplates that additional information may be sought from either **7–29** the judicial authority in the issuing State or the issuing State itself. Presumably this is to take account of the fact that the Framework Decision allows Member States to designate either their judicial authorities or their central authorities as being responsible for the transmission and administration of warrants. The courts have interpreted the terms of s 20 quite broadly.

In the case of *Minister for Justice, Equality and Law Reform v Ward*[21] additional **7–30** information had been provided in the form of an affidavit from a police constable from the United Kingdom which contained further details of the alleged offence in order that correspondence could be made out. The respondent submitted that the affidavit was inadmissible as it could not be said to have been provided by the judicial authority in the requesting State. The court considered such an objection to be "fanciful" on the basis that it was clear that the affidavit had not simply arrived "out of the blue" and that it had clearly been produced at the behest of the requesting judicial authority.

Notwithstanding the absence of any reference in s 12 to additional information **7–31** sought under s 20 the courts have taken the view that all other things being equal such material essentially proves itself. In *Minister for Justice, Equality and Law Reform v Sliczynski*[22] the court rejected a suggestion that the additional information would have to be formally proved in some way:

> "In my view s. 20(1) and (2) of the Act of 2003, as amended, are provisions by which the Oireachtas sought to give effect to the system of surrender envisaged by the Framework Decision so as to ensure that information could be furnished by the requesting Judicial Authority to the executing Judicial Authority, the High Court. If further information is transmitted by the requesting Judicial Authority either on its own initiative or following a request it is the function of the Central Authority to transmit it to the Executing Judicial Authority, in this country, the High Court. Section 20 must be interpreted in the light of the objectives of the Framework Decision and its provisions. In my view it specifically gives effect to Article 15(2) and (3) of the Directive. In so providing I am satisfied that the Oireachtas intended, consistent with the obligations of the State pursuant to the Framework Decision, that the High Court would have available to it the information provided by the issuing Judicial Authority and would have full regard to that information, in addition to information provided in the European Arrest Warrant itself, for the purpose of deciding whether a person should be surrendered on foot of a European Arrest Warrant. Moreover to interpret the provisions of the Act otherwise would render them meaningless

---

[21] [2008] IEHC 53.
[22] [2008] IESC 73.

since if direct evidence had to be given of the information concerned every Judge or member of the issuing Judicial Authority providing information would either have to give evidence personally or swear an Affidavit of matters within their own knowledge. If that were the case the provisions referred to would serve no purpose. Clearly in my view they were intended to ensure that the High Court would have, where required, information from the Judicial Authority concerned in addition to that already contained in the arrest warrant itself."

UNDERTAKINGS

7–32   Initially the European Arrest Warrant Act 2003 required that an application for surrender had to be accompanied by multiple undertakings to deal with the various bars to surrender which might possibly arise. This was so to the extent that it was highly questionable as to whether the 2003 Act achieved the goal of simplifying the system of extradition that pre-dated it. When one considers *Minister for Justice, Equality and Law Reform v Gokano*,[23] and the various undertakings required in that case, it is difficult to avoid the conclusion that the 2003 Act in fact rendered the system of surrender under the European arrest warrant complicated to the point of being practically unworkable. The requirement for undertakings was effectively dispensed with by the amendments brought about by the Criminal Justice (Terrorist Offences) Act 2005 which instead provided for a series of evidential presumptions to deal with the various matters which might otherwise give rise to an objection to surrender. This is not to say that the use of undertakings has been dispensed with entirely. Under the provisions of s 45 an undertaking may well be required to deal with the issue of a retrial subsequent to surrender where the respondent has been convicted in absentia. It is also quite possible that an undertaking might well be deployed for the purpose of dealing with an issue in respect of specialty or onward surrender.

7–33   The use of undertakings, whilst quite limited under the terms of the Act, is something of a novelty. Prior to the introduction of the 2003 Act, an undertaking given by a foreign executive power to do or refrain from doing something was not acceptable by the courts of this jurisdiction in the field of extradition law. The Supreme Court in *Bourke v Attorney General*[24] approved of the reasoning in *R. v Governor of Brixton Prison, Ex parte Armah*,[25] where the House of Lords considered undertakings given by the government of Ghana in relation to the subject of an extradition request. In his judgment in *Bourke*, O'Dalaigh CJ shared the concerns of Lord Upjohn in *Armah* in relation to undertakings given by foreign governments, as:

> "...there may be a change of government who may not feel bound by the acts of their predecessor. There may be a genuine difference of opinion as to the proper interpretation of the undertakings. Finally, it might in some circumstances be the duty of a government to depart from its expressed intention in the discharge of its duty in the good governance of the country and its inhabitants as a whole."

7–34   In *Bourke*, it was held that an undertaking by the Attorney General for England and Wales that the subject of the extradition request would be prosecuted for certain

---

[23] [2004] 3 IR 216.
[24] [1972] 1 IR 36.
[25] [1968] AC 192.

specified offences only should not be accepted by the Court as proof that this would in fact be the case. More recently, in *Attorney General v POC*,[26] O'Sullivan J was of the opinion that the *Bourke* principles were of general applicability to undertakings given by foreign executive powers, and so felt precluded from accepting the undertaking given by the Arizonian authorities in that case that the subject of the request would not be detained in a particular jail if extradited.

Undertakings are however acceptable by the Court where provided for by statute.   **7–35** Section 12 of the 2003 Act makes provision for the manner in which such undertakings are to be transmitted and the evidential status which they will be afforded. In *Minister for Justice, Equality and Law Reform v Dundon*[27] the respondent contended that the undertakings given in that case, which were at the time required in relation to the issues of non-surrender to a third State and of specialty, were invalid as they had not been made by the issuing judicial authority, but rather by a Parliamentary Under Secretary of State and by the Director of Public Prosecutions for England and Wales. Denham J rejected the argument that the requirement in s 45 that the issuing judicial authority *"gives"* an undertaking should be taken to mean that it must be the judicial authority itself that undertakes, even if it is not the relevant authority to undertake that, for example, a surrendered person will not be surrendered to a third State. Denham J found that the ordinary meaning of "give" is "to hand over, to transfer, to deliver". She went on to say:

> "There is no ordinary meaning that an undertaking "given" has to be made by the issuing judicial authority. It is required to be handed over, transferred or delivered, by the issuing judicial authority. Thus, I am satisfied that the certificate in this case, from the issuing judicial authority, with the attached undertakings from the two relevant authorities, meets the requirement under the Act".

This does not mean, however, that the court is obliged to take the undertaking at   **7–36** face value. In *Minister for Justice, Equality and Law Reform v Ficzere*[28] the court concluded that it could not act upon an undertaking given under s 45 in circumstances where it had not been given by the judicial authority as required by s 45 and where it was patent that the judicial authority was not permitted to give such an undertaking under the law of the requesting State. Whilst an undertaking had been provided by the Central Authority in the requesting State it had not been "given" in the sense contemplated in *Dundon*.

Similarly in *Minister for Justice, Equality and Law Reform v Gritunic*[29] the court   **7–37** declined to act on material forthcoming from Eurojust which dealt with the issue of retrial subsequent to conviction *in absentia* in lieu of an actual undertaking from the issuing judicial authority.

---

[26] [2007] 2 IR 421.
[27] [2005] 1 IR 261.
[28] [2009] 1 IR 486.
[29] [2009] IEHC 342.

CHAPTER 8

Surrender

Where the court decides to make an order for surrender there are a number of **8–01** formalities which must be observed. These are set out in s 16(4) of the Act:

> "When making an order under this section the High Court shall also make an order committing the person to a prison (or if he or she is not more than 21 years of age, to a remand institution) there to remain pending his or her surrender in accordance with the order under this section, and shall inform the person—
>
> > (a) that he or she will not, without his or her consent, be surrendered to the issuing state, before the expiration of the period of 15 days specified in *subsection (3)*, and
> >
> > (b) of his or her right to make a complaint under Article 40.4.2 of the Constitution at any time before his or her surrender to the issuing state."

In the case of consent surrender under s 15 the court is obliged to inform the **8–02** respondent of the same rights.[1]

---

[1] s 15(4).

TIME LIMITS WITHIN WHICH SURRENDER MUST BE EFFECTED

8–03   Irrespective of whether the respondent is on bail or in custody subsequent to the making of a surrender order, the 2003 Act sets out seemingly strict time limits within which orders for surrender made under s15(1) or s 16(1) must be complied with. These time limits, relating to the post-surrender order period, are to be contrasted with the 60 and 90 day time limits referred to in s 16(10) and s 16(11) of the 2003 Act and Art 17 of the Framework Decision, which were considered by the Supreme Court in *Dundon v Governor of Cloverhill Prison.*[2] In that case, Geoghegan J considered that:

> "…the 60 day and 90 day time limits are with a view to internal discipline within the member states and not with a view to conferring individual rights in individual cases."[3]

8–04   Denham J distinguished the 60 and 90 day time limits from the mandatory time limits provided for by ss 15(5) and 16(5):

> "The Act of 2003 does not establish mandatory time limits prior to the final order for surrender in the same way as it does to the period after the final order."[4]

8–05   As such the time limits which apply post-surrender will be applied in a considerably stricter fashion than the pre-surrender time limits which would appear to be largely aspirational.

Section 15 Time Limits

8–06   There are slightly different time limits which apply depending upon whether the consent procedure under s 15 has been adopted or the case has been contested under s 16. Section 15(3) provides that where a person consents to surrender the order shall not take effect for a period of 10 days:

> "An order under this section shall take effect upon the expiration of 10 days beginning on the date of the making of the order or such earlier date as the High Court, upon request of the person to whom the order applies, directs."

8–07   In other words there is a 10 day period subsequent to the making of the s 15 order during which nothing will happen. At the end of this period the order takes effect in the sense that at any point from thereon after the respondent may be surrendered to the requesting State. In effect at the conclusion of the first 10 day period the clock has started to run.

8–08   It is open to the respondent to waive this 10 day period or indeed consent to a shorter period before which the order takes effect. Given the consensual nature of

---

[2] [2006] 1 IR 518.

[3] p 541.

[4] p 529.

proceedings under s 15 it is almost invariably the case that the respondent will seek to waive this period.

Where the 10 day period has either been waived or has run its course the provisions **8–09** of s 15(5) apply. This provides that surrender must either be effected within 10 days or such longer period as may be agreed between the Central Authority and the issuing State.

Section 16 Time Limits

The provisions of s 16 in terms of the applicable time limits effectively mirror **8–10** those provided for in s 15 with the exception that the initial period before which the surrender order actually takes effect is 15 days[5] rather than 10. Again it is open to the respondent to seek to waive this period. Once this period has either expired or been waived surrender must be effected within 10 days or such longer period as may be agreed.

EXTENSION OF THE 10 DAY PERIOD

Both s 15 and s 16 contemplate the 10 day period during which surrender must be **8–11** effected as capable of being extended in the event that it is not possible to surrender the respondent within that period.

The relevant sub-section of s 16[6] provides as follows: **8–12**

> "(5) Subject to *subsection (6)*, subsection (7) and *section 18*, a person to whom an order for the time being in force under this section applies shall be surrendered to the issuing state concerned not later than 10 days after—
>
> (a) the order takes effect in accordance with subsection (3) (inserted by *section 75(b)* of the *Criminal Justice (Terrorist Offences) Act 2005*), or
>
> (b) such date (being a date that falls after the expiration of that period) as may be agreed by the Central Authority in the State and the issuing state."

Given that the provisions of s 15 are to all practical purposes virtually identical the **8–13** same considerations will apply irrespective of whether the original order was made under s 15 or s 16.

Section 16(5)(a) would appear to provide a general rule to the effect that surrender **8–14** ought to be effected, in the first instance, within 10 days[7] of the order taking effect. Section 16(5)(b) goes on to provide an exception to that rule in that it allows the Central Authority to agree a later date with the issuing State. The section is silent as to the circumstances in which an extension may be agreed.

Whilst it is not entirely clear, the provisions of s 16(7) would appear to presuppose **8–15** that where it is intended to agree a later date pursuant to s 16(5)(b) that it is also necessary to apply to the High Court in order to further remand the respondent either

---

[5] s 16(3).

[6] Subsections (5) and (7) of s 15 are in almost identical terms.

[7] The period of 10 days includes the day upon which the order was made. See s 18(h) of the Interpretation Act 2005.

in custody or on bail for that purpose. Unfortunately this provision provides no assistance as to the applicable criteria on such an application.

8–16   Sub-section (5) purports to implement the provisions of Art 23.3 of the Framework Decision which expressly contemplates the possibility of extending the time in which surrender is ordered:

> "23(3) If the surrender of the requested person within the period laid down in paragraph 2 is prevented by circumstances beyond the control of any of the Member States, the executing and issuing judicial authorities shall immediately contact each other and agree on a new surrender date. In that event, surrender shall take place within 10 days of the new date thus agreed."

8–17   It is immediately apparent from a cursory examination of Art 23.3 that the provisions of sub-sections (5) are in conflict with it. Specifically Art 23.3 supposes that an extension shall only be necessary where surrender has not been possible within the 10 day period due to "circumstances beyond the control" of the relevant States. Section 16(5) contains no such limitation. More jarringly, however, Art 23.3 envisages that the agreement to extend the period in which surrender might be effected must be made between the judicial authorities as opposed to the central authorities or some other emanation of the relevant States. It is not hard to understand why this might be so. The overwhelming majority of respondents will be remanded in custody at the point when an order under s 15 or 16 is made. Were it open to the respective central authorities to simply decide on a later date for surrender which could, in theory at least, be postponed indefinitely, then this would in effect amount to an open ended detention at the hands of the executive as opposed to judicial branch of government. It is reasonable to conclude that the drafters of the Framework Decision sought to expressly address this issue by requiring that the agreement of any extension of the period for surrender would be a matter that would fall within the judicial sphere rather than the executive sphere.

Rimsa v Governor of Cloverhill Prison

8–18   The relevant provisions of s 16 were scrutinised by the Supreme Court in *Rimsa v Governor of Cloverhill Prison*.[8] In that case the applicant had been the subject of an order under s 16 which required that he would be surrendered to Latvia on or before 7th January 2008. The original order under s 16 had been made on 13th December 2007.[9] It would appear from both the High Court[10] and Supreme Court judgments that little or nothing was done on the Latvian side between the making of the order and early January 2008 due to the intervening holiday period, notwithstanding a number of notifications having been sent by the Irish authorities. The Central Authority in Ireland and Latvia ultimately agreed on a new surrender date being 9th January which obviously fell outside the time period contemplated by s 16(5)(a). No application was made to the High Court under s 16(7) for any further remand of the applicant.

---

[8]   [2010] IESC 47.

[9]   The applicant had chosen not to waive the 15 day period before the s 16 Order came into effect.

[10]   [2008] IEHC 6.

The applicant then sought to challenge the legality of his detention on the **8–19** grounds, firstly, that s 16(5)(b) ought to be construed in light of Art 23.3 of the Framework Decision insofar as it required that any such agreement be entered into by the respective judicial authorities rather than the central authorities. As such the agreement reached was invalid and his detention on foot of same unlawful. Secondly, the applicant argued that there should have been no extension of the period for surrender as there had not been any "circumstances beyond the control" of the Irish and Latvian authorities that had prevented his surrender. Rather the failure to effect his surrender within that period was due to factors manifestly in the control of those parties. The High Court rejected these arguments.

When the matter came before the Supreme Court Murray CJ was quick to point **8–20** out the conflict between the provisions of the Framework Decision on the one hand and the provisions of s 16(5) on the other:

> "As pointed out earlier, it is manifest from the plain and express terms of Article 23.3 that an agreement for postponement of the surrender to a later date must be agreed between (a) the executing Judicial Authority (which in this case is the High Court) and (b) the issuing Judicial Authority (which here is the "First Instance Riga Vidzeme Suburb Court of the Republic of Latvia" as identified in the European arrest warrant in this case).
>
> On the other hand, as has been seen, s. 16(5)(b) of the Act excludes the High Court and permits a postponement of the date for surrender beyond the initial ten day period where that is agreed "(b) by the Central Authority in the State and the issuing State". While that clearly requires the Central Authority in this State to enter into the agreement the section does not specify what authority in the issuing State must agree to the postponement. It certainly does not specify that it be the Central Authority of the issuing State. The section does not, for example say 'be agreed by the Central Authority in the State and in the issuing State'."

Ultimately the court concluded that although s 16(5)(b) might well be construed as **8–21** requiring the agreement to be reached with the judicial authority in the issuing State on the basis of the doctrine of conforming interpretation it was clear in the present case that the agreement had been with the Central Authority in Latvia as opposed to the judicial authority there. Therefore even on such an interpretation of s 16(5)(b) the agreement was invalid:

> "Accordingly, even though paragraph (b) of s. 16(5) of the Act of 2003 expressly authorised the Central Authority in the State to reach an agreement on a new date for surrender, the agreement to do so could only be made by that Authority with the judicial authority of the issuing state, Latvia, as the subsection properly construed, requires.
>
> Since this was not done there was no valid or effective agreement to postpone the date of surrender within the meaning of s. 16(5)(b)."

The court went on to hold that quite apart from the agreement being invalid due to the **8–22** absence of the involvement of the judicial authority in the issuing State it was equally invalid due to the absence of involvement by the judicial authority in the executing State, i.e. the High Court. In effect the Supreme Court held that s 10 of the European

Arrest Warrant Act 2003 incorporated certain provisions of the Framework Decision in a directly effective way. One such provision was Art 23.3. Insofar as there was a direct conflict between a provision of the Act and a "directly effective" part of the Framework Decision then the latter must prevail having regard to the fact that the purpose of the 2003 Act was to give effect to the Framework Decision:

> "...the Central Authority in the State in entering into the agreement to postpone the date for surrender rather than taking steps to ensure that there was agreement between the *two respective judicial authorities* as Article 23(3) requires failed to act in accordance with the requirements of s. 10 of the Act. This is in addition to the earlier conclusion that the agreement was also contrary to s. 16(5)(b) insofar as it was made with the Central Authority of Latvia rather than the Latvian judicial authority as identified in the arrest warrant."

8–23 In light of the decision in *Rimsa* it very much remains an open question as to whether a valid agreement to extend the time in which surrender might be effected can ever be made under s 16(5)(b). Whilst it may be possible to require that the reference to the "issuing state" be construed as a reference to the judicial authority in the issuing State no such conforming interpretation is possible in relation to the reference to the role of the central authority.

8–24 An alternative view is that an application pursuant to s 16(7) is the practical means by which the possibility of reaching agreement with the judicial authority in the issuing State might be canvassed and that insofar as the Central Authority here enters into such an agreement it does and only can do so on the express instruction of the High Court.

Necessity

8–25 In *Rimsa* the Supreme Court, having found for the applicant on the first ground raised, felt it was not necessary to consider the second argument – namely whether an agreement to extend time for surrender could only be reached in circumstances where the necessity for an extension arose by reason of circumstances beyond the control of the relevant Member States as per Art 23.3 of the Framework Decision. The logic adopted by Murray CJ insofar as s 10 of the Act rendered Article 23.3 directly effective would seem to suggest that such an agreement may only be reached where the delay has been occasioned by reason of some extraneous factor. This may well be so notwithstanding the fact that s 16(5) does not seem to impose such a precondition.

8–26 As in Ireland, the relevant statutory provision in the United Kingdom[11] does not transpose the requirement of necessity contained in Art 23.3. However, in *R (Szklanny) v City of Westminster Magistrates' Court*,[12] Richards LJ came to a similar conclusion to that of Hedigan J at first instance in *Rimsa*:

> "The discretion must certainly be exercised with due regard to the wording and purpose of the Framework Decision and for that reason would no doubt fall normally to be exercised so as to extend the period where extradition was shown to have been prevented by circumstances beyond the control of the

---

[11] s 35(4)(b) of the *Extradition Act 2003*.
[12] [2008] 1 WLR 789.

member states. But I do not think that can be exhaustive of the circumstances in which the discretion may be exercised. Regard should be had not just to the wording of article 23 but also to the Framework Decision's underlying purpose of facilitating extradition and enhancing extradition procedures, based on a spirit of mutual co-operation. I see no reason why those considerations should not in an appropriate case tell in favour of the grant of an extension at the request of the judicial authority even if it has not been shown that circumstances beyond the control of the member states prevented extradition within the normal time limit, in the sense that the delay occurred without any fault on behalf of any of the state agencies concerned."[13]

It remains to be seen as to whether an extension of the time for surrender otherwise **8–27** than on the grounds set out in Art 23.3 could really be regarded as being compatible with the principles underlying the Framework Decision.

Application under Section 16(7)

Whilst s 16(5)(b) seems to leave it to the Central Authority to agree a new date for **8–28** surrender, s 16(7) appears to contemplate the making of an application to the High Court for a further remand of the respondent either in custody or on bail to that end. The precise purpose of such an application, the point at which it must be made and the applicable criteria remain frustratingly opaque however. Section 16(7) provides:

> "(7) Where a person (to whom an order for the time being in force under this section applies) is not surrendered to the issuing state within the relevant period specified in subsection (5) and the surrender is not prohibited by reason of subsection (6) the High Court may remand the person in custody or on bail for such further period as is necessary to effect the surrender unless it considers it would be unjust or oppressive to do so."

Whilst it is clear from the decision of the Supreme Court in *Rimsa* that no application **8–29** under s 16(7) was made in that case, such applications have been made in other cases. One of the few cases in which the provision was considered to any great degree was *Covaciu v Governor of Cloverhill Prison*[14] in which the court doubted the necessity for the bringing of such applications where there was a s 16 order, whether at first instance or affirmed on appeal, already in existence. The rationale was that such an order would allow for the detention of the respondent pending actual surrender whether this were done within the 10 day period or in the context of an agreement for the extension of that period. The High Court was, however, operating at a significant disadvantage in that it only became aware that the decision of the High Court in *Rimsa* had been over-turned but was not aware of the reasons for that decision.[15] As such it is a precedent of dubious value.

Section 16(7) would, on the face of it, seem to provide for the further remand of **8–30** the respondent in order to give effect to an agreement for an extension of time under s

---

[13] *ibid*, at 795.
[14] [2010] IEHC 182.
[15] The original decision of the High Court in *Rimsa* was given on 11 January 2008 ([2008] IEHC 6) and the appeal from it was heard shortly thereafter. The Supreme Court ordered the release of the applicant but did not give reasons for their decision until 28 July 2010.

16(5)(b). If the latter provision is ineffective subsequent to the decision in *Rimsa* then it would seem likely that applications under s 16(7) may be similarly ineffective.

Constitutionality of Section 16(5)

8–31   The applicant in *Rimsa* also brought parallel proceedings[16] to challenge the constitutionality of s 16(5) subsequent to the High Court (Hedigan J) having refused to order his release on foot of the earlier Art 40.4.2 enquiry. In the proceedings challenging the constitutionality of the section the applicant argued that s 16(5) as it stood essentially allowed for the indefinite detention of those whose surrender had been ordered at the whim of the executive in the form of the Central Authority. Peart J rejected the challenge:

> "However, it is not the case that the applicant is detained on foot of an executive decision rather than a judicial decision. It was the order of this Court which ordered his detention "pending the carrying out of his surrender". That order is made by the Court in full knowledge that his surrender may not actually occur within ten days following the taking effect of the surrender order, since the possibility of some later date thereafter being the date of actual surrender taking place is envisaged by the other provisions of s. 16 of the Act to which I have referred. It is for that reason that the Committal Warrant which was signed by the Court following the making of the order for surrender and committal to prison specifically authorises the Governor of Cloverhill Prison to detain the applicant for the period of fifteen days while the order takes effect and "such further period as may be necessary under law". This means that it is the High Court which has ordered that the applicant be detained in effect for such period as is reasonably necessary for appropriate and suitable arrangements to be put in place for the carrying out of the surrender.
>
> It is of course a necessary presumption inherent in the presumption of constitutionality of the Act, following *East Donegal Livestock Mart Ltd v. The Attorney General* [supra], and *McDonald v. Bord na gCon* [supra], that those in whose power or discretion it is to make those administrative arrangements necessary for surrender to take place, will exercise that power and exercise that discretion in good faith and in accordance with constitutional principles, such as that the detention will be for no period longer than is reasonably necessary for the purpose of achieving a successful surrender."

8–32   This conclusion must be open to doubt given the views expressed by the Supreme Court subsequently. Murray CJ having considered the very limited role enjoyed by the Central Authority pursuant to Recital 9 of the Framework Decision and the basis of the mutual trust between Member States being predicated on the judicial character of the orders being enforced observed as follows:

> "No doubt it was for the above considerations and with a view to achieving those objectives that any decision by agreement to delay the surrender of a requested person pursuant to judicial order beyond that ten day period, must, according to Article 23, be made by the judicial authorities of the two states concerned and not by any administrative authority. By this means the

---

[16] *Rimsa v Governor of Cloverhill Prison and the Attorney General* [2008] IEHC 125.

Framework Decision ensures that any postponement of the date on which the surrender is due to take place on foot of a judicial order already made remains under judicial control. It also avoids any extension of a period of custody pending surrender being decided by the executive authorities as a form of administrative detention."

It would seem that the Supreme Court would likely take a somewhat more jaundiced view of detention at the hands of the executive as envisaged by s 16(5).　　**8–33**

Effect of Non-compliance with Time Limits

The 2003 Act had previously made it clear that in the event that a respondent was not　**8–34** surrendered within the relevant period, the proceedings would effectively be at an end. Section 16(7) had originally[17] provided that a person who was not surrendered within the specified time period "shall be released from custody immediately". The strict manner in which this time limit was to be applied is clear from the case of *O'Falluin v Governor of Cloverhill Prison*[18] where the Supreme Court ordered the release of the applicant, a person in respect of whom a surrender order had been made under s 16(1), and who had lodged an appeal to the Supreme Court against that order. The respondent remained in custody pending the determination of his appeal. His application under Art 40.4.2° of the Constitution had been rejected by the High Court which found that, despite the fact that more than 10 days had passed since the order for surrender had come into effect, the respondent's pending appeal to the Supreme Court operated as a stay on the running of the 10 day time limit referred to in s16(5) of the 2003 Act, and thus that the applicant was not entitled to be released pursuant to s 16(7). The Supreme Court took a different view. Fennelly J dealt with the issue as follows:

> "I return to the words of sub-section (7). It mandates the release of the Appellant. That mandatory obligation is qualified only in the case that Article 40 proceedings are in being. Section 16(7) ordains release unless such proceedings are in existence and section 18(5) prohibits surrender until they are disposed of. It is noteworthy that the legislature has introduced no such qualification for the case of a pending appeal. The maxim, expressio unius est exclusio alterius, is strongly supportive of the conclusion that it was not intended to qualify the release obligation for the case of an appeal. I am satisfied that the Appellant was entitled to be released from custody immediately upon the expiry of the period of ten days after the coming into effect of the High Court, i.e., twenty five days after it was made."

Whilst the express and mandatory terms of ss 15(7) and 16(7) have been substantially　**8–35** softened by reason of ss 11 and 12 of the Criminal Justice (Miscellaneous Provisions) Act 2009 there is arguably little legal basis for detaining a requested person in excess

---

[17] s 16(7) had, prior to the amendments effected by the Criminal Justice (Miscellaneous Provisions) Act, 2009 provided:

"A person (to whom an order for the time being in force under this section applies) who is not surrendered to the issuing state in accordance with subsection (5) shall be released from custody immediately upon the expiration of the 10 days referred to in that subsection unless, upon such expiration, proceedings referred to in subsection (6) are pending."

[18] [2007] IESC 20.

of the 10 day period in the absence of an application pursuant to ss 15(7) and 16(7) first being made.

BAIL PENDING SURRENDER

8–36 Given the apparently mandatory terms of s 16(4) which required the High Court when making an order for surrender to commit the respondent to a prison or remand institution, it was generally assumed that it was not open to the court to grant bail once the surrender order had been made:

> "When making an order under this section the High Court shall also make an order committing the person to a prison (or if he or she is not more than 21 years of age, to a remand institution) there to remain pending his or her surrender..."

8–37 Such an interpretation was supported by the apparent differentiation between the situation which arose once a surrender order had been made on the one hand under s 16(4) and that where the s 16 hearing does not proceed for whatever reason as provided for by s 16(2A), on the other. In the latter event the High Court is empowered to:

> "...remand the person before it in custody or on bail and, for those purposes, the High Court shall have the same powers in relation to remand as it would have if the person were brought before it charged with an indictable offence."

8–38 In *Minister for Justice, Equality and Law Reform v Draisey*,[19] Peart J interpreted the terms of s 16(4) as unambiguously ousting the inherent jurisdiction of the High Court to grant bail to the respondent, in respect of whom an order for surrender pursuant to s 16(1) had been made. The learned judge found that s 16(4), interpreted in this way, was a proportionate restriction on the Court's power to grant bail, which was necessary to ensure that the State could fulfil its obligations under the Framework Decision.[20] Although the Framework Decision did not preclude the granting of bail to persons in respect of whom surrender orders had been made, it did demand that the relevant judicial authority:

> "...ensure that the material conditions necessary for effective surrender of the person remain fulfilled".[21]

8–39 In effect the Court sought to interpret the 2003 Act in a manner which it considered to be consonant with the State's obligations under the Framework Decision. One of the more obvious difficulties with such an approach was that the issue of proportionality

---

[19] [2007] 4 IR 163.

[20] Although the Minister was not objecting to bail in *Draisey*, Peart J clearly felt that, in light of the High Court's obligations under the Framework Decision, this was not a matter that should be decided on the basis of consent between the parties.

[21] Art 17 Framework Decision. Article 12 Framework Decision, entitled "Keeping the person in detention", clearly does not preclude the granting of bail, stating that "[t]he person may be released provisionally at any time in conformity with the domestic law of the executing Member State, provided that the competent authority of the said Member State takes all the measures it deems necessary to prevent the person absconding".

was not being considered in relation to the offences which were the subject matter of the warrant nor indeed the circumstances of the respondent.

The Supreme Court came to consider the issue in *Butenas v Governor of Cloverhill Prison*.[22] An order for surrender pursuant to s 16(1) had been made by the High Court as well as a consequential order pursuant to s 16(4) committing the respondent to prison pending his surrender. Neither order was appealed to the Supreme Court. The applicant however applied for his release pursuant to Art 40.4 of the Constitution, on the basis that s 16(4) of the 2003 Act was unconstitutional as it purported to oust the jurisdiction of the High Court insofar as the issue of bail was concerned, and thus that the detention order made pursuant to that section was invalid. Peart J refused the application, finding that s 16(4) was not unconstitutional and referring to his decision in *Draisey*. **8–40**

The applicant's appeal was ultimately unsuccessful. However, the Supreme Court disagreed with the view taken by Peart J of the phrase "there to remain pending surrender" in s 16(4), preferring instead the contention put forward by the State to the effect that these words could not be interpreted as ousting the inherent jurisdiction of the High Court to grant bail to a person pending his or her surrender. Murray CJ, giving judgment for the court, dealt with the issue in the following terms: **8–41**

> "A statute which confers a power on the High Court to deprive an individual of his or her liberty, particularly when the imprisonment as such is not the object of the provision must be strictly interpreted. In this instance there are no grounds for concluding, as counsel for the Minister made clear, that the purpose of the section would be undermined by a release on bail, subject to appropriate conditions, in cases where the Court is satisfied that the purpose of the section can be achieved without a remand in prison.

> The Court is of the view that if the Oireachtas had intended to oust the inherent jurisdiction of the High Court to grant bail in all cases where an order for surrender has been made, irrespective of the circumstances, it would have explicitly and unambiguously done so. To interpret the subsection otherwise would be to assume that the Oireachtas intended that persons should be detained for the purpose of their surrender even in cases where such detention was not necessary for such a purpose. Again the Court does not consider that the section discloses any grounds for such an assumption."

In the circumstances, the Supreme Court refused the application for release under Art 40.4 of the Constitution and held that the applicant was entitled to apply to the High Court for bail pending his surrender. Following *Butenas*, it is now clear that a person in respect of whom an order for surrender has been made under s 16(1) may be granted bail pending his surrender where the Court deems it appropriate. In reality, it seems likely that it was in fact the intention of the Oireachtas that all requested persons in respect of whom an order for surrender had been made should be kept in custody pending their surrender. The terms of s 16(2A) have already been noted in this regard and in particular the apparent differentiation to be drawn in terms of remand in custody or on bail in the case of a respondent whose s 16 hearing adjourns on the one hand and the respondent who is the subject of a surrender order **8–42**

---

[22] [2008] 4 IR 189.

on the other. Most significantly, however, there would now appear to be a very significant procedural lacuna in relation to the respondent who is granted bail but fails to make himself available to the Gardaí for the purpose of being transported out of the State. At what point do the time limits stop running? Can the recalcitrant respondent be arrested for the purpose of effecting surrender?

8–43   Ultimately it is difficult to regard the decision in *Butenas* as anything other than a reaction to the obvious difficulties created by the apparently mandatory terms of s 16(4). Any interpretation of that provision which precluded the granting of bail pending surrender would in all probability have to be regarded as unconstitutional as it would firstly oust the jurisdiction of the courts in relation to bail and secondly it would potentially be entirely disproportionate to the offence grounding the warrant in that the process of compelling the attendance of the respondent in the requesting State would quite possibly be significantly more punitive than the penalty finally imposed. In opting for the alternative interpretation of the provision which allows the possibility of bail being granted in such circumstances a host of practical questions arise to which there would not appear to be any obvious answers in the legislation, given that it is most likely predicated on the assumption that all respondents would necessarily be incarcerated pending surrender.

8–44   There is some slight difference as between the terms of s 16 insofar as it relates to the situation pending surrender and the equivalent provisions of s 15(4) which relate to the consent procedure in that the latter requires the Court to:

> "…commit the person to a prison (or, if the person is not more than 21 years of age, to a remand institution) pending the carrying out of the terms of the order."

8–45   However, the reasoning in *Butenas* would appear to apply with equal force here and as such there would seem to be little basis for drawing a distinction as between the two situations.

SEVERABILITY

8–46   More often than not a European arrest warrant will relate to a number of different offences in respect of which surrender is sought. The High Court may well take the view that surrender is permissible in relation to some of the offences but not in relation to others. In such circumstances the court is entitled to effectively sever the warrant and order surrender in respect of those offences which meet the requirements of the European Arrest Warrant Act 2003. This is provided for specifically by s 17:

> "Where, in relation to an offence specified in a European arrest warrant, the High Court decides not to make an order under *section 15* or *16*, it shall not be necessary for the issuing judicial authority to issue another European arrest warrant in respect of such other offences as are specified in that warrant, and, where such other offences are specified in the European arrest warrant, that warrant shall be treated as having been issued in respect of those other offences only."

8–47   The court is entitled to presume that the issuing State will observe the rule of specialty and not prosecute or punish in relation to the offences for which surrender has been refused.

DEDUCTION OF PERIOD SPENT IN CUSTODY

The Framework Decision specifically provides that the period of time spent in **8–48** custody in the executing State should be applied to the credit of the respondent once surrendered. Article 26 provides:

> "Deduction of the period of detention served in the executing Member State:
>
> 1. The issuing Member State shall deduct all periods of detention arising from the execution of a European arrest warrant from the total period of detention to be served in the issuing Member State as a result of a custodial sentence or detention order being passed.
>
> 2. To that end, all information concerning the duration of the detention of the requested person on the basis of the European arrest warrant shall be transmitted by the executing judicial authority or the central authority designated under Article 7 to the issuing judicial authority at the time of the surrender."

The terms of Art 26 suggest that the High Court has no actual role in relation to the **8–49** manner in which credit is given for time spent in custody in respect of a European arrest warrant. The extent of the role for either the High Court or the Central Authority relates to the transmission of sufficient information to the issuing State in order that the appropriate deduction may be made post-surrender. In *Minister for Justice, Equality and Law Reform v Power*[23] the respondent had spent a considerable amount of time in custody in Spain in relation to an extradition request (i.e. one which predated the introduction of the European arrest warrant) for the same offences in respect of which he was before the High Court and sought to avoid surrender on the basis that he was not guaranteed that he would be given credit for time served in Spain. The court noted that it had no role to play in relation to such issues:

> "But in any event there can be no question of this Court having any capacity or entitlement to review in any way the sentence of imprisonment imposed by the court in England. If there is any uncertainty in the actual time which the respondent will have to serve if returned, that is a matter to be taken up before the court in the United Kingdom which can clarify the matter in the event of such uncertainty existing."

A similar issue arose in *Minister for Justice, Equality and Law Reform v Abimbola*[24] **8–50** where the respondent had previously spent time in custody on foot of an extradition request by Germany which was ultimately unsuccessful. The respondent argued that his surrender should be refused in the absence of some guarantee or undertaking to the effect that the time spent in custody in relation to the extradition proceedings would be credited against his sentence in Germany. The court rejected this argument:

> "I am satisfied that the respondent is not entitled to be provided with this confirmation in advance of surrender being ordered. If the custody period had been on foot of a European arrest warrant, no such further confirmation would

---

[23] [2007] IEHC 285.
[24] [2008] IEHC 312.

be required as the Framework Decision provides for the deduction, and the issuing state must comply with its obligations thereunder. Under the previous extradition arrangements given effect to in Part II and Part III of the 1965 Act, it was never considered to be a breach of constitutional rights that there was no guarantee of such a deduction being given. It cannot suddenly become one now, simply because of the unusual history of this case. It will be a matter for the respondent to take up with the authorities in Germany upon surrender. This point of objection fails."

8–51   In *Minister for Justice, Equality and Law Reform v Horvath*[25] the respondent sought to argue that the failure on the part of the State to put in place a formal system whereby information in relation to time spent in custody could be communicated to the issuing State amounted to a failure to give effect to the terms of Art 26. Peart J rejected such an argument as amounting to a ground for resisting surrender:

"The obligation to deduct time spent by a respondent in detention pending surrender is an obligation on the issuing State, and this Court must presume that this will be done. If it is not done, the issuing state, and not the executing state would be in breach of its obligations under the Framework Decision. If the executing state was to fail to give the required information to the issuing state, then the latter also would be complicit in that breach. Perhaps certain consequences would flow from that, such that if there was to be a persistent breach of obligation to provide the information, steps would have to be taken at Council of Europe level to suspend the surrender arrangements in respect of this State, but there is no reason for concern simply because the Act here is silent as to whether it is the High Court here as the judicial authority, or the Central Authority, which must provide the information. That is a purely administrative matter arising under the Framework Decision, and not one which requires specific transposition under the Act, before this Court can exercise its functions under the Act in relation to the ordering of surrender."

8–52   It remains unclear as to whether it is the High Court or the Central Authority that is to be considered responsible for the transmission of such information.

POSTPONEMENT OF SURRENDER – SECTION 18

Postponement Due to Domestic Proceedings or Sentence

8–53   Frequently the respondent will either be the subject of charges within the State or will be serving a sentence within the State. In such circumstances an application will generally be made to postpone the surrender of the respondent until such time as either the domestic charges have been dealt with or the domestic sentence served. Section 18(3) sets out the relevant legislative mechanism:

"(3) Subject to *section 19*, where a person to whom an order under *section 15* or *16* applies—

(a)   is being proceeded against for an offence in the State, or

---

[25]   [2008] IEHC 411.

    (b) (i) has been sentenced to a term of imprisonment for an offence of which he or she was convicted in the State, and

        (ii) is required to serve all or part of that term of imprisonment,

the High Court may direct the postponement of that person's surrender to the issuing state until—

        (i) in the case of a person who is being proceeded against for an offence, the date of the final determination of those proceedings (where he or she is not required to serve a term of imprisonment), or

        (ii) in the case of a person who is required to serve all or part of a term of imprisonment, the date on which he or she is no longer required to serve any part of that term of imprisonment."

The terms of s 18(3) make it clear that an order for postponement can only be made once a surrender order under either s 15 or 16 has been made. In other words the court must first determine whether or not the respondent should be surrendered before entering upon a consideration of whether that order should be postponed. This logical sequence was considered in *Minister for Justice, Equality and Law Reform v Kinsella*[26]:
    8–54

"Both parties agree, as does the Court, that the provisions of s. 18 of the Act, which enable the Court, having made an order for surrender under either s. 15 or s. 16 of the Act, to postpone that order in certain circumstances, including where the respondent is required to serve a period of imprisonment arising from domestic charges, are not applicable at this point in time, since the court could not in the present circumstances make any order for surrender under either section. This section operates only after such an order has been made and has therefore no application at the present stage of the application for the surrender of this respondent."

On occasion the length of the postponement under s 18 will be extremely lengthy or even indefinite given the length of the domestic sentence in question. In *Minister for Justice, Equality and Law Reform v Machevicius*[27] the respondent was sought in Lithuania for what appeared to be a relatively minor offence in the nature of demanding with menaces. The respondent had been convicted in his absence but there was a sufficient undertaking in relation to a re-trial for the offence in question upon his return. Matters were, however, complicated by virtue of the fact that the respondent had also been indicted before the Central Criminal Court for murder. The applicant sought a postponement pursuant to the provisions of s 18 of the respondent's surrender until such time as the proceedings and sentence, if any, arising from the murder charge had concluded. The respondent argued that he should not be surrendered on the grounds that in the event of him being convicted of murder he would inevitably have to serve a lengthy sentence prior to his being surrendered thereby rendering his right to
    8–55

---

[26] [2007] IEHC 214.
[27] [2007] IEHC 78.

a re-trial effectively meaningless as too much time would have elapsed in the interim. Peart J rejected this argument:

> "In my view the Court cannot indulge in any speculation as to what may or may not happen in the future. The provision of a re-trial upon surrender is in ease of a person who has not attended for his trial in the first instance. If that person's own actions in another state give rise to a situation where his re-trial is delayed because of those actions, then it is certainly arguable that he cannot plead that in aid of an assertion that his right to an expeditious trial has been compromised. I do not consider that the Court is required to refuse surrender on this ground of objection."

8–56   A similar conclusion was reached in the case of *Minister for Justice, Equality and Law Reform v Wharrie*[28] where the respondent had been sentenced to a determinate but lengthy term of imprisonment within the State. Peart J did, however, suggest that it might be open to a respondent to seek to challenge his surrender anew as the period of postponement came to an end.

Postponement on Humanitarian Grounds

8–57   In addition to enjoying a jurisdiction to postpone surrender in order to accommodate the needs of the domestic criminal process the court can also postpone surrender on humanitarian grounds. Sections 18(1) and (2) provide as follows:

> "(1) The High Court may, if satisfied that circumstances exist that would warrant the postponement, on humanitarian grounds, of the surrender to the issuing state of a person to whom an order under *section 15* or *16* applies, direct that the person's surrender be postponed until such date as the High Court states that, in its opinion, those circumstances no longer exist.
>
> (2) Without prejudice to the generality of *subsection (1)*, circumstances to which that paragraph applies include a manifest danger to the life or health of the person concerned likely to be occasioned by his or her surrender to the issuing state in accordance with *section 15(5)* or *16(5)*."

8–58   Whilst the terms of s 18(2) are expressed to be without prejudice to the generality of s 18(1) it would appear from the Framework Decision that it was anticipated that this form of postponement would arise on an exceptional basis only. Article 23.4 is in somewhat more restrictive terms:

> "The surrender may exceptionally be temporarily postponed for serious humanitarian reasons, for example if there are substantial grounds for believing that it would manifestly endanger the requested person's life or health."

8–59   Necessarily, given the temporary nature of a postponement of this sort, the court will have to monitor the situation on an ongoing basis for the purpose of ascertaining when it may be possible to actually effect surrender.

---

[28] Unreported, High Court, Peart J, 22 January 2009.

As with postponement under s 18(3) an application for postponement on humanitarian   **8–60**
grounds can only be made subsequent to an order for surrender being made.[29]

CONDITIONAL SURRENDER – SECTION 19

Where a requested person is required to serve all or part of a prison sentence imposed   **8–61**
in the State, rather than postpone surrender to allow him to serve this sentence, the
High Court may order surrender within the normal time frame, but do so *"subject to
such conditions as it shall specify"*. It is not immediately apparent from the wording
of s 19(1) how broadly this provision should be interpreted, but presumably the
conditions should relate to the future return of the surrendered person to Ireland in
order to serve his domestic sentence.[30] Section 19 provides

> "(1) Where a person to whom an order under *section 15* or *16* applies—
>
> > (a) has been sentenced to a term of imprisonment for an offence of which he
> > or she was convicted in the State, and
> >
> > (b) is, at the time of the making of the order, required to serve all or part of
> > that term of imprisonment,
>
> the High Court may, subject to such conditions as it shall specify, direct that the
> person be surrendered to the issuing state for the purpose of his or her being
> tried for the offence to which the European arrest warrant concerned relates."

It would appear that the option of conditional surrender is only open to the High   **8–62**
Court where the requested person is sought *"for the purpose of his or her being
tried"*. Thus, where surrender is sought purely to enforce a sentence already imposed
on the requested person in the issuing State, postponement under s 18(3) will be the
only option available to the High Court should it desire the requested person to
serve the domestic sentence. This is a limitation not imposed by the Framework
Decision.[31] It is arguable that the words *"for the purpose of his or her being tried"*
in the 2003 Act restrict the scope of the conditions which can be imposed by the
High Court, in that the conditions imposed must direct the return of the surrendered
person after he has been tried, but before he is required to serve any sentence which
may be imposed in the issuing State. This would lead to a situation where a second
European arrest warrant from the issuing State, issued after the Irish sentence has
been served, would be necessary in order to have the requested person return to
serve his sentence there. The provisions of s 19 have yet to be considered by the
courts in any detailed manner.

DEFECTS IN THE ORDER FOR SURRENDER

Where there is a minor defect in the s 15 or 16 order it can generally be amended   **8–63**
by means of an application under the slip rule in the normal way. In *Minister for*

---

[29] See *Minister for Justice, Equality and Law Reform v Hall* [2008] IEHC 155.
[30] Art 24.2 of the Framework Decision is somewhat clearer in this regard, as it talks of
surrendering *"temporarily"* subject to conditions.
[31] Art 24.2 of the Framework Decision.

Justice, Equality and Law Reform v McArdle[32] Murray CJ considered that there should be no difficulty in correcting such minor errors:

> "In my judgment in *McMullen v. Clancy* [2002] 3 I.R. 493 I pointed out at p. 502 that "… there is a fundamental public interest in the due administration of justice which requires that the order of a court accord with what the court has decided and that the decision of a court should not be thwarted, by an accidental slip or error or clerical mistake". As I also pointed out in that case the courts have an inherent as well as an express (in the case of O. 28, r. 11) jurisdiction to amend a final order. In the ordinary course of events an application would be made to the judge who decided the case to correct an error or slip in the order but the courts' inherent jurisdiction to correct such errors made in orders, particularly where they are clear and manifest, is not confined to the judge or court from which the error emanated." [33]

8–64   In that case the order expressed itself to have been made pursuant to s 16(2) rather than s 16(1). The court went on to decide that, where no such amendment has been made prior to the matter coming on for appeal, the Supreme Court retained an inherent jurisdiction to correct the error at that stage:

> "Where a matter comes before this court on appeal and there is no dispute concerning the terms of the decision as set out in the judgment of the High Court and there is a clear and manifest error in the order made on foot of that judgment, this court has, in my view, an inherent jurisdiction, in the interests of the proper administration of justice, to amend the order so as to accurately reflect the decision made in the High Court. This is necessary so that the appeal can be determined on the basis of what was actually decided rather than on the basis of an erroneous order. There may be circumstances where this court, in its discretion, might consider it more appropriate for such an issue to be remitted for decision by the High Court but given the clear and manifest nature of the error in the order I do not think that this is one of those cases. Therefore in my view this court should exercise its inherent jurisdiction to amend the High Court order by substituting a reference to s. 16(1) for the reference s. 16(2) of the Act of 2003 in that order."[34]

SUBSEQUENT REQUESTS FOR SURRENDER

8–65   Where surrender has been refused because of a defect in proofs or some technical reason it will be open to the issuing State to issue a subsequent European arrest warrant, and to the Minister to make a further application under the Act. In *Minister for Justice, Equality and Law Reform v McArdle*,[35] the respondent argued that the application for surrender brought by the Minister was an abuse of process, as the respondent had previously, in 2001, been arrested and detained on a provisional arrest warrant issued pursuant to the provisions of the Extradition Act 1965. The earlier extradition request had been withdrawn, as the State at that time could not

---

[32] [2005] 4 IR 260.
[33] p 264.
[34] p 265.
[35] [2005] IEHC 222.

extradite one of its own citizens to Spain. The court found no abuse of process in the Minister's subsequent application pursuant to the European arrest warrant issued by the Spanish authorities.

In *Minister for Justice, Equality and Law Reform v C McG*[36] a previous application to **8–66** have the respondent surrendered to the United Kingdom[37] had been refused by the High Court due to concerns in relation to identification. The respondent argued that the new application, based on a new European arrest warrant but on the same domestic warrant, amounted to an abuse of process, as there was nothing in the 2003 Act or the Framework Decision to permit such a second application. Peart J rejected this argument:

> "[Counsel] refers to the fact that the applicant did not appeal the refusal of surrender on the first application, and that in those circumstances the applicant cannot simply bring a fresh application on foot of the same domestic warrant. I have already been satisfied that any difficulty which arose in relation to identity on the last occasion from the manner in which it was sought to satisfy the Court in that regard, does not arise on the present application. The issue of identity has been resolved on this application, and there can be no abuse of process in that regard. Neither is there any bar to bringing a second application for surrender in the present case".

Similarly a previous attempt to extradite a respondent under the provisions of **8–67** the Extradition Act 1965 will not give rise to a *res judicata* for the purpose of a subsequent application for surrender under the European Arrest Warrant Act 2003. In *Minister for Justice, Equality and Law Reform v Gorman*[38] there had been an unsuccessful attempt to extradite the respondent for the same offence in 1994. The Court rejected the argument that the determination in the earlier proceedings amounted to an estoppel in relation to the proceedings subsequently brought under the 2003 Act noting that entirely different considerations applied.

The issue of *res judicata* was considered by the Supreme Court in *Minister for Justice,* **8–68** *Equality and Law Reform v Ó Fallúin*[39] where the respondent had sought to argue an estoppel by analogy with criminal procedure. Finnegan J rejected the argument:

> "It is, of course, part of our jurisprudence that there should not be repeated attempts to procure a conviction: *E.S. .v. Judges of the Court Circuit Court and the Director of Public Prosecutions* [2008] I.E.S.C. 37. However proceedings under the European Arrest Warrant Acts are not criminal proceedings and the same principles will not apply. In the present case the attempted extradition was discontinued without any decision being made. Again the European arrest warrant of the 21st June 2004 resulted in an order for the appellant's surrender: all issues of law raised by him were determined against him and an order for his surrender made. His appeal against the order of the High Court was withdrawn. His surrender on foot of that European arrest warrant did not occur solely because of the failure to effect his surrender within the times stipulated in the Acts: again there was no decision on any issue which could create an estoppel in the appellant's favour or give rise to *res judicata*. Counsel for the appellant did not draw to the court's attention any issue either in the three judgments

---

[36] [2007] IEHC 47.
[37] See *Minister for Justice, Equality and Law Reform v McGrath* [2006] 1 IR 321.
[38] [2010] IEHC 210.
[39] [2010] IESC 37.

delivered in the High Court on the European arrest warrant of the 21st June 2004 or in the judgment in the Supreme Court on the application under Article 40.4.2 which could conceivably give rise to an estoppel or issues of *res judicata*. I am satisfied that neither estoppel nor *res judicata* arises."

8-69   However, this is not to say that a second application for surrender or extradition will not give rise to certain difficulties. *Minister for Justice, Equality and Law Reform v Aamond*[40] was a case where 12 years had passed between the initial, unsuccessful attempt to extradite the respondent to Denmark in 1993 and the application for surrender based on a European arrest warrant issued in 2005 based on the original domestic warrant from 1993. Given the circumstances of delay in that case, Peart J held that it would be oppressive to surrender the respondent, and thus found his surrender prohibited by s 37 of the 2003 Act. The circumstances of the delay in *Aamond* are best regarded as being somewhat exceptional — the alleged offence had been committed in 1988.

---

[40] [2006] IEHC 382. Note: the judgment incorrectly cites the respondent as "Aamond". He was in fact the "Aamand" of *Aamand v Smithwick* [1995] 1 ILRM 61.

CHAPTER 9

Appeals and Article 40

APPEALS

Prior to the introduction of the Criminal Justice (Miscellaneous Provisions) Act   **9–01**
2009 the right of appeal to the Supreme Court was unfettered. Necessarily this had
considerable practical consequences from the point of view of complying with the time
limits set out in the Framework Decision. Given that the waiting period in respect of
appeals to the Supreme Court in this jurisdiction is measured in years, the reference in
the Framework Decision to time limits measured in days became largely aspirational.

Scope of Appeal

Whilst the 2003 Act had expressed the appeal to be limited to an appeal on a point   **9–02**
of law, the decision of the Supreme Court in *Minister for Justice Equality and Law
Reform v SMR*[1] seemed to render this limitation largely irrelevant. In that case the
High Court had determined as a matter of fact that the respondent was at a very real
risk of death in the event of surrender. On appeal it was argued that the Supreme
Court was not entitled to interfere with such a finding of fact as it was beyond
the extent of the scope of the appeal contemplated by the Act. The case of *Hay v
O'Grady*[2] was cited in support of the contention that an appellate court should not
interfere with the findings of fact made by the trial judge at first instance. However,
the Supreme Court took the view that as the greater part of the evidence before the
High Court had been given by way of affidavit evidence it was in as good a position
as the trial judge to draw the appropriate inferences. It went on to overturn the
High Court's decision not to surrender the respondent. One of the consequences
of the decision in *SMR* was that the distinction between an appeal on a point of
law and what effectively amounted to a hearing *de novo* was effectively lost. The

---

[1] [2007] IESC 54.
[2] [1992] 1 IR 210.

practical result was a very significant increase in the number and extent of appeals with inevitable delays in the determination of cases.[3]

Certification

9–03   The amendments introduced by s 12 of the Criminal Justice Act 2009 are best regarded as a means of dealing with these difficulties insofar as it restricted the right of appeal to cases where the High Court certified a specific issue in the case as being a point of law of exceptional public importance. Additionally a certificate will only be granted if it is desirable in the public interest that an appeal be brought.

9–04   The statutory formulation of the right of appeal is not unique and indeed features in other comparable legislative schemes.[4] Section 16(12) provides:

> "An appeal against an order under this section or a decision not to make such an order may be brought in the Supreme Court if, and only if, the High Court certifies that the order or decision involves a point of law of exceptional public importance and that it is desirable in the public interest that an appeal should be taken to the Supreme Court."

9–05   Clearly the restriction on the right of appeal is significant and few cases are likely to meet the statutory threshold. The constitutionality of a similar restriction was considered on an Art 26 reference in the case of *In Re: The Illegal Immigrants (Trafficking) Bill, 1999*[5] where the Supreme Court held it to be an appropriate exercise of the legislative function reserved exclusively to the Oireachtas under Art 34.4.3 of the Constitution[6].

9–06   In *O'Sullivan v Governor of Cloverhill Prison*[7] the applicant sought to challenge the constitutionality of s 16(12) of the European Arrest Warrant Act 2003 on the grounds that it amounted to a disproportionate interference with his right of access to the courts. Following the decision of the Supreme Court in *In Re: The Illegal Immigrants (Trafficking) Bill, 1999* McKechnie J considered that the provision in question did not infringe the rights of the applicant on the grounds that:

---

[3] Although the approach taken in relation to the affidavit evidence before the High Court in *SMR* is very much to be contrasted with that taken in the later case of *Minister for Justice, Equality and Law Reform v Ó Fallúin* (Unreported, Supreme Court, 19 May 2010):

> "It is quite clear from these affidavits that there was before the learned High Court judge credible evidence upon which he could conclude that the underlying domestic warrant had not been executed and was not spent. This being so it is not the function of this court to re-try the issues of fact determined by the High Court but merely to review the evidence before the learned High Court judge in order to determine whether he erred in law in concluding that the underlying domestic warrant was not spent. This court will not review the weight of the evidence."

[4] Most notably s 5(3) of the Illegal Immigrants (Trafficking) Act 2000.

[5] [2000] IR 2 360.

[6] Art 34.4.3 provides:

> "The Supreme Court shall, with such exceptions and subject to such regulations as may be prescribed by law, have appellate jurisdiction from all decisions of the High Court, and shall also have appellate jurisdiction from such decisions of other courts as may be prescribed by law."

[7] Unreported, High Court, 25 May 2010, McKechnie J.

"...considering the EAW regime, I am satisfied that when considered *in toto* it does not unduly infringe the applicant's constitutional right of access to the Court; in particular given that:

i)   The hearing is in the High Court;

ii) The parties are or may be represented;

iii) It is in part a supervisory or facilitating judicial hearing;

iv) Despite this, there are express safeguards to ensure that an applicant's rights will not be infringed when surrendered; and furthermore,

v)   Some appeal or further judicial scrutiny is possible.

The High Court is therefore in a position to determine all matters relating to the surrender of the applicant. The s. 16 procedure is such as to allow *"all justiciable questions involving the administration of justice [to be] heard and determined"* before the High Court. The applicant's right of access to justice under Bunreacht na hÉireann has thus not been breached."

It is of note that particular significance was attached to the fact that s 16 hearings   **9–07**
took place before the High Court. McKechnie J distinguished this from the situation that pertained prior to the introduction of the 2003 Act:

"Previously matters relating to extradition would have been dealt with by the District Court initially. A hearing before the High Court therefore shows the serious and substantial nature of proceedings under s. 16 EAWA 2003, and a desire by the legislature that they be dealt with in a weighty and authoritative manner."

The restriction of the right of appeal contains two separate and distinct elements.   **9–08**
Firstly the party that wishes to appeal must be in a position to show that the point of law in issue of one of exceptional public importance. Thereafter he or she must go on to establish that it is in the public interest that an appeal be brought.

Applicable Criteria

An analogous provision under s 50(4)(f)(i) of the Planning and Development Act   **9–09**
2000 was considered in *Arklow Holidays v An Bord Pleananála*.[8] Clarke J set out the relevant considerations on such an application. These were summarised as follows:

"In a number of decisions of this court the requirements of the section have been analysed in some detail and it is clear that a number of tests must be met:-

(i) there must be an uncertainty as to the law in respect of a point which has to be of exceptional importance; see for example *Lancefort v. An Bord Pleanála* [1998] 2 I.R. 511;

(ii) the importance of the point must be public in nature and must, therefore, transcend well beyond the individual facts andparties of a

---

[8] [2007] 4 IR 112.

given case; see *Kenny v. An Bord Pleanála (No. 2)* [2001] 1 I.R. 704. It is the case that every point of law arising in every case is a point of law of importance; see *Fallon v. An Bord Pleanála* [1992] 2 I.R. 380. That, of itself, is insufficient for the point of law concerned to be properly described as of "exceptional public importance";

(iii) the requirement that the court be satisfied "that it is desirable in the public interest that an appeal should be taken to the Supreme Court" is a separate and independent requirement from the requirement that the point of law be one of exceptional public importance; see *Kenny v. An Bord Pleanála (No. 2)* [2001] 1 I.R. 704. On that basis, even if it can argued that the law in a particular area is uncertain, the court may not, on the basis, *inter alia*, of time or costs, consider that it is appropriate to certify the case for the Supreme Court; see *Arklow Holidays Ltd. v. Wicklow County Council* [2004] IEHC 75, (Unreported, High Court, Murphy J., 4th February, 2004)."

9–10   It is clear from the foregoing that the issue raised should be one of potentially broad applicability rather than one which turns on the particular facts of a given case. Necessarily it should be an issue which is not otherwise settled in law. Insofar as the court may have to determine whether it is in the public interest to certify such a point, regard will also be had to whether or not a certificate has already been granted in relation to an identical or similar point. It is unlikely that the court would consider it to be in the public interest to certify multiple cases in relation to the same point of law.

9–11   As a matter of practicality the application ought, wherever possible, be made to the judge who presided over the s 16 hearing. In *O'Sullivan v Governor of Cloverhill Prison*[9] it was suggested that this might give rise to an apprehension of bias and thereby render the provision unconstitutional. The court rejected such concerns noting that the High Court was not being asked to reverse itself or reconsider its decision but was rather being asked to assess the relative significance of the issue raised in the proceedings.

Effect of Certification

9–12   Whilst the Act is silent as to the specific procedure to be followed in the event of an appeal being certified by the High Court, it would seem reasonable to assume that the practice which has, heretofore, applied in relation to similar appeals from the Court of Criminal Appeal to the Supreme Court pursuant to s 29 of the Courts of Justice Act 1924 will apply. Accordingly it would not seem necessary to set out the actual point of law in the certificate. Moreover the decision of the Supreme Court in *People (Attorney General) v Giles*[10] would seem to suggest that the appeal will not be restricted to the point certified but rather all issues raised before the High Court can legitimately be the subject of the appeal.

9–13   Although the Act suggests a limited appellate jurisdiction it would seem by analogy with the Planning Acts that the Supreme Court is entitled to exercise the same powers as the High Court in order to give effect to its decision. In *Talbot v An*

---

[9] Unreported, High Court, 25 May 2010, McKechnie J.
[10] [1947] IR 422.

Bord Pleanála[11] Fennelly J concluded that a similar provision[12] had to be interpreted in light of Art 34.4.3 of the Constitution and Ord 58 of the Rules of the Superior Courts:

> "The right of appeal to this court derives in the first instance from Article 34.4.3 of the Constitution. The provisions of s. 50 of the Act, while limiting the right of appeal, cannot be interpreted so as to limit its effectiveness, once the necessary certificate has been granted.
>
> I am satisfied that s. 50, considered in the light of the Rules of Court, permits this court either to grant leave itself in appropriate cases or to make an order remitting the entire matter to the High Court. [Order 58] Rule 8 gives the court power 'to make such further or other order as the case may require'".

The relevant section of the Planning and Development Act 2000 had, on the face **9–14** of it, reserved to the High Court the function of determining whether a sufficient case had been made out to justify an application for judicial review. In *Talbot* the Supreme Court concluded that, notwithstanding the apparently limited nature of the appeal, it was entitled to make whatever order it considered appropriate to give effect to its decision including actually granting leave to apply for judicial review. In the context of the European Arrest Warrant Act 2003 the Supreme Court would, by analogy, be entitled to exercise any of the various functions reserved to the High Court under the Act. Whilst this might include seeking further information from the issuing State the reality is that the Supreme Court has been very slow to involve itself in the exercise of such powers presumably on the basis that it is undesirable that it would step into the role of executing judicial authority to such an extent.

Appeal without Certification

Whether by accident or design the amendments effected by the Criminal Justice **9–15** (Miscellaneous Provisions) Act 2009 did not restrict the right of appeal in relation to orders other than those made pursuant to ss 15 and 16. It would therefore seem that an unfettered right of appeal exists in relation to the granting or refusal to grant a postponement under s 18 and a waiver of specialty pursuant to s 22. An unfettered right of appeal in the latter circumstance is particularly anomalous given that the same issues as would be canvassed on a s 16 hearing will form the basis of any objection to a waiver of specialty. Similarly there would appear to be no restriction on the right of appeal in relation to interlocutory applications such as discovery or indeed bail.

Moreover, it would seem that by virtue of Art 34.4.4[13] of the Constitution it is **9–16** not permissible to limit the appellate jurisdiction of the Supreme Court in relation to any proceedings concerning the constitutionality of any legislation. In *O'Sullivan v Governor of Cloverhill Prison*[14] McKechnie J expressed the view that insofar as

---

[11] [2009] 1 IR 375.

[12] s 50(4) of the Planning and Development Act 2000.

[13] "No law shall be enacted excepting from the appellate jurisdiction of the Supreme Court cases which involved questions as to the validity of any law having regard to the provisions of this Constitution".

[14] Unreported, High Court, 25 May 2010, McKechnie J.

s 16(12) of the European Arrest Warrant Act 2003 did not include a saver in respect of proceedings in the nature of constitutional challenges, the provision must be read in light of the provisions of the Constitution:

> "Whilst section 16 has no saver, neither does it seek to disallow an appeal. It must therefore be presumed that, absent any express words seeking to remove such jurisdiction, such was not intended. If such words were inserted, they would have to be struck down. In my view the prohibition of Article 34.4.4° must be read into all legislation, so that there is in reality no question of the appellate jurisdiction of the Supreme Court, concerning the constitutionality of, in this case, the EAWA 2003 or amending legislation, being ousted by s. 16 or any section of that Act. I would therefore be of the opinion that, if the constitutionality of an Act legitimately arose in the course of a s. 16 application, no certificate would be needed to appeal such to the Supreme Court. However, given the nature of a s. 16 application, the circumstances in which this might arise would, to my mind, be limited and rare. Finally, I would note that if this be a correct view of Article 34.4.4°, it is unclear why a saver provision in that regard is ever present in most legislation".

9–17   It would seem to follow, then, that no certificate is required where the constitutionality of the Act is directly challenged in the course of a s 16 hearing.[15]

Stay Pending Appeal

9–18   Prior to the introduction of the Criminal Justice (Miscellaneous Provisions) Act 2009 difficulties had arisen in relation to the staying of surrender orders pending appeal. This was because in the absence of such a stay the time period in which surrender had to be effected started to run. The necessity of obtaining a stay was demonstrated in the case of *O Falluin v Governor of Cloverhill Prison*[16] when a major lacuna in the provisions governing the surrender of the requested person pending appeal came to light. In that case the applicant had been committed to prison pending his surrender. Thereafter he lodged an appeal against his surrender to the Supreme Court. However, given that no provision[17] was made in the Act to stop time running in respect of the period in which the applicant had to be physically surrendered, the period of 25 days[18] elapsed long before his appeal was ever likely to be determined. An application was brought pursuant Art 40 seeking an enquiry in relation to the lawfulness of his detention given the provisions of s 16(7) which entitled him to be

---

[15] An alternative view would be that the absence of any saver in relation to the right of appeal in cases of constitutional challenge amounts to an indication from the legislature that such challenges are simply not contemplated as being capable of being brought within the confines of the limited statutory hearing provided for by s 16.

[16] [2007] 3 IR 414.

[17] Section 16(6) originally provided that surrender shall not occur during the currency of an application under Art 40.4.2 of the Constitution but had been entirely silent in relation to the position whilst an appeal is pending. This has now been remedied by the Criminal Justice (Miscellaneous Provisions) Act 2009 which provides for an automatic stay in the event of an appeal.

[18] 25 days is the sum of the 15 day period during which the order must not take effect provided for in s 16(4)(a) and the 10 day period in which surrender must be effected pursuant to s 16(5).

released once the time for his surrender had run. Fennelly J ordered the release of the applicant as the Act had failed to make any provision in relation to the position pending appeal:

> "I return to the words of sub-section (7). It mandates the release of the Appellant. That mandatory obligation is qualified only in the case that Article 40 proceedings are in being. Section 16(7) ordains release unless such proceedings are in existence and section 18(5) prohibits surrender until they are disposed of. It is noteworthy that the legislature has introduced no such qualification for the case of a pending appeal. The maxim, *expressio unius est exclusio alterius,* is strongly supportive of the conclusion that it was not intended to qualify the release obligation for the case of an appeal. I am satisfied that the Appellant was entitled to be released from custody immediately upon the expiry of the period of ten days after the coming into effect of the High Court [order], i.e., twenty five days after it was made".[19]

In the aftermath of the decision in *O Falluin* a practical remedy of sorts was adopted by the Minister. As a matter of course he sought an order from the High Court in each case where surrender had been ordered granting a stay on the execution of the order in the event that a Notice of Appeal was filed within 15 days of the date of the order. Therefore if the respondent appealed time would stop running and the issue of release due to effluxion of time pursuant to s 16(7) would not arise.   **9–19**

It is no longer necessary to obtain a stay given the amendments to Section 16(6) brought about by the Criminal Justice (Miscellaneous Provisions) Act 2009 which now provides: **9–20**

> "(6) Where a person—
>
>   (a)   appeals an order made under this section, or
>
>   (b)   makes a complaint under Article 40.4.2 of the Constitution,
>
> he or she shall not be surrendered to the issuing state while proceedings relating to the appeal or complaint are pending."

The act of filing a notice of appeal once a certificate has been obtained pursuant to s 16(12) will itself act as a stay on the order for surrender.   **9–21**

BAIL PENDING APPEAL

The position of the respondent with regard to bail is now dealt with explicitly under s 16(13) of the European Arrest Warrant Act 2003 which provides as follows: **9–22**

> "Where a person lodges an appeal pursuant to subsection (12), the High Court may remand the person in custody or on bail pending the hearing of the appeal and, for that purpose, the High Court shall have the same powers in relation to remand as it would have if the person were brought before it charged with an indictable offence."

---

[19] p 420.

9–23   As a matter of logic the status of the respondent will generally only arise in circumstances where the respondent is the Appellant — otherwise an order discharging the respondent would presumably have already been made. In *Minister for Justice, Equality and Law Reform v Snela*[20] Denham J considered that a higher threshold for bail applied once a s 16 order had been made and that an unsuccessful respondent might be regarded as being in the same position as a prisoner seeking bail in the Court of Criminal Appeal subsequent to conviction. Reference was made to the case of *The People (DPP) v Corbally*[21] in which it was held that a convicted prisoner seeking bail from the Court of Criminal Appeal would have to show a clear and discrete point of appeal which had a reasonably strong prospect of success.

9–24   Given the amendments effected by the Criminal Justice (Miscellaneous Provisions) Act 2009 in relation to having to have point of law of exceptional public importance certified, it is likely that most, if not all, appellants will meet the criteria set out in *Corbally*. A more significant factor in relation to the decision whether or not to grant bail pending appeal is likely to be whether the respondent is sought for the purpose of serving a sentence or simply for the purpose of prosecution. In the former circumstance the respondent clearly does not enjoy a presumption of innocence and will, in any event, obtain the benefit of having any time in custody within the State taken into account pursuant to Art 26 of the Framework Decision.

ARTICLE 40 APPLICATIONS

9–25   Both ss 15 and 16 mandate the High Court to inform the respondent of the entitlement to bring an application pursuant to Art 40.4.2 of the Constitution after the order for surrender is made and the respondent is committed to prison. Whilst applications pursuant to Art 40 tended to be one of the principal means of appeal under the Extradition Act 1965 when the District Court was the court of first instance, the scope for such applications is more limited given the role of the High Court as court of first instance.

9–26   Such applications have tended to focus either on defects in the order committing the respondent to prison or on delays in actually effecting surrender. In *McArdle v Governor of Cloverhill Prison*[22] the applicant had been committed to prison to await his surrender. However, the order committing him recited that his surrender had been ordered pursuant to the provisions of s 16(2) of the Act as opposed to s 16(1).[23] It was patently clear that this error was of a technical and clerical nature as opposed to a substantive and fundamental defect. Peart J declined an application pursuant to Art 40.4.1 for the release of the applicant on the grounds that the error in the order was of a minor nature and of the sort that might otherwise be remedied as a matter of course under the slip rule. He cited the judgment of O'Higgins CJ in *State (McDonagh) v Frawley*[24]:

---

[20] *Ex tempore*, Supreme Court, 12 December 2008.

[21] [2001] 1 IR 180.

[22] [2005] 4 IR 249.

[23] The provisions in question are more or less identical save insofar as s 16(1) applies where a warrant has been duly endorsed for execution whereas s 16(2) applies where the respondent has been arrested without a warrant on the grounds of urgency.

[24] [1978] IR 131.

"The stipulation in Article 40, s. 4, sub-s. 1, of the Constitution that a citizen may not be deprived of his liberty save 'in accordance with law' does not mean that a convicted person must be released on *habeas corpus* merely because some defect or illegality attaches to his detention. The phrase means that there must be such a default of fundamental requirements that the detention may be said to be wanting in due process of law. For *habeas corpus* purposes, therefore, it is insufficient for the prisoner to show that there has been a legal error or impropriety, or even that jurisdiction has been inadvertently exceeded."

In *McArdle* the applicant had sought to argue that a distinction should be drawn   **9–27** as between a person who had been convicted of a criminal offence in accordance with law and a person, such as the applicant, who stood un-convicted and entitled to a presumption of innocence. It was suggested that in the latter circumstance even minor technical defects would be sufficient to lead to release pursuant to the provisions of Art 40. Whilst recognising the existence of such a distinction Peart J appears to have taken the view that the same principles that would apply to a convicted person in the context of a similar application would apply in the case of a person whose surrender had been ordered. It would appear, therefore, that little by way of practical distinction is to be drawn as between convicted prisoners and those awaiting surrender.

Part III
Objections to Surrender

Chapter 10

Correspondence

CORRESPONDENCE AND THE LIST SYSTEM

10–01   One of the more novel features of the European Arrest Warrant Act 2003 and the Framework Decision is that they combine two distinct elements which are features of extradition law generally: a list of offences and a correspondence requirement. This has the practical effect of broadening the scope of offences to which the European arrest warrant applies very considerably.

10–02   Practitioners in Ireland have long been used to the idea of correspondence of offences, or dual criminality, as one of the cornerstones of the extradition process whether it is pursuant to treaty or on foot of the mutual system of backing of warrants as applied between the State and the United Kingdom prior to the introduction of the European Arrest Warrant Act 2003. All of the bi-lateral treaties to which the State is party provide that extradition may occur in respect of any offence so long as there is correspondence between the offence which is the subject of the extradition request and an offence under the law of the State. This requirement for correspondence is expressed in similar terms in the various treaties.[1]

10–03   The necessity that the offence be a corresponding offence arose, not from any rule of international law, but rather by virtue of the provisions of s 10 of the Extradition Act 1965 which requires that the offence must be one which is "punishable under the laws of the requesting country and of the State". Similarly all of the multilateral treaties to which the State is a signatory are necessarily prescribed in that they will only apply once correspondence or dual criminality is established. Many of these multilateral treaties are further prescribed in that they will only apply to a limited range of offences.[2] The rationale underlying the imposition of a correspondence requirement is that one state should not be put in the position of being required to detain an individual and assist in that person's prosecution in circumstances where the conduct in question is not regarded as a crime under the law of that state. In essence it offends against the principle of sovereignty. In *Minister for Justice, Equality and Law Reform v Ferenca*[3] Murray CJ explained the nature of correspondence in the following terms:

> "For a very long time the law on extradition (to use that term in a generic sense) in this country stipulated that extradition could only be ordered in respect of an offence which was an offence against the law of this State or corresponded to such an offence. This is also the position generally adopted by other states. The underlying principle is that a country, as a general policy, often does not extradite persons to another country for the commission of an act which is not unlawful under its own law. In those circumstances, a Court, when considering whether to extradite verifies that the relevant offence corresponds to an offence

---

[1] e.g. Treaty on Extradition between the United States of America and Ireland, Article II.1: "An offence shall be an extraditable offence only if it is punishable under the law of both Contracting Parties by imprisonment for a period of more than one year, or by a more severe penalty". Treaty on Extradition between Ireland and Australia, Article II.1: "For the purposes of this Treaty, an extraditable offence is an offence however described which is punishable under the laws of both Contracting Parties by imprisonment for a period of at least one year or by a more severe penalty".

[2] e.g. The United Nations Convention Against Illicit Traffic in Narcotic Drugs and Psychotropic Substances, 1988.

[3] [2008] 4 IR 480.

under its law. Accordingly, in extradition proceedings generally in this country it was, and still is to a significant extent, necessary for a Court to verify that the offence or offences in respect of which extradition, or surrender under the Act of 2003, is sought corresponds to an offence under the law of the State."[4]

Traditionally in this jurisdiction the requirement to establish correspondence has **10–04** meant that the courts have been obliged to examine the offence which is the subject of the extradition request and consider, hypothetically, whether such conduct, if committed within the State, would amount to an offence. The alternative to such an approach is for the parties to an extradition treaty to indicate at the point when the treaty is drafted specifically what offences it is intended to relate to. Whilst such an arrangement may seem alien given the traditional requirement that correspondence be established it is in fact little different to the arrangements in respect of extradition (as opposed to backing of warrants) which were in force prior to the enactment of the Extradition Act 1965. The Extradition Acts 1870 to 1906 provided for a list of offences[5] in respect of which extradition would be granted although there appears to have been an additional requirement that some degree of correspondence must also be shown in relation to the offence.[6] Extradition on foot of a list of designated offences would, in fact, have been the norm in extradition treaties towards the end of the 19th century. Whilst such a system in the traditional form has the attraction of simplicity it is impractical in the context of multilateral treaties as constant amendments to the treaty would be required to take account of domestic legislative developments in each of the signatory States.

The Framework Decision incorporates both the traditional correspondence test[7] **10–05** and the list system in a novel way. It avoids the difficulties associated with a list system by stipulating a list of categories of offence, rather than offences themselves, which

---

[4] p 483.

[5] The Schedules to the various Acts specified the following offences: Murder, attempt or conspiracy to murder, manslaughter, counterfeiting, altering, uttering counterfeited or altered money, forgery, counterfeiting, altering, uttering what is forged, altered or counterfeited, embezzlement, larceny, obtaingin money or goods by false pretences, crimes by bankrupts against bankruptcy laws, fraud by bailee, banker, agent, factor, trustee, or director, member or public officer of any company made criminal by any act, rape, abduction, child-stealing, burglary, house-breaking, arson, robbery with violence, threats with intent to extort, piracy by law of nations, sinking or destroying a ship at sea, or attempting or conspiring so to do, assault on board a ship on the high seas with intent to destroy life or do grievous bodily harm, revolt or conspiracy to revolt by two or more persons on a ship on the high seas against the authority of the master, kidnapping, false imprisonment, perjury, subornation of perjury, indictable offences under the Criminal Law Consolidation Acts, 1861 and under bankruptcy laws, bribery.

[6] s 26 of the Extradition Act, 1870 provides: "The term 'extradition crime' means a crime which, if committed in England or within English jurisdiction, would be one of the crimes described in the first schedule to this Act".

[7] Albeit on an optional basis. The inclusion of a traditional correspondence test at s 38(1)(a) is in fact one of the optional grounds for refusal included within the Framework Decision at Art 2.4: "For offences other than those covered by paragraph 2, surrender may be subject to the condition that the acts for which the European arrest warrant has been issued constitute an offence under the law of the executing Member State, whatever the constituent elements or however it is described." This sentiment is echoed in Art 4.1 which allows, on an optional basis, Member States not to surrender on the grounds of non-correspondence.

it is then up to the issuing state to certify as being applicable in the circumstances of the particular case. Necessarily such a system reposes a considerable amount of faith in the issuing state and is best regarded as one of the more concrete examples of the principle of mutual trust which underpins the Framework Decision. Where the offence does not come within the list of offences, the ordinary rule in relation to correspondence will apply.

10–06   Given the rather broad description of some of the offences set out in the Art 2.2 list it quickly becomes apparent that the combination of a broad list system together with a general correspondence requirement in relation to any other offences means that the number offences that do not come within the terms of the European Arrest Warrant Act 2003 will in fact be quite limited.

SECTION 38

10–07   Article 2 of the Framework Decision is given effect by s 38 of the European Arrest Warrant Act 2003 which requires either that correspondence be established or that the offence be one to which Art 2.2 applies:

> "(1) Subject to *subsection (2)*, a person shall not be surrendered to an issuing state under this Act in respect of an offence unless—
>
> (a)   the offence corresponds to an offence under the law of the State…
>
> or
>
> (b)   the offence is an offence to which paragraph 2 of Article 2 of the Framework Decision applies…"

10–08   Whilst the traditional correspondence requirement and inclusion in the Art 2.2 list are expressed as alternatives the latter is probably better regarded as an exception to the former which is the general rule. In practical terms this will mean that in any given case the court will consider firstly whether a particular offence is an offence to which Art 2.2 applies. If it concludes that it is, then the issue of correspondence is essentially dealt with. If the offence is not an offence to which Art 2.2 applies then the court will move on to consider whether it is, nonetheless, a corresponding offence.

ARTICLE 2.2 OFFENCES — CERTIFICATION BY THE ISSUING STATE

10–09   The rather unhappy manner in which the Framework Decision has, in part, been incorporated into the European Arrest Warrant Act 2003 has already been commented on. Specifically the device of incorporating the Art 2.2 list into the Act by way of reference to it in s 38(1)(b) is somewhat unsatisfactory. To some extent the incorporation of part of the Framework Decision into an act of the Oireachtas serves to undermine, or at least confuse, the essential nature of a Framework Decision as an instrument of European Law without direct effect. Due to the manner in which the Act is drafted it is necessary to refer to the Framework Decision to ascertain the various categories of offence to which Art 2.2 applies. In reality there is little need for the court to give any detailed consideration to the terms in which the categories of offence are described because s 38(1) and the Framework Decision have in essence been interpreted as providing for a certification process whereby the issuing state certifies that the offence comes within Art 2.2. In practical terms such certification is conclusive save in the case of manifest error or absurdity.

Paragraph (e)I of the standard form warrant contained in the Annex to the **10–10** Framework Decision provides the mechanism whereby the issuing state can indicate whether an offence is one to which Art 2.2 applies. This is done by ticking a box next to the relevant category of offence to indicate that the offence comes within that category. This also has the effect of indicating that the offence in question is punishable by a maximum sentence of at least three years imprisonment. Thus the ticking of a box in relation to an offence brings it within the application of s 38(1) (b) of the 2003 Act, thereby obviating the need to establish correspondence. The courts have taken the approach that the ticking of a box in para (e)I of the warrant is conclusive as to the issue of whether the offence comes within Art 2.2, except in certain limited circumstances. Peart J, in *Minister for Justice, Equality and Law Reform v Butenas*[8] gave some indication of what such circumstances might be:

> "This is a case where the requesting state has ticked the appropriate box in relation to an Article 2.2 offence. The Court is precluded from looking at that question further, and there is absolutely no question in this case but that the facts set forth in the warrant justify the ticking of that box. There can be no question of it having been ticked through some manifest error, and neither is there any room for any suggestion of bad faith on the part of the requesting authority."

It would seem that arguments in respect of correspondence will only arise in relation **10–11** to a listed offence where it is apparent from the warrant or elsewhere that the offence for which the respondent is sought does not come within the scope of the Art 2.2 list. For example where the relevant box in relation to "fraud" was ticked in circumstances where the narrative of the offence set out in the warrant made it clear that what was alleged was an offence of personal violence then it would be entitled to regard the certification under Art 2.2 as a manifest error. Presumably in such a situation the court would then revert to the ordinary correspondence test under s 38(1)(a).

Such a situation arose in *Minister for Justice, Equality and Law Reform v* **10–12** *Horvath*,[9] where the *"fraud"* box was ticked in respect of all 17 offences referred to in the warrant. The respondent pointed out however that, according to the extracts of legislation provided in the warrant, four of these offences did not satisfy the minimum gravity requirement of a maximum sentence of at least three years imprisonment. Peart J stressed that, given the high level of mutual trust and confidence between Member States which underpinned the European Arrest Warrant system, "it would require very clear evidence to the contrary before this Court would find that an offence [marked as an Article 2.2 offence] in the warrant was not appropriately marked" and that the court would not normally look behind the ticking of the box in relation to an offence. However, he concluded that he was entitled to do so in this case:

---

[8] [2006] IEHC 378.
[9] [2008] IEHC 411.

> "I am satisfied that this Court is not obliged by virtue of the issuing judicial authority having marked all the offences as Article 2.2 offences, to not look behind that marking, when the warrant itself makes it clear that one or more of the offences do not in fact meet the minimum gravity requirement for the purpose of that Article".

10–13   The court then went on to consider the question of correspondence under s 38(1)(a) in the ordinary way.

10–14   In circumstances where there is an ambiguity as to whether the issuing state has actually sought to certify that the offence comes within Art 2.2 the court may also similarly decide to consider whether the offence meets the correspondence test. In *Minister for Justice, Equality and Law Reform v Paulauskas*[10] one of the boxes had been ticked by the judicial authority in the issuing state. However, under para (e)II of the warrant it had also given particulars in respect of offences not covered by Art 2.2. Clearly this amounted to an error although it was unclear as to whether the error lay in ticking the box at para (e)I or including the particulars at (e)II which were mutually incompatible. The court considered that the error was not fatal although insofar as there was an ambiguity as to whether or not it was an Art 2.2 offence this should be resolved in favour of requiring the Minister to prove that it is was a corresponding offence. A similar approach was adopted in *Minister for Justice, Equality and Law Reform v Nowakowski*.[11]

10–15   The corollary of the approach taken by the courts in relation to the conclusive nature of the certification by the issuing state is that where the issuing state has not ticked the relevant box the court here is not entitled to assume that it should have done so or that the offence in any event comes within the terms of Art 2.2. In *Minister for Justice, Equality and Law Reform v Ferenca*[12] the respondent had been sought in relation to three offences, two of which were corresponding offences, and one of which was not. In respect of the latter offence the warrant indicated that the respondent had been convicted of an offence consisting of handing over a document to a third party to be forged. Notwithstanding the fact that the offence appeared to have been committed with a general fraudulent intent, the issuing state had not invoked Art 2.2 by ticking the box in respect of "fraud". In the High Court Peart J had concluded that the terms of s 38(1) provided for three distinct bases upon which surrender could be ordered. The first was where there was correspondence in the ordinary way. The second was where the relevant box was ticked in respect of a listed offence. The third possibility was where the relevant box was not ticked but the offence was in any event one that in the words of s 38(1)(b)[13] "consists of conduct specified in" Art 2.2. In other words even if the box was not ticked the High Court would be entitled to conclude that it ought to have been as the conduct specified clearly came within one of the categories – in that case the relevant category was fraud.

---

[10] [2009] IEHC 32.
[11] [2008] IEHC 439.
[12] [2008] 4 IR 480.
[13] s 38(1)(b) has since been amended by the Criminal Justice (Miscellaneous Provisions) Act 2009 and the reference to offences that consist of conduct specified in Art 2(2) has now been deleted.

On appeal the Supreme Court had some sympathy for Peart J who had attempted **10–16** to give some meaning to the apparent distinction drawn in s 38(1)(b) between Art 2.2 offences and offences consisting of conduct specified in Art 2.2. However, Murray CJ concluded that such attempts were essentially in vain and that it was not up to the executing state to decide whether or not the offences came within the Art 2.2 list:

> "If there is no box ticked then the requested state has no basis for concluding that the offence in question is one of those specified in Article 2.2. On the contrary, it must conclude that it is not. That flows from the decision of the issuing state not to classify an offence as one of the offences in Article 2.2.
>
> The absence of a ticked box cannot simply be considered as an omission or failure. It is the choice of the issuing state. It knows its own law. The executing state does not know the other country's law."

The Court was fortified in its view by the decision of the Court of Justice in *Advocaten* **10–17** *voor de Wereld VZW v Leden van de Ministerraad*[14] which had considered the nature of the list of offences created by Art 2.2. The Court of Justice had specifically drawn attention to the fact that it was for the issuing Member States to decide which offences came within the categories set out in the list and which did not:

> "Consequently, even if the Member States reproduce word-for-word the list of the categories of offences set out in Article 2.2 of the Framework Decision for the purposes of its implementation, the actual definition of those offences and the penalties applicable are those which follow from the law of 'the issuing Member State'. The Framework Decision does not seek to harmonise the criminal offences in question in respect of their constituent elements or of the penalties which they attract."[15]

In relation to the reference in s 38(1)(b) relating to offences consisting of conduct **10–18** specified in the list the Chief Justice found that there was "great difficulty in attributing any effective meaning" to it and went on to describe it as an "impenetrable provision".

In a judgment on the same issue delivered by the Supreme Court on the same **10–19** date in the case of *Minister for Justice, Equality and Law Reform v Desjatnikovs*[16] Denham J was similarly perplexed by the meaning of s 38(1)(b) and ultimately reached an identical conclusion:

> "It would be an extraordinary leap, a major step, to give to an Irish High Court the role of deciding whether on the facts the warrant refers to an offence in the issuing state. The words of Article 2.2 of the Framework Decision are clear, and they do not establish such a system."[17]

Although it is clear from *Ferenca* and *Desjatnikovs* that the courts must regard as **10–20** significant the issuing judicial authority's failure to tick a box at para (e)I in respect

---

[14] (Case C 303/05) [2007] ECR I-3633.
[15] Para 52.
[16] [2009] 1 IR 618.
[17] p 636.

of an offence, the question arises as to what approach the courts take where the issuing judicial authority subsequently indicates by way of additional information that a box could and should have been ticked in respect of the offence. Such was the case in *Minister for Justice, Equality and Law Reform v Laks*.[18] The warrant in that case disclosed that the respondent was accused of having "swindled money". Notwithstanding this, neither the box marked "swindling" nor any other box in para (e)I of the warrant had been ticked, and instead details of the offence had been provided at para (e)II. Additional information from the issuing judicial authority obtained by the High Court pursuant to s 20 of the Act concluded "by stating in effect that even though the 'fraud' box has not been marked as such in the warrant, the offence comes within that category of offence and that therefore correspondence need not be verified under the Framework Decision". The Court rejected this attempt to effectively amend the warrant:

> "I am of the view that this Court must deal with the European arrest warrant on the basis of what it actually contains, and not on the basis of what it might have contained if it had been prepared differently. Fraud has not been marked. No offence has been marked, and accordingly correspondence must be made out".

10–21 The approach adopted by the courts in relation to Art 2.2 offences is that the certification on the face of the warrant is conclusive either way. The only exception may be in relation to cases of manifest error.

Inchoate Offences

10–22 Article 2.2 of the Framework Decision, somewhat surprisingly, does not explicitly state whether or not it also applies to inchoate offences. This issue was, however, put to rest in *Minister for Justice, Equality and Law Reform v Biggins*[19] where the respondent had been charged with attempted murder. Peart J held as follows:

> "Where the offence specified, being the offence for which the respondent will face prosecution, is inchoate in nature, such as attempted murder, it makes complete sense that the double criminality which is relevant, and which does not require verification, is that of the substantive offence, and not the inchoate. The offence ticked in the box is not to be seen as a contradiction of, or in conflict with, the offence stated to be that for which the respondent is to be prosecuted. The purpose of ticking the box is to indicate an offence the nature of which is common to all Member States, i.e. murder, and for that reason is one for which double criminality can be presumed and not in need of verification."

10–23 It would seem to follow that attempts and conspiracies to commit the underlying offence will also be amenable to certification.[20] The issue of conspiracy was

---

[18] [2009] IEHC 3.

[19] [2006] IEHC 351.

[20] See *Minister for Justice, Equality and Law Reform v Tighe* [2009] IEHC 33.

considered in *Minister for Justice, Equality and Law Reform v O'Sullivan*.[21] The court rejected the contention that conspiracy ought to be treated differently from other inchoate offences for the purposes of the Art 2.2 list:

> "The second submission made on behalf of the respondent in relation to these offences is whether the offence of "conspiracy to defraud" can be marked as being an offence within the "fraud" category for the purposes of Article 2.2. One leg of that submission is that conspiracy is an inchoate offence, an offence entirely different in nature to the substantive offence of fraud. [Counsel] submits that, given the manner in which conspiracy offences have, historically, been differently dealt with in extradition treaties, it must be presumed that Members States had intended conspiracy offences to be offences in respect of which double criminality was not required to be verified, and that they could therefore be regarded as offences coming within the list of categories in Article 2.2, it would have listed "conspiracy" as a specific heading or category within that list.
>
> ...in spite of the submissions of [Counsel] that, historically, conspiracy has been treated differently and that this court should therefore continue to treat it separately and differently by not regarding it as capable of coming within Article 2.2, this Court is required to respect the fact that it has been so marked, and, as I have said, it must be borne in mind that what is important is that the marking is by reference to how the particular offence or offences are defined in the issuing state."

10–24 It would appear that any attempt to second guess the certification by the issuing state of the offence for which surrender is sought as coming within the Article 2.2 list is unlikely to succeed.

CORRESPONDENCE — THE STATUTORY TEST

10–25 Where the offence in question is not certified as coming within the terms of Art 2.2, the court must turn to the terms of s 38(1)(a) and consider whether the offence satisfies the correspondence test. Whilst the Framework Decision makes reference to "dual criminality" and the European Arrest Warrant Act 2003 refers to "corresponding offences", there is in fact no distinction between these two expressions which may be used interchangeably. Although s 38 sets out the manner in which the list offences and corresponding offences interact, it is s 5 of the 2003 Act which defines a corresponding offence:

> "For the purposes of this Act, an offence specified in a European arrest warrant corresponds to an offence under the law of the State, where the act or omission that constitutes the offence so specified would, if committed in the State on the date on which the European arrest warrant is issued, constitute an offence under the law of the State."

10–26 Section 5 of the 2003 Act was substituted by s 70 of the Criminal Justice (Terrorist Offences) Act 2005. Prior to that s 5 had provided a definition of a corresponding offence which required the court to be satisfied not only that the act complained of was an offence

---

[21] Unreported, Peart J, 9 February 2010.

in the State but that the act was also an offence in the requesting State.[22] The definition very unhelpfully made reference to offences under the laws of the requesting and requested states corresponding with each other. This of itself seemed to invite the courts to engage in some degree of consideration of the terms in which offences were defined under the law of the requesting state. Such an exercise was necessarily fraught with the potential for great complexity and inevitable misunderstanding. The new definition provided for by s 5 is a considerably more simplified one which is exclusively based on a consideration by the court of the conduct giving rise to the offence set out in the warrant. As such this obviates the necessity for the court to engage in any serious consideration of the manner in which the offence is formally defined in the requesting state.

10–27   The amended definition is considerably more in accord with the terms of the Framework Decision which variously speak of corresponding offences as being considered with reference to "the acts for which the European arrest warrant has been issued"[23] and "the act on which the European arrest warrant is based".[24] The emphasis is, therefore, on the act or conduct rather than the statutory or other definition of the offence.

10–28   Section 5 also allows correspondence to be established even where the offence in respect of which surrender is sought would not have been an offence had the act been committed within the State on the date it was committed in the requesting state. All that is required is that the offence amounts to an offence within the State on the date that the warrant is issued. It remains to be seen as to whether it would be permissible for a requesting state to "re-issue" a European arrest warrant that had already been issued for the purpose of avoiding the temporal limitation created by s 5.

Correspondence under the Extradition Act 1965

10–29   The definition of a corresponding offence in the 2003 Act is something of an improvement on the situation as it pertained (and as it continues to in relation to Part II extraditions) under the Extradition Act 1965. Prior to the introduction of the 2003 Act the Act of 1965 had two differing definitions of corresponding offences. Part II of the 1965, which still applies to extradition to non-EU countries, dealt with the issue of correspondence by providing that extradition would only arise in relation to "an offence punishable under the laws of the State" which was defined by s 10(3) as:

---

[22] Prior to the amendment s 5 provided as follows:

"For the purposes of this Act—

    (a) an offence under the law of the issuing state corresponds to an offence under the law of the State, where the act or omission that constitutes the offence under the law of the issuing state would, if committed in the State, constitute an offence under the law of the State, and

    (b) an offence under the law of the State corresponds to an offence under the law of the issuing state, where the act or omission that constitutes the offence under the law of the State would, if committed in the issuing state, constitute an offence under the law of the issuing state."

[23] Art 2.4.
[24] Art 4.1.

> "(a)   an act that, if committed in the State on the day on which the request for extradition is made, would constitute an offence, or
>
> (b)   in the case of an offence under the law of a requesting country consisting of the commission of one or more acts including any act committed in the State (in this paragraph referred to as 'the act concerned'), such one or more acts, being acts that, if committed in the State on the day on which the act concerned was committed or alleged to have been committed would constitute an offence,"

A somewhat different approach was taken in relation to Part III of the 1965 Act   **10–30** which related to rendition arrangements between the State and the United Kingdom. Section 42(2) provided:

> "For the purposes of this Part an offence under the law of a place to which this Part applies corresponds to an offence under the law of the State where the act constituting the offence under the law of that place would, if done in the State, constitute an offence under the law of the State..."

Whilst both provisions deal with the issue of corresponding offences in a somewhat   **10–31** more opaque way than the 2003 Act it is, nonetheless, clear that the test as to what is a corresponding offence under either part of the 1965 Act is principally a conduct based test as it is under s 5 of the 2003 Act. To that extent the authorities in relation to correspondence under the 1965 Act are of relevance.

Case-Law: Extradition Act 1965

Much of the earlier case-law in relation to correspondence is beset with confusion   **10–32** in relation to the correct approach to the question of correspondence. This confusion can be traced to the decision of the Supreme Court in *The State (Furlong) v Kelly*[25] which was concerned with whether an offence of burglary under the English Theft Act 1968 corresponded with any offence under the Larceny Act 1916. O'Dalaigh CJ engaged in a laborious analysis of the relevant provisions of the offence as it was defined under English law and compared the requisite component parts of the offence to its equivalent under Irish law. Ultimately (and not surprisingly) he concluded that there were some slight differences in relation to the requisite intent set out in each statute. He concluded that correspondence had not been made out. Rather than looking at the conduct specified in the warrant O Dalaigh CJ had conducted his own review of the Theft Act 1968 and concluded that there must be a lack of correspondence because of the slightly different manner in which the offence was defined. He summarised the approach to be taken as follows:

> "The basic inquiry is to discover whether the several ingredients which constitute the offence specified in the warrant, or one or more of such ingredients, constitute an offence under the law of the State and, if they do, whether that offence (the "corresponding offence") is an indictable offence or, if not, whether it is punishable on summary conviction by imprisonment for a maximum period of at least six months. As to the first limb of the inquiry, the position may be illustrated algebraically as follows. If the English offence consists of, say, four essential elements a+b+c+d, then a corresponding Irish

---

[25]   [1971] IR 132.

offence exists only if it contains either precisely these same four essential elements or a lesser number thereof. If the only Irish offence that can be pointed to has an additional essential ingredient (that is to say, if the Irish offence may be defined as a+b+c+d+e), then there is no corresponding Irish offence to satisfy the requirements of s.47, sub-s. 2, of the Act of 1965 for the simple reason that, *ex hypothesi*, conduct a+b+c+d falls short of being an offence under Irish law or, in plainer words, is not an offence. It is fundamental to extradition that no one shall be extradited for acts or omissions (the offence alleged in the warrant) which, if repeated within the State, would not offend against our law."[26]

10–33   Such an approach inevitably leads to the conclusion that offences do not correspond. With the exception of a handful of common law offences there are now few statutory offences which are defined in more or less identical terms in both Ireland and the United Kingdom. The problem which would arise in relation to adopting such an approach in relation to offences from non-common law jurisdictions would be even more pronounced.

10–34   An altogether different approach was taken in the course of the same case by Walsh J who appears to have adopted a critical attitude to the approach of O Dalaigh CJ (albeit under the guise of criticising the District Judge):

"The next point which calls for consideration is how the District Justice is to ascertain and determine what is the corresponding offence under the law of this State. I do not for a moment think that the Act ever contemplated that a District Justice or indeed the High Court would be called upon in such cases to construe foreign law and indeed it would be manifestly impracticable to expect every District Justice in the country to undertake such a task even if he were competent to do so... The function of the District Justice is to examine the documents set before him and to see whether there is a sufficient statement of the particulars of the ingredients of the offence alleged to enable him to bring to bear on them his knowledge of the law of this State so that he may determine whether the acts alleged against the prisoner would constitute an offence under the laws of this State... Undoubtedly it is true that in respect of statutory provisions or common-law offences which were common to this country and other countries, under identical statutory provisions or identical common law at the time of the setting up of the State, there may be little difficulty because the District Justice will be versed in the law. But in respect of any offence created outside this jurisdiction subsequent to the setting up of this State the position is entirely different and it becomes immediately a question of foreign law. For this reason I do not find it necessary to enter into any examination of the Theft Act in England as, for the reasons I have given, I do not believe that that would be the concern of the District Justice in this case."[27]

10–35   This approach was echoed in subsequent cases. In *Hanlon v Fleming*[28] Henchy J at p 495 stated:

"...it is a question of looking at the factual components of the offence specified in the warrant, regardless of the name given to it, and seeing if those factual components, in their entirety or in their near-entirety, would constitute an

---

[26] p 141.

[27] pp 142 – 144.

[28] [1981] IR 489.

> offence which, if committed in this State, could be said to be a corresponding
> offence of the required gravity."

It is not feasible to seek to reconcile the two approaches of O'Dalaigh CJ and Walsh J   **10–36**
and there is evident confusion in much of the subsequent case-law concerning the issue
of correspondence. The issue was finally definitively dealt with by the Supreme Court
in *Attorney General v Dyer*.[29] In the course of his judgment Fennelly J diplomatically
dealt with two competing approaches:

> "It is apparent, therefore that O Dalaigh CJ conceived the inquiry into
> correspondence in terms of the legal elements of the offences created under the
> laws of the respective jurisdictions. Whatever force the reference to S. 10(3) of
> the Act of 1965 had at the time of the judgment in *The State (Furlong) v. Kelly*
> [1971] 1 IR 132, it must be greatly diminished by the fact that since 2001 there
> is a statutory definition of correspondence by reference to "the act constituting
> the offence" specified in the warrant."[30]

The issue before the Supreme Court in Dyer related to the fact that the warrant   **10–37**
which alleged offences in the nature of obtaining by false pretences failed to recite
that it had been committed with intent to defraud – a necessary element for the
offence in this jurisdiction. The Attorney General had sought to deal with this issue
by means of adducing evidence by way of an affidavit of law to the effect that an
intention to defraud was necessarily a part of the offence under the law of Jersey
but that the law there did not require that it be explicitly stated on the face of an
indictment. In substance the court was being invited to engage in an analysis of
the comparative elements of the offences in both jurisdictions. The Supreme Court
rejected this approach in favour of the fact based approach and concluded that there
was a lack of correspondence due to failure of the warrant to allege an intent to
defraud. Fennelly J went on to note that had such a fraudulent intent been stated
either on the face of the warrant or by way of an affidavit from a person involved in
the police investigation the court would probably have been able to make a finding
in favour of the offence corresponding, on the basis that there would then have been
sufficient factual material before the court to allow it to do so.

The decision in *Dyer* was informed principally by the statutory language used to   **10–38**
define what a corresponding offence was. In that case s 10(3)[31] of the Extradition Act 1965
referred to "the act constituting the offence", clearly indicating that it is what is alleged
rather than any statutory construction or definition of the offence that is important.

Case-Law: European Arrest Warrant Act 2003

Section 5 of the 2003 is equally clear in this regard in that it refers to "the act or   **10–39**
omission that constitutes the offence" as being the basis for correspondence. The
same approach as adopted in *Dyer* would seem also to apply to consideration of

---

[29] [2004] 1 IR 40.

[30] p 46.

[31] Strictly speaking the definition of a corresponding offence for the purposes of Part III of
the Extradition Act 1965 was governed by s 42(2) as inserted by s 26 of the Extradition
(European Union Conventions Act) 2001 and not s 10(3) which only applied to Part II
extraditions. Both provisions, in any event, refer to "the act constituting the offence".

correspondence in respect of a European arrest warrant and there would seem to be little basis for the court to embark upon an analysis of the constituent elements of the offence in the requesting state as compared with the constituent elements of whatever is said to be the Irish equivalent. The approach in *Dyer* was endorsed in relation to the European Arrest Warrant Act, 2003 in broad terms in *Minister for Justice, Equality and Law Reform v Altaravicius (No.2)*[32]:

> "This issue was fully examined by the Supreme Court in *Attorney General v. Dyer* [2004] IESC 1, [2004] 1 I.R. 40. In the course of his decision, Fennelly J. identified a number of principles set out in previous cases. These are:-
>
> 1. In considering whether correspondence has been established, the court looks to the facts alleged against the subject of their quest, as opposed to the name of the offence for which he or she is sought in the requesting state, and considers whether these facts or this conduct would amount in this State to a crime of the necessary minimum gravity;
>
> 2. In considering correspondence therefore the court is concerned not with the name of the offence in the requesting country but the criminal conduct alleged in the request or warrant, and;
>
> 3. In the absence of anything suggesting that the words used in a warrant had a different meaning in the law of the requesting state, the question of correspondence was to be examined by attributing to such words the meaning they would have in Irish law."[33]

10–40   Whilst the courts have, since the introduction of the 2003 Act, by and large adopted the conduct based test enunciated in *AG v Dyer* they have done so in a somewhat less formalistic way.

10–41   In *Minister for Justice, Equality and Law Reform v Dolny*[34] the warrant set out an allegation of an assault causing harm. However it did not go so far as to explicitly state that the assault was committed without the consent of the victim. The Supreme Court took the view that what should be looked at is the nature of the offence as it is described in the warrant and the question should be asked in general terms as to whether such conduct is contrary to the criminal law of the State:

> "In addressing the issue of correspondence it is necessary to consider the particulars on the warrant, the acts, to decide if they would constitute an offence in the State. In considering the issue it is appropriate to read the warrant as a whole. In so reading the particulars it is a question of determining whether there is a corresponding offence. It is a question of determining if the acts alleged were such that if committed in this jurisdiction they would constitute an offence. It is not a helpful analogy to consider whether the words would equate with the terms of an indictment in this jurisdiction. Rather it is a matter of considering the acts described and deciding whether they would constitute an offence if committed in this jurisdiction."[35]

---

[32]   [2007] 2 IR 265.
[33]   At p 280.
[34]   [2009] IESC 48.
[35]   As per Denham J.

This approach would appear to represent a gradual shift away from the somewhat **10–42** more formal approach adopted by the court in *Dyer* where the absence of an explicit allegation of fraudulent intent lead to a finding of an absence of correspondence.

A similar approach was taken by Peart J in *Minister for Justice, Equality and Law* **10–43** *Reform v Mazurkiewicz*[36] which concerned an allegation of robbery. The applicant contended that the offence corresponded with an offence under s 14 of the Criminal Justice (Theft and Fraud Offences) Act 2001. Whilst the warrant did not expressly allege a dishonest intent on the part of the respondent it was reasonably clear from the description of the offence that it in substance amounted to a robbery:

> "... the requested person mugged [the injured party] in such a way that by using
> violence involving holding the aggrieved party's arms, they went through his
> pockets and stole his wallet ..."

It would seem that the courts are prepared to draw the appropriate inferences from **10–44** the use of words such as *steal, rob, mug* and indeed from the circumstances as alleged in the warrant. In *Minister for Justice, Equality and Law Reform v Nowakowski*[37] the court similarly inferred from the general circumstances of the offences as described a dishonest intent to deprive the lawful owner of property for the purpose of establishing correspondence with s 4 of the Criminal Justice (Theft and Fraud Offences) Act 2001.

In *Minister for Justice, Equality and Law Reform v Fil*[38] the warrant described the **10–45** respondent as having stolen fuel from a vehicle. Peart J noted that the warrant did not simply allege a *taking* or *misappropriation* but rather it was specifically alleged that the respondent had stolen. In those circumstances the court was entitled to infer a dishonest intent to permanently deprive the owner of the goods and thereby establish correspondence with s 4 of the Criminal Justice (Theft and Fraud Offences) Act 2001. The Court in particular cited the following passage from *Attorney General v Dyer*:

> "Normally words used in an extradition warrant will be given their ordinary
> meaning. This enables the courts to give effect, without resort to extrinsic
> evidence, to extradition requests where words such as "steal", "rob" and
> "murder" are used. It is possible that such words have different meanings in the
> law of the requesting state, but, in the absence of anything like that, the courts
> will examine correspondence by attributing to such words, when used in the
> warrant, the meaning that they would have in Irish law."

The same passage was cited with approval in *Minister for Justice, Equality and Law* **10–46** *Reform v Sas*[39] by Geoghegan J who went on to note:

> "...as I have already indicated, I do not think that it is necessary to set out
> express words indicating mens rea if a word such as "stole" or its cognate

---

[36] [2008] IEHC 377.
[37] [2008] IEHC 439; see also *Minister for Justice Equality and Law Reform v Zukauskas* [2009] IEHC 341 and *Minister for Justice, Equality and Law Reform v Barry* [2009] IEHC 610.
[38] [2009] IEHC 120.
[39] [2010] IESC 16.

equivalent is used. The popular meaning of the word clearly brings in the mens rea."

10–47   In other cases the words used will not be quite so loaded. In *Minister for Justice, Equality and Law Reform v Tomella*[40] the court had to consider whether an allegation that the respondent had obtained goods for which he had not paid in circumstances which included "misleading" the supplier corresponded with s 6 of the Criminal Justice (Theft and Fraud Offences) Act 2001. The warrant did not include any express reference to a dishonest intent. Again, the court drew a distinction between the use of a "neutral" word such as *take* and the use of a more loaded expression such as *mislead*. It had been argued by the respondent that one might mislead either intentionally or unintentionally and that in the absence of any further information on the point it was not possible to conclude that there had been intentional misleading. Peart J concluded that where a word was open to two interpretations the court was entitled to look to the context which was otherwise ascertainable from the warrant for the purpose of deciding which was the appropriate interpretation. In that case the warrant disclosed that the respondent had purported to operate a business which did not employ anyone and did not otherwise respond to correspondence or other attempts to contact him. In those circumstances the court was prepared to adopt the more sinister interpretation of the respondent's motives in misleading the victim and thereby infer the appropriate fraudulent intent.

10–48   It will, however, be difficult for the court to infer a fraudulent intent in the absence of some words which at least go some way towards suggesting one. In *Minister for Justice, Equality and Law Reform v Wroblewski*[41] the offence in the warrant did little more than describe the respondent as having taken the property in question unlawfully. Apart from this there was little other information provided in relation to the offence. The High Court found itself unable to infer the necessary elements of dishonesty, absence of consent of the owner and an intention to deprive the owner permanently thereof from the rather terse description in the warrant. It is particularly noteworthy that the court took the view that the mere assertion of unlawfulness or illegality did not amount to a sufficient basis for inferring a fraudulent intent:

> "It is of no assistance in this regard that the warrant states that the taking of the property in question was respectively "for the purpose of unlawful taking" and "with intent of unlawful taking" because that unlawfulness is according to Polish law only. Such unlawfulness cannot be called in aid to presume into the facts behind the offences, elements of dishonesty, absence of consent of the owner, and an intention to deprive the owner of the property. It cannot simply be presumed that because what he did or is alleged to have done was contrary to the relevant Polish law that the concept of unlawfulness alone is sufficient to find that what he did on those occasions corresponds to 'theft' contrary to s. 4 of the 2001 Act."

10–49   The court went somewhat further in *Minister for Justice, Equality and Law Reform v Voznuka*[42] where the offence in the requesting state comprised as one of its elements the commission of an unlawful act, namely trespass. The court had to consider whether

---

[40] [2008] IEHC 443.
[41] [2008] IEHC 263.
[42] [2009] IEHC 195.

the act which comprised this particular element of the offence would amount to an unlawful act for the purposes of correspondence were it done in this jurisdiction. In that regard it concluded that it must consider the question of lawfulness from the perspective of domestic law as opposed to the law of the requesting state. Ultimately in that case it concluded that the entry in question did amount to a trespass having regard to the decision of *Whelan v Madigan*.[43]

A further example of the somewhat less formal approach to correspondence is **10–50** found in *Minister for Justice, Equality and Law Reform v Hahui*[44] where the warrant set out a description of an offence whereby the respondent had struck the victim with a "contusive tool" knocking him to the ground and had then taken from him a bag containing a large amount of money. It was suggested that the warrant had failed to explicitly state that the assault and theft had taken place without the consent of the injured party and that therefore correspondence with the offence of robbery had not been made out. The court rejected this argument as fanciful and held that the court was entitled to infer the absence of consent on the part of the victim from the circumstances as described in the warrant.

Quite apart from the manner in which the offence is described the different **10–51** manner in which Member States seek to apportion criminal liability in respect of criminal acts can also lead to difficulties. A good example is the case of *Minister for Justice, Equality and Law Reform v Laks*[45] where the respondent had written 13 cheques which, when presented, exceeded the overdraft facility on his bank account. The applicant contended that this set of circumstances corresponded with an offence contrary to s 6 of the Criminal Justice (Theft and Fraud Offences) Act 2001. However, the court took the view that in circumstances where the exceeding of the overdraft arose by virtue of the presentation of all 13 cheques it was not really possible to attribute a fraudulent intent in respect of the writing of all 13 cheques. There may have possibly been a fraudulent intent in respect of one or more of the cheques but the charge was not framed in such a way as to make clear which cheque or cheques had been written fraudulently. Presumably there was nothing unusual about framing charges in such a generic and broad fashion in the requesting state – however in circumstances where an equivalent set of circumstances in this jurisdiction would give rise to an offence a much clearer exposition of the offending behaviour would be required.

The emphasis on conduct for the purposes of establishing correspondence has **10–52** resulted in surrender being ordered even where there is an apparent inconsistency between the nature of the offence in the warrant and the proposed corresponding Irish offence. In *Minister for Justice, Equality and Law Reform v Stanzak*,[46] one of the offences contained in the warrant before the High Court was described as *"hiding a document...that [the respondent] had no right to dispose"*. It was apparent from allegations relating to other offences in the warrant that the respondent was accused of taking this document from a car which he had stolen. However, additional information received from the requesting state made clear that, since he had taken the document for the purposes of hiding it rather than to appropriate it, a theft had not taken place under Polish law. Nonetheless, the Court found that correspondence

---

[43] [1978] ILRM 136.
[44] [2008] IEHC 259.
[45] [2009] IEHC 3.
[46] [2010] IEHC 204.

was established with the offence of possessing stolen property contrary to s 18 of the Criminal Justice (Theft and Fraud Offences) Act 2001, notwithstanding the fact that s 18 did not include any element of "hiding" property, nor was the property "stolen" under the law of the requesting state.

EFFECT OF DEFENCES ON CORRESPONDENCE

10–53 The question as to whether the non-availability of a substantive defence in the requesting state can amount to an absence of correspondence has not been answered by the courts in this jurisdiction in a definitive fashion. Whilst it is to be expected that the courts will be reluctant to enter into any consideration of the merits of a defence which would be available in the State apparent on the face of the warrant, the fact remains that s 5 casts the issue of correspondence very much in terms of whether the *act* complained of would amount to an offence here. On any ordinary or literal interpretation of s 5 it would be difficult to justify discounting such considerations merely on the basis that the alleged lack of correspondence arose by virtue of a substantive defence rather than the terms in which the offence itself is defined.

10–54 In *State (McCaud) v Governor of Mountjoy Prison*[47] the court appeared to at least entertain the possibility that the absence of a substantive defence available in this jurisdiction might be a basis for refusing surrender on the grounds of a lack of correspondence. In that case the prosecutor had been requested by the United States of America under Part II of the 1965 Act [48] in relation to *inter alia* a murder charge. He advanced the argument that, since the New York Penal Code did not provide for the defence of provocation to reduce murder to manslaughter, the crime of murder in the State of New York did not correspond to the crime of murder under Irish law. Egan J commented that he might have been influenced by such an argument if he had had before him an affidavit from an expert in American law stating that provocation would never be sufficient to reduce murder to manslaughter. However, in rejecting the argument, he pointed out that there was equally no specific Irish statutory provision relating to provocation, and it may well be that case-law exists in the US providing for such a defence:

> "The Statute goes on to enumerate two affirmative defences none of which are applicable to the facts of this case. I have considered the express wording of the statute itself as [Counsel] advanced an argument on behalf of the prosecutor that there did not appear to be complete identity between the crime of murder in this country and that of murder in the United States of America. He argued that in certain circumstances proof of provocation could reduce murder to manslaughter in this country whereas the same would not be so in the U.S. There is no express reference to this factor in Mr. Quinlan's affidavit nor can I find it dealt with specifically in the extracts from the Statutory Code exhibited. It must be said, however, that there is no statutory provision in this country either relevant to provocation and it may well be that case law exists in the U.S.

---

[47] [1985] 1 IR 68.

[48] At that time correspondence was governed by the provisions of s 10(3) of the Extradition Act 1965 which provided: "In this section references to an offence punishable under the laws of the State shall be construed as including references to an act which, if it had been committed in the State, would constitute such an offence". Substantively the test to be applied was similar to that under the 2003 Act.

> to the same effect. I might have been influenced by [Counsel's] argument if an affidavit had been sworn on behalf of the prosecutor by an expert on American law stating that provocation would never be sufficient to reduce murder to manslaughter but I leave open the question as to whether or not I might still have required some proof or averment that the question of provocation was relevant to the charge in this case. In the end result, the argument is rejected."

The approach of the court in *McCaud* is obviously problematic in that it did **10–55** not approach the question of correspondence on the basis of the act alleged but rather on the basis of the specific legislative provisions in the requesting state. In this regard the decision must be viewed in the context of the confusion as to the correct approach arising from the decision of the Supreme Court in *The State (Furlong) v Kelly*.[49] It would appear from the passage quoted above that there was nothing to suggest that provocation was in any sense a live issue in the case and the court left it open as to whether it would have to be shown that it was in issue before an objection to correspondence on the basis of the absence of a substantive defence of provocation could be raised. Applying the more correct conduct based test of correspondence it would seem that as a first step the court would have to regard the substantive defence as having been made out in the warrant, or from some other source, before addressing the more difficult question as to the consequences of the absence of such a substantive defence in the requesting state.

In *Harris v Wren*,[50] it was argued that the English offence of indecent assault **10–56** did not correspond with that under Irish law, since consent was a defence available in England only where the alleged victim was 16 years of age or more at the time, whereas Irish law prohibited consent as a defence only where the alleged victim was under 15 years of age. Finlay P found firstly that he was not entitled to take judicial notice of the legal situation in England, nor had any expert evidence been adduced to prove it. Furthermore, he was not convinced that a lack of parity in the extent of the consent defence available in the different jurisdictions precluded correspondence:

> "Even if it were established by proper proof to my satisfaction that upon being tried on this charge the Plaintiff would be in the event of the offence being established as having occurred whilst the injured party was under 16 years of age be deprived of a defence which he would have in this country on the same set of facts it would not in my view have led me to the conclusion that this was not a corresponding offence. The word contained in the Act of 1965 is corresponding and it is not necessary to establish total identity".

Whilst the possibility that the absence of a substantive defence might lead to a **10–57** want of correspondence was entertained at some length in *McCaud* the opposite approach appears to have been taken in *Harris v Wren* albeit not on the basis of any particularly detailed consideration of the issue. A similarly brief consideration was given to the issue under the 2003 Act in *Minister for Justice, Equality and Law Reform v Walas*[51] where the court concluded that the fact that there exists in this

---

[49] *supra*, n 25.
[50] [1984] ILRM 120.
[51] [2009] IEHC 129.

jurisdiction a specific statutory defence in relation to an equivalent domestic offence that is regulatory in character but which does not arise in relation to the offence as defined in the requesting state will not matter. In other words the description of the offence in the warrant cannot be expected to negative possible statutory defences to corresponding domestic offences.

10–58   It is difficult to fault such an approach in relation to the finer points of technical defences that might arise in the context of a regulatory offence, but the position is much less clear when the defence relates to an important substantive element of the offence. It is not difficult to imagine a situation arising in relation to, for example, an allegation of sexual assault where it was clear from the warrant that the complainant who was above the age of 15 but less than 17 had actually consented to the sexual contact. Whilst such conduct might well be an offence in the requesting state where the age of consent in relation to sexual contact (as opposed to sexual intercourse) is higher, it is quite clear that it is not an offence in this jurisdiction. In such a situation it is difficult to see how a court could conclude that such an offence "would, if committed in the State...constitute an offence under the law of the State".

10–59   Even more troublesome is the prospect of a similar situation where the fact of consent is not apparent on the face of the warrant but is something which is in dispute. In that event the warrant will presumably allege conduct which would amount to an offence in the State in that it will allege sexual contact without consent, but the fact remains that the respondent faces the prospect of surrender and ultimately conviction not on the basis of the absence of consent as alleged in the warrant but rather irrespective of the absence of consent. In other words the respondent may be surrendered on the basis that the conduct alleged corresponds but in due course be convicted on the basis of conduct which does not correspond to an offence. The courts have yet to deal with this difficult issue in a comprehensive manner.

CORRESPONDENCE IN RELATION TO PENALTY

10–60   It is a notable feature of the provisions relating to correspondence that they do not contain any minimum gravity requirement in relation to the domestic offence in respect of which the comparison is made. In other words it is not necessary to show that the domestic offence which is said to correspond to the offence in the warrant carries a penalty of a particular level. Therefore whilst the offence contained in the warrant may be very serious, correspondence will nonetheless be made out if it can be shown that the same act would be criminal in this jurisdiction albeit in circumstances where the domestic offence was of an altogether less serious nature. A good example is the case of *Minister for Justice, Equality and Law Reform v Ward*[52] where the respondent had been charged with an offence of "causing death by causing another to drive a mechanically propelled vehicle dangerously" in the United Kingdom. Although the offence bore similarities to the domestic offence of causing death by dangerous driving it, was not possible to make out correspondence largely on the basis that the respondent had not actually been driving the vehicle which had been in a dangerous condition. Instead the court found that there was correspondence with the summary offence of being the owner of a defective vehicle

---

[52] [2008] IEHC 53.

which was being driven in a public place contrary to s 54(2) of the Road Traffic Act 1961. Whilst it may seem somewhat incongruous to compare offences which are so disparate in terms of seriousness it would, nonetheless, appear to be a legitimate exercise.

The fact that a higher penalty may be imposed on the respondent by virtue of him **10–61** or her having a previous conviction for the same offence does not go to the issue of correspondence. In *Minister for Justice, Equality and Law Reform v Koncis*[53] it was clear from the warrant that in the case of a person who had a previous conviction for robbery a higher penalty could be imposed. The court rejected the argument that this amounted to an additional element of the offence in respect of which correspondence had to be shown, namely an equivalent aggravation of penalty in relation to a domestic offence. Whilst similar provisions are relatively rare in this jurisdiction they are not unknown.[54]

In general it is true to say that so far as the issue of correspondence is **10–62** concerned the courts will, by and large, be unconcerned in relation to the question of penalty. This is because the issue of correspondence relates solely to the criminal act alleged and not to other surrounding circumstances which may have an effect on sentence. In *Minister for Justice, Equality and Law Reform v Pavlovs*[55] the respondent was sought in Lithuania for a drunk driving offence. The warrant, however, disclosed that because he had been convicted of a similar offence in the preceding 12 months he would be subject to a prison sentence of up to one year. It was argued that in reality he was being sought in respect of a type of compound offence which did not correspond with any offence known to Irish law. The court dealt with this argument by simply asking the question as to whether, had the act complained of been done in this jurisdiction, an offence would have been committed. Given that the answer to this was in the affirmative, there was correspondence of offences and the issue of the previous conviction aggravating the potential sentence to be imposed was not pertinent to the issue of correspondence.

CORRESPONDENCE AND REVENUE OFFENCES

Traditionally it was extremely difficult to succeed in extraditing a fugitive for revenue **10–63** offences on the basis that to do so would amount to one state acting as tax collector for another state. This was thought to amount to an affront to the sovereignty of the requested state. The principle found rather blunt expression in s 13 of the Extradition Act 1965 as originally passed which provided that "extradition shall not be granted for revenue offences".

The position has changed very considerably since that time with many treaties **10–64** now providing for extradition for revenue offences and s 13 of the Extradition Act

---

[53] [2006] IEHC 379.

[54] s 3 of the Misuse of Drugs Act 1977 insofar as it relates to cannabis provides for higher penalties for those with previous convictions. Similarly s 15A of the same act provides for a more stringent sentencing regime in the case of those who have previous convictions under that section.

[55] [2007] IEHC 363.

1965 has been amended to allow for extradition for such offences if the relevant treaty allows for it.[56]

10–65   Neither the Framework Decision nor the 2003 Act purport to preclude surrender in the case of revenue offences. Not only would it seem that revenue offences are very much intended to come within the ambit of the European arrest warrant but both the Framework Decision and the Act make special provision in relation to how the court should approach the issue of correspondence in relation to such cases. Section 38(2) provides:

> "The surrender of a person to an issuing state under this Act shall not be refused on the ground that, in relation to a revenue offence –
>
> (a)   no tax or duty of the kind to which the offence relates is imposed in the State, or
>
> (b)   the rules relating to taxes, duties, customs or exchange control that apply in the issuing state differ in nature from the rules that apply in the State to taxes, duties, customs or exchange control."

10–66   Section 38(3) provides a definition of "revenue offence" in the following terms:

> "In this section "revenue offence" means, in relation to an issuing state an offence in connection with taxes, duties, customs or exchange control."[57]

10–67   Because the non-payment of tax or duty involves the breach of a purely legal duty it is by definition necessary for the court to consider, to some extent, the fact of that legal duty for the purpose of establishing correspondence. Notwithstanding that consideration of the law of the requesting state in the context of correspondence is generally deprecated, revenue offences are best regarded as a special case in that the effect of s 38(2) is in substance to allow the court to assume that the same legal provisions that give rise to the tax and the rules which are used to calculate and levy the extent of the liability also apply within the State. The court then goes on to consider whether if, for the sake of the exercise, the same tax, calculated and levied on the same basis, were to apply

---

[56]   s 13 as substituted by s 13 of the Extradition (European Union Conventions) Act 2001 now provides: "Extradition shall not be granted for revenue offences unless the relevant extradition provisions otherwise provide".

[57]   The definition of a "revenue offence" provided for by s 3(1) of the Extradition Act 1965 as substituted by s 13 of the Extradition (European Union Conventions) Act 2001 is considerably more elaborate:

> "revenue offence, in relation to any country or place outside the State, means an offence in connection with taxes, duties, customs or exchange control but does not include an offence involving the use or threat of force or perjury or the forging of a document issued under statutory authority or an offence alleged to have been committed by an officer of the revenue of that country or place in his capacity as such officer or an offence within the scope of Article 3 of the United Nations Convention Against Illicit Traffic in Narcotic Drugs and Psychotropic Substances done at Vienna on the 20th day of December, 1988".

here, the respondent would also have committed an offence here had he acted in the manner set out in the warrant.

Whilst it is not explicit in s 38(2)(b), it would seem to follow as a matter of logic **10–68** that the "rules" referred to therein can only be a reference to rules associated with the calculation of the amount of tax, when it arises, payable by the person who is liable. It presumably cannot refer to "rules" which give rise to criminal liability. Were it do so it would never be necessary to establish correspondence in the first place.

DETERMINING CORRESPONDENCE FROM THE WARRANT

As is apparent from the standard form of the European arrest warrant, it is designed **10–69** to be a document which provides all of the information necessary for the judicial authority in a requested state to make a decision as to surrender. In that regard s 11(1A)(f) requires that the European arrest warrant specify:

> "...the circumstances in which the offence was committed or is alleged to have been committed, including the time and place of its commission or alleged commission, and the degree of involvement or alleged degree of involvement of the person in the commission of the offence."

Any argument concerning correspondence is likely to be based upon the information **10–70** provided under this heading. This requirement finds expression in para (e) of the standard form of the European arrest warrant as appended to the Framework Decision.

The amount of detail required in relation to the circumstances of the commission **10–71** of the alleged offence in a European arrest warrant is considerably more extensive than in an extradition request made under Part II of the 1965 Act, s 25(1)(b) of which requires:

> "...a statement of each offence for which extradition is requested specifying, as accurately as possible, the time and place of the commission, its legal description and a reference to the relevant legal provisions of the law of the requesting country."

In effect, a request under Part II need only give as much detail as might be found in **10–72** an indictment, and this can give rise to difficulties when considering correspondence, particularly when attempting to apply a conduct-based test. In contrast, the standard form European arrest warrant, contained in the Annex to the Framework Decision, requires a very significant amount of information to be provided in relation to the circumstances surrounding the offence. As a result the court will generally have before it an account of the events leading up to and subsequent to the commission of the offence. From this account, the court will examine the alleged acts of the requested person and identify whether such acts, if performed in the State on the date on which the warrant was issued, would constitute an offence under the law of the State.

When one compares the provisions of the European Arrest Warrant Act 2003 and **10–73** the Extradition Act 1965 it is at once clear that the amount of information contained in the European arrest warrant is much greater than was traditionally the case in relation to extradition under Parts II and III of the 1965 Act. One of the principal reasons that correspondence issues arose with such frequency particularly in relation to Part III of the Extradition Act 1965 appears to have been a degree of reticence in relation to the level of detail provided in such warrants. Frequently it was not possible to glean much information as to what it was that was alleged against the fugitive. It was necessary to *"dress up"*[58] warrants prior to their being endorsed for execution in order that they would contain sufficient particulars to allow the courts here to come to a view that the offence alleged corresponded with an offence in this jurisdiction. In many ways the necessity to dress up the warrant arose because an arrest warrant, the function of which historically was to do little more than state in a minimalist way the barest outlines of an allegation, was being used as the principal means to convey what might be quite detailed information to the Irish courts in order to allow them to be satisfied as to correspondence. This difficulty is much less pronounced in the case of a European arrest warrant.

10-74   Whilst most of the authorities on the issue of correspondence in relation to the 1965 Act deal with the consequences of providing inadequate particulars of the offence, one of the novel difficulties which the format of the European arrest warrant throws up is the problem of actually identifying the offence which should be the subject of the correspondence inquiry. It is not unusual for European arrest warrants to contain several pages of narrative in relation to the alleged offence before citing a relatively anonymous provision of the relevant penal code. In such situations it is often exceedingly difficult to actually extract the portion of the narrative which relates to the offence. This would not of itself be a difficulty if the warrant clearly indicated which parts of the narrative identified the actual offence and which parts simply referred to incidental matters. A warrant in respect of one offence may set out a narrative of events which discloses a number of distinct and separate criminal offences under Irish law. However, unless the court is told which of the possibly numerous offences is the one in respect of which surrender is sought, it will not be able to assess whether or not correspondence exists.

---

[58] See the decision of Walsh J in *Wyatt v McLoughlin* [1974] 1 IR 378 at 395:

> "I should like first to deal with what I might call the"dressing up" point. The gist of this submission is that if this charge were not one for which extradition was being sought its wording would have been quite different. The basis of this submission is that English law does not require the proof of the ingredients set out in the charge. Be that as it may, and I am not saying whether English law does so or not because, for the reasons I shall later deal with, this Court and any other court in proceedings such as these is not at all concerned with the construction of English law. It appears to me to be quite clear that the wording of the charge as laid in the warrant identifies it with the offence of simple larceny in this country. It is quite clear that the charge was drafted by following, word for word, what I said such a warrant ought to contain in the course of my judgment in *Furlong's Case* at p. 144 of the report. Whether such wording is or is not necessary in England is a matter the Court need not concern itself with and is quite irrelevant. The District Court here has to be satisfied that an offence laid in a warrant sent here and endorsed for execution is so stated as to be recognizable as corresponding with an offence under our law. It must, therefore, contain such essential factual material as may be necessary to recognize whether or not the acts complained of are ones which, if committed in this country, would amount to a criminal offence."

The converse of this situation may also throw up difficulties. In *Minister for* **10–75** *Justice, Equality and Law Reform v Wawrzyniak*[59] the respondent was sought in relation to an offence of "tormenting" his spouse. The warrant alleged conduct of different sorts over a protracted period of time. Some of the conduct, in the form of physical assaults, clearly corresponded with criminal offences in the State, whilst other parts of the conduct, in the nature of verbal abuse and unkindness, did not. The court concluded that so long as some part of the criminal act alleged corresponded, this would be sufficient:

> "The reason behind the rule regarding correspondence in extradition matters is so that the requested state can make sure that a person whose surrender is sought does not face prosecution for, or a sentence to be served in respect of, an act or acts which is not an offence in the requested state. I am of the view that if one looks at the description of the tormenting offence in this warrant a person here, including me, would clearly recognise the acts said to have given rise to the 'tormenting' as being criminal acts under Irish law, such as s. 3 assault. I think that it is also relevant to draw attention to the way in which s. 5 is worded. The Court by reference to that section looks at the facts contained in the warrant and if any one or more of those acts would constitute "an offence" in this State that is sufficient. It does not have to be "the offence" i.e. the same offence as that committed in the issuing state."

SEVERABILITY OF NON-CORRESPONDING OFFENCES

A difficulty may arise where the warrant relates to multiple offences and there is **10–76** no correspondence in relation to at least one. In such circumstances s 17 allows the court to essentially sever the warrant and order surrender in relation to the corresponding offences:

> "Where, in relation to an offence specified in a European arrest warrant the High Court decides not to make an order under Section 15 or 16, it shall not be necessary for the issuing judicial authority to issue another European arrest warrant in respect of such other offences as are specified in that warrant, and, where such other offences are specified in the European arrest warrant, that warrant shall be treated as having been issued in respect of those other offences only."

Section 17, however, is predicated on the assumption that it is possible to distinguish **10–77** between the various offences. Frequently it is not. The respondent in *Minister for Justice, Equality and Law Reform v Kondratevas*[60] had been sentenced in Lithuania in respect of two offences. The first was a "ticked" offence pursuant to Art 2(2) of the Framework Decision, and as such, there was no requirement to show correspondence. However, in respect of the other offence, which was not "ticked" and concerned the purchase and storage of a quantity of "denatured ethyl alcohol", the applicant conceded that there was no corresponding offence in the State – as such surrender was prohibited in respect of the latter offence. The High Court noted that an immediate difficulty arose as a result of the manner in which the respondent had been sentenced in the issuing state:

---

[59] [2009] IEHC 381.
[60] [2006] IEHC 456.

> "The warrant discloses that in the absence of the respondent the sentence of two years and six months was imposed together with a fine of LTL 3, 750 on the 27th August 2003 and that this punishment is *the combined sentence of imprisonment imposed on him for both crimes*". This phrase is underlined and highlighted in the text of the warrant. In the warrant there is no indication of any division of the period of the sentence as between the two offences".

10–78   The Minister had sought clarification from the Lithuanian authorities regarding the sentence imposed in respect of each offence, but the reply merely stated that the sentence of two years and six months satisfied the minimum gravity requirement for the purposes of Art 2.1 of the Framework Decision. This did little to resolve the difficulty as the court found itself in a position where it could not be satisfied that the respondent would be required to serve only the sentence imposed in relation to the corresponding offence:

> "[T]he surrender of the respondent is sought so that he can serve one sentence of which two years and four months or thereabouts remains to be served, imposed in respect of one offence for which there is no corresponding offence in this State. This Court is not permitted to surrender a person for an offence unless satisfied that it corresponds to an offence here. This is clear from the clear meaning of s. 38 of the Act which I have set forth.
>
> Since it is not possible to sever the offences by reference to a period of the sentence imposed which is applicable to the non-corresponding offence, so that surrender could be ordered so that the respondent would return to serve only a sentence for the offence in respect of which correspondence does not require verification, the Court must refuse to order surrender on this ground".

10–79   The High Court essentially saw the problem as engaging the rule of specialty – the respondent would have to serve a sentence in respect of an offence for which he was not surrendered (i.e. the non-corresponding offence).

10–80   A similar view was taken in *Minister for Justice, Equality and Law Reform v Ferenca*.[61] A sentence of two years and nine months had been imposed in relation to three offences one of which did not correspond. The warrant did not indicate how much of the sentence related to the non-corresponding offence and as such Murray CJ concluded that the court was not in a position to order surrender:

> "As I pointed out at the outset and which is clear from the terms of the European arrest warrant, the sentence imposed is a single sentence, what one might call a composite sentence, imposed for the three offences collectively. If the appellant were to be surrendered to serve that sentence he would be surrendered to serve a sentence which was in part imposed for the first offence. I have already concluded above that the first offence is an offence for which s. 38(1) says the appellant should not be surrendered. There is obviously no basis on which this Court can apportion part of the sentence of two years and nine months among the three offences so that he could be surrendered for the purpose of serving the amount of the sentence which related to the second and third offence."[62]

---

[61]   [2008] 4 IR 480.

[62]   p 498.

In relation to the possibility of invoking the provisions of s 17 Murray CJ noted: **10–81**

> "That section is clearly only intended to apply where the request in relation to
> each offence in the warrant is distinct and separate."[63]

A similar conclusion was reached in *Minister for Justice, Equality and Law Reform v*   **10–82**
Kizelavicius.[64] Interestingly, some authority in the United Kingdom suggests that surrender
can be ordered even where a composite sentence had been imposed in respect of two or
more offences and one of those offences was not an *"extradition offence"* under UK
law because it did not satisfy the dual criminality requirement. This was the situation in
Kucera v District Court of Karvina, Czech Republic,[65] where the Queen's Bench Division
ordered surrender for only one of two offences in respect of which a composite sentence
had been imposed. This approach raises obvious problems in relation to specialty, as it
would seem to necessitate the surrendered person serving a composite sentence imposed
in part in respect of an offence for which surrender was not ordered. The court in *Kucera*
did not face this particular difficulty however, as information received from the Czech
authorities indicated that a re-sentencing would take place should the requested person
be surrendered, and it was presumed that the Czech court would honour the relevant
specialty requirements.

EXAMPLES OF CORRESPONDING OFFENCES

Precedent is of obvious value for the purpose of demonstrating correspondence or   **10–83**
its absence in a given case. Below are examples of cases where correspondence has
been considered in relation to various different types of offence. It should be noted
that some of the decisions cited below were subsequently overturned on appeal but
on grounds unrelated to the issue of correspondence.

Assault

Minister for Justice, Equality and Law Reform v M(M)[66]: Causing "grievous bodily   **10–84**
harm" was held to correspond with an offence under s 3 of the Non-Fatal Offences
Against the Person Act 1997.

    Minister for Justice, Equality and Law Reform v Paulauskas[67]: Stabbing causing   **10–85**
"serious health impairment" was found to correspond to an offence under either s 3
or s 4 of the Non-Fatal Offences Against the Person Act 1997.

    Minister for Justice, Equality and Law Reform v Dolny[68]: There was no express   **10–86**
statement in the warrant that the victim of the alleged assault did not consent to
it. Correspondence with an offence under s 3 of the 1997 Act was found to exist
nonetheless, as absence of consent is not an essential ingredient of that offence,
unlike an offence under s 2 of the Non-Fatal Offences Against the Person Act 1997.

---

[63] p 499.
[64] [2009] IESC 74.
[65] [2009] 1 WLR 806.
[66] [2007] IEHC 443.
[67] [2009] IEHC 32.
[68] [2009] IESC 48.

10–87   *Minister for Justice, Equality and Law Reform v Wawrzyniak*[69]: The respondent had been convicted of the Polish offence of "tormenting" his spouse. The description of acts constituting this offence included punches to the face and offensive language. Correspondence was made out with an offence of assault causing harm under s 3 of the Non-Fatal Offences Against the Person Act 1997.

Conspiracy to Defraud Contrary to Common Law (UK)

10–88   *Minister for Justice, Equality and Law Reform v Fallon*[70]: Correspondence was established with the offence of conspiracy to defraud contrary to common law in this jurisdiction which, it was held, had not been abolished by the enactment of s 3 of the Criminal Justice (Theft and Fraud Offences) Act 2001.

Conspiracy to Commit an Offence (UK)

10–89   *Minister for Justice, Equality and Law Reform v Tighe*[71]: Correspondence was made out with the offence of conspiracy to commit an offence contrary to common law.

Drugs

10–90   *Minister for Justice, Equality and Law Reform v Nowakowski*[72]: "Sharing" drugs with another was found to correspond with the offence of supply of drugs under s 15 of the Misuse of Drugs Act 1977.

Drunk Driving

10–91   *Minister for Justice, Equality and Law Reform v Serdiuk*[73]: The respondent was alleged to have had 310mg of alcohol per 100ml of his blood while driving, contrary to Polish law. It was argued that there was no corresponding Irish offence since the relevant time for the blood/alcohol reading under s 49(2) of the Road Traffic Act 1961 was within three hours of driving rather than at the time of driving, in contrast to the Polish offence. Unsurprisingly the court rejected this argument and found that correspondence was made out with s 49(2) of the 1961 Act.

10–92   *Minister for Justice, Equality and Law Reform v Pavlovs*[74]: Correspondence was made out with an offence under s 49 of the Road Traffic Act 1961.

Escape from Lawful Custody Contrary to Common Law (UK)

10–93   *Minister for Justice, Equality and Law Reform v Brennan*[75]: The offence of escape contrary to common law was found to correspond to the same offence in this jurisdiction.

10–94   *Minister for Justice, Equality and Law Reform v Breen*[76]: No distinction was drawn between escape from a normal prison and leaving an "open prison" for the purposes of the offence of escape from lawful custody contrary to common law.

---

[69] [2009] IEHC 381 (affirmed *ex tempore* on appeal).
[70] [2005] IEHC 323.
[71] [2009] IEHC 33.
[72] [2008] IEHC 439.
[73] [2010] IEHC 242.
[74] [2007] IEHC 363.
[75] [2006] IEHC 94.
[76] [2008] IEHC 54.

Failing to Answer Bail

Minister for Justice, Equality and Law Reform v Brennan[77]: The offence of failing   **10–95**
to answer bail was found to correspond to an offence under s 13 of the Criminal
Justice Act 1984.

   Minister for Justice, Equality and Law Reform v McDonagh[78]: Correspondence   **10–96**
was made out with an offence under s 13 of the Criminal Justice Act 1984.

Forgery/Using a False Instrument

Minister for Justice, Equality and Law Reform v Ferenca[79]: The respondent was   **10–97**
accused of being an accessory to the production of a forged instrument, by handing
a bank card to someone who then forged it. It was held that correspondence was
not made out with an offence under s 25(1) of the Criminal Justice (Theft and
Fraud Offences) Act 2001 as there was no allegation that the respondent played any
part in the act of forging. In relation to another offence alleged in the warrant, the
respondent had attempted to purchase a digital camera using a credit card which he
knew to be forged. Correspondence was found to exist with an offence under s 26 of
the Criminal Justice (Theft and Fraud Offences) Act 2001.

   Minister for Justice, Equality and Law Reform v LG[80]: The respondent was alleged   **10–98**
to have cut off the end of genuine receipts in order to create false instruments. It was
held that correspondence was made out with an offence under s 25(1) of the Criminal
Justice (Theft and Fraud Offences) Act 2001 – the definition of "false instrument" in
s 30 of the 2001 Act was relied upon.

   Minister for Justice, Equality and Law Reform v Nowakowski[81]: Correspondence   **10–99**
was made out with an offence under s 25(1) of the Criminal Justice (Theft and
Fraud) Offences Act 2001 where the respondent was alleged to have replaced the
original owner's photo in a bus pass with his own in order to use it himself.

Handling Stolen Goods

Minister for Justice, Equality and Law Reform v Nowakowski[82]: Correspondence   **10–100**
was made out with s 17 of the Criminal Justice (Theft and Fraud Offences) Act
2001 where the respondent was alleged to have bought a bicycle "from theft" in
circumstances where he might have thought it was obtained through unlawful
activity.

"Hiding" a Document

Minister for Justice, Equality and Law Reform v Nowakowski[83]: There was held to   **10–101**
be no corresponding offence where the respondent had been convicted of "hiding
driving licence...issued to [another] acting thus to his detriment".

---

[77] [2006] IEHC 94.
[78] *Ex tempore*, High Court, 11 July 2007, Peart J.
[79] [2007] IEHC 199.
[80] [2005] IEHC 310.
[81] [2008] IEHC 439.
[82] *ibid.*
[83] *ibid.*

10–102   However, in *Minister for Justice, Equality and Law Reform v Stanzak*[84] a different conclusion was reached where there was additional information which allowed the court to conclude that what was alleged was more in the nature of handling stolen property.

Indecent Assault on a Female/Indecency with a Child (UK)

10–103   *Minister for Justice, Equality and Law Reform v S(JS)*[85]: The conduct alleged in the warrant constituting "indecent assault on a female" was found to correspond with an offence under s 2 of the Criminal Law (Rape) (Amendment) Act 1990. However, the conduct said to amount to the separate offence of "indecency with a child" was found not to correspond with s 12 of the Children Act 1908 nor with any other offence.

Infringement of Copyright

10–104   *Minister for Justice, Equality and Law Reform v Hogyi*[86]: The European arrest warrant related to a number of copyright offences. Section 140(1) of the Copyright and Related Rights Act 2000 provides for an offence where the accused, *inter alia*, infringes copyright in the course of business or makes available to the public material gained by way of copyright infringement. It was held that such conduct could not be inferred from the facts in the warrant in this case.

Making Gain or Causing Loss by Deception

10–105   *Minister for Justice, Equality and Law Reform v Ferenca*[87]: An attempt to knowingly use a forged instrument was found to correspond with the offence at common law of attempting to commit an offence under s 6 of the Criminal Justice (Theft and Fraud Offences) Act 2001.

10–106   *Minister for Justice, Equality and Law Reform v Laks*[88]: No correspondence was found to exist with an offence under s 6 of the Criminal Justice (Theft and Fraud Offences) Act 2001 where the conduct consisted of writing cheques which caused a bank overdraft limit to be exceeded. The respondent had cashed some of the cheques himself, but it was unclear which cheques had breached the overdraft limit.

10–107   *Minister for Justice, Equality and Law Reform v Tomella*[89]: It was held that the word "misled" can in some instances imply dishonesty and in others have no such implication and that in such a case the court was entitled to choose the appropriate meaning in the context of the facts contained in the warrant. In this case, correspondence was made out with an offence under s 6 of the Criminal Justice (Theft and Fraud Offences) Act 2001 where the respondent was alleged to have "misled" a vendor about his intention to pay for purchased cement.

---

[84] [2010] IEHC 204.
[85] [2006] IEHC 403. See also *Minister for Justice, Equality and Law Reform v SR*, unreported, High Court, 15 November 2005, Peart J.
[86] [2006] IEHC 373.
[87] [2007] IEHC 199.
[88] [2009] IEHC 3.
[89] [2008] IEHC 443.

Minister for Justice, Equality and Law Reform v Desjatnikovs[90]: The respondent **10–108** was alleged to have taken money "for his own economic needs" from the cash desk in the pawnshop where he worked, and to have filled out dockets in relation to this, confirming that he was the recipient of the money, which was never repaid. It was held that, although a civil action might lie in such circumstances in this jurisdiction, no correspondence with either Section s 4 or Section s 6 of the Criminal Justice (Theft and Fraud Offences) Act 2001 was made out as no dishonest intent was evident. This finding was upheld on appeal.

Negligent Accounting in the Course of a Business

Minister for Justice, Equality and Law Reform v Busjeva[91]: Correspondence found **10–109** with an offence under s 202 of the Companies Act 1990.

Perverting the Course of Justice

Minister for Justice, Equality and Law Reform v Hill[92]: Correspondence was **10–110** found with the equivalent Irish common law offence of perverting the course of justice.

Minister for Justice, Equality and Law Reform v Ward[93]: A positive act was **10–111** required in order for correspondence with the common law offence of perverting the course of justice to be made out. In this case, the giving of a misleading statement in relation to a road accident in which information was withheld constituted a positive act and correspondence was made out.

Possession of Alcohol

Minister for Justice, Equality and Law Reform v Kondratevas[94]: The respondent **10–112** was alleged to have bought and stored "denatured ethyl alcohol". No corresponding offence was found in this jurisdiction.

Public Order

Minister for Justice, Equality and Law Reform v Kasprowicz[95]: The respondent **10–113** was sought for an offence of insulting a police officer alleged in the following terms:

> "On 27th November 2005 in Stara Wisnlowa, having been placed in a police patrol car, he insulted [named police officers] by using vulgar and scurrilous words towards them while they were carrying out their official duties."

The only candidate offence for the purposes of establishing correspondence was s 6 of the Criminal Justice (Public Order) Act 1994. It was held that not only did

---

[90] [2007] IEHC 332.
[91] [2007] 3 IR 829.
[92] [2009] IEHC 159.
[93] [2008] IEHC 53.
[94] [2006] IEHC 456.
[95] [2010] IEHC 207.

the offence fail the correspondence test on the grounds that the alleged offence did not occur in a public place but also that conduct amounting to insulting another was insufficient for the purposes of establishing criminal conduct in this jurisdiction.

Removing Chassis Number from Vehicle

10–114   *Minister for Justice, Equality and Law Reform v Walas*[96]: Correspondence was made out with the offence of breach of ministerial regulation under s 139 of the Finance Act 1992. The fact that the respondent might have a defence open to him in the issuing state was not relevant to the issue of correspondence.

Road Traffic Offences

10–115   *Minister for Justice, Equality and Law Reform v Tobin*[97]: The fact that the Irish driving offence to which the conduct alleged in the warrant corresponds may be seen as less serious than the offence charged in the issuing state does not preclude correspondence being made out. In this case, it was held that conduct could correspond to a number of different Irish road traffic offences.

10–116   *Minister for Justice, Equality and Law Reform v Ward*[98]: Correspondence was not made out with the Irish offence of counselling or procuring the offence of dangerous driving where the respondent, the owner of the vehicle alleged to have been driven dangerously, was not actually said to have been aware of any defects in the vehicle. However, correspondence was made out with a more minor offence under s 54(2) of the Road Traffic Act 1961. It was not relevant that the corresponding offence was summary in nature.

10–117   *Minister for Justice, Equality and Law Reform v Anderson*[99]: There was held to be no meaningful distinction to be drawn between "driving while disqualified" and the Irish offence of driving without a licence. Correspondence was made out.

Robbery

10–118   *Minister for Justice, Equality and Law Reform v Hahui*[100]: Inferences were drawn from the facts outlined in the warrant enabling correspondence to be made out with an offence under s 14 of the Criminal Justice (Theft and Fraud Offences) Act 2001, notwithstanding the absence of an express reference to dishonest intent or absence of consent.

10–119   *Minister for Justice, Equality and Law Reform v Mazurkiewicz*[101]: Correspondence was made out with an offence under s 14 of the Criminal Justice (Theft and Fraud Offences) Act 2001 notwithstanding the absence of an express reference in the warrant to any dishonest intent or intention to deprive the owner of the property.

---

[96] [2009] IEHC 129.
[97] [2008] 4 IR 42.
[98] [2008] IEHC 53.
[99] [2006] IEHC 95.
[100] [2008] IEHC 259.
[101] [2008] IEHC 377.

These elements of the offence could be inferred from the facts outlined, as well as from the use of the word "stole".

Theft

Minister for Justice, Equality and Law Reform v Dunkova[102]: The warrant alleged that the respondent "took away" money belonging to the victim. Correspondence was not made out with an offence under s 4 of the Criminal Justice (Theft and Fraud Offences) Act 2001 as there was no allegation or implication that money was taken without the consent of the owner and with the intention of depriving the owner of it.   **10–120**

Minister for Justice, Equality and Law Reform v Wroblewski[103]: An allegation of "unlawful taking" in the warrant was not sufficient to establish correspondence with the offence of theft under s 4 of the Criminal Justice (Theft and Fraud Offences) Act 2001.   **10–121**

Threat to Kill or Cause Serious Harm

Minister for Justice, Equality and Law Reform v Machevicius[104]: It was clear from the facts in the warrant that it was alleged that the respondent intended the threat to be believed. Correspondence was made out with s 5 of the Non-Fatal Offences Against the Person Act 1997.   **10–122**

Trespass

Minister for Justice, Equality and Law Reform v Slonski[105]: It was alleged that the respondent broke the door of a shop and was scared away by an alarm. Correspondence was made out with an offence under s 11 of the Criminal Justice (Public Order) Act 1994 despite the absence of an express reference to "trespass" in the warrant.   **10–123**

Minister for Justice, Equality and Law Reform v Voznuka[106]: Inferences from facts outlined in the warrant enabled correspondence to be made out with an offence under s 11 of the Criminal Justice (Public Order) Act 1994.   **10–124**

Unlawful Fishing

Minister for Justice, Equality and Law Reform v Wroblewski[107]: Correspondence was made out with an offence under s 95(1) of the Fisheries Consolidation Act 1959 (although minimum gravity was not satisfied).   **10–125**

---

[102] [2008] IEHC 156.
[103] [2008] IEHC 263.
[104] [2007] IEHC 78.
[105] [2009] IEHC 116.
[106] [2009] IEHC 195.
[107] [2008] IEHC 263.

CHAPTER 11

Minimum Gravity

It goes without saying that European arrest warrant proceedings can cause **11–01** considerable disruption to the life of a requested person. Furthermore, the arrest and detention of requested persons, as well as applications to court for surrender, inevitably involve a significant financial cost to the executing State. In view of this, the Framework Decision, in common with most other systems of rendition or extradition, provides for surrender only in respect of non-trivial offences. This has long been a feature of extradition arrangements[1] and can best be regarded as a feature of the principle of proportionality. Both the 2003 Act and the Framework Decision provide that a person may only be surrendered where the offence in question meets the relevant minimum gravity requirement which is prescribed in relation to that particular category of offence.

SECTION 38

Section 38(1) of the 2003 Act lays out the minimum gravity requirements that must **11–02** be satisfied. The test is expressed in negative terms and requires that the requested person shall not be surrendered unless:

"(a)…

    (i)   under the law of the issuing state the offence is punishable by imprisonment or detention for a maximum period of not less than 12 months, or

    (ii)   a term of imprisonment or detention of not less than 4 months has been imposed on the person in respect of the offence in the issuing state, and the person is required under the law of the issuing state to serve all or part of that term of imprisonment,

---

[1] See for instance s 10 of the Extradition Act 1965.

or

(b) the offence is an offence to which paragraph 2 of Article 2 of the Framework Decision applies and under the law of the issuing state the offence is punishable by imprisonment for a maximum period of not less than 3 years."

11–03 This mirrors the minimum gravity requirements provided for by the Framework Decision.[2] It is of particular note that the two situations provided for in s 38(1)(a) are not mutually exclusive – in the case of a warrant which relates to an offence where a sentence has been imposed it will be sufficient to show that the maximum applicable penalty either exceeds 12 months or the penalty imposed exceeds four months. Section 38(1)(a)(i) and 38(1)(a)(ii) do not require the court to apply the former threshold to accusation cases and the latter one to conviction and sentence cases. The issue was considered by Macken J in *Minister for Justice, Equality and Law Reform v Dus*[3] who concluded that:

"...the provisions of section 38(1)(a) are disjunctive, the appellant can be surrendered provided that the minimum gravity thresholds under either (a)(i) or (a)(ii) is met. In the present case the minimum gravity is significantly exceeded in respect of the offences, one offence having a maximum penalty of 10 years, and one offence of having a maximum penalty of 12 years. I am satisfied also that a term of imprisonment or detention of not less than four months had been imposed on the person in respect of the offences arising in the present case."[4]

11–04 It follows that an offence in respect of which a sentence of for example three months was imposed will satisfy the minimum gravity requirement so long as the maximum potential sentence exceeded 12 months.

11–05 Obviously where a requested person has not yet been sentenced in the issuing State, no such issue will arise. In such cases surrender may only be ordered in respect of an offence if the maximum sentence which it carries in the issuing State is a term of at least 12 months imprisonment or detention.[5]

Article 2.2 Offences

11–06 Where the warrant recites one or more of the offences as coming within the terms of Art 2.2 then a different regime applies. Section 38(1)(b) provides that such offences must be punishable by a maximum sentence of at least 3 years. This provision relates solely to the maximum possible sentence and is not concerned with the sentence actually imposed as such. Therefore it will be irrelevant if the sentence imposed in respect of such an offence is less than 4 months so long as the three year threshold is met in respect of the maximum possible penalty.

---

[2] See Art 2.1 and 2.2.

[3] [2009] IESC 67.

[4] This decision had the effect of clarifying certain obiter comments which Macken J had made in *MJELR v Ferenca*: "On their face these are not mutually exclusive, but in the scheme of the Framework Decision and the Act of 2003, I think it is probable that [(i)] refers to warrants sought in respect of the prosecution of offences and [(ii)] refers to warrants sought in respect of sentences imposed".

[5] s 38(1)(a)(i) of the 2003 Act.

Pre-conviction Cases

The fact that the penalty that will actually be imposed in a pre-conviction case is **11–07** not capable of being ascertained or predicted does not alter the minimum gravity requirement – although as noted above the four month threshold in respect of sentences actually imposed cannot apply as a matter of logic. The fact that a penalty less than the maximum carried by the offence might be imposed is not relevant to considerations of minimum gravity, so long as the maximum penalty which may be imposed satisfies the relevant requirements of s 38(1). In *Minister for Justice, Equality and Law Reform v Brennan,*[6] the respondent argued that, although the maximum sentence for the offence for which his surrender was sought by the UK authorities (escape from lawful custody) was life imprisonment, an unspecified lesser sentence would in all probability be imposed. The court found that this did not affect its consideration as to minimum gravity, which did not go beyond establishing that the maximum sentence which could be imposed satisfied the requirements of s 38(1):

> "The Court must be satisfied that the offence for which he is sought is one for which it is possible to receive a sentence which satisfies the minimum gravity under the Act. Clearly a potential life sentence comes within that meaning, and the fact that any sentence of a length less than life might be imposed in any particular case does not take it out of that category."

Similarly in *Minister for Justice, Equality and Law Reform v Gorman*[7] the respondent **11–08** argued that he would be released from whatever sentence might be imposed in the event of conviction within two years under the terms of the Good Friday agreement even though he was sought for prosecution for the offence of murder. This was in circumstances where another person who had already been convicted and sentenced in respect of the same offence had been granted early release. The Court rejected this argument:

> "The warrant in this case indicates at paragraph c thereof that the maximum penalty for murder and for conspiracy to murder is life imprisonment. In my view, even though Mr Magee benefited from the prisoner release provisions of the Good Friday Agreement, being considered a qualifying prisoner, that does not alter in the respondent's case the fact that when imposing sentence following conviction on these charges, the Court could impose a life sentence. The question of whether following sentencing the UK executive would or even must consider that the respondent is also entitled to the benefit of that Agreement and be released after two years does not in my view mean that his surrender is prohibited by the provisions of s. 38 of the Act. The question of early release is an executive decision and is discretionary in nature, as far as I recall. I could usefully refer to *the offence* (i.e. murder/conspiracy to murder) being within Article 2.2, and the *offence* being punishable by a maximum of not less than three years. It makes no reference to the particular respondent actually receiving a sentence or being punished with a sentence of not less than three years. That is another reason why I believe that this point of objection should also fail."

---

[6] [2006] IEHC 94. This decision was appealed to the Supreme Court—see [2007] 3 IR 732.
[7] [2010] IEHC 210.

11–09 It would seem to follow that in any pre-conviction case the court will, as a matter of logic, only be concerned with the maximum penalty applicable as opposed to the penalty that will actually be imposed even where it is possible to predict it with some degree of certainty.

MINIMUM GRAVITY OF CORRESPONDING IRISH OFFENCE

11–10 In cases where an examination as to correspondence is required, there is no minimum gravity requirement in relation to the Irish offence which corresponds to the offence for which surrender is sought. This is in contrast to the position under the Extradition Act 1965, as was noted in *Minister for Justice, Equality and Law Reform v Tobin*[8]:

> "What must be noted for the purposes of the present case is that minimum gravity is considered only in respect of the offence in the requesting state, and not in relation to the corresponding offence in this State. This is a clear change, and cannot be regarded as accidental or unimportant. It follows that even if the offence charged in Hungary is one carrying the required minimum punishment, it matters not at all that the offence in this State with which it is found to correspond carries a much lighter penalty, even one involving no term of imprisonment. Under s. 10 of the 1965 Act that would not be so."[9]

11–11 A similar conclusion was reached in *Minister for Justice, Equality and Law Reform v Ward*[10] where the surrender of the respondent was sought in relation to an offence of dangerous driving causing death. Correspondence was established with the summary offence of being the owner of a defective vehicle.

SENTENCES FOR AGGRAVATED OFFENCES

11–12 The examination of minimum gravity concerns either the actual or maximum sentence which either was or could be imposed upon the requested person should he be surrendered, and in this regard, the requested person's degree of involvement or personal circumstances insofar as they may pertain at sentencing stage in the issuing State do not really arise. However, the court may on occasion have to have regard to some aspect of the respondent's circumstances where the law of the issuing State provides for the imposition of a sentence which is predicated on some particular aspect of the respondent's circumstances. In *Minister for Justice, Equality and Law Reform v Pavlovs*,[11] surrender was sought by the Lithuanian authorities for an offence of drunken driving. The offence was punishable in the issuing State by a maximum term of imprisonment of 12 months, but only in circumstances where it was the second such offence committed within a year. The warrant disclosed that the respondent did have a relevant previous conviction within the 12 months prior to the offence in respect of which surrender was sought. In the respondent's particular circumstances he would be liable if surrendered to be sentenced to a maximum of 12 months imprisonment. Accordingly the court was satisfied as to minimum gravity.

---

[8] [2008] 4 IR 42.
[9] p 60.
[10] [2008] IEHC 53.
[11] [2007] IEHC 363.

COMPOSITE SENTENCES

In the case of the respondent who has already been sentenced one difficulty which **11–13** has arisen in the past is that the warrant will purport to relate to a number of offences in respect of which one sentence was imposed. It is frequently unclear as to whether this means that multiple concurrent sentences were imposed, that consecutive sentences were imposed or that a global sentence was imposed. This gives rise to a difficulty in ascertaining whether each of the offences for which surrender is sought satisfies the minimum gravity requirement.

The court avoided tackling this issue directly in *Minister for Justice, Equality* **11–14** *and Law Reform v Sakalauskis*[12] in which the European arrest warrant had been issued in respect of multiple offences, but referred to a single composite sentence of two years, one month and five days imprisonment which the respondent was required to serve, without specifying what period of imprisonment had been imposed in respect of each offence. Unlike in *Minister for Justice, Equality and Law Reform v Kondratevas*,[13] correspondence had been shown in respect of all three offences, and so there could be no objection to surrender on that basis. However, the respondent argued that, given the lack of information in the warrant as to what sentence had been imposed in respect of each offence, it could well be the case that less than four months had been imposed in respect of one of the offences, with the remainder of the stated period being made up of the sentences imposed for the other two offences. Thus, the respondent submitted, there could be no certainty that the minimum gravity requirement had been satisfied in respect of each offence for which surrender was sought. The court rejected this argument, relying on the presumption contained in s 4A of the 2003 Act that the issuing State would comply with the requirements of the Framework Decision. It also found it relevant that the respondent had been present at his sentence in Lithuania, and so should know what sentence was imposed in respect of each offence. In this regard, the court effectively imposed a burden of proof on the respondent to show that minimum gravity had not been shown for each offence:

> "The warrant states that the period required to be served is two years, one month and five days. That is sufficient in order to satisfy the minimum requirement. If the respondent wishes to demonstrate that more than three separate periods of imprisonment were imposed, namely one in respect of each offence making a combined total period of two years and three months, it is up to him to do so and in that way discharge the onus of proof. No attempt to so do has been made, and the objection must fail accordingly."

Given the inquisitorial nature of proceedings under the 2003 Act it is difficult to **11–15** regard the issue of minimum gravity as being one in respect of which an onus can be cast onto the respondent. Moreover the decisions of the Supreme Court in *Minister for Justice, Equality and Law Reform v Altaravicius*[14] and *Minister for Justice, Equality and Law Reform v Sliczynski*[15] would tend to cast doubt on the applicability of the presumption under s 4A to the question of minimum gravity.

---

[12] [2007] IEHC 364.
[13] [2006] IEHC 456.
[14] [2006] 3 IR 148.
[15] [2008] IESC 73.

11–16   In *Minister for Justice, Equality and Law Reform v Ferenca*,[16] the Supreme Court refused surrender principally on the basis that one of the offences in respect of which a composite sentence was imposed did not correspond and as such it was not possible to disentangle the remaining offences. However, Macken J went on to comment that a similar difficulty arose in respect of the issue of minimum gravity:

> "The difficulty arises because of the fact that the warrant gives the details of the sentences in the form of a global sentence. It is, on the face of the warrant, unclear whether the 2 years and 9 months sentence imposed was made up of the same sentence in respect of all three individual offences, each to run concurrently with the other, or is composed of separate and different sentences in respect of each of the three convictions, all to run consecutively, and therefore combining to make up the term, or simply that it is a single global sentence imposed in respect of all three offences...Having regard to the fact that there is no information upon which the court can be satisfied that the threshold set out in s.38(1)(a)(ii) is met, I am satisfied that the appellant cannot be surrendered pursuant to this warrant".

11–17   Whilst such comments were presumably obiter having regard to the conclusion of the court in respect of correspondence they nonetheless had the effect of suggesting that in the case of offences which were the subject of a composite sentence it was necessary to show that a sentence of at least four months had been imposed in respect of each individual offence. However, the subsequent decision of the court in *Minister for Justice, Equality and Law Reform v Dus*[17] implicitly rejected such an approach and allows the court to have regard to the maximum applicable sentence rather than the sentence actually imposed, if the latter is unclear.

11–18   The issue of minimum gravity and composite sentences was dealt with definitively by the Supreme Court in *Minister for Justice, Equality and Law Reform v Sas*.[18] Geoghegan J made it clear that insofar as *Ferenca* might have been regarded as an authority for the proposition that composite sentences rendered impossible the exercise of determining minimum gravity the relevant comments had been made obiter:

> "Even though Peart J. was mindful of the distinction there is nothing in his ex tempore judgment to suggest that the judgments of this court in the Ferenca case were cited and, in particular, the last cited passage from the judgment of the Chief Justice, even though the Supreme Court judgments had been delivered several months earlier. It would seem to me to have been implicit in that passage from the Chief Justice's judgment in Ferenca that he would have seen no problem with the composite sentence if surrender was being effected in respect of each of the offences the subject matter of the sentence, provided of course, that the composite sentence exceeded the threshold or *"minimum gravity"*. The minimum gravity test as provided for in the Framework Document and enacted in the European Arrest Warrant Act, 2003 was concerned with the length of a particular sentence the offender was called upon to serve. Provided there was the necessary correspondence, it is immaterial that the sentence related to more than one offence.

---

[16] [2008] 4 IR 480.

[17] [2009] IESC 67.

[18] [2010] IESC 16.

> Although the view which I have expressed seems to me to be implicit, for the reasons indicated, in the judgment of the Chief Justice in Ferenca, it is true that the precise point did not directly arise in Ferenca and in that sense the implicit view might be regarded as obiter dicta. But it is difficult to see how such a view could be challenged."

He went on to consider and apply a recent House of Lords decision on the same **11–19** issue:

> "As pointed out in the written and oral submissions on behalf of the Minister, the point did directly arise in a House of Lords appeal, *Pilecki v. Circuit Court of Legnica, Poland* [2008] 1 WLR 325. Lord Hope of Craighead in an opinion with which the other members of the appellate committee concurred, held that where a Polish court had aggregated a number of sentences for the purposes of its final judgment, the aggregated sentence exceeding four months and where it was not possible to say how much of the aggregated sentence was attributable to each offence, it was the length of the sentence alone that determined whether or not it fell within the scope of a European Arrest Warrant. If there was a composite sentence in respect of two offences for which otherwise surrender should lawfully be made, there was no necessity to make any further enquiry into the sentence. That opinion was primarily based on the Framework Document. I am satisfied, for the reasons which I have indicated, that Irish law is no different and I would dismiss the appeal."

As a result the difficulty that presents itself in such cases is considerably less **11–20** pronounced than the equivalent difficulty that will arise in respect of correspondence and composite sentences. Before an issue can arise one of the offences in respect of which the composite sentence is imposed must fail to meet the minimum gravity requirement. Given the relatively low thresholds set by s 38(1)(a)(i) and 38(1)(a)(ii) such situations are inevitably going to be relatively rare.

MINOR OFFENCES AND PROPORTIONALITY

Where the minimum gravity requirements are met, it remains open to question **11–21** as to whether or not the court is entitled to refuse surrender on the grounds of proportionality having regard to the trivial nature of the offence. Such an argument is necessarily predicated upon the fact that the respondent may be obliged to spend some period of time in custody in order that surrender can actually be effected. In such circumstances the respondent might argue that whilst minimum gravity has been satisfied his surrender would be disproportionate having regard to the fact that there is little or no reality to the imposition of a custodial sentence in the requesting State. To date the courts have been very slow to entertain such arguments.

In *Minister for Justice, Equality and Law Reform v Krasnovas*,[19] the respondent **11–22** sought to rely on the fact that a co-accused had been given a sentence of just six weeks imprisonment as an indication that the offences for which his surrender was sought were extremely minor and that it would be a breach of his constitutional rights to surrender him in such circumstances. Peart J declined to enter into a consideration of whether the offences in question were minor in nature:

---

[19] [2006] IEHC 377.

"I am satisfied first of all that there is no question of this Court on an application such as this reaching a view that the offences for which surrender is sought are of a minor nature. They are offences for which the issuing state is entitled to seek surrender under the Framework Decision and there is no basis for refusal to comply with that request simply because a person said to have been an accomplice of the respondent received a sentence of only six weeks. The question of any sentence to be imposed in respect of the offences is a matter entirely within the competence of the court in Lithuania, and provided that the offences are such as meet the required minimum gravity, that is sufficient".

11–23   In that case, however, the argument put forward by the respondent was not explicitly grounded on the application of the European Convention on Human Rights or the principle of proportionality. Quite how the courts would deal with such an argument very much remains to be seen. The courts of England and Wales would appear to entertain some degree of argument as to proportionality in respect of trivial offences insofar as surrender might amount to a breach of Art 8 of the Convention. However, a stringent test has been adopted in relation to this. In *Zak v Regional Court of Bydgoszcz Poland*[20] the court described the applicable test in the following terms:

"The relevant test as regards Article 8 is to be found in the case of *Jaso, Lopez and Hernandez v Central Criminal Court No.2 Madrid* [2007] EWHC 1983 (Admin), at paragraph 57 of which Dyson LJ said this, applying decisions of the House of Lords in Razgar and Huang:

'What is required is that the court should decide whether the interference with a person's right to respect for his private or (as the case may be) family life which would result from his or her extradition is proportionate to the legitimate aim of honouring extradition treaties with other states. It is clear that great weight should be accorded to the legitimate aim of honouring extradition treaties made with other states. Thus, although it is wrong to apply an exceptionality test, in an extradition case there will have to be striking and unusual facts to lead to the conclusion that it is disproportionate to interfere with an extraditee's Article 8 rights.'"

11–24   The court went on to conclude that the surrender of the respondent in *Zak* would not breach his Art 8 rights. It is of note that the High Court of England and Wales had on a previous occasion commented in relation to this case that the underlying offence was extremely trivial in character[21] being one of handling a mobile telephone.

Principle of Proportionality

11–25   The principle of proportionality is a maxim which states that no layer of government should take any action that exceeds that which is necessary to achieve the objective

---

[20] [2008] EWHC 470 (Admin).

[21] See "Bar of Triviality in European Arrest Warrant Cases", 31 Crim LR [2009] where the following comment is noted as having been made by Maurice Kay LJ on an adjourned appeal hearing: "...one is becoming used to European extradition cases for less serious offences than used to come before the courts for extradition, but in my reasonable experience of cases under the 2003 Act I have never seen one quite as low down the calendar as this".

of government (regardless of the intent underlying the objective). It was initially developed in the German legal system. It is a fundamental principle of European Union law. According to this principle, the EU may only act to the extent that is needed to achieve its objectives, and no further. This principle has underpinned the European Communities since their inception in 1957. Under the TEU from which the Framework Decision derives, the principle of proportionality was clearly formulated in the third paragraph of Art 5 as follows:

> "Any action by the Community shall not go beyond what is necessary to achieve the objectives of this Treaty."

The principle of proportionality is expressly recited in para 7 of the Recitals to the **11–26** Framework Decision[22] and undoubtedly applies to the operation of the European arrest warrant procedure. The principle applies not only to the measures adopted to achieve the implementation of the relevant objectives but also to the means. This was a theme which was briefly touched on by the European Court of Justice in *Advocaten voor de Wereld VZM*[23]:

> "It must be noted at the outset that, by virtue of Article 6 TEU, the Union is founded on the principle of the rule of law and it respects fundamental rights, as guaranteed by the European Convention for the Protection of Human Rights and Fundamental Freedoms, signed in Rome on 4 November 1950, and as they result from the constitutional provisions common to the Member States, as general principles of Community law. It follows that the institutions are subject to review of the conformity of their acts with the Treaties and the general principles of law, just like Member States when they implement the law of the Union..."

The Council of the European Union has, in the past, expressed concern[24] in relation **11–27** to use of the European Arrest Warrant for what are patently minor offences and would appear to be of the view that the deployment of the European arrest warrant in such circumstances breaches the principle of proportionality. The following examples were listed:

- seizure of 0.45 grams of cannabis;
- seizure of 1.5 grams of marijuana;
- seizure of 0.15 grams of heroin;
- seizure of three ecstasy tablets;
- theft of two car tyres;

---

[22] "(7) Since the aim of replacing the system of multilateral extradition built upon the European Convention on Extradition of 13 December 1957 cannot be sufficiently achieved by the Member States acting unilaterally and can therefore, by reason of its scale and effects, be better achieved at Union level, the Council may adopt measures in accordance with the principle of subsidiarity as referred to in Article 2 of the Treaty on European Union and Article 5 of the Treaty establishing the European Community. In accordance with the principle of proportionality, as set out in the latter Article, this Framework Decision does not go beyond what is necessary in order to achieve that objective".

[23] Case C-303/05.

[24] 9 July 2007 – Memorandum from the Council of the European Union to the Working Party on Cooperation in Criminal Matters (10975/07).

- driving a car under the influence of alcohol;
- theft of a piglet.

11–28   Whilst the Council expressed concern in relation to such trivial offences it did not suggest that the minor nature of the underlying crimes would give rise to a basis for refusing surrender in an individual case. Rather the Council went on to suggest that the issue of proportionality should be considered by the issuing State. The implication was that it would be undesirable for the requested state to sit in judgment over what was or was not to be considered a disproportionate use of state power. It remains to be seen whether the courts will exhibit any great appetite for considering proportionality as a basis for refusing surrender in an individual case. There is some evidence that the European Court of Justice is prepared to entertain arguments in relation to proportionality in the context of individual rights. In the case of *Kadi*[25] the court considered whether certain asset freezing measures imposed amounted to a disproportionate interference with fundamental rights. Specifically it made reference to the case-law emanating from Strasbourg:

> "In this respect, according to the case law of the European Court of Human Rights, there must also exist a reasonable relationship of proportionality between the means employed and the aim sought to be realised. The Court must determine whether a fair balance has been struck between the demands of the public interest and the interest of the individuals concerned. In so doing, the Court recognises that the legislature enjoys a wide margin of appreciation, with regard both to choosing the means of enforcement and to ascertaining whether the consequences of enforcement are justified in the public interest for the purpose of achieving the object of the law in question."[26]

11–29   Given that such rights as liberty and the right to private and family life may well be adversely affected by on order of surrender there would appear to be some basis for supposing that the courts may be entitled to engage in a balancing exercise for the purpose of giving effect to the principle of proportionality.

---

[25] Joined cases C-402/05 P and C-415/05 P.
[26] Paragraph 360.

CHAPTER 12

Extra-Territorial Offences

It may seem obvious that the requesting State must have jurisdiction to try a **12–01** particular offender for a particular offence. As a common law country where jurisdiction has, traditionally at least, been based on the offence having occurred within the territory of the State, issues of jurisdiction have tended not to arise too frequently in a domestic context. The situation is, however, somewhat less straightforward in other Member States where jurisdiction can be exercised on grounds other than commission of the offence within the territory of the State in question.

CRIMINAL JURISDICTION

12–02   Prior to the abolition of trial by ordeal by the 4th Lateran Council in the 13th century, criminal jurisdiction was not necessarily linked to the place of the offence or the habitual residence or birthplace of the offender. Presumably the divine intervention which was assumed to underlie the criminal process was available irrespective of the forum. However, subsequent to the introduction of more rational evidence based procedures it became logical to base jurisdiction in the place where the evidence was available, namely the place where the offence had been committed. Territorial jurisdiction increased in importance, particularly in the common law jurisdictions where juries were expected to make use of local knowledge in discharging their function.

12–03   In more recent times and specifically in the civil law countries jurisdiction has been exercised on a considerably broader basis than that of territorial jurisdiction. This is in part a response to the increasingly international nature of crime and also the extent to which sovereign States consider themselves to be more inter-dependent on each other in relation to their response to crime. Such extra-territorial jurisdiction can be exercised on the basis of a number of different principles.

The Active Personality Principle

12–04   Most commonly States will reserve to themselves the entitlement to prosecute their own citizens in respect of offences committed outside their own territory. This is known as the active personality principle. In practice the manner in which various States operate this principle varies with some requiring that the criminal act be an offence under both the law of the territory where it is committed and under the territory of the offender's State.

The Passive Personality Principle

12–05   This purports to grant jurisdiction on the basis of the nationality of the victim of the offence. Typically this will only arise in relation to cases of a serious nature such as murder. The exercise of jurisdiction on this basis is comparatively rare and inherently problematic as it generally involves the requesting State seeking to assert jurisdiction in relation to an offence which the requested State has a very real interest in prosecuting itself for the purpose of maintaining public order.

The Protective Principle

12–06   Some States will also consider themselves entitled to prosecute and punish those who commit crimes against the interests of the State. For example in the US case of *Layton* the accused was tried for the murder of a US Congressman even though the offence had taken place in Guyana. On the broadest application of this principle the State of Israel prosecuted Adolf Eichmann in respect of war crimes committed during the Holocaust even though the victims of his crimes were not citizens of Israel as that State did not exist at the time. Israel considered itself entitled to exercise jurisdiction on the grounds that it was the State most concerned with the crimes in question.

ARTICLE 4.7 OF THE FRAMEWORK DECISION

The Framework Decision deals with the difficulties presented by requests for **12–07** surrender in relation to extra-territorial offences by providing two optional grounds for non-surrender. Member States are free to decline to surrender:

> "4(7) Where the European arrest warrant relates to offences which:
>
> (a) are regarded by the law of the executing Member State as having been committed in whole or in part in the territory of the executing Member State or in a place treated as such; or
>
> (b) have been committed outside the territory of the issuing Member State and the law of the executing Member State does not allow prosecution for the same offences when committed outside its territory."

Article 4.7 contains two separate and distinct grounds for refusing surrender, only **12–08** the second of which has been implemented by way of s 44 of 2003 Act.

Article 4.7(a)

The optional ground for non-surrender contained in Art 4.7(a), namely that the **12–09** offence was committed in the territory of the Member State, can be traced back to Art 7 of the European Convention on Extradition 1957 and initially was concerned with ensuring that crimes would first and foremost be prosecuted in the country where they occurred. It has been suggested[1] that the reason for the inclusion of such a ground for optional non-surrender in the context of the European arrest warrant had more to do with concerns which arose from the partial abolition of the double criminality requirement as a result of the list of excepted offences appearing at Art 2.2 of the Framework Decision. Specific concerns had been expressed by the Netherlands and Belgium that in the absence of such an exception it would be possible to seek surrender in respect of abortion or euthanasia committed in the requested State in circumstances where the requesting State certified the offence amounted to murder or grievous bodily harm.

It would appear that the Oireachtas opted not to implement the optional ground for **12–10** refusal provided for in Art 4.7(a) in that s 44 which appears to be the only provision in the 2003 Act which deals with extraterritoriality is clearly a transposition of Art 4.7(b) only. However, it would seem that on at least one occasion the courts have entertained, albeit briefly, an argument which was predicated on the basis of Art 4.7(a).

In *Minister for Justice, Equality and Law Reform v Devlin*[2] the respondent **12–11** suggested that the provisions of Art 2 of the Constitution effectively meant that any offence committed within Northern Ireland fell foul of Art 4.7(a) of the Framework Decision as the offence was committed within the territory of the executing Member State. This argument was disposed of in short order:

---

[1] Keijzer and Van Sliedregt, "The European Arrest Warrant in Practice", (2009) at p 93.

[2] [2008] IEHC 12.

> "In my view this ground of objection is untenable in light of the provisions of Article 3 (prior to its amendment) which prohibited the enactment of any laws by the Oireachtas beyond, in effect, the extent of the twenty six counties comprising the Republic of Ireland. It cannot possibly be argued that this State regards the offence referred to in the warrant as having been committed in this State. The fact that the then Article 3 of Bunreacht na hEireann was worded as it was at the date of the offence does not alter that in any way. This is an imaginative, yet far-fetched submission, about which I need say no more in order to conclude that it is devoid of merit."

12–12   The court would appear to have entertained the argument on the basis of s 16(2)(d) of the 2003 Act which appears to require that surrender be refused where to grant it would conflict with the Framework Decision. In reality such considerations should not arise as Art 4 sets out a number of *optional* grounds for refusing surrender. Insofar as an option actually arises it is one to be availed of by the Oireachtas in implementing the Framework Decision rather than the courts on a discretionary basis.

Article 4.7(b)

12–13   The rationale underlying Art 4.7(b) which is implemented by s 44 of the 2003 Act is quite different. Provisions of this type can be found in extradition agreements from the late 19th century onwards.[3] Such provisions are based on the principle of reciprocity which held that one State should not be required to extradite for an offence if it could not request extradition for the same offence were the roles reversed. The principle is directed at ensuring that an almost perfect balance of mutual obligations as between States is maintained.

12–14   The principle of reciprocity is distinct from that of double criminality in that there will be many cases where the extra-territorial offence will be one where either double criminality has been established or does not need to be established as it is an offence that comes within Art 2.2. This distinction, however, is not altogether clear in some of the case-law.

SECTION 44

12–15   Where a request is received by way of a European arrest warrant in respect of an offence where the requesting State is exercising extra-territorial jurisdiction then the provisions of s 44 may be engaged:

> "A person shall not be surrendered under this Act if the offence specified in the European arrest warrant issued in respect of him or her was committed or is alleged to have been committed in a place other than the issuing state and the act or omission of which the offence consists does not, by virtue of having been committed in a place other than the State, constitute an offence under the law of the State."

12–16   In essence s 44 prohibits surrender in circumstances where the State would not be entitled to prosecute the same offence on an extra-territorial basis. This necessarily

---

[3] The earliest example being the Belgian Extradition Act of 1874.

requires the court to engage in a hypothetical exercise of considering whether, if the respondent committed the offence in a third country, he could be prosecuted for that offence within the State on the basis of his nationality or some other feature of the offence which gives rise to an extra-territorial jurisdiction. It is immediately obvious that such an exercise is far from straightforward and will require the court to consider first whether or not the offence is in fact an extra-territorial one and second, on the assumption that it is, on what basis it might be hypothetically prosecuted in this jurisdiction.

"COMMITTED IN A PLACE OTHER THAN THE ISSUING STATE"

In many cases it will be clear that the offence specified in the European arrest **12–17** warrant is an extra-territorial offence *vis-à-vis* the requesting State. Paragraph (f)[4] of the standard form of the warrant would appear to be the appropriate part of the warrant by which the requesting State can indicate clearly to the executing State that the offence in question is an extraterritorial one. Rather unhelpfully the information to be included under this heading is described as "optional information" and as such there would not appear to be a clear obligation on the requesting State to indicate in definitive terms whether or not the offence is extraterritorial. It may also be necessary to consider the information supplied at para (e) insofar as it may disclose the locus of the offence.

In *Minister for Justice, Equality and Law Reform v Walas*[5] the offence was **12–18** alleged to have occurred in a place unknown. As such the prosecuting authorities were not in a position to State whether the offence had actually occurred within the requesting State or not. The issue arose as to whether or not the offence should therefore be considered an extra-territorial offence. The court took the view that in circumstances where it was not really possible to State where the offence took place the court was entitled to proceed on the basis that it was not an extra-territorial offence and that the terms of s 44 were not engaged:

> "...it is not stated in the warrant that this offence was committed outside Poland or that it is alleged that this is the position. Additional information provided by the issuing judicial authority in a letter dated 27th May 2008 states in this regard there is no information available which indicate [*sic*]that the offence was committed outside Poland. That is not being alleged. In my view this Court is entitled to take the view, in the absence of anything to the contrary being stated in the warrant, that this offence is alleged to have occurred in Poland. It is not a case that comes within s. 44 of the Act, even though the warrant does not state specifically that the offence occurred in Poland."

It would seem to follow that s 44 only arises where the warrant makes it clear that **12–19** the offence "was committed or is alleged to have been committed" in a place other than the requesting State. On a purely literal interpretation, therefore, no issue would appear to arise where the offence is either non-specific as to the *locus in quo* or

---

[4] Under the heading "Other circumstances relevant to the case (optional information)" there appears the following notation "NB: This could cover remarks on extraterritoriality, interruption of periods of time limitation and other consequences of the offence".

[5] [2009] IEHC 129.

where the *locus in quo* is simply unknown.[6] In such circumstances a respondent who wishes to raise the issue will be obliged to do so on an evidential basis which may give rise to obvious difficulties from the point of view of being seen to make admissions in respect of the substantive offence.

12–20   Even where the warrant makes it clear that some or perhaps all of the criminal conduct took place outside the jurisdiction of the requesting State, this will not necessarily mean that the offence is extraterritorial in nature. In *Minister for Justice, Equality and Law Reform v Hill*[7] the respondent was alleged to have posted from Ireland a number of packages to a jury which had been empanelled to hear a trial relating to the London Underground Bombings. The warrant alleged an offence of attempting to pervert the course of public justice and the warrant was silent as to whether or not the offence was extraterritorial in nature. Having considered the UK decisions of *R. v Doot*[8] and *DPP v Stonehouse*[9] the court concluded that the offences in question were not committed outside the territory of the requesting State as the object of the offence, namely the jury it was sought to influence, was within the territory of the requesting State. The decision might be criticised on the grounds that it essentially amounted to a finding by an Irish court as to whether the offence in the warrant was an extraterritorial offence under the law of the requesting State.

THE TEST TO BE APPLIED

12–21   Where it is clear that the offence in the warrant is an extraterritorial offence, the court must consider whether the offence would be amenable to prosecution on an extraterritorial basis in this jurisdiction. This, clearly, amounts to the court engaging in a hypothetical test whereby it essentially substitutes the State for the position of the requesting State in relation to the offence described in the warrant. Quite how far this translation of the different elements of the offence must go is not made entirely clear by s 44. Presumably where the place of commission of the offence is Ireland the court must essentially ignore this fact and assume for the sake of the exercise that the place of the offence is another State. It is less clear what the position is where the requesting State has asserted extraterritorial jurisdiction on a particular basis, such as active personality (i.e. the respondent is a citizen of the requesting State and as such criminally liable for offences committed abroad). Is the court restricted to considering whether the State would exercise extraterritorial jurisdiction on the same basis or can it consider whether extraterritorial jurisdiction might be exercised on an alternative basis? The Act provides little assistance in this regard. However, the underlying principle of reciprocity would seem to predicate in favour of the court being restricted to considering whether extraterritorial jurisdiction could be exercised in theory on a similar basis as opposed to on some other ground.

12–22   The circumstances in which the State exercises extraterritorial jurisdiction are quite varied and are not informed by any one particular underlying theory or approach. More often than not they arise by virtue of the need to fulfil some obligation under international law. It may, therefore, be necessary for the court to

---

[6] A similar point was raised and disposed of in short order in *Minister for Justice, Equality and Law Reform v Tighe* [2009] IEHC 33.

[7] [2009] IEHC 159.

[8] [1973] AC 807.

[9] [1978] AC 55.

consider any one of a number of different provisions which are capable of giving rise to the exercise of extraterritorial jurisdiction by the State.

EXTRATERRITORIAL JURISDICTION PURSUANT TO STATUTE

Whilst it is generally presumed that a criminal offence created by the Oireachtas **12–23** will only have effect within the territory of the State unless otherwise provided, the legislature is unrestricted in relation to the creation of extraterritorial offences. It had been argued in the case of *In re Article 26 and the Criminal Law (Jurisdiction) Bill, 1975*[10] that legislative competence was restricted to the creation of offences within the national territory. This argument was rejected in unambiguous terms:

> "...every sovereign State has power to legislate with extraterritorial effect in the sense that it may enact that acts or omissions done outside its borders are criminal offences which may be successfully prosecuted within its borders – this is sometimes called the jurisdiction to prescribe – provided that the events, acts or persons to which its enactment applies bear on the peace, order and good government of the legislating State..."[11]

Whilst the court seemed to suggest that the entitlement to create extraterritorial **12–24** offences must be linked to the public order of the State it would, nonetheless, appear that the Oireachtas enjoys a broad entitlement to create extraterritorial offences by statute. Below are some of the situations where the State is entitled to exercise extraterritorial jurisdiction.

Murder and Manslaughter

Section 9 of the Offences against the Person Act 1861 provides an extremely broad **12–25** jurisdiction to try a person for murder and is not predicated upon the nationality of the victim:

> "Where any Murder or Manslaughter shall be committed on Land out of the United Kingdom, whether within the Queen's Dominions or without, and whether the Person killed were a Subject of Her Majesty or not, every Offence committed by any Subject of Her Majesty, in respect of any such Case, whether the same shall amount to the Offence of Murder or of Manslaughter, may be dealt with, inquired of, tried, determined, and punished in any County or Place in England or Ireland in which such Person shall be apprehended or be in Custody, in the same Manner in all respects as if such Offence had been actually committed in that County or Place; provided that nothing herein contained shall prevent any Person from being tried in any Place out of England or Ireland for any Murder or Manslaughter committed out of England or Ireland, in the same Manner as such Person might have been tried before the passing of this Act."

It should be noted that s 16 of the Criminal Law Act 1997 deleted the words "or of **12–26** being accessory to murder or manslaughter" from s 9. The implication would appear

---

[10] [1977] IR 129.
[11] p 149.

to be that extraterritorial jurisdiction could not be asserted in respect of accessories. However, this amendment has been superseded in practical terms by the amendment of s 7 of the Criminal Law Act 1997[12] which provides for extraterritorial jurisdiction in relation to aiding and abetting generally.

12–27   In addition s 10 of the Offences Against the Person Act 1861 gives jurisdiction to try murder or manslaughter cases where the victim dies within the State:

> "Where any Person, being feloniously stricken, poisoned, or otherwise hurt upon the Sea, or at any Place out of England or Ireland, shall die of such Stroke, Poisoning, or Hurt in England or Ireland, or, being feloniously stricken, poisoned, or otherwise hurt at any Place in England or Ireland, shall die of such Stroke, Poisoning, or Hurt upon the Sea, or at any Place out of England or Ireland, every Offence committed in respect of any such Case, whether the same shall amount to the Offence of Murder or of Manslaughter, or of being accessory to Murder or Manslaughter, may be dealt with, inquired of, tried, determined, and punished in the County or Place in England or Ireland in which such Death, Stroke, Poisoning, or Hurt shall happen, in the same Manner in all respects as if such Offence had been wholly committed in that County or Place."

Conspiracy or Soliciting to Commit Murder

12–28   Section 4 of the Offences Against the Person Act 1861 makes provision for extraterritorial effect in respect of conspiracy and solicitation to commit murder in terms similar to s 9 of the same Act.

> "All Persons who shall conspire, confederate, and agree to murder any Person, whether he be a Subject of Her Majesty or not, and whether he be within the Queen's Dominions or not, and whosoever shall solicit, encourage, persuade, or endeavour to persuade, or shall propose to any Person, to murder any other Person, whether he be a Subject of Her Majesty or not, and whether he be within the Queen's Dominions or not, shall be guilty of a Misdemeanor, and being convicted thereof shall be liable, at the Discretion of the Court, to be kept in Penal Servitude for any Term not more than Ten and not less than Three Years,—or to be imprisoned for any Term not exceeding Two Years, with or without Hard Labour."

Offences Aboard Irish Registered Ships and Aircraft

12–29   At common law there is a recognised jurisdiction to prosecute in respect of offences that occur on Irish registered ships irrespective of where the offence occurs.[13] In addition the offence of piracy on the high seas may also be prosecuted extraterritorially by operation of the principal of *jure gentium*.

12–30   The Maritime Security Act 2004 creates a number of offences in respect of which extraterritorial jurisdiction may be invoked. Section 2(1) criminalises the following conduct:

> "A person who unlawfully and intentionally does any of the following acts is guilty of an offence:

---

[12] See s 7(1A) as inserted by s 19 of the Criminal Justice (Amendment) Act 2009.
[13] See R.L. Sandes, "Criminal Law and Procedure in Eire"(3rd ed 1951) at p 21.

(a) seizing or exercising control over a ship or fixed platform by force or threat of force or any other form of intimidation;

(b) performing an act of violence against a person on board a ship or fixed platform if that act is likely to endanger the safe navigation of the ship or the safety of the fixed platform;

(c) destroying a ship or fixed platform;

(d) causing damage—

 (i) to a ship or its cargo which is likely to endanger its safe navigation, or

 (ii) to a fixed platform which is likely to endanger its safety;

(e) placing or causing to be placed on a ship or fixed platform, by any means, a device or substance which is likely to—

 (i) destroy the ship or fixed platform, or

 (ii) cause the damage referred to in *paragraph (d)*;

(f) destroying or seriously damaging maritime navigational facilities or seriously interfering with their operation, if the destruction, damage or interference is likely to endanger the safe navigation of a ship;

(g) endangering the safe navigation of a ship by communicating information which the person knows to be false;

(h) or killing any person in connection with doing any of the acts mentioned elsewhere in this subsection;

(i) with the aim of compelling a person to do or not to do any act, threatening to endanger the safe navigation of a ship by doing any of the acts mentioned elsewhere in this subsection;

(j) attempting to do any of the acts mentioned in this subsection."

The basis upon which extraterritorial jurisdiction can be exercised is set out in s 3(1): **12–31**

"Section 2 (1) applies to an act done outside the State in relation to a ship or a fixed platform if it is done—

(a) by any person on board or against an Irish ship,

(b) by a citizen of Ireland on board or against a ship (other than an Irish ship) or a fixed platform, or

(c) subject to *subsection (2)*, by a person who is not a citizen of Ireland on board or against a ship (other than an Irish ship) or a fixed platform."

Section 2(1) of the Air Navigation and Transport Act 1973 essentially extends the **12–32** jurisdiction of the Irish courts in respect of any offence committed aboard an Irish registered aircraft:

"Any act or omission which, if taking place in the State, would constitute an offence under the law of the State, shall, if it takes place on board an Irish controlled aircraft while in flight elsewhere than in or over the State, constitute that offence."

Criminal Law (Jurisdiction) Act 1976

12–33   Whilst the Criminal Law (Jurisdiction) Act 1976 does provide for the prosecution of extraterritorial offences it is highly unlikely to arise practically in the context of the European arrest warrant given that its scope is restricted to criminal acts committed in Northern Ireland.

Explosives

12–34   Section 3 of the Explosives Act 1883 makes it an offence for any person, being an Irish citizen who:

> "...outside the State unlawfully and maliciously -
>
> (a)   does any act with intent to cause, or conspires to cause by an explosive substance an exposion of a nature likely to endanger life, or cause serious injury to property, whether in the State or elsewhere, or
>
> (b)   makes or has in his possession or under his control an explosive substance with intent by means thereof to endanger life, or cause serious injury to property, whether in the State or elsewhere, or to enable any other person so to do..."

12–35   Specific provision is also made in respect of aiders, abettors and accessories in s 5 of the Act.

Terrorism Offences

12–36   The Criminal Justice (Terrorist Offences) Act 2005 creates a number of offences which are by and large predicated upon the exercise of extraterritorial jurisdiction as a consequence of the very broad definition of "terrorist activity" provided for in s 4 of the Act. The definition includes conduct outside the State.

Sexual Offences Involving Minors

12–37   Limited extraterritorial jurisdiction is enjoyed in respect of certain sexual offences involving children. Section 2(1) of the Sexual Offences (Jurisdiction) Act 1996 provides:

> "Where a person, being a citizen of the State or being ordinarily resident in the State, does an act, in a place other than the State ("the place") against or involving a child which –
>
> (a)   constitutes an offence under the law of the place, and
>
> (b)   if done within the State, would constitute an offence under, or referred to in, an enactment specified in the Schedule to this Act,
>
> he or she shall be guilty of the second mentioned offence."

The Act also makes provision for the prosecution of attempts, incitement of offences, aiding and abetting etc.   **12–38**

Offences in Respect of Organised Crime

Section 74 of the Criminal Justice Act 2006[14] provides for extraterritorial effect in respect of the substantive offences of participating in or directing a criminal gang created by ss 71A and 72.   **12–39**

Offences Against the State Acts

Section 18 of the Criminal Justice (Amendment) Act 2009 extends extraterritorial jurisdiction in respect of the offence of obstruction of government contrary to section of the Offences Against the State Act 1939 but solely on the basis that the offending conduct takes place on an Irish registered ship or aircraft or that the offender is an Irish citizen or resident within the State.   **12–40**

Treason

Section 1 of the Treason Act 1939 allows for the prosecution for treason of any person ordinarily resident within the State irrespective of where the actual offence was committed.   **12–41**

Bigamy

Section 57 of the Offences Against the Person Act 1861 would seem to provide for the prosecution of the offence of bigamy wherever it is committed. However, it has been suggested[15] that the reference to any "subject of her majesty" in relation to the definition of the extraterritorial element of the offence has not been the subject of any legislative adaptation which might have the effect of applying it to citizens of the State and as such the continued existence of the extraterritorial version of this offence is open to doubt.   **12–42**

Conspiracy

There is authority for the proposition that extraterritorial jurisdiction may be exercised in respect of a conspiracy to commit an offence within the State even though the conspiracy takes place outside the State. In *Ellis v O'Dea (No. 2)*[16] it was held: **12–43**

> "...it is a fundamental principle of the Irish common law, applicable to the criminal jurisdiction of the Irish courts, that a person entering into a conspiracy outside Ireland in furtherance of which an overt act is done in Ireland is amenable to trial in the courts of Ireland. I am equally satisfied that a person who, though located outside Ireland, does an act which either in itself or by

---

[14] As amended by s 11 of the Criminal Justice (Amendment) Act 2009.
[15] See Ryan and Magee, "The Irish Criminal Process", (1983) at p 32.
[16] [1991] 1 IR 251.

reason of the conduct of an accomplice has the effect of completing a criminal offence in Ireland, is amendable to the Irish courts."[17]

12–44　The offence of conspiracy has now been largely codified by means of s 71 of the Criminal Justice Act 2006 which also provides for extraterritorial effect.

Aiding and Abetting

12–45　Section 7 of the Criminal Law Act 1997 which provides for criminal liability on the part of aiders and abettors now includes detailed provision in respect of offences committed outside the jurisdiction of the State. Section 7(1A)[18] provides:

> "Any person who, outside the State, aids, abets, counsels or procures the commission of an indictable offence in the State shall be liable to be indicted, tried and punished as a principal offender if –
>
> (a)　the person does so on board an Irish ship,
>
> (b)　the person does so on an aircraft registered in the State,
>
> (c)　the person is an Irish citizen, or
>
> (d)　the person is ordinarily resident in the State."

12–46　Provision for extraterritorial jurisdiction in respect of accessories after the fact and the withholding of information is made in ss 7(2A) and 8(1A) respectively of the same Act.

Interference with Witnesses and Jurors

12–47　The offence of intimidating or putting in fear prospective witnesses and jurors created by s 41 of the Criminal Justice Act 1991[19] now also enjoys extraterritorial effect in circumstances similar to those as apply in respect of ss 7 and 8 of the Criminal Law Act 1997.

War Crimes

12–48　Section 12 of the International Criminal Court Act 2006 allows for the exercise of extraterritorial jurisdiction in relation to war crimes, grave breaches of the Geneva Convention and International Criminal Court offences.

Fraud and Corruption Affecting the European Communities

12–49　The offences of fraud and corruption insofar as they affect the financial interests of the European Communities can be prosecuted on an extraterritorial basis pursuant to s 45 of the Criminal Justice (Theft and Fraud Offences) Act 2001.

---

[17]　p 258.

[18]　As inserted by s 19 of the Criminal Justice (Amendment) Act 2009.

[19]　As amended by s 20 of the Criminal Justice (Amendment) Act 2009.

Drug Trafficking Offences at Sea

Part V of the Criminal Justice Act 1994 creates an offence of drug trafficking on **12–50** a ship registered in a State which is a signatory to the United Nations Convention against Illicit Traffic in Narcotic Drugs and Psychotropic Substances. Section 33 provides:

> "A person is guilty of a drug trafficking offence if the person does, on an Irish ship, a ship registered in a Convention State or a ship not registered in any country or territory, any act which, if done in the State, would constitute such an offence."

Given that the vast majority of countries have now ratified the Convention, s 33 **12–51** covers nearly all drug trafficking offences at sea.[20]

EXTRA-TERRITORIALITY AND RETROSPECTIVITY

Section 44 is not explicit as to whether the issue of reciprocity should be considered **12–52** by reference to a hypothetical set of facts at the time of the offence or at the time of the issue of the European arrest warrant or even at the time of the hearing. Given that the exception to surrender contained in s 44 is concerned with the principle of reciprocity and the goal of maintaining the balance of obligations as they existed at the time of the offence, there is a certain logical attraction in approaching the question on the basis of whether or not a reciprocal entitlement to prosecute for the offence would have existed at the time of the offence. This is particularly so when one considers that the Oireachtas saw fit to specifically allow the courts to have regard to the position in respect of correspondence as of the date of issue of the warrant rather than the date of the offence.[21]

However, it has been suggested, given the history of the Art 4.7 and the **12–53** purpose of the optional grounds for refusing to surrender having been included in the Framework Decision by way of compensating for the partial loss of the dual criminality requirement, that it is more appropriate to consider the issue of reciprocity as of the time of the s 16 hearing.[22] The issue was determined in this jurisdiction in *Minister for Justice, Equality and Law Reform v Aamond*.[23] In that case the surrender of the respondent was sought in respect of an international drug trafficking offence which had taken place on the high seas some years earlier. It was only possible to seek his surrender once the island State of Vanuatu, where the boat used in the course of the drug trafficking offence had been registered, had signed the United Nations Convention against Illicit Traffic in Narcotic Drugs and Psychotropic Substances. Thereafter it became possible to argue that the State would have been entitled to prosecute on a reciprocal basis in respect of an offence under s 33 of the Criminal Justice Act 1994.

---

[20] See *Minister for Justice, Equality and Law Reform v Aamond* [2006] IEHC 382.

[21] s 5.

[22] See Keijzer and van Sliedregt, "The European Arrest Warrant in Practice" (2009) at p 97.

[23] [2006] IEHC 382. Note: The name of the respondent is misspelled in the judgment. The respondent, Poul John Aamand, had previously been the subject of an unsuccessful attempt to extradite pursuant to Part II of the Extradition Act 1965 as to which see *Aamand v Smithwick & Others* [1995] 1 ILRM 61.

12–54   It was common case that the State would have jurisdiction to try such an offence were it committed at the time of the s 16 hearing but would not have had jurisdiction to try such an offence were it to have been committed at the time the offence alleged in the warrant was said to have been committed. The court held that it was not restricted to considering the hypothetical issue only in relation to the date of the offence but could consider it on a contemporary basis. Particular emphasis was laid on the use of the present tense in the words "does not" as used in s 44. Peart J concluded:

> "It must be remembered that it is not the ratification of that Convention which has given rise to the offence under the laws of Denmark and for which he is sought to face trial. The ratification of the Convention has relevance only as to whether the acts committed in 1988 *now* would be an offence under Irish law. That is the basis which the Oireachtas has laid down for deciding whether or not the surrender of a respondent should be prohibited in respect of an extra-territorial offence. That is clear from the words used. According to those words, the surrender is not prohibited, and I am satisfied that this is consistent also with the terms of Article 7.4 of the Framework Decision."

12–55   It is, therefore, permissible to surrender for an extraterritorial offence even though the same offence could not, strictly speaking, give rise to a prosecution in this jurisdiction by virtue of the offence not having been amenable to prosecution at the time of its commission. A similar conclusion was reached in *Minister for Justice, Equality and Law Reform v Cidylow*.[24]

---

[24] *Ex tempore*, High Court, Peart J, 22 April 2010.

CHAPTER 13

Trials in Absentia

Trial *in absentia* denotes the conviction and/or sentencing of a person in his or her **13–01** absence. Whilst the concept arises very rarely in practice in this jurisdiction (on indictment at least) it is a much more common occurrence in most other Member States. This differentiation most likely has its roots in 19th century French criminal procedure which influenced many legal systems across the continent. It distinguished between two different circumstances which might give rise to the trial of an accused person in his or her absence. In the first instance where the person simply could not be located a form of default judgment or conviction could be entered. This was subject to a right of appeal which was to some extent circumscribed. The other situation which might arise was where the accused person was deemed to have fled. The accused was then considered to be a rebel and the procedure adopted in such cases (trial *in contumacio*) inevitably lead to conviction and by and large obviated the necessity to call witnesses or hear evidence. It is the first of these procedures, the default procedure, which has in one form or another found its way into various modern continental criminal justice systems.

This is not to say, however, that the approach to trial *in absentia* amongst **13–02** continental Member States is in any sense uniform. Traditionally many countries have sought to reserve their position in relation to extradition of those who have been convicted in their absence. In such instances extradition has been conditional upon an examination of the procedures adopted in the case of the person sought in the requesting State . This approach ultimately found expression in the Second Additional Protocol to the 1957 European Convention on Extradition (17th March 1978) which expressly allowed the requested State to conduct an examination of the procedure adopted in the requesting State to ensure that it met the appropriate minimum safeguards.[1] Moreover, even a brief examination of the jurisprudence of the European Court of Human Rights suggests that the manner in which the various signatories approach the question of trial *in absentia* differs enormously.

---

[1] The protocol allowed signatories to refuse extradition in relation to convictions *in absentia* if in the view of the requested State "…the proceedings leading to the judgment did not satisfy the minimum rights of defence recognised as due to everyone charged with a criminal offence".

THE FRAMEWORK DECISION: ARTICLE 5.1

13-03   Article 5.1 of the Framework Decision allows individual Member States to qualify their obligation to surrender in such cases to some extent. The terms of Art 5.1 are permissive as opposed to mandatory:

> "Where the European arrest warrant has been issued for the purposes of executing a sentence or a detention order imposed by a decision rendered and if the person concerned has not been summoned in person or otherwise informed of the date and place of the hearing which led to the decision rendered *in absentia*, surrender may be subject to the condition that the issuing judicial authority gives an assurance deemed adequate to guarantee the person who is the subject of the European arrest warrant that he or she will have an opportunity to apply for a retrial of the case in the issuing Member State and to be present at the judgment."

13-04   The exception to surrender provided for in Art 5.1 is not absolute and is ultimately subject to any guarantees as regards a re-trial which may be provided by the requesting State. In this regard it is to be differentiated from the grounds for optional non-execution set out in Art 4 none of which may be *trumped* by the provision of some type of guarantee. Moreover, the Framework Decision seems to envisage that the issue of the provision of such guarantees be dealt with at the conclusion of the proceedings to determine whether surrender should be ordered. Article 15 appears to set out a procedural sequence of events in this regard. This sequence is perhaps of little enough significance in the context of the 2003 Act given that all matters in dispute are contested in the course of the s 16 hearing and the court in any event retains an entitlement to seek further information, including the provision of guarantees, at any point pursuant to the provisions of s 20.

13-05   The principal difficulty with Art 5.1 is that it fails to define any of the terms it uses. Quite what is meant by "otherwise informed" or "retrial" is unclear and it would seem that the term "judgment" is used interchangeably with the term trial or perhaps is simply used in error. These difficulties are particularly unfortunate as trial *in absentia* is perhaps the most contentious issue that arises in the context of the European arrest warrant due to the divergence of practice amongst Member States. It might be observed that given the very vague terms of Art 5.1 it may be difficult for domestic courts to obtain much assistance in interpreting domestic legislative provisions on a purposive basis.

SECTION 45

13-06   Article 5.1 is given effect by s 45 of the 2003 Act which essentially sets out a two stage enquiry process for the court. Firstly the court must decide if the respondent was convicted *in absentia*. It is clear that what is contemplated here is not simply that the respondent was not present at his trial but rather that he was not informed of its time and place or for some other reason was prevented from attending. In other words if the respondent was aware of the time and place of his trial and chose not to be present he is not a person to whom s 45 applies. Secondly, where the court decides that the respondent is a person to whom s 45 applies it must go on to consider whether an adequate guarantee as to a retrial has been provided. Section 45 provides as follows:

"A person shall not be surrendered under this Act if—

(a) he or she was not present when he or she was tried for and convicted of the offence specified in the European arrest warrant, and

    (i) he or she was not notified of the time when, and place at which, he or she would be tried for the offence, or

    (ii) he or she was not permitted to attend the trial in respect of the offence concerned,

unless the issuing judicial authority gives an undertaking in writing that the person will, upon being surrendered—

    (I) be retried for that offence or be given the opportunity of a retrial in respect of that offence,

    (II) be notified of the time when, and place at which any retrial in respect of the offence concerned will take place, and

    (III) be permitted to be present when any such retrial takes place."

As with the Framework Decision s 45 provides no assistance in identifying what is meant by either "notification" or "retrial".   **13–07**

The *in absentia* exception to surrender will only apply where the respondent was absent for *both* the trial and conviction. Therefore a respondent who may have attended for the first part of his or her trial and thereafter absconded would not appear to be covered. Such a person would, in any event, presumably have received sufficient notice to allow him or her to attend in the first instance.   **13–08**

NOTIFICATION

No difficulty will arise in relation to the issue of notification where it is apparent from the warrant or other material before the court that the respondent was personally summonsed. However the situation where some other form of notification is relied upon is much less clear. Article 5.1 of the Framework Decision appears to draw a distinction between being "summonsed in person" and "otherwise informed". It has been suggested that the failure to make explicit the requirement that a person may be "otherwise informed" by means other than personal service is in fact an error in the drafting of the Framework Decision.[2] Given that many civil law jurisdictions contemplate such modes of service as posting a notice at the town hall or court registry sufficient where the wanted person is effectively untraceable, the issue as to whether such indirect means of notification are sufficient is potentially of critical importance.   **13–09**

The suggestion that Art 5.1 contains an error in that it fails to apply the requirement of personal knowledge to other forms of notification is very much in line with the jurisprudence of the European Court of Human Rights which expressly criticised   **13–10**

---

[2] See Blekxtoon and Ballegooij, "Handbook on the European Arrest Warrant", (2005) at p 239.

signatory States which allow for the conviction of accused persons *in absentia* on the basis of constructive notice of the proceedings – most recently in *Sejdovic v Italy*[3]:

> "In previous cases concerning convictions *in absentia*, the Court has held that to inform someone of a prosecution brought against him is a legal act of such importance that it must be carried out in accordance with procedural and substantive requirements capable of guaranteeing the effective exercise of the accused's rights; vague and informal knowledge cannot suffice (see *T. v. Italy*, cited above, p. 42, § 28, and *Somogyi*, cited above, § 75). The Court cannot, however, rule out the possibility that certain established facts might provide an unequivocal indication that the accused is aware of the existence of the criminal proceedings against him and of the nature and the cause of the accusation and does not intend to take part in the trial or wishes to escape prosecution. This may be the case, for example, where the accused states publicly or in writing that he does not intend to respond to summonses of which he has become aware through sources other than the authorities, or succeeds in evading an attempted arrest (see, among other authorities, *Iavarazzo v. Italy* (dec.), no. 50489/99, 4 December 2001), or when materials are brought to the attention of the authorities which unequivocally show that he is aware of the proceedings pending against him and of the charges he faces."[4]

13–11 In that case the applicant had been proceeded against in his absence in circumstances where there was little positive evidence to suggest he had fled although he had become untraceable in the immediate aftermath of the killing of which he was convicted.

13–12 The decision is instructive in that it highlights the importance which ought to be attached to the entitlement of the accused to be made expressly aware of the proceedings against him or her. Most of the other procedural rights which arise under Art 6 of the Convention necessitate the presence of the accused i.e. the right to legal assistance, the right to an interpreter, the right to challenge witnesses etc. It follows that a denial of an accused's right to be present at trial or to be expressly informed of same is tantamount to a denial of those other fundamental rights. As such the European Court of Human Rights, not surprisingly, took the view that a trial *in absentia* is only permissible where the accused has expressly waived his or her right to be present. In practical terms this means in circumstances where the accused has deliberately chosen not to attend his/her trial:

> "The Court has further held that the duty to guarantee the right of a criminal defendant to be present in the courtroom – either during the original proceedings or in a retrial – ranks as one of the essential requirements of Article 6 (see *Stoichkov v. Bulgaria*, no. 9808/02, § 56, 24 March 2005). Accordingly, the refusal to reopen proceedings conducted in the accused's absence, without any indication that the accused has waived his or her right to be present during the trial, has been found to be a "flagrant denial of justice" rendering the proceedings "manifestly contrary to the provisions of Article 6 or the principles embodied therein" (ibid., §§ 54-58)."[5]

---

[3] ECHR, Case 56581/00.

[4] Paragraph 99.

[5] Paragraph 84.

The requirement that an accused person expressly waive such a right has been an **13–13** established feature of the jurisprudence of the European Court of Human Rights for some time[6] and it would be surprising given the terms of para 12 of the Recitals to the Framework Decision, which in effect imports the provisions of the Convention, if the Framework Decision were to be interpreted in a manner which did not take adequate account of this.

The courts in this jurisdiction initially took quite a different approach to that of **13–14** the European Court of Human Rights in dealing with convictions *in absentia* in the context of the European arrest warrant. In effect the courts here were content to assume that the respondent waived his Art 6 right to be present at his trial on the basis of what the ECtHR might characterise as "vague and informal knowledge". In *Minister for Justice, Equality and Law Reform v Ciobanica*[7] the respondent said that he had never received any of the postal notifications in relation to his trial at an address which he described as being one that he used for "official purposes". The High Court referred to the decision of the European Court of Human Rights in *Hennings v Germany*[8] which concerned the question of whether actual as opposed to constructive notice of a penal order was required by Art 6 of the Convention. In *Hennings* it had been held that the domestic provisions providing for service of such orders by post were permissible and that it was ultimately up to the applicant to ensure that he took the appropriate steps to collect his post. Mr Hennings, who had been convicted in relation to a minor altercation with a train ticket collector and fined, claimed that he had been unaware of the notice of the proceedings against him which was sitting in his letter box because his wife had the keys to the letter box and was away on holidays.

In *Ciobanica* the court took the view that once it was established that the **13–15** respondent had been notified in accordance with the provisions of the relevant penal code of the requesting State, this of itself was sufficient to show that he had been notified in accordance with the terms of s 45:

> "He has stated that this is the address which he used for official purposes, and this Court is entitled to assume therefore that any document required to be sent to him, including a letter notifying him of the date time and a place that his trial would take place, could be sent to him at that address. Thereafter it is a matter for himself as to whether he produces a situation whereby the contents of a letter addressed to him at that address remain unknown to him by reason of his having left the country, or otherwise not keeping in touch with his mother in relation to any post which may have been directed to him at her address. I am satisfied that he was "notified" in accordance with the requirements of the Romanian Code of Criminal Procedure, and that this court is not required to look beyond that in order to be certain that he was actually aware of the contents of the letter in question."

Obviously such an approach was at odds with that taken by the European Court of **13–16** Human Rights in relation to convictions *in absentia*.[9]

---

[6] See also *Colozza v Italy* (12 February 1985) and *Poitrimol v France* (23 November 1993).

[7] [2008] IEHC 61.

[8] 16 December 1992, Application No. 12129/86.

[9] See also *Minister for Justice, Equality and Law Reform v Gheorgie* [2008] IEHC 115.

Minister for Justice, Equality and Law Reform v Sliczynski

13–17   In *Minister for Justice, Equality and Law Reform v Sliczynski*[10] the High Court went even further and specifically adopted the position that the issue of service was one which was to be considered not in the context of what would normally be considered to amount to service in this jurisdiction, nor even to commonly accepted norms across the European Union, but rather by reference to the provisions in relation to service in the requesting State:

> "The position therefore as I see it is that a question arises as to whether under Polish law this person was notified in accordance with Polish law of the trial. Now, the Polish authority indicates that as far as they are concerned he was notified by communication through his mother. This Court is not in a position to decide that matter of fact."

13–18   In effect the court eschewed any role in determining whether the service referred to in the warrant was in any way effective or meaningful. In *Sliczynski*, as in many other cases, the respondent deposed to the fact that he was unaware of his trial and this assertion was essentially un-contradicted. Given that it is considered sufficient in many continental jurisdictions to effect service by way of posting notice of trial at the town hall local to the accused the effect of the decision was that the requirement of notification contained in s 45 would vary depending upon the level of procedural safeguards applicable in the requesting State and might frequently be more notional than real. In other words the interpretation which the courts had adopted in relation to s 45 did not seek to hold the requesting State to any objective standard of fairness but rather simply sought to hold it to the terms of its own procedure which was then assumed to be adequate.

13–19   Such an approach was highly problematic. In the first instance many cases involving convictions *in absentia* were historic in nature and the provisions in relation to notification which may have been in force at the time may well have left a lot to be desired when considered in light of the more recent jurisprudence emanating from Strasbourg. Moreover from a historical point of view a requested State would generally look at the procedure adopted in the requesting State and ask whether it considered such notification adequate in the light of its own constitutional norms and imperatives.[11] Indeed it might be said that there is little point in a State reserving its position in relation to convictions *in absentia* on the basis of a concern that such convictions may be unfair unless it is going to apply its own yardstick in considering whether a difficulty arises. Applying the yardstick of the requesting State will, by definition, never lead to a refusal to surrender in such a case. It has been suggested that the Framework Decision itself mandates such an approach:

> "...the wording of Article 5, taken in conjunction with paragraph (12) of the Preamble (which guarantees Member States' powers to apply their

---

[10] [2008] IESC 73.

[11] The case of *Sejdovic* cited above is directly in point in this regard. After leaving Italy Mr Sejdovic had travelled to Germany where he was ultimately arrested for the purposes of extradition under the 1957 convention. The German courts ultimately refused to extradite him, however, on the grounds that his conviction *in absentia* did not adhere to the appropriate standards in terms of procedural safeguards.

constitutional rules relating to due process), determines that the requesting and the requested State (i.e. the issuing and the executing authority) retain their national procedural machinery which – in the executing State – has competence to assess aspects of fundamental fairness regarding the concerned person's trial or punishment in the issuing State and to postpone surrender until the issuing authority adequately ensures that the surrendered person will not be denied certain standards of justice."[12]

By simply providing for an option to refuse surrender on the grounds that the trial **13–20** of the respondent took place *in absentia* the Framework Decision addresses itself to particular concerns held by some Member States. It is apparent that the Oireachtas had such concerns in that it availed of what essentially amounts to a reservation contained in Art 5.1. Presumably such concerns arose from what we would consider to be the minimum applicable safeguards in relation to the entitlement of an accused person to be present for trial. Consequently it was difficult to see how such concerns can be satisfied by reference to compliance with the domestic procedure applicable in the requesting State which may well be what has given rise to the concerns in the first place.

Ultimately the Supreme Court overturned the decision of the High Court in **13–21** *Sliczynski* on appeal. It considered that whilst it may well have been established on the evidence that the respondent had been notified so far as the law of the requesting State was concerned, the issue under the 2003 Act was for the court to consider whether such notification met the standard set out in s 45. In that regard Murray CJ noted:

> "The ordinary meaning of that language is that it is the person to be tried who must be notified. It must be actual notification and not any other notification. I cannot read into s. 45 a meaning that envisaged notification to a person's mother or other person being presumed sufficient, especially when there is no evidence that the person concerned received any notification. If it was intended that any other form of notification or some form of constructive notification, particularly where trial for a criminal offence is concerned, the Oireachtas would have expressly said so.
>
> Under Polish law it may be sufficient, for the purpose of trying somebody in Poland in their absence, to give them notification by delivering it to some person at their place of residence and even that does not seem to have been done in this case but that is not the kind of notice to which s. 45 refers. It would, as I say, require some express provision in our Act, along the lines of that expressly stated in the Polish Article 132, to deem that kind of notice sufficient for the purpose of s. 45."

It is clear, therefore, that the notice of the respondent's trial must represent an **13–22** actual rather than constructive notification. Moreover, the fact that the notification afforded to the respondent may satisfy the domestic procedural requirements of the requesting State is more or less irrelevant to the exercise which must be carried out under s 45.

---

[12] Blekxtoon and Ballegooij, "Handbook on the European Arrest Warrant" (2005) at p 120.

GUARANTEE OF A RETRIAL

13–23   Where the court has concluded that either the respondent was not notified of the time and place of this trial or was otherwise prevented from attending it may still order surrender subject to receiving an undertaking in writing that the respondent will be retried or given the opportunity of a retrial. At the outset it should be noted that the terms of s 45 in this regard would appear to go somewhat further than what is envisaged by the Framework Decision, which requires the requesting State to give an adequate assurance that the respondent will have "an opportunity to apply for a retrial." The distinction between being entitled to a retrial and being entitled to apply for a retrial is obvious. Once more it would appear that the drafting of the Framework Decision leaves something to be desired in this regard. The European Court of Human Rights would appear to regard it as virtually a *sine qua non* that where an accused person is convicted *in absentia,* but has not expressly waived the right to be present at trial, there be an entitlement to a retrial once the person has been made amenable:

> "Although proceedings that take place in the accused's absence are not of themselves incompatible with Article 6 of the Convention, a denial of justice nevertheless undoubtedly occurs where a person convicted *in absentia* is unable subsequently to obtain from a court which has heard him in accordance with the requirements of Article 6 a fresh determination of the merits of the charge, in respect of both law and fact, where it has not been established that he has waived his right to appear and to defend himself…"[13]

13–24   The entitlement to apply for a retrial contained in Art 5.1 does not in any meaningful way address this issue. On the contrary this provision which is self evidently incorporated in the Framework Decision for the purpose of vindicating the rights of the respondent would, on the face of it, appear to have the effect of diluting those rights. It has been suggested that the correct interpretation of Art 5.1 is to require that a right to a retrial be provided as opposed to an opportunity to apply for one.[14] If such an analysis is correct it would appear that the requirement of s 45 that a retrial be guaranteed may not be as far out of step with the provisions of the Framework Decision as it may have seemed at first glance.

13–25   The terms of s 45 are quite specific in that they require that the judicial authority in the requesting State to provide a written undertaking in respect of a retrial. In *Sliczynski* there was no written undertaking given as such although the following translation of Art 482 of the Code of Criminal Procedure of Poland had been furnished by the issuing judicial authority:

> "The sentence issued in absentia will be served by the Defendant. The Defendant may appeal against the sentence in absentia within seven days after the copy has been duly served and the appeal should contain justification of the Defendant's absence from the trial. The Defendant may combine the appeal with a request for sentence justification in case that the appeal is rejected."

---

[13]   *Sejdovic v Italy*, ECHR Case 56581/00.

[14]   See Blekxtoon and Ballegooij, "Handbook on the European Arrest Warrant" (2005) at p 128.

Even allowing for translation it would be difficult to construe the foregoing as amounting to a guarantee of retrial or even a guarantee of an opportunity to apply for a retrial. Notwithstanding this the High Court, at first instance, considered that a construction of s 45, s 4A and Art 5 of the Framework Decision allowed it to do just that:

> "...the point has been made in submission that that is not a guarantee of a retrial, but I am satisfied that a proper interpretation of Section 45 and the Framework Decision in Article 5 is that the procedure available in Poland whereby the respondent may apply to the court there for a retrial is a sufficient guarantee for this court to ensure that there is compliance with the Framework Decision. I rely on Section 4A of the European Arrest Warrant Act, 2003... Now that presumption is in relation to future events, and in the circumstances of this case it entitles me to presume or this court to presume that in relation to any application that may be made by this respondent under Article 482 of the Code of Criminal Procedure in Poland for a retrial, that any decision made by the Polish court on that application will be one that complies with Poland's obligations under the Framework Decision, and I am entitled to take that view in my view by virtue of Section 4A of the Act as inserted by the 2005 Act."

13–26

On appeal the Supreme Court rejected such an approach and held that the undertaking envisaged by s 45 must be just that:

13–27

> "This is what Ireland has done by virtue of s. 45 and that pre-condition can only be met in the form of a written undertaking which the section requires. The section is very specific. It requires that " *...the issuing Judicial Authority gives an undertaking in writing*" that the person surrendered will be retried for the offence or be given an opportunity of a retrial in respect of the offence. The section does not require proof that the law of the requesting State provides for a retrial of the offence, or provides for the surrendered person to have an opportunity of a retrial, (and in any event Polish law appears to provide for a review of sentence only on appeal, if taken within time) but requires the Judicial Authority to give a written undertaking. The absence of an undertaking is a fatal flaw in the request concerning the fourth offence."

A similar conclusion was reached in *Minister for Justice, Equality and Law Reform v Gritunic*.[15] In that case the warrant suggested that in the event of his surrender the respondent "may enjoy the benefit of a new trial if the above judgment is set aside". Although expressing some doubts as to the accuracy of the translation of the warrant Peart J was not satisfied that this was a sufficient guarantee for the purposes of s 45:

13–28

> "The use of the word *"may"* falls short of a guarantee, and the reference to *"if the above judgment is set aside"* suggests a measure of discretion on the part of a judge on an application to set aside the judgment."

The court, thereafter, procured further correspondence between the Central Authority and the issuing judicial authority for the purpose of clarifying the situation. The confusing and somewhat tortuous nature of the correspondence is apparent from the

13–29

---

15 [2009] IEHC 342.

judgment and serves to highlight the difficulties which can arise in relation to what should be a relatively straightforward issue.

WHAT AMOUNTS TO A RETRIAL

13–30   As noted above little assistance is to be found in either the Act or the Framework Decision as to what is meant be a "retrial". In *Minister for Justice, Equality and Law Reform v Machevicius*[16] the warrant recited a portion of the Lithuanian Penal Code which dealt with the entitlement to appeal a conviction which would presumably be open to a respondent who was surrendered. Specifically the relevant provision required that:

> "…the court of appeal must once again conduct those actions of investigating evidence which were carried out by the court of first instance, on which the judgment of conviction was based, if the convicted person objects to the assessment of evidence in his/her appeal."[17]

13–31   The court held that in the circumstances this provision amounted to a guarantee of a re-trial. The High Court considered that even though what was provided for was an appeal the nature of it was appeal by way of re-hearing:

> "There is no requirement that such a re-trial be a first instance re-trial with the potential of an appeal thereafter. What the Framework Decision requires is that the person has an opportunity upon surrender to be tried again in his presence. The Code referred to provides specifically that if the person is unhappy with the assessment of the evidence by the judge who dealt with the hearing in absentia, he can require the appeal court to "once again conduct those actions of investigating evidence which were carried out by the court of first instance.""

13–32   That decision is to be contrasted with the decision in *Minister for Justice, Equality and Law Reform v Gokano*[18] where it was held that the provision of an appeal as opposed to a retrial was not sufficient for the purpose of s 45:

> "In addition, that document speaks only of a right of "appeal" and not "retrial". Certainly in this jurisdiction there is a world of difference between a retrial and an appeal against a conviction and it would not be possible for this court to reach a conclusion … that the guarantee required under art. 5 of the Framework Decision and as given effect to by s. 45 of the Act, has been provided."

13–33   Ultimately the court must look at what is proposed by way of "retrial" and consider whether it amounts to a substantive reconsideration of the evidence in the case such as to allow the respondent to exercise the due process rights that his or her earlier absence prevented being exercised. In the case of *Minister for Justice, Equality*

---

[16] [2007] IEHC 78.
[17] Given the decision of the Supreme Court in *Sliczynski* and specifically the requirement that a written undertaking be given rather than simply reciting the relevant legislative provision, the decision in *Machievicius* may be of questionable weight.
[18] [2004] 3 IR 216.

and Law Reform v Marek[19] the Supreme Court were not satisfied that the "re-trial" proposed by the requesting State was sufficient. Murray CJ commented:

> "...a re-trial in its ordinary and natural meaning refers to a trial de novo, that is to say, a trial of the accused as if he was on trial for the first time for the offence or offences in question.

> The requesting Judicial Authority in drafting and setting out the terms of the European Arrest Warrant did state that there was a particular legal guarantee available to the appellant namely that he will after delivery have the right to a new trial in his presence. This right, it was stated, is guaranteed by S. 306A, Part 2 of the Code of Criminal Procedure of the Czech Republic and it then proceeds to quote from that provision. What the Judicial Authority means be a re-trial in that respect is indicated by s. 1 of that Code which in translation includes the following statement:

> > "That if the defendant so demands new evidence shall be admitted to the Court which had not been presented in previous proceedings whose character can allow it or which cannot be prevented by other relevant matters otherwise the statements of evidence will be read to the accused and he will have the possibility to comment on them."

> That raises a question in the mind of the Court as to the meaning and effect and the interpretation to be given to the undertakings provided by the requesting Judicial Authority pursuant to s. 45. Simply reading statements of evidence rather than hearing witnesses does not suggest a re-trial."

The court expressed itself not to be satisfied that the undertaking complied with **13–34** the provisions of s 45 and ultimately remitted the matter to the High Court for the purpose of ascertaining whether a proper undertaking might be obtained from the issuing State.[20] The comments of Murray CJ in relation to the nature of a re-trial being akin to being put on "trial for the first time" were clarified in the subsequent case of *Minister for Justice, Equality and Law Reform v Gheorghe*[21]:

> "It is important to recall that what section 45 requires is that the person surrendered should have the benefit of an undertaking that he or she will be *retried for the offence* of which he or she has been convicted *in absentia*. It is axiomatic that the retrial will take place in accordance with the rules of criminal law and procedure of the issuing state. The statement of the Chief Justice upon which reliance is placed should not be read, in itself, as if it were a section of the statute. Clearly, the Chief Justice did not intend to add words to the statute. The notion that the retrial should take place *"as if he was on trial for the first time for the offence or offences in question"* could not mean that the first trial had been obliterated from history. Even in our law, there are circumstances in which the

---

[19] Unreported, Supreme Court, 5 February 2009.

[20] In due course further information was forthcoming from the authorities in the issuing State to allow the High Court to conclude that in fact the respondent would be granted a re-trial that was *de novo* in nature. See *Minister for Justice, Equality and Law Reform v Marek* [2010] IEHC 198.

[21] [2009] IESC 76.

evidence at a previous trial may be referred to. The provision of article 405.2 to the effect that the prosecution may use again evidence that was *"prepared during the first trial"* does not take away the character of a retrial."

13–35   Once it is clear that the respondent will be entitled to a re-hearing of the substantive issues of fact and law the court will, by and large, be satisfied. The mere fact that the retrial may take place before the same judge who originally convicted the respondent will be immaterial. In *Minister for Justice, Equality and Law Reform v Ster*[22] the respondent sought to argue that any retrial would be unsatisfactory as it would possibly be before the judge who had already convicted him in his absence. As such the respondent was attempting to add an additional gloss to the provisions of s 45 – namely that any retrial contemplated by the undertaking would be conducted before a judge other than the one who had been involved in the original trial. Not surprisingly the court rejected this line of argument.

---

[22]   [2008] IEHC 15.

CHAPTER 14

Specialty

NATURE OF THE RULE OF SPECIALTY

It is in the nature of any system of extradition or rendition that once the respondent **14–01** has been surrendered the role of the requested State is essentially at an end. In that regard the various reservations and exceptions to surrender that arise in relation to correspondence, minimum gravity and so on will be largely meaningless if the respondent could be prosecuted, subsequent to surrender, for offences in respect of which surrender was not sought. This has given rise to what is described as the rule of specialty. In short this allows the requested State to surrender subject to the requirement that the respondent will not be prosecuted for any offence other than that for which he was surrendered. The rationale underlying the rule was considered by the Supreme Court in *Minister for Justice, Equality and Law Reform v Gotszlik*[1]:

> "The specialty rule, which has long been part of extradition law, arises to protect
> the person surrendered from being prosecuted or sentenced for another offence
> on which he has not been surrendered. Thus, a State could not request a person
> for one offence and then prosecute or sentence him for another offence on which
> he had not been surrendered. This protection is and was important to protect
> persons. It has arisen especially to protect persons from being prosecuted for
> political offences or for offences on which there was no double criminality."[2]

---

[1] [2009] 3 IR 390.
[2] p 401.

14–02   Whilst it is frequently described as a "rule" the specialty provisions contained in the Framework Decision are in fact expressed as an optional ground for refusing surrender. Article 27.1 is drafted on the basis that Member States may actually choose to opt out of the specialty provisions in respect of their relations with other Member States who have also opted out:

> "Each Member State may notify the General Secretariat of the Council that, in its relations with other Member States that have given the same notification, consent is presumed to have been given for the prosecution, sentencing or detention with a view to the carrying out of a custodial sentence or detention order for an offence committed prior to his or her surrender, other than that for which he or she was surrendered, unless in a particular case the executing judicial authority states otherwise in its decision on surrender."[3]

14–03   Specialty is more appropriately regarded as a policy which informs the majority of extradition agreements rather than a rule as such. It should not be regarded as a general right which the requested person is entitled to invoke as deriving either from international law or domestic law but rather an exception to surrender that can only be considered in the specific terms of the statute or agreement that gives rise to it. The version of the *rule* which appears in the Framework Decision and the European Arrest Warrant Act 2003 is subject to a significant number of exceptions and a waiver procedure which can be invoked subsequent to surrender.

Onward Surrender

14–04   The provisions of the Framework Decision and the 2003 Act that deal with the prohibition of surrender, where it is anticipated that the respondent may either be surrendered under another European arrest warrant to another Member State or extradited to a non-Member State subsequent to surrender, can also be regarded as aspects of the general rule of specialty. Whilst the rule of specialty in its traditional form concerns itself with the prosecution of offences in the requesting State in respect of which surrender would not have been ordered, the provisions of ss 23 and 24 concern themselves with the prosecution of the surrendered person in a place other than the requesting State for such offences.

SECTION 22

14–05   In the absence of a Member State having made a notification in accordance with Art 27.1 of the Framework Decision the rule of specialty as set out in the remainder of that provision will apply. Unlike many other parts of the Framework Decision, Art 27 is quite particular in terms of the detail which it requires to be transposed into domestic legislation for the purpose of giving it the appropriate domestic effect. Whilst many of the other optional grounds for surrender leave a considerable margin to the Member State in relation to the terms, scope and mechanism of the provision in question, Art 27 sets out all of the essential detail which must be included if the rule of specialty is to be given effect in domestic legislation. It is not surprising, therefore, that s 22 of the 2003 Act follows almost precisely the terms of Art 27.

---

[3] As of the Commission's report of 11 July 2007 in relation to the implementation of the Framework Decision, only Austria and Estonia had made such a notification.

The general prohibition on surrender which might otherwise result in a breach of **14–06** the rule of specialty is contained in s 22(2):

> "(2) Subject to this section, the High Court shall refuse to surrender a person under this Act if it is satisfied that—
>
> (a) the law of the issuing state does not provide that a person who is surrendered to it pursuant to a European arrest warrant shall not be proceeded against, sentenced or detained for the purposes of executing a sentence or detention order, or otherwise restricted in his or her personal liberty, in respect of an offence, and
>
> (b) the person will be proceeded against, sentenced, or detained for the purposes of executing a sentence or detention order, or otherwise restricted in his or her personal liberty, in respect of an offence."

The first observation to be made in relation to the general prohibition contained **14–07** in s 22(2) is that it, in theory at least, requires the court to undertake a two stage enquiry before the prohibition is actually engaged. Firstly it must be satisfied that the law of the requesting State does not actually protect the surrendered person from prosecution for other offences. Secondly the court must be satisfied that the surrendered person will actually be prosecuted. It is clear that the conditions described in s 22(2)(a) and 22(2)(b) are cumulative.[4] As to whether these conditions exist in a given case is ultimately a matter of fact to be established on the evidence. Section 22(3) does, however, provide for an evidential presumption in that regard:

> "It shall be presumed that, in relation to a person to whom a European arrest warrant applies, the issuing state does not intend to—
>
> (a) proceed against him or her,
>
> (b) sentence or detain him or her for a purpose referred to in subsection (2)(*a*), or
>
> (c) otherwise restrict him or her in his or her personal liberty,
>
> in respect of an offence, unless the contrary is proved."[5]

---

[4] See *Minister for Justice Equality and Law Reform v Breen* [2008] IEHC 54 which concerned the provisions of s 24(1). The same logic applies with equal force to the provisions of s 22(2).

[5] There is a similar presumption in respect of onward surrender at s 23(3):

> "It shall be presumed that, in relation to a person to whom a European arrest warrant applies, the issuing state does not intend to surrender him or her to a Member State pursuant to a European arrest warrant issued by a judicial authority in that Member State in respect of an offence, unless the contrary is proved."

whilst in respect of onward extradition an almost identical provision appears at s 24(2):

> "It shall be presumed that, in relation to a person to whom a European arrest warrant applies, the issuing state does not intend to extradite him or her to a third country, unless the contrary is proved".

14–08   Even where there is material in the warrant itself from which an intention to prosecute for other offences might be inferred the presumption under s 22(3) may still apply. In *Minister for Justice, Equality and Law Reform v O'Sullivan*[6] the warrant recited that the judge who had presided over the trial at which the respondent had been convicted had commented that when the respondent was brought before him he would impose a consecutive sentence for an offence relating to the breach of his bail terms. It was argued that this amounted to an expression of an intention to see the respondent prosecuted for an offence not contained in the warrant. The court rejected such an argument on the basis that a comment by the presiding judge was not such as to displace the presumption created by s 22(3).

14–09   A similar approach was taken in *Minister for Justice, Equality and Law Reform v Mika*,[7] where additional information received from the requesting State alluded to further offences which the requested person was said to be guilty of but which had not been mentioned in the warrant. The Court referred to the s 22(3) presumption and found that, in order to rebut it, proof of an intention on the part of the requesting State authorities to disregard specialty obligations rather than mere speculation would be required.

14–10   The rule of specialty will only apply to offences committed prior to the surrender of the respondent.[8] If, once surrendered, the respondent commits further offences in the law of the requesting State then he or she may be proceeded against without engaging the rule. As such it will not be necessary in such a situation for the requesting State to make any application for waiver of specialty under s 22(7).

14–11   Having set out the general rule in s 22(2) the Act goes on to set out a number of exceptions to it in the following subsections. As a matter of logic these will only actually arise for consideration where it has been established that, firstly, the law of the requesting State allows for the prosecution of the respondent in respect of offences other than those in the warrant and, secondly, that he or she will be prosecuted for such offences.

Imposition of a Non-Custodial Penalty

14–12   Section 22(4) allows a surrendered person to be prosecuted where that prosecution will not result in the imposition of a custodial penalty:

> "The surrender of a person under this Act shall not be refused under subsection (2) if—
>
> (a)   upon conviction in respect of the offence concerned he or she is not liable to a term of imprisonment or detention, or
>
> (b)   the High Court is satisfied that, where upon such conviction he or she is liable to a term of imprisonment or detention and such other penalty as does not involve a restriction of his or her personal liberty, the said other penalty only will be imposed if he or she is convicted of the offence."

14–13   Little difficulty arises in relation to s 22(4)(a) as it will, presumably, be made clear what the applicable penalty in a given case is. Section 22(4)(b) on the other hand

---

[6]   Unreported, Peart J, 9 February 2010.

[7]   [2010] IEHC 208.

[8]   See s 22(1).

would appear to require some form of indication or assurance in advance as to what the applicable penalty might be. Precisely who might give such an assurance and in what terms is not specified by the Act.

Proceedings Resulting in Default Custody

No difficulty arises where it is clear that that anticipated prosecution cannot result **14–14** in the imposition of a sentence or detention order. However, as is the case in this jurisdiction, the failure to comply with a non-custodial penalty, such as a fine or indeed an order made other than in criminal proceedings, may of itself result in the imposition of a custodial penalty as a default mechanism. Such a situation is expressly contemplated by s 22(5) which makes it clear that proceedings that may result in the imposition of a non-custodial sanction ought not be regarded as proceedings that can give rise to a sentence or detention order even where custody may well follow a failure or refusal to comply with the sanction:

> "(5) The surrender of a person under this Act shall not be refused under subsection (2) if it is intended to impose in the issuing state a penalty (other than a penalty consisting of a restriction of the person's liberty) including a financial penalty in respect of an offence of which the person claimed has been convicted, notwithstanding that where such person fails or refuses to pay the penalty concerned (or, in the case of a penalty that is not a financial penalty, fails or refuses to submit to any measure or comply with any requirements of which the penalty consists) he or she may, under the law of the issuing state be detained or otherwise deprived of his or her personal liberty."

In *Minister for Justice, Equality and Law Reform v McCague*[9] the respondent was **14–15** sought for the purpose of serving a custodial sentence in the requesting State . In addition it was clear from the warrant that a confiscation order had been made at the conclusion of his trial. The law of the requesting State provided that if he did not satisfy the confiscation order he would be imprisoned for a period in default. The court concluded, *inter alia*, that the terms of s 22(5) applied and as such the surrender of the respondent was ordered.

Where a Waiver of Specialty will be Sought

Section 22(7) provides for a procedure whereby the issuing State can, subsequent to **14–16** surrender, apply to the High Court for a waiver of specialty which will be granted where the offence is one in respect of which surrender would have been ordered had it been the subject of a European arrest warrant. Consequently s 22(6) provides that a respondent may be surrendered where it is anticipated that he will be prosecuted for an offence other than that contained in the warrant but the court is satisfied that the requesting State will apply for such a waiver of specialty prior to bringing such proceedings:

> "The surrender of a person under this Act shall not be refused under subsection (2) if the High Court—

---

[9] [2008] IEHC 154 — the decision was subsequently affirmed *ex tempore* by the Supreme Court.

(a) is satisfied that—

    (i) proceedings will not be brought against the person in respect of an offence,

    (ii) a penalty will not be imposed on the person in respect of an offence, and

    (iii) the person will not be detained or otherwise restricted in his or her personal liberty for the purposes of an offence,

without the issuing judicial authority first obtaining the consent thereto of the High Court"

14–17 This exception to the general rule is of considerable significance when considered in conjunction with the provisions of s 4A of the Act which allows the court to presume future compliance by the requesting State with the terms of the Framework Decision. Given that the exception contained in s 22(6) essentially mirrors Art 27.3(g) of the Framework Decision the courts have considered themselves entitled to presume that the surrendered person will not be prosecuted in the absence of an application for waiver of specialty on the basis that were the issuing State to do otherwise it would be in breach of the Framework Decision. In *McCague* the court concluded:

> "This Court is entitled to presume that the issuing state will comply with its obligations under the Framework Decision. In that regard, it is to be presumed that if the confiscation order application constitutes the prosecution of the respondent for an additional offence, which I believe it does not, then the issuing judicial authority will comply with its obligation under the Framework Decision to obtain the consent of the High Court before doing so."

14–18 A similar conclusion was reached in *Minister for Justice, Equality and Law Reform v Pavlovs*.[10] The effect of this provision is that even if the respondent goes so far as to overcome all of the evidential hurdles created by s 22(2) and shows that none of the other exceptions apply, surrender will still be ordered unless he can show on the basis of some degree of cogent evidence that the issuing State will not apply for a waiver of specialty under s 22(7). Given the near impossibility of overcoming the various evidential presumptions it must be concluded that the operation of the rule of specialty as a bar to surrender under the 2003 Act is more imagined than real. Rather the Oireachtas has opted for a system whereby the issuing State will apply, post-surrender, for consent to the prosecution of the surrendered person. In circumstances where such consent is not forthcoming the court is entitled to presume that the surrendered person will not be proceeded against.

Waiver by the Respondent

14–19 Section 22(6)(b) also provides for an exception in respect of the general rule where the respondent, who has not yet been surrendered, in fact wishes to waive it:

---

[10] [2007] IEHC 363.

"The surrender of a person under this Act shall not be refused under subsection (2) if the High Court—

   (b)   is satisfied that—

        (i)   the person consents to being surrendered under section 15,

        (ii) at the time of so consenting he or she consented to being so proceeded against, to such a penalty being imposed, or being so detained or restricted in his or her personal liberty, and was aware of the consequences of his or her so consenting, and

        (iii) the person obtained or was afforded the opportunity of obtaining, or being provided with, professional legal advice in relation to the matters to which this section relates."

There may well be compelling reasons for a respondent to wish to waive the rule of specialty in the circumstances of his or her particular case particularly where he or she has been charged or sentenced in respect of offences which do not meet the minimum gravity or correspondence requirements. The respondent may well take the view that it is desirable to deal with all outstanding matters – indeed there may well be some tangible benefit in terms of serving sentences concurrently or seeking to merge a series of sentences. Also, it may well be the intention of the respondent to seek to appeal or have reviewed all matters in respect of which sentence has been imposed. The prospect of being surrendered to serve a sentence in the requesting State and still not having the slate wiped clean, so to speak, may well be highly undesirable for a given respondent. **14–20**

Even respondents who have not yet been convicted may well wish to seek to waive the rule of specialty. There can frequently be a tactical advantage in being prosecuted for a number of offences, particularly in circumstances where there is some prospect of the court or jury, as the case may be, convicting in respect of one of the less serious offences available. In such a scenario it may well be to the respondent's advantage to ensure that he or she can be prosecuted for a larger number of offences even where they do not correspond or meet the minimum gravity requirement. **14–21**

The exercise of such a waiver of specialty is conditional upon the respondent having been provided with legal advice in advance. One of the difficulties, however, which faces practitioners advising a respondent who might wish to waive specialty is as to whether or not such a waiver is a general waiver of the rule or applies only to specific offences. In other words where a respondent indicates such a waiver, can he or she be proceeded against for any offence in the issuing State or can he or she be proceeded against solely in respect of those offences he or she indicates as being the subject of the waiver? On the one hand the references to "being so proceeded against", "such a penalty" and being "so detained" in s 22(6)(b)(ii) would tend to suggest that the waiver is intended to be specific in its effect. As against this however Art 27.3(e) of the Framework Decision refers to the respondent renouncing the "specialty rule" rather than its specific application in respect of one or more offences. Similarly Art 13.1 provides for the transmission of the waiver in the following terms: **14–22**

"If the arrested person indicates that he or she consents to surrender, that consent and, if appropriate, express renunciation of entitlement to the 'speciality rule', referred to in Article 27.2, shall be given before the executing judicial authority, in accordance with the domestic law of the executing Member State."

14–23   There is no form prescribed by the Rules of the Superior Courts whereby the respondent might record such a waiver of consent. This is somewhat surprising given that the Rules provide for such a form in respect of a waiver of specialty under s 20 of the Extradition Act 1965.[11] That form seems to contemplate only a general waiver. In the absence of some degree of certainty as to the effect of such a waiver it would appear to be problematic to comply with the requirement that the respondent understands the effect of such a waiver.

14–24   Section 22(6)(d) also provides a waiver of the rule by the respondent subsequent to surrender. Whilst the court will not be concerned with the practicalities of such a waiver given that it will necessarily take place subsequent to surrender, some of the same issues in terms of the effect of such a waiver will apply.

Where the Respondent has had the Opportunity to Leave the Requesting State

14–25   The final exception to the rule of specialty is that contained in s 22(6)(c) which provides that s 22(2) will not apply where the court is satisfied that:

> "(i)   such proceedings will not be brought, such penalty will not be imposed and the person will not be so detained or otherwise restricted in his or her personal liberty before the expiration of a period of 45 days from the date of the person's final discharge in respect of the offence for which he or she is surrendered, and
>
> (ii)   during that period he or she will be free to leave the issuing state,"

14–26   In essence once the proceedings for which the respondent has been surrendered have been determined and the relevant sentence served, the respondent has 45 days within which to leave the issuing State. If he or she does not, he or she may thereafter be prosecuted for any other offence.

CONSENT TO FURTHER PROSECUTION OR SENTENCE – SECTION 22(7)

14–27   Of the various exceptions to the general rule that are set out in both Art 27 of the Framework Decision and s 22 of the Act, arguably the most important relates to the situation where the court is satisfied that the issuing State will not proceed against the surrendered person until consent to do so is obtained from the High Court. This exception envisages the procedure provided for at s 22(7) and 22(8) of the 2003 Act. In essence this allows the issuing State to apply to the High Court, subsequent to surrender, for permission to either prosecute the surrendered person for other offences or to impose a sentence in respect of other offences. It is this mechanism which allows the requested State to surrender in the knowledge that it will be consulted in respect of any future proceedings or sentence against the respondent.

14–28   The Act does not spell out the detail of the procedure to be adopted in such circumstances. Section 22(7) simply provides that:

> "(7)   The High Court may, in relation to a person who has been surrendered to an issuing state under this Act, consent to—

---

[11] See Ord 98, r 17(2) and Appendix AA, Form 12.

    (a)   proceedings being brought against the person in the issuing state for an offence,

    (b)   the imposition in the issuing state of a penalty, including a penalty consisting of a restriction of the person's liberty, in respect of an offence, or

    (c)   proceedings being brought against, or the detention of, the person in the issuing state for the purpose of executing a sentence or order of detention in respect of an offence,

upon receiving a request in writing from the issuing state in that behalf."

As such the only express requirement laid down by s 22(7) in respect of such a **14–29** request from the issuing State is that it must be in writing. In practice such requests have substantially followed the format of the European arrest warrant and the same degree of information has tended to be supplied. Such an approach makes sense when one considers that the criteria which the court will apply to such a request are in effect the same as apply to a request for surrender under s 16. In this regard s 22(8) imposes an almost identical obligation on the court to refuse to give consent as appears in s 16:

> "The High Court shall not give its consent under subsection (7) if the offence concerned is an offence for which a person could not by virtue of Part 3 of the Framework Decision (including the recitals thereto) be surrendered under this Act."

Therefore the court will have to examine the application for consent in much the **14–30** same way as it would approach an application for surrender under s 16. All of the potential bars to surrender that would be available to a respondent on a surrender hearing will similarly be available for the purpose of resisting an application for consent. Also the wording of the provision would seem to have the practical consequence of rendering the Framework Decision directly applicable insofar as the prohibitions on surrender contained therein are concerned.

Procedure

From a procedural point of view the most obvious difficulty which arises from the **14–31** respondent's perspective is that an application under s 22(7) will only arise subsequent to surrender. As a matter of practicality this will mean that the respondent will in all likelihood no longer be in the State. Frequently, by this stage in proceedings, the respondent will be in custody in the issuing State . It is clear from the terms of s 22(8) that the court will have to consider whether any legitimate bar to consent arises and as such the respondent must be entitled to litigate any issues of concern in this regard.

    As a matter of practice once a request for consent is received by the Central **14–32** Authority in the State an *ex parte* application will be made to the High Court seeking directions as to the manner in which the respondent ought to be notified. Generally some sort of personal service will be required particularly where the respondent is in custody in the issuing State . In general the court will also direct that the former solicitors of the respondent will also be notified and served with the relevant papers for the consent application. The court will also fix a hearing date for the purpose of the application for consent.

14-33　　Whilst it is difficult to speculate as to the manner in which the issuing State may approach such applications it seems reasonable to suppose that they will only arise in circumstances where the respondent has been given an opportunity to consent to his further prosecution and has declined to do so. This being so most such applications for consent will be resisted by the respondent.

14-34　　The practical difficulties that will be faced by the legal representatives of the respondent in obtaining instructions from their client, particularly where the respondent is in custody and there is also a language barrier, are significant. Neither the Act not the Framework Decision makes any particular provision for this notwithstanding the clear entitlement of the respondent to contest such an application.

ONWARD SURRENDER

14-35　　A similar formulation to that which appears in s 22 is used in both ss 23 and 24 which prohibit surrender where it is anticipated that the respondent may be subject to either onward surrender or onward extradition. In respect of onward surrender from the requesting State to another Member State under a European arrest warrant s 23(2) provides:

> "Subject to this section, the High Court shall refuse to surrender a person under this Act if it is satisfied that—
>
> (a)　the law of the issuing state does not provide that a person who is surrendered to it pursuant to a European arrest warrant shall not be surrendered to a Member State pursuant to a European arrest warrant issued by a judicial authority in that Member State in respect of an offence, and
>
> (b)　the person will be surrendered to a Member State pursuant to a European arrest warrant issued by a judicial authority in that Member State in respect of an offence."

14-36　　Before any objection to surrender can succeed under this heading the court must be satisfied on a cumulative basis both that the law of the requesting State is deficient in terms of its provisions in respect of onward surrender and that the person will be so surrendered. In practical terms this will require the respondent to show that there is a European arrest warrant or Schengen alert in existence for him in respect of another Member State. As with s 22 the reference to an "offence" is confined to offences committed prior to the surrender of the respondent. Therefore the warrant or alert will have to relate to such a pre-existing offence. Section 23(2) also makes provision for an evidential presumption which allows the court to presume that the conditions described in s 23(1) do not arise.

14-37　　As with the provisions of s 22 a number of specific exceptions are provided for in respect of the general prohibition on surrender contained in s 23(2). These are in essentially identical terms to those provided for in s 22 and as such much of the commentary above applies *mutatis mutandis* to these exceptions. They may be summarised as follows:

- The bar on surrender will not apply where the court is satisfied that the issuing judicial authority will not surrender the respondent without first obtaining the consent of the High Court.[12]
- Where the respondent consents to onward surrender either before his surrender from the State[13] or afterwards.[14]
- As with section 22 the bar in respect of onward surrender will not apply where the person has, subsequent to his discharge in respect of the offence for which he was originally surrendered, remained in the issuing State for a period of in excess of 45 days.

A near identical procedure for an application to waive the prohibition on onward **14–38** surrender is provided for in s 23(5) and 23(6). Again the criteria that the court will apply on such an application will be more or less identical to those that arise in respect of a s 16 application, namely whether the granting of consent would contravene either Part 3 of the Act or the Framework Decision.

ONWARD EXTRADITION

In near identical terms to s 23, the provisions of s 24(1) which relate to the onward **14–39** extradition of the surrendered person to a non-Member State provides:

> "The High Court shall refuse to surrender a person under this Act if it is satisfied that—
>
> (a) the law of the issuing state does not provide that a person who is surrendered to it pursuant to a European arrest warrant shall not be extradited to a third country without the consent of the High Court and the Minister first being obtained, and
>
> (b) the person will be extradited to a third country without such consent first being obtained."

Both sections require the court to prohibit surrender where the law of the requesting **14–40** State does not itself prevent onward surrender or extradition and the court is satisfied that the respondent will be so surrendered or extradited subsequent to his or her surrender to the requesting State . As with ss 22 and 23 the conditions set out in s 24(1) are cumulative.

One notable distinction that arises in respect of s 24 is that the prohibition on **14–41** surrender where onward surrender is anticipated is not restricted to extradition in respect of offences committed prior to surrender but would seem to extend to offences committed subsequent to surrender also. This is due to the omission of the definition of "offence" which features in both ss 22 and 23.

Similarly the detailed exceptions to the general rules reflected in ss 22 and 23 are **14–42** absent in s 24. This necessarily means that there is significantly less scope for the operation of the presumption in s 4A to allow the court to presume that the issuing State will seek the consent of the High Court prior to onward surrender. There does,

---

[12] s 23(4)(a).
[13] s 22(4)(b).
[14] s 22(4)(d).

however, remain the evidential presumption contained in s 24(2) which allows the court to presume that no onward extradition will take place.

14–43   Section 24 was examined in detail in *Minister for Justice, Equality and Law Reform v Breen*,[15] where the court concluded that the conditions set out in ss 24(1)(a) and 24(1)(b) were cumulative. The respondent in *Breen* had been sentenced to a term of imprisonment in Jersey but had subsequently been transferred to an open prison in the United Kingdom to serve his sentence. Shortly afterwards, he absconded from that prison and travelled to Ireland. His surrender was sought not in relation to the sentence which he had been serving, but for the purposes of being prosecuted in the United Kingdom for the offence of escape from lawful custody. However, it was stated in the European arrest warrant that the Attorney General of Jersey intended to apply for his transfer to Jersey following the completion of any sentence imposed in the United Kingdom for escape from lawful custody. The respondent pointed to the system of backing of warrants which existed between Jersey and the United Kingdom,[16] which, it appeared, would allow for his transfer from the United Kingdom to Jersey on an arrest warrant from Jersey, without the consent of the Irish High Court first being obtained. Thus the respondent based his objection to surrender on s 24, submitting that the presumption contained in s 24(2), that the issuing State did not intend to extradite him to a third country following surrender, had been rebutted by the reference in the warrant to the intentions of the Attorney General of Jersey, and further that no provision of English law would require the consent of the Irish High Court to be obtained before he could be extradited to Jersey.

14–44   Although the warrant made reference to provisions of English law which would require the consent of the Irish High Court before the requested person could be extradited to another Member State or to a "Category 2" country, it was established from affidavit evidence provided that Jersey was neither of these.[17] However, a number of affidavits were filed by the Minister which stated that the reference in the warrant to the Attorney General of Jersey's intention to seek the transfer of the respondent from the United Kingdom had been inserted in error, and that the Attorney General in fact had no such intention. Significantly, a letter from the Attorney General was put before the Court, which stated that he would not, and in fact could not under the law of Jersey, seek the transfer of the respondent from the United Kingdom for the purposes of having him serve the remainder of the sentence which had originally been imposed in Jersey. Peart J was therefore satisfied that there was no practical likelihood of the respondent being transferred to Jersey following his surrender, and furthermore that the evidence did not show any intention on the part of the issuing State to extradite him to a third country following surrender:

> "In my view, the presumption contained in s. 24(2) of the Act has not, in the light of all the facts now available to this Court been rebutted, and s. 24 therefore presents no reason why the surrender of the respondent must be refused".

---

[15] [2008] IEHC 54.

[16] This system of backing of warrants appeared to be largely similar to that which had existed between Ireland and the United Kingdom under Part III of the *Extradition Act 1965*.

[17] Peart J commented that, had Jersey been a "Category 2" country, whereby English law would have required the consent of the Irish High Court before extraditing the respondent there, then surrender would not have been prohibited, *"even though the intention to surrender him to Jersey was made known in the warrant"*.

It seems clear from the judgment in *Breen* that the first leg of the test under s 24(1) **14–45** was satisfied in that the law of the requesting State clearly did not provide for a prohibition in relation to onward surrender in the absence of the consent of the High Court. However the second leg of that test was not satisfied in that the respondent did not satisfy the court that he actually would be extradited if surrendered. In fact all of the evidence in the case was to the contrary. Whilst the courts have expressed some disinclination to rely upon undertakings in the context of extradition cases[18] ss 22, 23 and 24 seem to require the court to assess the likelihood of prosecution/ surrender/extradition for the purpose of carrying out the enquiry that each section envisages. It seems inevitable that a part of that process will be the seeking of some form of indication from the requesting State as to the relevant legal provisions and indeed what the practical position will be in relation to any attempt to subsequently prosecute, surrender or extradite the surrendered person.

Waiver

Sections 24(3) and 24(4) contain a consent procedure similar to the terms of the **14–46** procedures that are provided for in ss 22 and 23. However, the criteria to be applied in respect of such an application is for the court to determine whether it would order the extradition of the person had the request for extradition been received in the State.

PRESUMPTION UNDER SECTION 4A

As noted previously the general presumption provided for under s 4A is limited in **14–47** its scope to the actions of the requesting State and is only prospective in that it can only be applied to future conduct:

> "It shall be presumed that an issuing state will comply with the requirements of the Framework Decision, unless the contrary is shown."

Whilst, as a general rule, it will not operate to allow the court to presume that a given **14–48** bar on surrender does not arise, it does have significant effect in relation to the operation of ss 22, 23 and 24 in that it allows the court to presume that the issuing State will not contravene the corresponding provisions of the Framework Decision. On a number of occasions the courts have applied this presumption for the purpose of concluding that there was no basis for supposing that the respondent would be proceeded against in a manner contrary to any of the relevant provisions in the event of surrender.

In *Minister for Justice, Equality and Law Reform v Pavlovs*[19] the court briefly **14–49** considered the manner in which the specialty provisions of s 22 operate as a matter of practice. In that case the respondent had raised the possibility that a suspended sentence which had previously been imposed on him might be activated if he was surrendered. The court pointed out that it was always open to the requesting State to seek the permission of the High Court to proceed against a respondent after surrender had been effected. Prior to surrender the High Court was entitled to take the view that the respondent would not be proceeded against for any offence other than that contained in the warrant on the basis of mutual trust and understanding.

---

[18] *Bourke v Attorney General* [1972] 1 IR 36; *Attorney General v POC* [2007] 2 IR 421.
[19] [2007] IEHC 363.

14–50   Similarly in *Minister for Justice, Equality and Law Reform v Puta and Sulej*[20] the respondents had adduced evidence to the effect that apart from the offences contained in the warrants on foot of which they were sought they were both suspected of other offences in the issuing State and as such there was some prospect of them being proceeded against contrary to the rule of specialty. They were, however, unable or unwilling to adduce any evidence in relation to the provisions of the law of the issuing State concerning specialty. Fennelly J concluded that the effect of Art 27 of the Framework Decision which precluded the prosecution of surrendered persons contrary to the rule of specialty and s 4A of the 2003 Act had the effect of giving rise to a presumption against the respondents:

> "The appellants have not suggested that this aspect of the Framework Decision has not been implemented in Czech law. This Court must presume, until the contrary is proved, that it has. Section 4A of the Act of 2003, as amended in 2005, provides:
>
> > *"It shall be presumed that an issuing state will comply with the requirements of the Framework Decision, unless the contrary is shown."*
>
> It should be clearly stated that the Framework Decision prohibits the prosecution or imprisonment of persons surrendered in respect of matters committed prior to their surrender other than the charges for which they have been surrendered. The Czech Republic would be acting in breach of its obligations under the Framework Decision, if it were to prosecute or otherwise pursue either of the appellants in respect of such matters other than the offences specified in the warrant. However, the appellants have not shown that this will happen."

14–51   It might be observed that it was almost certainly unnecessary for the courts to invoke the provisions of s 4A in respect of either of the above cases as the basic cumulative criteria set out in s 22(2) had not even been established. The courts have applied the presumption set out in s 4A to the exception to the rule provided for by in s 26(6)(a)[21] in such a way as to give rise to a presumption that this exception will always apply. There is no reason why the courts would not apply a similar logic to the exception to the general rule provided for in respect of s 26(6)(d).[22] The practical effect of this is that the court will presume that the issuing State will honour and observe the rule of specialty as it is set out in Art 27 of the Framework Decision. Once that presumption is made in a given case then there would appear to be little basis for prohibiting surrender as one or more of the exceptions to the rule will necessarily apply.

MULTIPLE WARRANTS

14–52   The terms of s 22 do not preclude surrender where more than one European arrest warrant is received from the same issuing State . In the case of *Minister for Justice,*

---

[20] [2008] IESC 30.

[21] i.e. that the general rule does not apply where the requesting State first apply to the High Court for a waiver of specialty under s 22(7).

[22] i.e. where the issuing State obtains a waiver of specialty from the respondent.

Equality and Law Reform v Gotszlik[23] the High Court at first instance decided that s 22 applied in such a manner as to preclude surrender where two warrants were received from the same issuing State on the basis that surrender in respect of one warrant would inevitably lead to a situation whereby the respondent would be prosecuted for offences not referred to in that warrant, namely the offences referred to in the other warrant. The court felt obliged to refuse surrender whilst at the same time acknowledging the difficulties that might result from this. The decision was, however, overturned by the Supreme Court on appeal. The Supreme Court adopted a more purposive approach as to the interpretation of s 22:

> "Bearing in mind the words of section 22, and taking a purposive interpretation, noting especially the qualifying words "except where the context otherwise requires", considering the Framework Decision which could not be construed as requiring all offences to be on a single warrant, and the European principles of law enunciated in *Pupino,* I am satisfied that a court may order the surrender of a person on more than one European arrest warrant. Thus, as existed in the High Court in this case, the respondent may be ordered to be surrendered on two warrants. Such an approach preserves the rule of specialty and is consistent with the terms of section 22 and with the purpose of the Framework Decision."[24]

The provisions of s 22, therefore, will not extend to cover offences that are the subject **14–53** of one or more other European arrest warrants emanating from the same issuing State.

INWARD SURRENDER

Unlike most other aspects of extradition law the rule of specialty has potential **14–54** significance in the context of domestic criminal proceedings. Article 27 of the Framework Decision is predicated upon the assumption that Member States will include as part of their domestic criminal law a prohibition on the prosecution of a surrendered person for offences other than those for which he or she has been surrendered subject to the various exceptions already discussed. Unfortunately it would appear that any such presupposition in relation to the law of the State is unfounded. Neither the 2003 Act nor any other piece of domestic legislation makes provision for the operation of a rule of specialty.

Given the highly specific and technical manner in which the rule of specialty operates **14–55** it is not feasible to suggest that it operates as part of the common law. Moreover, it is clear form the decision in *The State (Sumers Jennings) v Furlong*[25] that the rule of specialty is a principle of international rather than domestic law which does not enjoy any domestic effect. As to whether the courts would be prepared to give effect to the State's obligations under Art 27 of the Framework Decision vis-à-vis other Member States that operate the rule of specialty very much remains to be seen. On the one hand there is no clear obligation under domestic law to do so, whilst on the other a failure to give effect to the rule of specialty would effectively preclude surrender into the State for any offence from a large number of other Member States.

On the assumption that the courts were to give effect to the rule of specialty in **14–56** some way the most obvious question which arises is whether or not the preferring of

---

[23] [2009] 3 IR 390.
[24] p 404.
[25] [1966] 1 IR 183.

an additional or amended charge actually amounts to a breach of the rule of specialty. In the case of *Criminal proceedings against Artur Leymann et Aleksei Pustovarov*[26] the European Court of Justice considered that fairly substantial amendments to the nature of the charges in respect of which surrender had been granted could be made before the rule of specialty was offended.

> "In order to establish whether the offence under consideration is an 'offence other' than that for which the person was surrendered within the meaning of Article 27(2) of Council Framework Decision 2002/584/JHA of 13 June 2002 on the European arrest warrant and the surrender procedures between Member States, requiring the implementation of the consent procedure referred to in Article 27(3)(g) and 27(4) of that Framework Decision, it must be ascertained whether the constituent elements of the offence, according to the legal description given by the issuing State, are those in respect of which the person was surrendered and whether there is a sufficient correspondence between the information given in the arrest warrant and that contained in the later procedural document. Modifications concerning the time or place of the offence are allowed, in so far as they derive from evidence gathered in the course of the proceedings conducted in the issuing State concerning the conduct described in the arrest warrant, do not alter the nature of the offence and do not lead to grounds for non-execution under Articles 3 and 4 of the Framework Decision."

14–57   In that case the accused had been surrendered from Poland to Finland for the purpose of being prosecuted for specified offences of trafficking in amphetamines. However, when an indictment was subsequently preferred it referred not to amphetamines but rather to hashish. The Court took the view that this did not amount to an "other offence" for the purpose of Art 27 as it was sufficiently proximate to the offences in respect of which surrender had originally been ordered.

14–58   Any issues in relation to the operation of the rule of specialty in the domestic context can, in principle, be overcome by means of a waiver of specialty in accordance with the procedure set out in Art 27.4 of the Framework Decision whereby the executing judicial authority that ordered the surrender of the accused is asked to consent to the prosecution of the accused for further offences. In *Adams v DPP & Others*[27] the applicant sought to quash a certificate issued by the United Kingdom Home Secretary granting consent under equivalent rendition arrangements under Part III of the Extradition Act 1965. Not surprisingly the Supreme Court declined to entertain the application on the basis that it had no jurisdiction to seek to hold the administrative act of a foreign State up to scrutiny. As such, a consent given by an executing judicial authority in this context is essentially unreviewable.

---

[26] Case C-388/08 PPU.

[27] [2001] IESC 27.

CHAPTER 15

Ne Bis in Idem and Equivalent Domestic Proceedings

NE BIS IN IDEM

A principle common to the criminal justice systems of all Member States is that **15–01** a person may not be prosecuted for conduct in respect of which he has previously been acquitted or convicted. This is referred to as *ne bis in idem*.[1] The *ne bis in idem* principle is applied to varying degrees amongst the Member States. In the common law jurisdictions it finds expression in the rule against double jeopardy which, in general, tends to militate against substantive prosecution appeals albeit with certain exceptions. Such appeals are considerably more common in civil law jurisdictions which do not regard them as a breach of the general principle. Whilst the principle is applied in different ways amongst the various Member States its universality is clear. Article 4(1) of the Seventh Protocol to the European Convention on Human Rights is explicit in this regard:

> "No one shall be liable to be tried or punished again in criminal proceedings under the jurisdiction of the same State for an offence for which he has already been finally acquitted or convicted in accordance with the law and penal procedure of the State."

It is, however, notable that the terms of Art 4(1) of the Seventh Protocol expressly **15–02** confine themselves to the domestic legal order. The reference to "the jurisdiction of the same State" is quite deliberate. The fact is that whilst it is relatively easy to apply the principle of *ne bis in idem* to any self contained domestic legal system the effect on the interactions of that legal system with other legal systems who purport to observe the same principal is considerably more nuanced and complex. There is little point being immune from further prosecution in one Member State on the basis of *ne bis in idem* or double jeopardy if one is liable to multiple and possibly

---

[1] Literally "not twice for the same matter".

sequential prosecutions for the same acts in some or all of the other Member States. At best it would offend against the free movement of persons, at worst it would undermine confidence in the domestic legal order.

Article 3.2

15–03   It is such concerns that Art 3.2 of the Framework Decision seeks to address by including as a mandatory ground for the refusal of surrender the rendering of final judgment in respect of the same acts in another Member State:

> "The judicial authority of the Member State of execution (hereinafter 'executing judicial authority') shall refuse to execute the European arrest warrant in the following cases:

> …(2) if the executing judicial authority is informed that the requested person has been finally judged by a Member State in respect of the same acts provided that, where there has been sentence, the sentence has been served or is currently being served or may no longer be executed under the law of the sentencing Member State;"

15–04   The importance of ensuring a consistent and coherent application across the European Union is obvious, particularly in the context of attempting to create a common area of security, freedom and justice. It is, therefore, unsurprising that the *ne bis in idem* principle has been raised to the status of a positive right by Art 50 of the EU Charter of Fundamental Rights:

> "No one shall be liable to be tried or punished again in criminal proceedings for an offence for which he or she has already been finally acquitted or convicted within the Union in accordance with the law."

15–05   This general prohibition upon surrender in circumstances where final judgment has already been given in another Member State finds expression in s 41 of the 2003 Act.

STATUTORY PROVISIONS – *NE BIS IN IDEM*

15–06   The principle of *ne bis in idem* as it applies as between Member States is given effect by s 41 of the 2003 Act under the heading "double jeopardy":

> "41(1) A person shall not be surrendered under this Act for the purpose of his or her being proceeded against in the issuing state for an offence consisting of an act or omission that constitutes in whole or in part an offence in respect of which final judgment has been given in the State or a Member State."

15–07   It is, perhaps, unfortunate that the section in question is headed "double jeopardy" as that is a concept which is limited in its application to common law jurisdictions. The principle of double jeopardy has little application in its traditional form in civil law jurisdictions which contemplate all manner of substantive prosecution appeals and revisions, frequently long after the apparent conclusion of a case. The purpose of the section is not to seek to give effect to our own domestic equivalent of the *ne bis in idem* principle, namely the double jeopardy rule, but rather to give effect to the principle as it is expressed in the domestic legal orders of all of the other Member States.

It remains open to argument as to whether any real distinction should be drawn **15–08** as between *ne bis in idem* and double jeopardy. In the case of *Minister for Justice, Equality and Law Reform v Dillon*[2] it had been argued by the Minister that s 41 was not engaged where the original prosecution of the respondent and the intended new prosecution were both situate in the issuing Member State. In other words the Minister contended that the purpose of the *ne bis in idem* principle was confined to situations where there had been a conviction or acquittal in one Member State and it was now sought to surrender the respondent to a different Member State. The court declined to decide on the issue as to whether or not there was any such distinction to be drawn as between the rule against double jeopardy and the principle of *ne bis in idem*.

Section 41(1) of the European Arrest Warrant Act 2003 is not without difficulties **15–09** in terms of the manner in which it has sought to implement Art 3.2 of the Framework Decision. First it precludes surrender for the purpose of "being proceeded against" in the issuing State. On the face of it this would appear to confine its scope to cases where it is intended to prosecute the respondent as opposed to execute a sentence. It would, however, be difficult to reconcile such an interpretation with the terms of Art 3.2 or indeed Art 50 of the Charter of Fundamental Freedoms.

More significantly, unlike the corresponding provision of the Framework **15–10** Decision, s 41(1) does not require the requested person to have served any sentence imposed on him or her in respect of the conduct in question or for the sentence to no longer be capable of execution. The prohibition on surrender provided for by s 41(1) is considerably broader than that contemplated by Art 3.2 of the Framework Decision.[3] This deviation is, however, somewhat less significant when considered in light of Art 4.3 of the Framework Decision which provides for a number of optional grounds for refusing surrender including "where a final judgment has been passed upon the requested person in a Member State, in respect of the same acts, which prevents further proceedings". It is unclear whether s 41(1) is an implementation of the basic rule set out in Art 3.2 or the somewhat broader exception provided for in Art 4.3. Given that both provisions are directed towards the general principle of *ne bis in idem* such distinctions are, perhaps, of purely academic interest.

The fact that s 41(1) prohibits surrender where a person has undergone trial, but **15–11** not necessarily punishment, in relation to the offence in the warrant must be seen as intentional on the part of the Oireachtas. It affords a prominence to the *ne bis in idem* principle not required, *per se*, by the Framework Decision and would seem to seek to prevent any possibility of a person being tried twice within the Member States in relation to the same conduct. The position may be justified by virtue of the fact that it remains open to the Member State which initially prosecuted the respondent to seek surrender in order to have the respondent serve the previous sentence imposed.

---

[2] [2010] IEHC 196.

[3] This is in contrast to the situation under s 41(2) in respect of final judgment in relation to the same conduct in a third country (i.e. a non-Member State), where there is an express requirement that any sentence imposed must have been served or no longer be required to be served.

From a strict *ne bis in idem* standpoint, this would be more desirable than having the person tried for the same conduct in another Member State, notwithstanding the previous final judgment in the first Member State.

Non-Member States

15–12 Both the Framework Decision and the 2003 Act also apply the *ne bis in idem* principle to convictions and sentences imposed in respect of the offence contained in the warrant from countries other than Member States. Section 41(2) provides as follows:

> "A person shall not be surrendered under this Act for the purpose of his or her being proceeded against in the issuing state for an offence consisting of the act or omission that constitutes an offence in respect of which final judgment has been given in a third country, provided that where a sentence of imprisonment or detention was imposed on the person in the third country in respect of the second-mentioned offence—
>
> (a) the person has completed serving the sentence, or
>
> (b) the person is otherwise no longer liable under the law of the third country to serve any period of imprisonment or detention in respect of the offence."

15–13 The foregoing is an implementation of Art 4.5 of the Framework Decision which is in the following terms:

> "The executing judicial authority may refuse to execute the European arrest warrant:
>
> ...(5) if the executing judicial authority is informed that the requested person has been finally judged by a third State in respect of the same acts provided that, where there has been sentence, the sentence has been served or is currently being served or may no longer be executed under the law of the sentencing country."

15–14 Unlike the situation in relation to Member States the Oireachtas explicitly included reference to the additional requirement that the respondent must either have served the sentence or no longer be amenable to execution before the exception to surrender will apply.

FINAL JUDGMENT

15–15 The position in Ireland in relation to what constitutes a "final judgment" for the purposes of double jeopardy is relatively straightforward. Only a previous acquittal or conviction will be seen as final judgment. Thus, in *DS v Judges of the Cork Circuit*,[4] the Supreme Court found that the existence of a previous trial where the

---

[4] [2008] 4 IR 379.

jury was unable to decide on a verdict did not engage the double jeopardy principle. Kearns J explained as follows:

> "In Ireland, the principle of double jeopardy has only been seen as applying in cases where a person tried for a criminal offence has been either acquitted or convicted. In either situation, a plea of autrefois acquit or autrefois convict will operate to prevent any further steps by the prosecution."[5]

However, for the purposes of s 41, the court may be asked to consider whether **15–16** a particular judgment in another Member State or in a third State should be considered "final judgment". In this regard, problems may arise in certain circumstances, such as, for example, where surrender is sought by a Member State for the purposes of carrying out an appeal against an acquittal. Clearly if the court were to apply the Irish definition of final judgment, such surrender would have to be refused on the basis that the requested person has been acquitted of the offence in question, and as such enjoyed the benefit of what would, in purely domestic terms, be considered to be a final judgment in respect of the offence. However, it would seem logical that the concept of final judgment must be considered not in the context of the executing Member State but rather of the State where the final judgment was rendered. Therefore, it may well be perfectly permissible to seek surrender in circumstances where the law of the State in question permits an appeal from a judgment, and the surrender is sought for the purposes of pursuing that lawful appeal.

Whilst there is little by way of definition provided in relation to the expression **15–17** "final judgment" there is some potentially useful authority in relation to the expression "finally disposed of" as used in Art 54 of the Schengen Agreement which also gives effect to the principle of *ne bis in idem*. In the context of that provision a number of cases have been referred to the European Court of Justice.

There is little difficulty with the idea that a conviction and sentence for an offence **15–18** amount to a final judgment for the purpose of the *ne bis in idem* rule. Similarly there is ample authority for the proposition that an acquittal on the grounds of a lack of evidence will also be regarded as a final judgment. In *Van Straaten v Netherlands and Italy*[6] the ECJ held:

> "59. Furthermore, in the case of a final acquittal for lack of evidence, the bringing of criminal proceedings in another Contracting State for the same acts would undermine the principles of legal certainty and of the protection of legitimate expectations. The accused would have to fear a fresh prosecution in another Contracting State although a case in respect of the same acts has been finally disposed of."

Similarly an acquittal on the basis of the prosecution becoming time barred will be **15–19** regarded as final judgment for the purposes of the general rule.[7]

---

[5] At p 409. The Supreme Court did ultimately prohibit a third trial where there had been two previous hung juries, but this was expressly on the grounds of a potential unfairness which might otherwise arise.

[6] Case C-150/05.

[7] See *Criminal Proceedings against Gasparini*, Case C-467/04.

15–20   In the joined cases of *Gozutok and Brugge*[8] the Court was considering the issue of whether or not an out of court settlement of criminal proceedings[9] with the duly appointed prosecutor in a given member State amounted to a bar on prosecution for the same offence in another member State. In other words, the court was being called on to consider what was actually meant by the expression "finally disposed of" in the context of Art 54 of the Schengen Agreement. The Court concluded that a person who had been the subject of criminal proceedings which had been compromised by a duly appointed prosecutor could avail of the *ne bis in idem* principle as a bar to prosecution in another Member State on the basis of mutual trust and recognition:

> "In those circumstances, whether the *ne bis in idem* principal enshrined in Article 54 of the CISA is applied to procedures whereby further prosecution is barred (regardless of whether a court is involved) or to judicial decisions, there is a necessary implication that the member States have mutual trust in their criminal justice systems and that each of them recognises the criminal law in force in the other member States, even when the outcome would be different if its own national law were applied.
>
> For the same reasons the application by one member State of the *ne bis in idem* principal as set out in Article 54 of the CISA to procedures whereby further prosecution is barred, which have taken place in another member State without a court being involved, cannot be made subject to a condition that the first State's legal system does not require such judicial involvement either.
>
> The aptness of that interpretation of Article 54 of the CISA is borne out by the fact that it is the only interpretation to give precedence to the object and purpose of the provision rather than to procedural or purely formal matters, which, after all, vary as between member States concerned, and to ensure that the principal has proper effect."

15–21   It remains to be seen whether the ECJ would take a similar view in relation to the Framework Decision which makes reference to a person being "finally judged" rather than "finally disposed of". Whilst there may appear to be some difference of terminology that would militate against an identical interpretation, a teleological or purposive approach must inevitably identify similar objectives underlying both the Schengen Agreement and the Framework Decision – namely the free movement of persons and the creation of a common area of freedom, justice and security.

15–22   Whilst some form of discharge or compromise with a public prosecutor in a Member State may amount to final judgment it would appear that it is essential that the manner in which the proceedings are discontinued has the effect under the law of that State of precluding the institution of further proceedings. In *Criminal Proceedings against Turansky*[10] the police in the relevant Member State decided to discontinue the investigation

---

[8] Cases C-187/01 and C-385/01.

[9] It is not uncommon in civil law jurisdictions for an accused person to reach an agreement with the prosecutor generally involving the payment of compensation or some other form of redress which then results in the criminal proceedings being discontinued. This may sometimes involves some degree of oversight by the judiciary but will frequently occur without the making of any formal court order.

[10] Case C-491/07.

having considered the available evidence. Under the law of the Member State such a determination did not preclude the investigation being reopened at some future point. As such the ECJ concluded that the *ne bis in idem* provisions of the Schengen Agreement did not bar the prosecution of the accused in another Member State:

> "A decision which does not, under the law of the first Contracting State which instituted criminal proceedings against a person, definitively bar further prosecution at national level cannot, in principle, constitute a procedural obstacle to the opening or continuation of criminal proceedings in respect of the same acts against that person in another Contracting State."

The Court went on to consider the underlying rationale of the *ne bis in idem* rule: **15–23**

> "That interpretation of Article 54 of the CISA is compatible with the objective of the article, which is to ensure that a person whose trial has been finally disposed of is not prosecuted for the same acts in the territory of several Contracting States on account of his having exercised his right to freedom of movement (see, to that effect, Gözütok and Brügge, paragraph 38).
>
> The application of that article to a decision to suspend criminal proceedings such as that taken in the main proceedings would have the effect of precluding, in another Contracting State, in which more evidence may be available, any possibility of prosecuting and perhaps punishing a person on account of his unlawful conduct, even though such a possibility is not ruled out in the first Contracting State, in which the trial of the person is not considered to have been finally disposed of under national law.
>
> Such an outcome would, as pointed out by the Swedish and United Kingdom Governments in their written observations, be contrary to the very purpose of the provisions of Title VI of the Treaty on European Union as stated in the fourth indent of the first paragraph of Article 2 thereof, that is, to take 'appropriate measures with respect to … prevention and combating of crime' while developing the Union as an area of freedom, security and justice in which the free movement of persons is assured."

The theme of mutual trust as being the foundation of the *ne bis in idem* principle was **15–24** further underlined in another case concerning Art 54 of the Schengen Agreement. In *Criminal Proceedings against Bourqain*[11] the European Court of Justice was concerned with a prosecution for murder that had been the subject of a conviction and sentence in absentia in 1961. The issue which arose for consideration was whether or not an *in absentia* judgment could be considered a final judgment for the purpose of the Schengen Agreement in circumstances where the proceedings would have had to have been re-opened if Mr Bourqain had been arrested on foot of the original order of sentence and conviction. The court concluded that in order to give effect to the free movement of persons within the European Union the conviction and sentence *in absentia* ought to be regarded as final. The fact that under the law of the Member State concerned with the first trial, France, the conviction and sentence could not be enforced due to a domestic limitation period and an amnesty law was irrelevant as

---

[11] Case C-297/07.

one of the consequences of a *ne bis in idem* regime as between Member States was that each Member State had to respect the outcome of proceedings of each other's criminal justice system even if the outcome of their own might have been different.

15–25   The High Court considered the issue of what amounted to a "final judgment" in *Minister for Justice, Equality and Law Reform v Dillon*.[12] In that case the respondent had, some years previously, been acquitted of the offence in respect of which consent[13] for prosecution was latterly being sought. The law of the issuing State, the United Kingdom, allowed for a re-trial by the prosecution in circumstances where new evidence, not available at the time of trial, had come to light. Such a re-trial could only be granted on application to the Court of Appeal. Such an application had been brought and the Court of Appeal considered that a re-trial was justified under the relevant statutory provisions. However, it expressed the view that were it to make an order for a re-trial prior to an application for a waiver of specialty being made to the High Court of Ireland this would, of itself, amount to a breach of the rule of specialty. This resulted in a situation where the respondent, at the time of the application to the High Court still, for the time being at least, enjoyed the benefit of his acquittal. The issue which arose for consideration was whether or not the judgment, i.e. the acquittal, amounted to a final judgment. Peart J resolved what otherwise appeared to be a forensic chicken and egg scenario in the following terms:

> "The resolution of the question on this application is to be found in the meaning to be given to "finally judged" or "final order". While obviously an acquittal or a conviction can be considered a final order, that is not the end of the matter. I must interpret Section 41 of the Act in conformity with the aims and objectives of the Framework Decision under the well known principles of conforming interpretation...
>
> In my view there is nothing in the Framework Decision which indicates that one objective of that instrument is to protect a person, whose surrender is sought by an issuing state, from being surrendered for the purpose of being tried for an offence in respect of which he has been already acquitted in that issuing Member State, and where it is beyond doubt that such a trial will not take place until the earlier acquittal has been quashed and a re-trial ordered in accordance with the procedures available in the issuing state. In such a circumstance it is perfectly clear that the surrendered person is not faced with double jeopardy. He will not be tried again in the face of an extant acquittal for the same offence. That mutual trust in the legal system of the United Kingdom referred to by Fennelly J above mandates that this Court presumes, and may safely do so if I may say so, that the respondent will not be exposed to a double jeopardy.
>
> Where a person is convicted of an offence, and appeals successfully against that conviction and is ordered by an appeal court to be re-tried for the same offence, it cannot possibly be said that the accused is exposed to double jeopardy; yet until that conviction was quashed it exists as a "final order". But it was never a final order in the sense of one that could never be set aside, as the convicted person has a right of appeal.

---

[12] [2010] IEHC 196.

[13] This was not an application for surrender but rather an application for consent to prosecute the respondent for further offences in circumstances where he had previously been surrendered to the United Kingdom.

> In the same way in the present case, the acquittal for the 1982 offence was a "final order", but given the jurisdiction to set aside an acquittal at the suit of the DPP in the United Kingdom, it is not necessarily a final order for all time and in all circumstances, since under certain circumstances, such as the emergence later of fresh and compelling evidence it may be set aside and quashed."

It would seem to be implicit in the foregoing that the purpose of s 41(1) and indeed the various provisions of the Framework Decision which address themselves to the *ne bis in idem* principle is solely related to the manner in which that principle operates as between Member States rather than how Member States give effect to the principle in the context of their own domestic legal order. This is not surprising when one considers that the purpose of the Framework Decision is not directed at any harmonization of substantive criminal law. A corollary would appear to be that *ne bis in idem* issues will, in general, not arise where the final judgment in issue was given in the Member State which is seeking surrender. Rather the final judgment in issue will either have been given here or in a third Member State. **15–26**

Given the propensity of civil law jurisdictions to exercise extra-territorial jurisdiction in respect of their own citizens and similarly the greater prevalence of trials *in absentia* in such jurisdictions it is not difficult to envisage situations whereby one Member State will seek the surrender of an individual who has been convicted or acquitted in another State. The issue in such a scenario will be whether the judgment in the third Member State, which is not actually represented in the proceedings, amounted to final judgment. In other words the courts here may well find themselves being asked to construe the procedural niceties of a foreign legal system without any input from the authorities in that jurisdiction. **15–27**

THE SAME OFFENCE

The *ne bis in idem* exception will only apply in circumstances where the respondent is sought to be surrendered for the same offence in respect of which there has already been final judgment. Whilst the Framework Decision makes reference to the "same acts" s 41(1) makes reference to: **15–28**

> "...an offence consisting of an act or omission that constitutes *in whole or in part* an offence in respect of which final judgment has been given"

Section 41(2) precludes surrender in respect of: **15–29**

> "...an offence consisting of the act or omission that constitutes an offence in respect of which final judgment has been given".

Quite why a distinction is drawn as between the definition of what constitutes the same offence in s 41(1) as opposed to s 41(2) is a best unclear particularly in circumstances where the Framework Decision does not draw any such distinction.[14] It remains to be seen how significant the distinction between **15–30**

---

[14] s 41(1) gives effect to Art 3.2 of the Framework Decision whilst s 41(2) gives effect to Art 4.5.

conduct that consists "in whole or in part" of the offence for which final judgment has been given and conduct that simply amounts to that offence will be. It is not difficult to envisage circumstances where the distinction may take on some considerable importance.

15–31   It goes without saying that the same act can often give rise to a prosecution for more than one offence. However, following an acquittal or conviction in respect of one offence, it would be manifestly unfair to allow the prosecuting authorities to circumvent the effect of the *ne bis in idem* principle by prosecuting a person for a second offence which, although legally a different offence from that in respect of which the person has been previously acquitted or convicted, arises from the same acts.

15–32   Some assistance in determining what amounts to the same acts may be gleaned from domestic case-law in relation to double jeopardy although, as noted above, it is far from clear as to whether such domestic principles are of general applicability having regard to the context of *ne bis in idem* as applied in the Framework Decision. The position in this jurisdiction regarding when a plea of *autrefois acquit* or *autrefois convict* will be accepted has its basis in the House of Lords decision in *DPP v Connelly*.[15] In that case, it was held that a previous acquittal for murder did not give rise to an entitlement to a plea of *autrefois acquit* in a subsequent prosecution for robbery based on the same factual scenario. After an extensive examination of the authorities, Morris LJ laid down a number of principles in relation to the pleas of *autrefois acquit* and *autrefois convict*. One of these was:

> "…that the same rule applies if the crime in respect of which he is being charged is in effect the same, or is substantially the same, as either the principal or a different crime in respect of which he has been acquitted or could have been convicted or has been convicted."[16]

15–33   In prosecutions based on the same factual background, where the offence in the second prosecution is precisely the same as the offence in the first (in respect of which the accused has been acquitted or convicted), an issue of double jeopardy will clearly arise. However, the principle also arises where the second offence *"is in effect the same, or is substantially the same"* as the first offence, or an offence in respect of which the accused was in danger of being convicted in the first prosecution.[17] Whether this is so can be difficult to determine. In *Connelly*, Morris LJ held:

> "…one test as to whether the rule applies is whether the evidence which is necessary to support the second indictment, or whether the facts which constitute the second offence, would have been sufficient to procure a legal conviction

---

[15] [1964] 1 AC 1254.

[16] p 1305.

[17] Thus, a plea of *autrefois acquit* would be available where the first prosecution, which was for theft, ended in an acquittal, and there was an attempt to subsequently prosecute for handling stolen goods. As it would have been open to a court to convict of the latter offence on an indictment for theft as an alternative verdict, the acquittal on the theft charge would act as a bar to a later prosecution for handling stolen goods.

upon the first indictment either as to the offence charged or as to an offence of which, on the indictment, the accused could have been found guilty".[18]

In that case, the accused had not been in jeopardy of conviction for robbery on the murder indictment, and the facts necessary to prove murder would not have proved robbery. The House of Lords therefore held that the double jeopardy principle was not infringed. **15–34**

Whilst the foregoing may well be persuasive authority in terms of how a court ought to approach the issue of what constitutes the same offence it should be borne in mind that the case of *Connelly* is perhaps of less assistance when considered in light of the particular and distinct reference in s 41(1) to acts or omissions which constitute "in whole or in part" the offence in question. Had the House of Lords been applying such a specific statutory test which appeared to lay such particular emphasis on the concept of a partial identity of offence then, perhaps, a different conclusion would have been reached. **15–35**

It remains to be seen whether the courts will take a narrow interpretation of s 41(1) in order to avoid departure from the well-established *Connelly* principles. It is more probable that the courts will look to the body of case-law already developed by the European Court of Justice in relation to the Schengen Agreement. Article 54 of the Schengen Agreement precludes prosecution is successive States for "the same acts" – as such it uses terminology which is identical to that appearing in both the Framework Decision and the 2003 Act. **15–36**

In the case of *Criminal Proceedings Against Kraaijenbrink*[19] there had been a suspended sentence imposed in Holland for an offence of handling the proceeds of drug trafficking. Subsequently Ms Kraaijenbrink was convicted and sentenced to two years imprisonment in Belgium for carrying out specific financial transactions in relation to the same proceeds of drug trafficking. She claimed that this amounted to a breach of the *ne bis in idem* provisions of Art 54 of the Schengen Agreement. The European Court of Justice disagreed: **15–37**

> "It follows that the starting point for assessing the notion of 'same acts' within the meaning of Article 54 of the CISA is to consider the specific unlawful conduct which gave rise to the criminal proceedings before the courts of the two Contracting States as a whole. Thus, Article 54 of the CISA can become applicable only where the court dealing with the second criminal prosecution finds that the material acts, by being linked in time, in space and by their subject-matter, make up an inseparable whole.
>
> On the other hand, if the material acts do not make up such an inseparable whole, the mere fact that the court before which the second prosecution is brought finds that the alleged perpetrator of those acts acted with the same criminal intention does not suffice to indicate that there is a set of concrete circumstances which are inextricably linked together covered by the notion of 'same acts' within the meaning of Article 54 of the CISA.

---

[18] p 1305. He went on to say that this test *"must be subject to the proviso that the offence charged in the second indictment had in fact been committed at the time of the first charge; thus if there is an assault and a prosecution and conviction in respect of it there is no bar to a charge of murder if the assaulted person later dies".*

[19] Case C-367/05.

As the Commission of the European Communities in particular pointed out, a subjective link between acts which gave rise to criminal proceedings in two different Contracting States does not necessarily mean that there is an objective link between the material acts in question which, consequently, could be distinguished in time and space and by their nature."

15–38   Ultimately the Court concluded that it was for the domestic court to assess all of the relevant factors:

"In the light of the foregoing, the answer to the first question must therefore be that Article 54 of the CISA is to be interpreted as meaning that:

– the relevant criterion for the purposes of the application of that article is identity of the material acts, understood as the existence of a set of facts which are inextricably linked together, irrespective of the legal classification given to them or the legal interest protected;

– different acts consisting, in particular, first, in holding in one Contracting State the proceeds of drug trafficking and, second, in the exchanging at exchange bureaux in another Contracting State of sums of money also originating from such trafficking should not be regarded as 'the same acts' within the meaning of Article 54 of the CISA merely because the competent national court finds that those acts are linked together by the same criminal intention;

– it is for that national court to assess whether the degree of identity and connection between all the facts to be compared is such that it is possible, in the light of the said relevant criterion, to find that they are 'the same acts' within the meaning of Article 54 of the CISA."

15–39   A somewhat clearer and more helpful exposition of the Court's view as to what might constitute the "same acts" is to be found in the case of *Criminal Proceedings against Van Esbroeck*.[20] That case concerned a sentence of imprisonment imposed in Norway for importation of drugs. When Mr Van Esbroeck was subsequently returned to Belgium the authorities there sought to prosecute him for having exported the same drugs. The Court regarded this as a breach of Art 54 and as such the *ne bis in idem* principle:

"...punishable acts consisting of exporting and importing the same narcotic drugs and which are prosecuted in different Contracting States to the CISA are, in principle, to be regarded as 'the same acts' for the purposes of Article 54 of the Convention, the definitive assessment in that respect being the task of the competent national courts."[21]

---

[20]   Case C-436/04.

[21]   See also *Criminal Proceedings against Van Straaten* Case C-150/05.

STATUTORY PROVISIONS – EQUIVALENT DOMESTIC PROCEEDINGS

Quite apart from circumstances where a respondent has been the subject of final **15–40** judgment elsewhere, the Framework Decision allows the executing Member State to refuse to surrender in circumstances where it is intended to prosecute the respondent in the executing Member State in respect of the same offence. Article 4.2 of the Framework Decision provides:

> "4. The executing judicial authority may refuse to execute the European arrest warrant:
>
> ...(2) where the person who is the subject of the European arrest warrant is being prosecuted in the executing Member State for the same act as that on which the European arrest warrant is based."

This optional ground for refusing surrender is given effect by means of s 42 of the **15–41** Act:

> "A person shall not be surrendered under this Act if—
>
> (a) the Director of Public Prosecutions or the Attorney General is considering, but has not yet decided, whether to bring proceedings against the person for an offence, or
>
> (b) proceedings have been brought in the State against the person for an offence consisting of an act or omission of which the offence specified in the European arrest warrant issued in respect of him or her consists in whole or in part."

It is doubtful as to whether the situation provided for in s 42(a) is really contemplated **15–42** by the Framework Decision, namely where domestic proceedings for the same offence are merely being considered by the prosecuting authorities here. Given that s 42 provides that surrender shall be refused in such circumstances rather than deferred it would appear to potentially allow for an almost open-ended period of time during which a person may not be surrendered.

In *Minister for Justice, Equality and Law Reform v Brennan*[22] s 42(a) was **15–43** considered briefly at first instance by Peart J in the context of an argument by the respondent that his surrender should be refused as certain domestic criminal charges against him were being considered by the Director of Public Prosecutions or the Gardaí. The respondent submitted that surrender was prohibited by s 42(a) in such circumstances. Peart J rejected this submission on the facts, finding that the considerations of An Garda Síochána were not relevant for the purposes of s 42(a):

> "In this regard evidence has been given to the Court by Sgt. Anthony Linehan that he has made enquiries of the DPP's office and that he is satisfied that there

---

[22] [2006] IEHC 94. The decision was subsequently appealed (unsuccessfully) on other grounds.

> are no matters still being considered against the respondent. All such matters as
> were being considered have been decided upon and necessary directions given.
> [Counsel's] concern was that there may be matters still being considered by the
> Gardaí as opposed to the DPP. But in my view the only matters of relevance
> are those still under active consideration by the DPP's office, and not An Garda
> Síochána, and accordingly I am satisfied that there is nothing relevant for the
> purpose of s. 42 of the Act which would require this Court to refuse to make
> the order sought."

15–44   In respect of the second scenario which s 42 is intended to cover, namely where a
prosecution is actually in being, it is of note that such domestic proceedings need not
be brought at the suit of either the Director of Public Prosecutions or the Attorney
General. It would seem that a private prosecution for the same offences would of
itself be sufficient. It is important to distinguish the effect of s 42 from the provisions
relating to postponement of surrender under s 18. Section 42 requires the court to
actually refuse to surrender the respondent whereas s 18 only comes into play once
an order under either s 15 or 16 has been made. That said, where a prosecution has
been instituted, depending upon the manner in which the case is ultimately disposed
of, it may then be possible subsequent to the finalisation of the prosecution to seek
the surrender of the respondent. If, for example, the prosecution were struck out,
discontinued or the subject of a *nolle prosequi*, it would then potentially be possible
to seek surrender in respect of the same underlying offence. Obviously in the event
of either acquittal or conviction the provisions of s 41 and the *ne bis in idem* principle
would come into play.

15–45   Prior to the Criminal Justice (Terrorist Offences) Act 2005, surrender also had to
be refused in the event of the proceedings ending in circumstances other than those
amounting to a conviction or an acquittal.[23] However, the repeal of s 42(c) is a clear
indication that a decision by the prosecution to discontinue the proceedings or a
decision not to institute proceedings in the first place will not preclude subsequent
surrender in respect of the same offence. However, in such a situation an issue
may well arise as to whether the decision to discontinue the proceedings *de facto*
amounted to a final judgment for the purposes of the *ne bis in idem* rule.

15–46   The repeal of s 42(c) was commented upon by Peart J in *Minister for Justice,
Equality and Law Reform v Kinsella*[24]:

> "An interesting question might arise, though so far not in this case, in the event
> that the Director of Prosecutions was to at some stage prior to the trial enter a
> nolle prosequi. It could be argued presumably in such an event that although
> proceedings were brought in the historical sense, they were no longer 'brought'
> since they were discontinued. Furthermore, since the Act makes no provision in
> respect of the optional circumstance set out in paragraph 3 of Article 4 [of the

---

[23] Prior to the Criminal Justice (Terrorist Offences) Act 2005 s 42(c) had provided that
surrender must be refused where: "…the Director of Public Prosecutions or the Attorney
General, as the case may be, has decided not to bring, or to enter a nolle prosequi under
section 12 of the Criminal Justice (Administration) Act 1924 in proceedings against the
person for an offence consisting of an act or omission that constitutes in whole or in part the
offence specified in the European arrest warrant issued in respect of him or her, for reasons
other than that a European arrest warrant has been issued in respect of that person".

[24] [2007] IEHC 1.

Framework Decision] set out above, effect has not been given to the terms of
that paragraph which refers to a decision to "halt" proceedings".

Given that the part of the Framework Decision upon which s 42(c) is based (namely **15–47**
Art 4.3) amounts to an optional ground for refusing surrender, it would appear that
the Oireachtas having initially decided to include it in the domestic legislation as
a basis upon which surrender might be refused subsequently opted to repeal it. As
such it is unlikely that it could really be argued that the reference in s 42(b) to
proceedings which had been "brought" could also encompass proceedings which
had been halted or otherwise struck out without a final result.

The practical manner in which s 42(b) operates was also considered in *Kinsella*. **15–48**
The respondent's surrender was sought by the Belgian authorities in relation his
alleged role in organising the transport of 48 kilos of heroin from a Belgian airfield
to Ireland. Meanwhile, the Director of Public Prosecutions had made a decision
to prosecute the respondent for organising the importation of the same drugs into
Ireland, and the respondent had been charged and was awaiting trial in relation
to this charge. The Minister applied for an adjournment of the European arrest
warrant proceedings until after the domestic trial had concluded. It was on this
application that the High Court gave judgment. The respondent submitted that the
s 16 application should proceed as normal. The High Court had little hesitation in
refusing to adjourn the proceedings. Referring to Art 4.2 and 4.3 of the Framework
Decision, it held:

> "The Framework Decision itself does not have direct effect, but clearly s. 42
> has given effect to those provisions whereby this State has chosen to require
> this Court to refuse to order surrender to the issuing state where the Director
> of Public Prosecutions has decided to prosecute the respondent for an offence
> arising from the facts underlying the offence referred to in the warrant. Curiously
> the Act is silent as what is to happen in the event that the respondent is either
> acquitted or convicted of the offences for which proceedings are brought here.
> The section refers simply to proceedings which are "brought". That suggests
> that once proceedings have been "brought", it is sufficient for a refusal of
> surrender regardless of the outcome of those proceedings...
>
> ...it is quite clearly provided in s.42 that once the Director of Public Prosecutions
> has decided to prosecute the charge here, then this Court shall not order
> surrender. In such circumstances, it seems to me that it is inappropriate that the
> Court should grant an adjournment of the application for the order of surrender,
> since such an adjournment can serve no useful purpose."

The court then went on to discuss the options open to the Minister following his **15–49**
decision to refuse the adjournment:

> "In my view the applicant is left with two possible courses of action. He
> can proceed now with his application under s. 16 and make submissions on
> that application that despite the provisions of s. 42 of the Act, and the view
> which I have expressed for the purpose of this application for adjournment
> that this Court may nevertheless order surrender, or he can apply to withdraw
> the present warrant in the knowledge that, should the requesting state choose
> to issue a fresh European arrest warrant at some future date, same can be

> endorsed for execution leading to the arrest again of the respondent and the hearing of an application for his surrender, when the outcome of the present prosecution has become known. But of course the question of double jeopardy might then emerge in relation to any further prosecution of him in Belgium on foot of offences arising from the same facts, given the provisions of s. 41(1) of the Act."

15–50 The conclusion of the court is not surprising when it is considered that the purpose of s 42 is clearly aimed at preventing anticipated breaches of the *ne bis in idem* rule.

CHAPTER 16

Protection of Rights

PROTECTION OF RIGHTS PRIOR TO THE 2003 ACT

Although the Extradition Act 1965 has never contained a specific protection for **16–01** fundamental rights protected by the Constitution or any international agreements, it is clear that the courts considered themselves entitled to exercise a jurisdiction to refuse to order extradition where this would lead to a breach of a constitutionally protected right. Although the existence of a bilateral extradition treaty with a particular country does give rise to a presumption that the extradited person will not have his constitutional rights breached in the requesting State,[1] where this presumption is rebutted, the courts have not been slow to intervene. In *Larkin v O'Dea*,[2] the Supreme Court prevented the extradition of the requested person to the United Kingdom in circumstances where it was likely that evidence obtained by unconstitutional means in Ireland would be used at his trial for murder in Northern Ireland. Hamilton CJ, having referred to the judgment of Henchy J in *Shannon v Ireland*,[3]

---

[1] See for instance the comments of McCarthy J at 262 in *Ellis v O'Dea* (No.2) [1991] IR 251.

[2] [1995] 2 IR 485.

[3] [1984] IR 548.

found an overriding duty on the courts to uphold the Constitution, notwithstanding the provisions of the 1965 Act:

> "Having regard to the presumption referred to in the said judgment, *viz.* that the Act will not be operated in such a manner as to violate the constitutional rights of those affected by its operation and the statement that "if it were shown in a particular case that the provisions of Part III of the Act were being used . . . in a manner, inconsistent with such constitutional rights, the courts would be bound to refuse to give effect to Part III", there is an obligation on all organs of the State, and in particular the judicial arm thereof, to ensure that in the operation of the provisions of the Act the constitutional rights of persons affected thereby are not violated but defended and vindicated."[4]

16–02 Similarly, in *Ellis v O'Dea*,[5] Walsh J in the Supreme Court referred to a residual jurisdiction to protect constitutional rights in the context of extradition proceedings:

> "All persons appearing before the courts of Ireland are entitled to protection against all unfair or unjust procedures or practices. It goes without saying therefore that no person within this jurisdiction may be removed by order of a court or otherwise out of this jurisdiction, where these rights must be protected, to another jurisdiction if to do so would be to expose him to practices or procedures which if exercised within this State would amount to infringements of his constitutional right to fair and just procedures. The obligation of the State to save its citizens from such procedures extends to all acts done within this jurisdiction and that includes proceedings taken under the Extradition Act, 1965."[6]

16–03 It is somewhat ironic that the courts have taken a much less active role in relation to the protection of the requested person's rights under the 2003 Act which actually explicitly mandates the court to refuse surrender where there is a real concern that fundamental rights might be infringed as a result of surrender.

LEGISLATIVE PROVISIONS

16–04 This obligation to protect and vindicate constitutional rights has been given statutory footing by s 37 which prohibits surrender where this would contravene the Constitution or the European Convention on Human Rights. However, as discussed below, the interpretation given by the courts to s 37 of the 2003 Act, coupled with the principle of mutual trust and confidence between Member States, has resulted in a significantly less active role for the courts in relation to the protection of fundamental rights than arose under the 1965 Act.

The Framework Decision

16–05 Whilst Arts 3 and 4 of the Framework Decision list a number of circumstances in which the executing State is relieved of the obligation to surrender under a European

---

[4] p 504.
[5] [1989] 1 IR 530.
[6] *ibid*, at 537.

arrest warrant, the situation where surrender would contravene either the Convention or the constitutional principles of the executing State is not contained in any of these exceptions. Similarly the Framework Decision does not explicitly state that Member States are entitled to refuse to surrender on the grounds of an anticipated breach of the European Convention on Human Rights. However, Art 1.3 provides that nothing in the Framework Decision, including the obligation to surrender, affects the duty of Member States to respect :

> "fundamental rights and fundamental legal principles as enshrined in Article 6 of the Treaty on European Union."

Additionally, Recital (12) of its Preamble makes clear that the Framework Decision: **16–06**

> "respects fundamental rights and observes the principles recognised by Article 6 of the Treaty on European Union and reflected in the Charter of Fundamental Rights of the European Union, in particular Chapter VI thereof."[7]

Accordingly, although a potential breach of fundamental rights is not prescribed **16–07** in the Framework Decision as a mandatory or even optional ground for refusing surrender, Member States are given a wide discretion as to how such a potential breach might affect the decision on whether to surrender.[8]

The Member States have taken various different approaches to the protection **16–08** of fundamental rights in their implementing legislation. Three distinct approaches of various Member States have been identified[9] in relation to the protection of fundamental human rights and the implementation of the Framework Decision. First, there are those containing an unrestricted human rights exception such as the Extradition Act 2003 in the United Kingdom where surrender *must* be refused if it would be incompatible with the requested person's Convention rights. Secondly, there are implementing Acts without a human rights exception, which provide that the obligation to surrender be weighed against any potential violation of human rights, with surrender only being refused where the latter carries greater weight. Lastly, certain implementing Acts contain a restricted human rights exception. An example of this is Art 11 of the Dutch implementing Act which prohibits surrender only where there has been a *flagrant* violation of the requested person's fundamental rights, with violations of Arts 2 and 3 of the Convention considered flagrant *per se*, and non-flagrant violations being left over to be remedied in the issuing State.

---

[7] Chapter VI of the said Charter is less broad than Art 6 TEU in that it specifically guarantees the following: the right to an effective remedy and to a fair trial; the presumption of innocence and right of defence; the principles of legality and proportionality of criminal offences and penalties; and the right not to be tried or punished twice for the same criminal offence.

[8] The Framework Decision's own conformity with Art 6 of the Treaty on European Union is justiciable in the European Court of Justice in the circumstances mentioned below, and was upheld in the context of the Art 2.2 of the Framework Decision in *Advocaten voor de Wereld* C-303/05 (ECJ Grand Chamber Judgment of 3 May 2007).

[9] Professor Nico Keizjer, "The European Arrest Warrant and Human Rights", published on www.eurowarrant.net.

16–09   Adopting the above analysis, it seems clear that Ireland has chosen to implement an unrestricted human rights exception by means of s 37 which covers three distinct sets of circumstances which give rise to a refusal of surrender:

- Section 37(1)(a) and 37(1)(b) are best regarded as a catch all ground in that they require the court to refuse surrender in circumstances where to do otherwise would result in the breach of a constitutional or convention right.
- Section 37(1)(c)(i) and 37(1)(c)(ii) both prohibit surrender where there are grounds to believe that the requested person might be discriminated against in the issuing State.
- Section 37(1)(c)(iii) precludes surrender where this might result in a threat to the right to life or bodily integrity as a result of the imposition of the death penalty, torture or inhuman or degrading treatment.

16–10   Each of these categories is considered in turn below.

BREACH OF CONSTITUTIONAL AND CONVENTION RIGHTS

16–11   Section 37(1) of the 2003 Act speaks in terms of mandatory refusal where surrender would result in any violation of fundamental rights:

> "(1)   A person shall not be surrendered under this Act if—
>
> > (a)   his or her surrender would be incompatible with the State's obligations under—
> >
> > > (i)   the Convention, or
> > >
> > > (ii)   the Protocols to the Convention,
> >
> > (b)   his or her surrender would constitute a contravention of any provision of the Constitution (other than for the reason that the offence specified in the European arrest warrant is an offence to which *section 38(1)(b)* applies),"

16–12   It is, perhaps, difficult to imagine how the Oireachtas[10] might have more widely defined the circumstances in respect of which the court might refuse surrender on the basis of a concern that fundamental rights might be infringed.

---

[10] It certainly appears to be the view of the legislature that no more could have been done to protect fundamental rights, as evidenced by the following reply of Deputy John Curran, Minister of State at the Department of Justice, Equality and Law Reform, to questions in the Seanad regarding proposed amendments to the 2003 Act by the *Criminal Justice (Miscellaneous Provisions) Act 2009*: *"Senator Walsh expressed concern about the adequacy of human rights protection in the provisions...However, I draw the Senator's attention to section 37 of the European Arrest Warrant Act 2003, which prohibits surrender where the person's rights under either the Constitution or the Convention on Human Rights would be breached. On any objective assessment, it is difficult to imagine what greater protection of human rights could be given."* Seanad Debates, Vol. 196 No 10, 3 July 2009.

APPROACH OF THE COURTS TO SECTION 37

In contrast to the broad terms and mandatory nature of s 37, what might be seen **16–13** as the equivalent provision of Part III of the 1965 Act, s 50(2)(bbb), was framed in narrow terms, without reference to the Constitution or the Convention, and merely gave the court a discretion to direct the release of a person where:

> "...by reason of the lapse of time since the commission of the offence specified in the warrant... and other exceptional circumstances, it would, having regard to all the circumstances be unjust, oppressive or invidious to deliver him up under section 47..."

The courts had on a number of occasions[11] held that in order to successfully resist **16–14** extradition by reliance on s 50(2)(bbb), the person sought would have to address each element of the test, showing not only delay but also other, separate, exceptional circumstances, and showing that a combination of these would make it unjust, oppressive or invidious to extradite him or her.

It initially appeared from the case of *Minister for Justice, Equality and Law* **16–15** *Reform v Aamond*[12] that s 37 of the 2003 Act would be given a much broader application than s 50(2)(bbb) of the 1965 Act. The case concerned an application for surrender on foot of a European arrest warrant in circumstances where there had been a previous unsuccessful extradition application under the 1965 Act. Peart J compared the 1965 and 2003 regimes in the context of delay. He concluded that:

> "...in the absence of Section 50(2)(bbb) there exists a wider discretion to the Court as to the manner in which it might consider a sufficient unfairness to exist to justify a refusal to surrender. It is also clear from the Framework Decision itself that Member States have agreed that Member States can apply their own constitutional rules in this and other matters as necessary, and so these questions are not necessarily to be overridden or trumped in all cases by any imperative derived from the objectives of the Framework Decision as set forth in the recitals thereto."

Notwithstanding the recognition in *Aamond* of the much broader terms in which **16–16** s 37 is drafted, the Supreme Court's interpretation of the section in subsequent cases has undoubtedly taken a much less forgiving approach to a respondent who attempts to resist surrender on the basis of a potential breach of fundamental rights than those who previously sought to invoke s 50(2)(bbb) of the 1965 Act.

In interpreting s 37 of the 2003 Act, the Supreme Court has emphasised that **16–17** surrender should be refused only where *the surrender itself* (as opposed to the future trial and/or imprisonment in the issuing State) would constitute a contravention of the Convention or the Constitution. Thus, so long as neither the act of ordering surrender nor the physical surrender of the requested person involves a contravention of his or her fundamental rights, his or her surrender will not be prohibited by s 37. The effect of the decisions of the Supreme Court in *Minister for Justice, Equality*

---

[11] See for example *Coleman v O'Toole* [2003] 4 IR 222 and *Bolger v O'Toole* [2008] 4 IR 780.

[12] [2006] IEHC 382. Note that the judgment incorrectly cites the respondent as "Aamond". He was in fact the "Aamand" of *Aamand v Smithwick* [1995] 1 ILRM 61.

and Law Reform v Stapleton[13] and *Minister for Justice, Equality and Law Reform v SMR*,[14] discussed below, is that, given the principle of mutual trust and confidence amongst the Member States, two presumptions arise in practice. Firstly, the court can generally assume that no fundamental right of the requested person will be infringed following his or her surrender. Secondly, even if the evidence tends to show that the trial and/or imprisonment of the requested person in the issuing State *would* involve an infringement of his or her fundamental rights, it can be presumed that such infringement can and will be remedied or prevented in the issuing State following surrender.

Constitutional Rights – Extent of Protection

16–18   Moreover it is clear form the various cases that have come before the courts that notwithstanding the apparently broad terms of s 37 it does not extend protection to all rights contained in the Constitution and the European Convention on Human Rights. In *Minister for Justice, Equality and Law Reform v Brennan*,[15] the surrender of the respondent was sought by the UK authorities so that, *inter alia*, he could be prosecuted for the offence of escape from lawful custody contrary to common law, which according to the warrant before the court was punishable by a maximum term of life imprisonment. At para (h) of the warrant, it was stated that *"the offender has to serve an appropriate minimum period (the tariff) that reflects the punitive element of the sentence"*. The respondent argued that, if convicted of the offence of escape from lawful custody, he would have to serve an unspecified mandatory minimum sentence, and the sentencing judge would not have discretion to alter this minimum period to reflect the particular circumstances of his case. He therefore objected to his surrender on the basis that for the court to order his surrender to face the potential imposition of such a mandatory minimum period would be in breach of his constitutional rights, and thus would be contrary to s 37(1)(b) of the 2003 Act.

16–19   The Supreme Court found firstly that it was not in fact apparent from the warrant that there was any question of a mandatory minimum sentence.[16] Murray CJ, giving judgment for the court, went on however to consider the question of whether s 37 might have been of assistance to the respondent had the court been satisfied that he *would* face a potential mandatory minimum penalty in the UK. Having cited his own judgment in *Minister for Justice, Equality and Law Reform v Altaravicius*[17] in relation to the State's obligations under the Framework Decision and the "high level of confidence between Member States" referred to in Recital (10) thereof, he concluded that the due process rights provided for by Art 38 of the Constitution were rights which were applicable primarily in domestic proceedings, and which

---

[13] [2008] 1 IR 669.

[14] [2008] 2 IR 242.

[15] [2007] 3 IR 732.

[16] The court found that the reference to a minimum tariff was made solely in the context of the requirement to address issues of parole and clemency in para (h) of the standard form warrant. Paragraph (h) deals with the issues of parole or clemency where the offence in question is punishable by or has led to the imposition of a life sentence.

[17] [2006] 3 IR 148.

therefore could not generally be relied upon by a respondent in the context of s 37 of the 2003 Act:

> "There is no doubt that the operation of the process for surrender as envisaged by the Act of 2003, as amended, is subject to scrutiny as to whether in any particular case it conforms with constitutional norms and in particular due process so that, for example, the respondent in such an application has an opportunity to be duly heard in the proceedings.
>
> However the argument of the respondent goes much further. He has contended that the sentencing provisions of the issuing state, in this case the United Kingdom, did not conform to the principles of Irish law, as constitutionally guaranteed, governing the sentencing of persons to imprisonment on conviction before our courts for a criminal offence.
>
> The effect of such an argument is that an order for surrender under the Act of 2003, and indeed any order for extradition, ought to be refused if the manner in which a trial in the requesting state including the manner in which a penal sanction is imposed, does not conform to the exigencies of our Constitution as if such a trial or sentence were to take place in this country. That can hardly have been the intention of the Oireachtas when it adopted Section 37(1) of the Act of 2003 since it would inevitably have the effect of ensuring that most requests for surrender or extradition would have to be refused. And indeed if that were the intent of the Framework Decision, which the Act of 2003 implements, and other countries applied such a test from their own perspective, few, if any, would extradite to this country."[18]

He went on to note that the general prohibition on extradition contrary to constitutional **16–20** rights that had existed previously had not thrown up any authority for the proposition that the due process rights contained in Art 38 were capable of application to foreign judicial systems:

> "Indeed it may be said that generally extradition has always been subject to a proviso that an order for extradition, as with any order, should not be made if it would constitute a contravention of a provision of the Constitution. I am not aware of any authority for the principle that the extradition or surrender of a person to a foreign country would contravene the Constitution simply because their legal system and system of trial differed from ours as envisaged by the Constitution".

However, he did not entirely rule out s 37 coming into play to prohibit surrender in **16–21** extreme cases of incompatibility between the criminal justice system of the issuing State and the Irish Constitution:

> "That is not by any means to say that a court, in considering an application for surrender, has no jurisdiction to consider the circumstances where it is established that surrender would lead to a denial of fundamental or human rights. There may well be egregious circumstances, such as a clearly established and fundamental defect in the system of justice of a requesting state, where

---

[18] p 743.

a refusal of an application for surrender may be necessary to protect such rights. It would not be appropriate in this case to examine further possible or hypothetical situations where this might arise. The sole matter which I wish to make clear here is that the mere fact that a trial or sentence may take place in a requesting state according to procedures or principles which differ from those which apply, even if constitutionally guaranteed, in relation to a criminal trial in this country does not of itself mean that an application for surrender should be refused pursuant to s. 37(2) of the Act."[19]

16–22　The mere fact, therefore, that the requesting State does not observe the same constitutional norms will not of itself result in a refusal of surrender under s 37.

16–23　The decision of the High Court in *Minister for Justice, Equality and Law Reform v Stapleton*[20] predated that of the Supreme Court in *Brennan*. The respondent in *Stapleton* sought to resist his surrender to the United Kingdom on the grounds that it would be in breach of his right to an expeditious trial, in circumstances where more than 28 years had passed since the alleged commission of the fraud offences on which the European arrest warrant was based. Peart J, giving judgment before the Supreme Court decision in *Brennan*, took a different view of the application of s 37 to due process rights to that of the Supreme Court, finding it appropriate to consider such rights when deciding on surrender:

> "My view in this regard is that if the respondent enjoys a convention and a constitutional right to a trial of offences with which he is charged within a reasonable time, that is a right which he is entitled to invoke and have protected on the first occasion on which it becomes relevant for argument, and that it is not a matter to be postponed so that it can be ventilated at some date in the future in another country, and after the respondent has been returned in custody to that place."[21]

16–24　As regards the issue of whether the respondent's *surrender*, as opposed to his trial, would be in breach of his right to an expeditious trial, he found little justification in such a distinction:

> "There is in my view no meaningful distinction to be drawn between surrendering the respondent to the requesting state to face a trial which would be either unfair or not within a reasonable time, and him actually facing such a trial."[22]

16–25　It is important to note however that, in making these comments, the court had been satisfied on the evidence before it (including an affidavit from an English lawyer) that the right to an expeditious trial was afforded less protection under English law than was the case in Ireland, and thus that there was a real risk that the respondent's

---

[19]　p 744.
[20]　[2006] 3 IR 26.
[21]　pp 49-50.
[22]　p 50.

trial would not be prohibited on delay grounds in the United Kingdom even though it might well be on the same facts in Ireland.[23] He stressed that this finding was:

> "...not an indication in any way that this court does not have the high level of confidence in the neighbouring jurisdiction which is referred to in the framework decision. That aspiration, if I can call it that for the moment, was not sufficient for the Oireachtas to decide that it was unnecessary to enact Section 37 of the Act of 2003."[24]

The High Court ultimately refused to order the surrender of the respondent to the United Kingdom on the grounds that such surrender would lead to a breach of his constitutional and convention right to an expeditious trial and was thus prohibited by s 37 of the 2003 Act.   **16–26**

The Minister appealed to the Supreme Court.[25] Prior to the hearing of the appeal the decision in *Brennan* was handed down. It was unsurprising then that Fennelly J, giving judgment for the Court, allowed the appeal and ordered the surrender of the respondent. In particular he made reference to the principle of mutual trust and the fact that the court was entitled to presume that the authorities in the issuing State would not subject the requested person to a trial which would be in breach of his fundamental rights: **16–27**

> "The principle of mutual recognition applies to the judicial decision of the judicial authority of the issuing Member State in issuing the Arrest Warrant. The principle of mutual confidence is broader. It encompasses the system of trial in the issuing Member State. The Court of Justice has ruled, in its recent decision in Case C-303/05 Advocaten voor de Wereld v Leden van de Ministerrad, delivered in 3rd May 2007 (since the hearing of this appeal) that the issuing Member State, as is 'stated in Article 1(3) of the Framework Decision, must respect fundamental rights and fundamental legal principles as enshrined in Article 6 EU'. It follows, in my view, that the courts of the executing Member State, when deciding whether to make an order for surrender must proceed on the assumption that the courts of the issuing Member State will, as is required by Article 6.1 of the Treaty on European Union, 'respect...human rights and fundamental freedoms'. Article 6.2 provides that the Union is itself to 'respect fundamental rights, as guaranteed by the European Convention on Human Rights and Fundamental Freedoms... and as they result from the constitutional traditions common to the Member States, as general principles of Community law."[26]

Only rights affected by the *surrender* of the requested person (as opposed to his trial or imprisonment) were protected by s 37, and thus due process rights under Art 38 did not come into play when the court was considering whether to surrender, save insofar as the requested person was entitled to due process in the hearing of the   **16–28**

---

[23] The decision of the High Court in *Stapleton* also predated the decision of the Supreme Court in *H v DPP* [2006] IESC 55 which substantially overturned much of the pre-existing case-law in relation to delay in domestic proceedings.

[24] p 51.

[25] [2008] 1 IR 669.

[26] p 689.

proceedings under the 2003 Act. Fennelly J therefore disagreed with Peart J in his interpretation of s 37:

> "Article 1.3 of the Framework Decision, read with the recitals to the Framework Decision and, as further explained by the Court of Justice in the decision in Advocaten voor de Wereld, imposes these obligations, which in turn impose the obligations found in Article 6 of the Convention on each issuing Member State when seeking the surrender of a person and, necessarily in any subsequent trial process. It follows that I am satisfied that the learned trial judge was mistaken in holding that there was 'no meaningful distinction to be drawn between surrendering the respondent to the requesting state to face a trial which would be either unfair or not within a reasonable time, and him actually facing such a trial'. Equally, he was mistaken in holding that the Respondent was entitled to have his right to a speedy trial '…protected on the first occasion on which it becomes relevant for argument, and that it is not a matter to be postponed so that it can be ventilated at some date in the future in another country, and after the respondent has been returned in custody to that place.'"[27]

16–29   There would, therefore, appear to be a very significant reluctance on the part of the courts to engage themselves in any consideration of the potential infringement of rights on the grounds that such issues can be litigated in the requesting State. Whilst such a position has the merit of simplicity and convenience in respect of convention rights, it is much less clear how a respondent might be expected to litigate an issue concerning rights under the Constitution in the requesting State.

RIGHT TO A FAIR TRIAL

16–30   Obviously a large number of issues can arise in the context of the constitutional entitlement to a fair trial. Specific consideration is given to the issue of delay below. In respect of other objections raised in relation to the trial process in the issuing State the courts have shown a marked reluctance to engage in any consideration of such issues citing the principal of mutual trust.

16–31   In *Minister for Justice, Equality and Law Reform v Michael Gerard Ward*,[28] the respondent contended that, as a member of the travelling community, he would not receive a fair trial in the United Kingdom. In support of this contention, he submitted an article concerning the unfair treatment of travellers in the UK criminal justice system. It was held that much stronger evidence than this article would be necessary to dislodge the faith the court was entitled to have in the UK criminal justice system.

16–32   Similarly in *Minister for Justice, Equality and Law Reform v Koncis*[29] the court declined to entertain such an argument where the respondent failed to adduce evidence sufficient to show that he would not receive a fair trial in the issuing State. In that case, it appeared from the information contained in the European arrest warrant that the offence of robbery with which the respondent was charged in Latvia carried a higher penalty where the accused had a previous conviction for the same

---

[27]   pp 689-690.
[28]   Unreported, High Court, 4 July 2006, Peart J.
[29]   [2006] IEHC 379.

offence. Furthermore, it was stated in the warrant that the respondent had in fact been convicted of robbery before. The respondent argued that he would not get a fair trial as it was a basic principle of fairness that evidence of previous criminal convictions should not be given at criminal trials. Peart J agreed with the Minister, who pointed out that the respondent had not shown that he would be tried by jury or that even if he was, any jury would be aware of his previous conviction, and furthermore that the previous conviction for robbery was not an ingredient of the offence which was concerned with guilt or innocence but was rather concerned with the severity of the penalty which might be imposed. Again, the court referred to the "high level of confidence between Member States", all of which were presumed to have certain minimum standards of fair procedures and for the protection of fundamental rights. The respondent was found not to have rebutted this presumption:

> "A respondent seeking to unsettle such a presumption and understanding has a heavy onus to discharge and a high hurdle to overcome before his/her surrender will be refused. This respondent has fallen well short of discharging that onus".[30]

In *Minister for Justice, Equality and Law Reform v Devlin*,[31] the respondent sought **16–33** to rely on a combination of his ill health, including potential future complications arising from liver transplant surgery, and a delay of almost 10 years between the date of the alleged revenue offences and the issuing of the European arrest warrant to resist his surrender based on the risk of an unfair trial in the United Kingdom. Peart J rejected these arguments finding firstly that the delay issue was dealt with by the Supreme Court's decision in *Stapleton*:

> "I am satisfied that since the Supreme Court judgment in Stapleton, the position now is that if the respondent wishes to claim that any delay in seeking his surrender has resulted in a situation where it is not possible for him to obtain a fair trial in respect of the offences contained in the European arrest warrant, this is a matter which must be dealt with by way of an application to prohibit trial in the issuing state, and is not a matter which can be the subject of a determination in this jurisdiction under section 37 of the European Arrest Warrant Act 2003, as amended."

In relation to the evidence of ill health, Peart J found that there was: **16–34**

> "... no evidence whatsoever to suggest that his medical condition in any way contributes to any inability to receive a fair trial".

It is clear that any evidence which purports to show that a requested person will not **16–35** receive a fair trial in the issuing State must be substantial in nature, ideally specific to the person's own particular circumstances and will in most cases be required to be independently corroborated. In *Minister for Justice, Equality and Law Reform v*

---

[30] The facts of *Koncis* might be considered in light of the subsequent enactment of s 25 of the Criminal Justice Act 2007, which imposes certain mandatory sentences in cases where certain specified crimes are committed for the second time within a specified period. This provision appears to be quite similar to the Latvian laws which were examined by the Court in *Koncis*, and, had it been in force at the time, may have strengthened the Court's view that the Latvian laws did not breach fair procedures.

[31] [2008] IEHC 12.

Puta and Sulej,[32] the surrender of the respondents was sought on several charges by the Czech authorities. One of the points of objection submitted by both respondents was that they would not receive a fair trial because of what they alleged was the pervasive corruption and brutality of the political and criminal justice system of the Czech Republic. Fennelly J put little store on the respondents' affidavits in this regard, which questioned the Czech Republic's fitness to be a Member State of the European Union and included averments such as:

> "The Czech Republic is more like the Wild West and those in charge are more like the Italian mafia".

16–36   The court described the affidavits filed as containing:

> "...a large number of largely incomprehensible allegations of corruption and violence (including murder) against, on the whole, unnamed persons"

> and

> "...wild and irresponsible allegations"

16–37   The court concluded that the allegations made by the respondents were unsubstantiated by any independent evidence and fell far short of discharging the heavy onus on the respondents to show that they would not receive a fair trial in the issuing State:

> "It is, of course, clear that persons in the position of the appellants are entitled to resist the making of the order by producing proof that they face the risk of mistreatment on their return. That is clear from the recitals to the Framework Decision and from section 37 of the Act of 2003. But they must discharge a heavy onus. They must rebut the presumption that the issuing state generally respects human rights. The evidence must be cogent. That is that it must be coherent and persuasive. It is easy to make unsupported and unverifiable assertions about the state of affairs in another country".

16–38   In *Minister for Justice, Equality and Law Reform v Stapleton*,[33] the respondent maintained that he was at real risk of receiving an unfair trial in the United Kingdom because certain evidence had been excluded from the trial of his wife on similar charges in 1986, on the grounds of some form of public interest immunity, and it was likely that this evidence would also be excluded by the judge in his trial. The Court found that this consideration was entirely a matter for the trial judge in the issuing State:

> "What did or did not happen in the trial of his wife can have no bearing for the purpose of the present application, and this court cannot make any assumptions as to what evidence will or will not be admitted by the trial judge at any trial which would take place. That is manifestly a matter for the trial judge, and the respondent, if surrendered, would have available to him all his rights to due process in that trial".[34]

---

[32] [2008] IESC 30.
[33] [2006] 3 IR 26.
[34] p 40.

Such an approach is in line with domestic jurisprudence which suggests that any **16–39**
issue of admissibility in the course of a criminal trial must be left to the trial judge
and cannot be litigated in advance in isolation.[35]

RIGHT TO LIFE AND BODILY INTEGRITY

In a number of cases the respondents have argued that their lives may be in danger **16–40**
if surrendered. In *Minister for Justice, Equality and Law Reform v SMR*,[36] the
respondent's suggestion that the delay in his case engaged the provisions of s 37 was
rejected by the Supreme Court for the same reasons as in *Stapleton* and *Brennan*.
However, the respondent also contended that his surrender would be in breach of
his constitutional right to life and/or bodily integrity, in circumstances where the
surrender would constitute a serious risk to his health. He argued that his surrender
was therefore prohibited by s 37(1)(b). This argument was accepted by the High
Court, which made the following finding of fact:

> "I have concluded that the Respondent is at real risk of dying if placed in any
> situation of severe stress, and also that it is reasonable to assume not only that
> any trial would constitute such a severely stressful situation, but also the whole
> pre-trial period, including his surrender to the U.K., where he would be involved
> in instructing solicitor and counsel in preparation for his trial."

On this point, the court stressed the fact that the breach of rights would be caused, **16–41**
not only by the trial in the issuing State, but also by the act of surrender itself.
In this way, the court's approach to the potential breach of the right to life and/
or bodily integrity of the respondent was reconcilable with the Supreme Court's
view in *Stapleton* and *Brennan* that the issuing State was the appropriate venue for
consideration of whether the *trial* of the applicant would involve a breach of rights.[37]
Although s 16(12) provided, at that time, for an appeal on a point of law only, the
Supreme Court essentially substituted its own finding of fact on the medical evidence
and concluded that there was insufficient evidence to substantiate the suggestion
that the respondent's life would be put at risk were he to be surrendered.

> "While [the respondent's doctor] is of opinion that stress may precipitate acute
> coronary disease and should be avoided I am satisfied that something much
> more definite by way of threat to life would be required in this jurisdiction
> before the courts would involve article 40.3.2° of the Constitution and prohibit
> a trial. The possibility that stress may precipitate acute coronary disease, I
> am satisfied, is insufficient...The report, as I understand it, is to the effect
> that a further acute coronary event might well prove catastrophic in further
> limiting heart muscle pump function. The report read in conjunction with the
> other medical reports relied upon does not justify the learned trial judge's

---

[35] i.e. *Byrne v Grey* [1988] IR 31.

[36] [2008] 2 IR 242.

[37] However, Peart J also found that surrender was prohibited on account of the breach of fair
procedures arising from the delay on the part of the UK authorities in seeking the surrender
of the respondent. The Supreme Court disagreed with this finding as the issue of delay was
in its view one which could and should be left over for consideration by the courts in the
issuing State.

conclusion that the Respondent is at a real risk of dying if placed in any situation of severe stress."[38]

16–42 Significantly the court described the necessity of engaging in a balancing exercise which the court must perform, again noting that the only relevant health consequences were those which would arise from the surrender itself:

> "The court, I am satisfied, must balance the risk to the health of the respondent directly related to his surrender on the one hand and the obligations of the State under the Framework Decision."[39]

16–43 The conclusion of the Supreme Court to the effect that the right to life and bodily integrity of the respondent ought, in some way, be balanced with the State's obligations under the Framework Decision is open to significant criticism. Whilst certain rights may well have to be balanced against each other it is difficult to see how the right to life or bodily integrity can be subjected to what amounts to a proportionality test in the context of the obligation to surrender. The subsequent decision of the Supreme Court in *Minister for Justice, Equality and Law Reform v Rettinger*[40] which spoke of the absolute protection of certain rights and referenced the relevant decisions of the European Court of Human Rights in that regard would seem to signal a somewhat more principled approach.

16–44 The decision in *SMR* was referred to in the subsequent case of *Minister for Justice, Equality and Law Reform v Johnston*,[41] where one of the grounds on which the respondent sought to resist his surrender was that he suffered from a serious psychiatric condition which put him at risk of self harm in the event of surrender. The court compared the circumstances of the two cases and concluded that the condition of the respondent in *Johnston* was substantially less serious than that of the appellant in *SMR*. Given the extensive and thorough nature of the medical evidence before the court in *SMR* and the fact that it is likely to be regarded as something of a benchmark by the courts, one might well ask the question as to what level of evidence would be required before the courts were persuaded to exercise the jurisdiction under s 37 where a risk to the health of a respondent is concerned.

DELAY

16–45 As is clear from the discussion above of *Minister for Justice, Equality and Law Reform v Stapleton*,[42] a requested person seeking to resist surrender on the basis of a delay in issuing the warrant on the part of the prosecuting authorities in the issuing State faces an uphill struggle. The issue of delay in that case was discussed primarily in the context of the constitutional right to an expeditious trial which the respondent claimed engaged s 37.

16–46 Even prior the Supreme Court's decision in *Stapleton* to the effect that delay was a matter most appropriately argued before the courts of the issuing State, objections

---

[38] p 254.
[39] p 252.
[40] [2010] IESC 45.
[41] [2008] IESC 11.
[42] [2008] 1 IR 669.

based on delay were unlikely to succeed in circumstances where the respondent could not show actual prejudice. In *Minister for Justice, Equality and Law Reform v TMC*[43] the underlying offences involved charges of rape and indecent assault in the United Kingdom. The offences against two young girls were alleged to have been committed between 1989 and 2001. Having found that the deterioration in the respondent's health was not so significant as to give rise to a risk of an unfair trial, Peart J further rejected the argument that the passage of time alone would lead to such a risk, citing the relevant jurisprudence of the Supreme Court:

> "As far as delay since the date of the alleged offences is concerned, and that delay to create a serious risk of an unfair trial is concerned, the recent judgments of the Supreme Court in *PM v. DPP* [2006] 2 ILRM 361, *H v. DPP*, unreported, Supreme Court, 31st July 2006 make it clear that the reasons for the delay do not have to be inquired into, and that real prejudice must be demonstrated".

As regards prosecutorial as opposed to complainant delay, Peart J disregarded the **16–47** lapse of time from 2001 to 2004 as one caused by the respondent himself in leaving the UK. In this regard, he disbelieved the respondent's evidence that he had been in contact with the UK and Irish authorities during this period. Peart J did however criticise the delay between March 2004, when the UK authorities learned of the respondent's whereabouts, and March 2006, when the European arrest warrant was issued. Such a delay however, again in the absence of any significant prejudice, was found to be insufficient to justify refusing surrender:

> "That delay is not explained. There would inevitably be some time required to process the paperwork for the preparation of that warrant, but it would be unreasonable, in the absence of a particular explanation, to accept that it could take two years. There appears to have been an inordinate delay in that process. However, I am not satisfied that the lapse of time or passage of time or delay, whichever it is to be termed, is such that the respondent can be said to have been prejudiced to the extent that his surrender should be refused. There has been no breach of his constitutional rights or his Convention rights in this regard and as such his surrender is not prohibited by Part 3 of the Act or the Framework Decision".

An even longer period of unexplained prosecutorial delay was held not to prohibit **16–48** surrender in *Minister for Justice, Equality and Law Reform v Draisey*,[44] in a judgment delivered on the same day as that in *TMC*. In *Draisey*, despite the UK domestic warrant issuing in December 2000, the European arrest warrant was not issued until almost five years later, in December 2005. Although the court felt that there had been no proper explanation given for this delay, it again referred to the "necessity even in cases of substantial delay to establish real prejudice", and found that such prejudice had not been shown by the respondent. In those circumstances, it found that surrender was not prohibited by s 37. A similar finding was made in relation to a delay of eight years in *Minister for Justice, Equality and Law Reform v Krasnovas*.[45]

---

[43] [2006] IEHC 372.

[44] [2006] IEHC 375.

[45] [2006] IEHC 377.

16–49 Minister for Justice, Equality and Law Reform v JBF[46] was another case in which the respondent did not appear to have contributed in any way to the delay, which in his case was almost four years. Allegations had been made against him in May 2002. However, he was never questioned in relation to these allegations, and the European arrest warrant was not received from the UK authorities until February 2005. Before applying for the respondent's surrender, the Minister sent certain queries to the UK authorities, but a reply was not received until nine months later. An application for the respondent's surrender was finally made in February 2006. Peart J, although noting that there certainly had been delays for which the respondent was not in any way responsible, found that the delay was not sufficient to give rise to an issue under s 37 particularly as no risk of an unfair trial had been shown:

> "I cannot regard the sort of delay which occurred in this case as coming anywhere near the sort of length of delay which could give rise to a breach of constitutional right such that would warrant a refusal of the obligation to order surrender under the Act of 2003 and the framework decision. It requires something quite exceptional both in terms of length and consequence/ prejudice to bring the s. 37 provisions into play. There is nothing of any significance contained in the respondent's affidavit as to how he is prejudiced in the ability to defend himself. There is no suggestion that any witness is no longer available, and I suspect that he is in the same position now to defend himself as he would have been at any stage since May, 2002."[47]

16–50 In *Minister for Justice, Equality and Law Reform v Gardener*,[48] having examined the Supreme Court decision of *PM v DPP*[49] in relation to blameworthy prosecutorial delay, the court rejected the respondent's argument that a blameworthy prosecutorial delay of five years gave rise to a presumed prejudice which prohibited surrender. Peart J quoted Kearns J in *PM* to the effect that, as well as blameworthy prosecutorial delay,

> "...one or more of the interests protected by the right to expeditious trial must also be shown to have been so interfered with such as would entitle the applicant to relief."[50]

16–51 As the respondent in *Gardener* had put forward no evidence whatsoever relating to any interference with such rights, Peart J found that his surrender could not be

---

[46] [2006] 3 IR 411.

[47] p 418. The decision of Peart J to order surrender was upheld on appeal by the Supreme Court in an *ex tempore* judgment of 29 June 2006.

[48] [2007] IEHC 35.

[49] [2006] 3 IR 172.

[50] pp 185-186. As noted by Kearns J, the interests protected by the right to an expeditious trial were set out by Powell J in the US Supreme Court judgment of *Barker v Wingo* 407 U.S. 514 (1972) as (i) the right to prevent oppressive pre-trial incarceration; (ii) The right to minimise anxiety and concern to the accused; and (iii) the right to limit the possibility that the defence will be impaired.

prohibited on grounds of blameworthy prosecutorial delay.[51] The respondent's appeal to the Supreme Court was dismissed in a short judgment[52] of Finnegan J, delivered just three days after the Supreme Court's decision in *Stapleton*. Referring to the latter case, Finnegan J noted that

> "...the issue of delay is one to be dealt with in the court of trial unless the respondent can establish by clear and cogent evidence a clear and fundamental defect in the system of justice of the requesting state such that the refusal of the application for surrender is necessary to protect his constitutional rights."

The present position is most conveniently summarised by Denham J in *Minister for* **16–52**
Justice, Equality and Law Reform v Hall[53]:

> "There may be situations where a court in this requested State would consider the issue of a delay, it would depend on the circumstances. However, in general, issues such as prosecutorial delay and its consequences, are more appropriately litigated in the requesting state, which is the state of trial. This presumption is based on the existence of remedies, such as access to judicial review or a process to review an allegation of abuse of process. It is grounded on the foundation of mutual trust of the European Arrest Warrant scheme. It all depends on the circumstances of the case."

The foregoing passage does seem to suggest that if there were evidence before the **16–53**
court to the effect that there was no forum in which the respondent might agitate an issue of prosecutorial delay upon his return, a different attitude might be taken here.

Athough the courts in this jurisdiction have shown a marked reluctance to **16–54**
consider issues of delay, it should be borne in mind that whilst delay will generally not of itself give rise to a ground of objection, it may well feed into other grounds. In *Minister for Justice, Equality and Law Reform v Gorman*[54] a delay in applying for a European arrest warrant was considered to be something that might be taken account of in balancing the respondent's right to family life under Art 8 of the European Convention on Human Rights and the obligation to surrender:

> "...the period of 8 years from the enactment of the 2003 Act is something to weigh in the balance when considering the extent of the pressing social need in a democratic society to achieve the surrender of the respondent...In my view the pressing social need or other obligation to surrender the respondent is diluted by the delays which have been encountered in this case..."

It may, therefore, still be worthwhile pursuing issues of delay in conjunction with **16–55**
other anticipated breaches of s 37.

---

[51] In *Gardener*, there was also a significant period of complainant delay. On the basis of the Supreme Court decision in *SH v DPP* [2006] 3 IR 575, Peart J found that, since no actual prejudice to the respondent had been shown to have arisen from the complainant delay, such delay did not prohibit his surrender.

[52] [2007] IESC 40.

[53] [2009] IESC 40.

[54] [2010] IEHC 210.

EUROPEAN ARREST WARRANTS ISSUED IN BAD FAITH

16–56   In extradition proceedings under the 1965 Act requests which were shown to have been made in bad faith or to have involved deception were, from time to time, refused. In *The State (Hully) v Hynes,*[55] the Supreme Court accepted the prosecutor's unanswered claim that the English warrant upon which he was sought for an offence of forgery was in fact a "*cloak*" by means of which he could be transferred to England to be prosecuted for revenue offences. The transfer of a person out of the jurisdiction to face prosecution for revenue offences was prohibited by the relevant legislation at the time. The Court considered that it had the power to intervene in such circumstances:

> "It cannot be doubted that it would be well within the jurisdiction of the High Court, and of this Court, to grant habeas corpus to a person who was about to be sent out of the country to answer a charge not made bona fide but with the object of getting the person accused into the foreign jurisdiction for another purpose."[56]

16–57   Kingsmill Moore J found that the *mala fides* made the entire process invalid:

> "…when the facts are revealed, this Court must treat the endorsement [of the warrant] as a nullity."[57]

16–58   In *Ellis v O'Dea,*[58] Walsh J in the Supreme Court referred to *The State (Hully) v Hynes* and observed that:

> "Extradition being a matter of reciprocity requires good faith from each side. The courts must not be subjected to requests for extradition which in fact conceal some other purpose or some totally different charge."[59]

16–59   In England, there was formerly a specific statutory basis for the principle that the extradition of a person must be refused where it was established that the accusation made against him in the requesting State was not made in good faith in the interests of justice.[60] Even though the present legislation, the Extradition Act 2003, contains no such specific provision, it has been held that the courts in that jurisdiction retain a residual power to refuse to surrender on grounds of abuse of process by the authorities of the requesting State.[61] Furthermore, it is likely that the general fundamental rights protection contained in that Act mandates a refusal of surrender where bad faith can be shown.[62]

---

[55]   100 ILTR 145 (1966).

[56]   p 172.

[57]   p 166.

[58]   [1989] 1 IR 530.

[59]   p 539.

[60]   s 11(3)(c) of the Extradition Act 1989. That Act has now been repealed by the Extradition Act 2003.

[61]   *Symeou v Public Prosecutor's Office, Patras, Greece* [2009] 1 WLR 2384, at 2388.

[62]   See further s 21 of the Extradition Act 2003 and *Handbook on the European Arrest Warrant* (TMC Asser Press, 2005) at p 180.

There is little reason to suppose that the above-quoted principle espoused by **16–60** Walsh J in *Ellis v O'Dea* should not also apply to proceedings under the 2003 Act. In *O Fallúin v Governor of Cloverhill Prison*,[63] Peart J spoke of the eventuality where an extradition request is made by fraudulent means as:

> "one against which any person present in this State would be entitled to protection against the deprivation of his/her liberty".

However, the major difference between proceedings under the 1965 Act and those **16–61** under the 2003 Act is the enhanced trust and respect due in the latter to the authorities in the issuing State. Accordingly, where bad faith on the part of the issuing State is alleged, this will have to be substantiated by convincing and weighty evidence.

Typically a bad faith prosecution will arise where, due to lack of evidence, there **16–62** is no reasonable likelihood of a conviction and the main motive for bringing the prosecution is to vex the accused by causing major disruption to his life and potential damage to his good name. In the United Kingdom, a request for surrender will not be seen as having been made in bad faith simply because certain evidence alleged against the requested person seems likely to be inadmissible at trial. In *Symeou v Public Prosecutor's Office, Patras, Greece*,[64] evidence that witness statements implicating the requested person were obtained by coercion by the Greek police was not evidence that the request for surrender by the Greek authorities amounted to an abuse of process. It was to be presumed that the trial court in Greece would not admit improperly obtained evidence. Effectively, for surrender to be refused on this basis, the bad faith or abuse of process should relate to the making of the request for surrender rather than any other deficiencies or misconduct in relation to the investigation of the offence.

In *Minister for Justice, Equality and Law Reform v Dundon*,[65] the respondent **16–63** contended that the case against him was essentially a "one witness case", and that one witness, his wife, had withdrawn her earlier testimony against him. Furthermore, as his wife, she was not compellable as a witness. One of the grounds on which the respondent sought to resist his surrender was that it would be an abuse of process to surrender him in circumstances where there was no realistic chance of the prosecution against him succeeding. However, Denham J in the Supreme Court declined to engage in any form or assessment of the likelihood of the respondent being convicted in the issuing State:

> "I would, first of all, note on the facts that there is no basis to find that this is a one witness case. However, on the law, I am satisfied that the adequacy of the evidence against the person sought is not a matter for consideration on these proceedings under the Act. Further, there is no requirement that the requesting state establish a prima facie case."[66]

A similar situation arose subsequently in *Minister for Justice, Equality and Law Reform* **16–64** *v Dubikatlis*,[67] where the respondent was sought by the Lithuanian authorities for an

---

[63] [2005] IEHC 284.
[64] [2009] 1 WLR 2384.
[65] [2005] 1 IR 261.
[66] p 272.
[67] [2006] IEHC 332.

offence of extortion. A certificate purporting to be from the complainant was produced in evidence by the respondent. The complainant stated that the respondent had never made any demand for money from him, and stated that they were in fact good friends. The respondent submitted that, notwithstanding the obligations arising from the 2003 Act and the Framework Decision, the court retained an inherent jurisdiction to prevent an abuse of process by refusing to order surrender. Peart J did not disagree with this, but quoted the above passage from Denham J in *Dundon* in finding that there was no abuse of process in circumstances where the prosecuting authority in Lithuania had confirmed, in a letter submitted to the court by the applicant, that it intended proceeding with the prosecution of the respondent following his surrender. Peart J found that:

> "…it is not open to this Court to determine or even consider whether or not the prosecution can or cannot succeed at trial".

16–65   It will obviously be difficult to prove *mala fides* on the part of the authorities in the issuing State. Actual evidence of actions in bad faith would seem to be necessary before an objection under this heading is likely to succeed. Evidence of the withdrawal of the complaint by the complainant will, by and large, be insufficient.

LEGITIMATE EXPECTATION

16–66   On occasion it has been argued that surrender ought to be refused by virtue of some understanding or indication obtained from the authorities in the requesting State to the effect that the criminal proceedings underlying the European arrest warrant were at an end or would otherwise not be pursued.

16–67   A domestic warrant had been issued for the arrest of the respondent in *Minister for Justice, Equality and Law Reform v Johnston*[68] due to his failure to appear in respect of certain charges at the High Court of Glasgow in 2001. The respondent's own evidence was that he had fled to Ireland after being granted bail. He had re-entered the United Kingdom from Ireland in 2005, when his car was stopped at Holyhead by police officers exercising powers under UK anti-terrorism legislation, who noted that the respondent was a person in respect of whom a domestic warrant had issued. Enquiries were made with the police in Scotland, who it seems incorrectly advised that the respondent was no longer wanted. Accordingly, he was allowed to proceed on his way. One of the respondent's grounds of objection to his surrender was that, as a result of being allowed to proceed from Holyhead on that occasion, he held a legitimate expectation that he would not be subsequently prosecuted for the Scottish offences. This expectation, he argued, was sufficient to prohibit his surrender.

16–68   The Supreme Court rejected this argument. Although appearing to proceed on the basis that a genuine and properly held expectation could possibly be a bar to surrender in some cases, the court found no reasonable basis for the respondent's belief. Macken J stressed that even an honest and genuine belief that one will not in future be prosecuted does not amount to a legitimate expectation unless it is in fact "legitimate" — that is to say reasonable in the circumstances. She found that the law was clear on this point:

> "The law relating to legitimate expectation has long been the subject of judgments in this jurisdiction, in the United Kingdom and undoubtedly in

---

[68] [2008] IESC 11.

Scotland and in many other jurisdictions. It is true also that it has been an evolving area of the law and it may well be that the principles applicable to the doctrine of legitimate expectation have not yet been fully expounded. What is however clearly established in the case law in this jurisdiction, in Northern Ireland and elsewhere is the following primary principle. The expectation which a person is entitled to hold is one which must in all the circumstances of the case be reasonable or legitimate for him to hold".

The court went on to distinguish the case before it from the case of *Eviston v DPP*,[69] **16–69** where a road traffic prosecution had been prohibited on legitimate expectation grounds. In *Eviston*, there had been evidence that the prosecutor had made a decision not to prosecute the accused, and had communicated this decision to her. In *Johnston* however, Macken J noted that there was no evidence that any such decision had been made or communicated with any effect:

"There was before the learned High Court judge no evidence whatsoever that any decision had been made by the appropriate decision maker, that the prosecution would not or could not proceed. Still less could it be concluded from the evidence adduced to the High Court that the exchanges, in Scottish law or under the law of the United Kingdom (if otherwise applicable), had as their legal consequence that the warrant could not be pursued, if not executed in Holyhead at that time".

However, the issue of legitimate expectation in a more general sense may well be **16–70** of relevance in assessing whether there has been a breach of Art 8 of the European Convention on Human Rights.

INTERFERENCE WITH FAMILY LIFE – ARTICLE 8

In a number of cases respondents have sought to argue that their surrender will **16–71** disproportionately interfere with their right to family life and thereby result in a breach of Art 8 of the European Convention on Human Rights. On the grounds that imprisonment inevitably amounts to a gross interference with family life and as such is no more than the consequence of the trial process the courts have, in general, dismissed such objections out of hand:

"...I would also dismiss the third ground of appeal in limine. It is a regrettable but inescapable incident of extradition in general and, as in this case, surrender pursuant to the system of the European arrest warrant, that persons sought for prosecution in another state will very often suffer disruption of their personal and family life. Some states have historically refused to extradite their own nationals, but that is a special case. The Framework Decision expressly provides that, in Article 1, that it does not "have the effect of modifying the obligation to respect fundamental rights and fundamental legal principles as enshrined in Article 6 of the Treaty on European Union." No authority has been produced to support the proposition that surrender is to be refused where a person will, as a consequence, suffer disruption, even severe disruption of family relationships".[70]

---

[69] [2002] 3 IR 260.
[70] *Minister for Justice, Equality and Law Reform v Gheorghe* [2009] IESC 76.

16–72   However, such an objection succeeded in *Minster for Justice, Equality and Law Reform v Gorman.*[71] The respondent was sought in the United Kingdom for an offence of murder alleged to have been committed in 1992 as part of the INLA campaign then ongoing at the time. The respondent had been arrested in 1994 with a view to his extradition for the same offence but the State had offered no evidence on that application in circumstances where a related case[72] had already determined that a prospective co-accused should not be extradited as the offence fell into the political offence exception and there had been inordinate pre-trial publicity so as to render any trial unfair. In the intervening years the respondent had married and started a family.

16–73   Subsequently a European arrest warrant was issued for the respondent in 2007 although it was not endorsed for execution until 2009. Thereafter he was arrested. He resisted his surrender principally on the basis that his surrender would amount to a disproportionate interference with his right to private and family life in circumstances where he was entitled to assume that he would not be subject to any further attempt to effect his extradition or surrender.

16–74   Peart J reviewed the various decisions of the European Court of Human Rights and considered that the following test should be applied in such cases:

> "It seems to me to follow that for the purposes of the present application for the respondent's surrender, this Court is required to consider the following questions in arriving at a conclusion as to whether an order for the surrender of the respondent to the United Kingdom would constitute a breach of the State's obligations under the Convention or its Protocols: (1) does a surrender constitute an interference with the respondent's private/ family right; (2) if so, is that interference one that is in accordance with law; (3) if further so, is the interference, by surrender of the respondent, in pursuit of a legitimate aim or objective (4) and further if so, whether that interference is necessary in a democratic society (the latter meaning that it is justified by a pressing social need) and proportionate to the legitimate aim pursued."

16–75   The court went on to consider each of the questions it had posed. In relation to the first question it concluded that were the respondent to be surrendered this, of itself, would result in a significant period of incarceration prior to trial and as such amounted to an interference with family life. On the second question there was little doubt but that the interference, if it were to occur, would be in accordance with law. The aim or objective underlying the surrender of the respondent was identified as that of public order and national security thereby answering the third question.

16–76   It was, however, the fourth question which proved determinative of the issue. Necessarily this involved a balancing of the interests of the State parties in seeking to have the respondent surrendered and his right to private and family life:

> "The Court's task involves striking a fair balance in the present case between the respondent's right to family life, and this State's obligation, as it appears, under the Framework Decision, and subject inter alia to the provisions of Section 37 of the Act, to surrender the respondent under the European arrest

---

[71] [2010] IEHC 210.

[72] See *Magee v O'Dea* [1994] 1 IR 500.

warrant. In my view it cannot be the case that the obligation of this State to surrender the respondent so that he can be prosecuted for serious offences in the United Kingdom would on all occasions trump any family or other rights of a respondent, as otherwise the provisions of Section 37 of the Act would have no relevance or meaning. That section requires the Court in cases such as the present one, where facts are established, to determine whether the surrender of the respondent would constitute a breach of a Convention right of the respondent, and if so, to prohibit surrender."

Ultimately the Court concluded that, in the circumstances of the particular case, that balance lay in favour of the respondent: **16–77**

"In assessing the question of the balance to be struck between this State's obligation to surrender and the rights of the respondent to family and private rights, I am of the view that proportionality is not satisfied on the unique and exceptional facts of this case. In my view, the obligation to surrender which this State is under by virtue of its international obligations must yield to the Article 8 rights of the respondent, and in my view, therefore, his surrender is prohibited by the provisions of Section 37 of the Act."

The decision is of particular significance in that it considers the right of the individual respondent as being capable of comparison with the obligations of the State. In that regard it is in contrast to some of the dicta emanating from the Supreme Court which have tended to suggest that the concerns of the individual are generally subservient to those of the State. **16–78**

DISCRIMINATION

Sections 37(1)(c)(i) and 37(1)(c)(ii) of the 2003 Act prohibit the surrender of a person where **16–79**

"...there are reasonable grounds for believing that—

    (i)   the European arrest warrant was issued in respect of the person for the purposes of facilitating his or her prosecution or punishment in the issuing state for reasons connected with his or her sex, race, religion, ethnic origin, nationality, language, political opinion or sexual orientation, or

    (ii) in the prosecution or punishment of the person in the issuing state, he or she will be treated less favourably than a person who—

        (I)   is not of his or her sex, race, religion, nationality or ethnic origin,

        (II)   does not hold the same political opinions as him or her,

        (III) speaks a different language than he or she does, or

        (IV) does not have the same sexual orientation as he or she does,".

As such two distinct scenarios are envisaged by the provision which require to be considered in turn. **16–80**

Section 37(1)(c)(i)

16–81   It would seem that the circumstances envisaged by s 37(1)(c)(i) are intended to deal with the prosecution of offences that are discriminatory *per se*. It is probably unlikely to arise with any great frequency in practice as it would be extremely difficult to show that the relevant law of the issuing State is *in itself* (as opposed to in its application) discriminatory.[73]

16–82   In *Minister for Justice, Equality and Law Reform v Biggins*[74] the court was required to examine the meaning of the words "connected with" in the context of s 37(c)(i). The surrender of the male respondent was sought for the attempted murder of his female partner. The respondent submitted that his surrender was prohibited by s 37(c)(i), since the alleged offence arose out of his relationship with his partner, and thus was connected with his "sex" or "sexual orientation". The court noted that the logical conclusion of this argument was that any person in a relationship, be it heterosexual, homosexual or other, who murdered his or her partner and fled to another Member State to avoid prosecution would have his or her surrender prohibited because of the proposed interpretation of the words "connected with". The court concluded that such a result:

> "…would be a classic absurdity arrived at by an interpretation so literal, and out of context, that it could not be open to the respondent".

16–83   The fact that the words "connected with" appeared at first instance to give a wider protection to a requested person than the equivalent words "on the grounds of" in Recital (12) of the Preamble to the Framework Decision did not alter the obvious context of the words and the absurdity which would result from an acceptance of the respondent's proposed interpretation of the words "connected with".

16–84   Similarly the mere fact that a given offence arises in a political context will not of itself engage the provisions of s 37(1)(c)(i). In *Minister for Justice, Equality and Law Reform v Gorman*[75] the respondent was sought in respect of an alleged murder that had clearly arisen in a political context. The court rejected the argument that the respondent was sought for prosecution in connection with his political beliefs:

> "There must be a distinction between being prosecuted or punished on account of one's political opinions, and the commission of a political or politically motivated offence, the latter being no longer an offence for which surrender is prohibited as such. In the present case, there can be little doubt that in so far as the offences in 1992 are concerned they were political offences within the meaning which would have been given to that term at the time when his extradition was first requested. They appear to be offences which were committed in the context of the political troubles extant at that time, and are similar to offences which were the subject of judicial decisions in those days which found them

---

[73] However, such discriminatory laws within the European Union are not unthinkable — for example, some of the laws of certain former Soviet Member States have been shown in the past to be openly discriminatory towards ethnic Russians. However, most discriminatory laws tend to be in the civil rather than the criminal sphere, and so would be unlikely to be the subject of examination in the context of European arrest warrant proceedings.

[74] [2006] IEHC 351.

[75] [2010] IEHC 210.

to be political offences. But in order to come within the ambit of s. 37 of the Act, it would, in my view, be necessary to establish not simply that the offences committed or alleged to have been committed were political offences, as understood by that term, but that the warrant has been issued in order to facilitate prosecution which is brought not simply in respect of such an offence but "on account of his political opinions". There is a distinction. I suggest that it would be necessary to show that the respondent, holding certain political opinions, is being prosecuted for an offence because he holds those opinions, whereas another person, not holding those particular opinions and who might commit the same offence, would not be prosecuted for that same offence. In my view, Section 37 provides a protection from this type of discrimination, as well as the others set forth therein, and is not intended to embrace, *sub silento*, the former political exception."

It follows that in order to invoke the provisions of s 37(1)(c)(i) it is firstly necessary **16–85** to prove that the offence is related to one of the categories set out therein and further to show that a person not coming within such a category would not be subject to such a prosecution all other things being equal.

Section 37(1)(c)(ii)

Discrimination is more likely to arise in the application of laws rather than their **16–86** wording, and thus s 37(1)(c)(ii) would seem to be a more potentially fruitful avenue for those seeking to resist surrender on discrimination grounds. It prohibits surrender where there are reasonable grounds for believing that, in the prosecution or punishment of the requested person, he or she would be "treated less favourably" because of his or her status under any of the relevant headings. Given the widely varying political outlooks across the ever-changing governments of the Member States, as well as the religious and ethnic makeup of the populations, discriminatory practices may well arise from time to time notwithstanding the well intended recitals of the Framework Decision. Although the principle of mutual trust may well entitle the court to assume otherwise objective evidence from international media and non-governmental organisations may highlight such discrimination where it occurs, thus possibly giving a requested person independent evidence with which to rebut such assumptions and the principle of mutual trust.

Attempts to resist surrender on the basis of discrimination contrary to s 37(c)(ii) **16–87** have thus far been unsuccessful. In *Minister for Justice, Equality and Law Reform v Michael Gerard Ward*,[76] an article alleging that travellers were treated unfairly within the UK criminal justice system was considered insufficient to rebut the presumption that the said system was fair and non-discriminatory. Similarly *Minister for Justice, Equality and Law Reform v Iordache*,[77] the Court rejected the proposition that it was entitled to presume that a three year sentence of imprisonment to which the Roma respondent had been sentenced in Romania for an apparently relatively minor theft was indicative of discrimination against persons of Roma ethnicity within the Romanian criminal justice system. Peart J noted that there was nothing before him other than the respondent's own assertions in this regard, and suggested that independent information or case-law from the European Court of Human Rights

---

[76] Unreported, High Court, 4 July 2006, Peart J.
[77] [2008] IEHC 186.

would have been required to interfere with the recognition and respect which was due to the sentencing decision of the Romanian court.

TORTURE AND OTHER INHUMAN OR DEGRADING TREATMENT

16–88   The final leg of s 37 prohibits surrender where it would result in the execution of the respondent or exposure to inhuman and degrading treatment. Section 37(1)(c)(iii) provides that surrender shall be refused where there are reasonable grounds for believing that:

> "...were the person to be surrendered to the issuing state—

> (I)   he or she would be sentenced to death, or a death sentence imposed on him or her would be carried out, or

> (II)   he or she would be tortured or subjected to other inhuman or degrading treatment."

16–89   Given the abolition of the death penalty across Europe since the mid 1960s it is unlikely that the possibilities mentioned in s 37(1)(c)(iii)(I) will arise.

16–90   Section 37(1)(c)(iii)(II), on the other hand, has arisen for consideration on a number of occasions. This provision transposes Recital (13) of the Preamble to the Framework Decision,[78] which in turn echoes the wording of Art 3 of the ECHR. Given the principle of mutual trust and the presumption under s 4A of the 2003 Act a question arises as to the extent to which that principle allows the courts to presume that a surrendered person will not be subjected to inhuman or degrading treatment on surrender.

16–91   Prison conditions in Lithuania came under scrutiny in *Minister for Justice, Equality and Law Reform v Busjeva*,[79] where the respondent submitted two reports, compiled in 2000 and 2004 for the Council of Europe by the European Committee for the Prevention of Inhuman or Degrading Treatment, on conditions in Lithuanian prisons and pre-trial detention centres. The reports pointed to a general lack of hygiene, lack of access to medical treatment, overcrowding and ill-treatment by prison guards. The respondent contended that her surrender would be in breach of Art 3 of the European Convention on Human Rights.[80] Peart J commented that:

> "...there is no doubt that these reports present a bleak picture and that in places the report itself describes aspects of the prison regime as inhuman and degrading."[81]

---

[78]   "(13) No person should be removed, expelled or extradited to a State where there is a serious risk that he or she would be subjected to the death penalty, torture or other inhuman or degrading treatment or punishment." The absence of the words "or punishment" at the end of s 37(c)(iii)(II), although in contrast with Recital (13), is probably not of any significance.

[79]   [2007] 3 IR 829.

[80]   No mention appears to have been made of s 37(c)(iii)(II) of the 2003 Act, although the effect of the argument would undoubtedly have been the same under that section.

[81]   p 834.

He also referred to some European Court of Human Rights cases brought by **16–92** applicants who suffered ill-treatment in Lithuanian prisons in the late 1990s. The evidential onus on the respondent was set out as follows by Peart J:

"In order to succeed in her objection, the respondent would have to show a real risk that she would suffer inhuman or degrading treatment or punishment if surrendered. This is clear from cases such as *Soering v. The United Kingdom* (1989) 11 E.H.R.R. 439, as well as cases here such as *Attorney General v. Skripakova* [2006] IESC 68, (Unreported, Supreme Court, 24th April, 2006). Clear and cogent evidence must be established in this regard. Mere speculation or uncorroborated assertion is insufficient."[82]

Although the reports submitted by the respondent seemed to go a considerable way **16–93** towards discharging the evidential burden, Peart J was impressed by a 2006 document submitted by the applicant which showed the response by the Lithuanian authorities to the earlier critical reports. It appeared to show that certain improvements had been carried out, and that further improvements were planned:

"One way or another the [2006] response document is evidence of intent on the part of the Republic of Lithuania to continue to put in place the programme of renovation and overall improvement in the prison regime and buildings. This will take time, but the important matter is that it is under way, and many improvements have already been made".

The court also saw great significance in the fact that the 2000 and 2004 reports had **16–94** been compiled before Lithuania's accession to the European Union:

"...that accession has had many consequences, but one relevant to the present application is that it is to be assumed that certain minimum standards of human rights now exist in that country."[83]

A third reason for his finding that the respondent had not shown that she was at risk **16–95** of inhuman or degrading treatment or punishment was that, pursuant to s 4A of the 2003 Act, it could be presumed that Lithuania would comply with its obligations under the Framework Decision:

"This court must have regard also to the fact that Lithuania has been designated for the purpose of the European Arrest Warrant Act 2003. There is a presumption in s. 4A of the Act that the requesting state will comply with its obligations under the framework decision. Nevertheless, that alone cannot absolve this court of the need to examine whether the presumption might have been rebutted in a given case. But there has to be taken into account the fact that the European arrest warrant regime is based on a high level of mutual trust and confidence, as set forth in the recital to the framework decision. The fact that Lithuania joined the European Union after the framework decision was adopted does not detract from that level of trust and confidence. It must be paid due regard, while at the same time not excluding, in a truly exceptional circumstance and on foot of clear cogent evidence, a determination that to order surrender would breach rights guaranteed by the Constitution or the

---

[82] p 835.
[83] p 835.

European Convention on Human Rights. This is not such a case given the clear expression of intent contained in the Lithuanian government's response document, and the progress already noted to have been made".[84]

16–96 It is unclear whether, in the absence of the 2006 "response document", the mere fact that Lithuania had become a Member State of the European Union and a designated State under s 3 of the 2003 Act would have been sufficient to justify rejecting the respondent's argument under Art 3 of the European Convention on Human Rights. Arguably, real objective evidence of a risk of inhuman or degrading treatment should outweigh the abstract notion that a State has been recognised as Convention-compliant. However, the fact that the reports submitted by the respondent in *Busjeva* were a number of years old and the fact that they appeared to relate largely to male-only prisons (whereas the respondent was female) undoubtedly served to weaken the respondent's argument. The respondent was ultimately surrendered.

16–97 A number of months after the decision in *Busjeva*, the High Court was again called upon to examine the risk to a respondent of inhuman or degrading treatment at the hands of the Lithuanian authorities who were seeking his surrender. In *Minister for Justice, Equality and Law Reform v Raustys*,[85] the respondent gave evidence on affidavit that he had been assaulted and hospitalised in 2001 by the police officers who were investigating his case, one of whose mother owned the shop which it was alleged the respondent had stolen from. Two medical reports were submitted which purported to, at least partly, corroborate the assault claims. The respondent maintained that he was at real risk of being assaulted again by these same police officers if surrendered to Lithuania, and thus that his surrender would be in breach of Art 3 of the European Convention on Human Rights and s 37(1)(c)(iii) of the European Arrest Warrant Act 2003. He submitted the same documents relating to the ill-treatment of persons in custody in Lithuania which had been submitted by the respondent in *Busjeva*.

16–98 The respondent sought to distinguish *Busjeva* on the basis that the point raised was not merely a general one relating to general conditions in Lithuanian prisons, but related rather to a fear derived from a specific assault perpetrated by specific police officers. On the facts of the case the court was not satisfied that the assault had taken place in the way described by the respondent, and accordingly found that the respondent had:

> "…failed to establish facts to the necessary degree upon which to make his submission that he has shown to exist reasonable grounds for this Court to consider as a matter of probability that if surrendered the respondent's rights will be infringed in the way suggested".

16–99 However, the court went on to state that, even if it had been satisfied as to the factual basis of the respondent's claims, it would have been satisfied by the principle of mutual trust and the positive steps taken by the Lithuanian authorities since the alleged assault that the respondent was not at risk of being subjected to torture or other inhuman or degrading treatment if surrendered.

---

[84] pp 835-836.
[85] [2007] IEHC 370.

Prison conditions in the United Kingdom were sought to be impugned in **16–100** *Stapleton*,[86] where the High Court dismissed as "fanciful in the extreme" the respondent's submission that he would be at risk of inhuman or degrading treatment as a "Category A" prisoner in the United Kingdom. Apart from the fact that no evidence tended to show that the respondent was in fact likely to be treated as a "Category A" prisoner, there was also no evidence that such a prisoner, or in fact any prisoner in a UK prison, would be subjected to inhuman or degrading treatment.

The respondent in *Minister for Justice, Equality and Law Reform v Brady*[87] **16–101** similarly failed to prevent his surrender as a result of a lack of evidence when he argued that there was no guarantee that, as a person who was paralysed from the waist down, he would have access to appropriate medical facilities in custody in the United Kingdom if surrendered. An affidavit was before the court from a barrister attached to the Crown Prosecution Service, who attested to the prison conditions in the UK, including their compliance with Art 3 of the European Convention on Human Rights. Peart J found that this affidavit was in fact not even necessary, as the situation was covered by the principle of mutual trust and confidence between Member States:

> "It would take a truly exceptional circumstance and a very high degree of proof in my view to dislodge what must be almost a presumption (though it is not expressed as a presumption in the Framework Decision or in the Act) that participating member states designated under Section 3 of the Act by the Minister for Foreign Affairs here observe fundamental rights, whether with regard to prison conditions or otherwise".

This approach, however, would seem not to be valid in light of subsequent authority **16–102** from the Supreme Court.

MJELR v Rettinger

In *Minister for Justice, Equality and Law Reform v Rettinger*[88] the respondent **16–103** appeared to have a wealth of material at his disposal for the purpose of showing that prison conditions in Poland fell considerably short of the requisite international standards. He relied upon a US State Department Report from 2009 and a report compiled by Greifswald University in Germany. In addition the respondent had direct personal experience of the Polish prison system which he was able to aver to and most significantly was able to point to the recent decision of the European Court of Human Rights in *Orchowski v Poland*[89] which dealt specifically with the issue of overcrowding in Polish prisons. Notwithstanding such evidence the High Court rejected the respondent's objection:

> "Given the general situation gleaned from the material provided and from the Orchowski judgement, there is no reason to cast doubt on what the respondent has stated or to consider that he has exaggerated the conditions under which he was held while on remand. But it is another matter altogether to go further

---

[86] [2006] 3 IR 26.
[87] [2007] IEHC 209.
[88] [2010] IEHC 206.
[89] Application No. 17885/04: 22 October 2009.

and reach a conclusion in the present case, which would, if correct, mean that until such time as this Court was satisfied by evidence that prison conditions had improved substantially, no person sought by Poland on foot of a European arrest warrant transmitted to this State, in particular to serve a sentence, could be surrendered. We do not know to which prison the respondent will be sent. Those conditions in which he was detained for six months or so in one particular prison, described in as brief a way as they are, even if corroborated by what appears in Orchowski, could not be sufficient in my view to establish to the required standard that if surrendered to Poland now there is a real risk that his Article 3 rights would be breached, and therefore that his surrender is incompatible with this State's obligations under Article 3 of the Convention."

16–104   It was notable that none of what the respondent had averred to on affidavit was really in dispute nor was it disputed that Polish prison conditions had, in the very recent past, fallen well below international norms. The court went on to suggest that before it could act on such concerns it would have to be proven in some conclusive fashion that the problematic prison conditions would continue into the future:

"It is inevitable that a respondent seeking to establish to the necessary standard of proof that in the future his rights will be breached if surrendered has a more difficult probative task than a person complaining of what has already occurred. But that inevitability must not be allowed to lower the standard by which this Court must examine the question. The averments made by the respondent and the material he has referred the Court to are probably the best the respondent could do. But in my view neither the respondent's own evidence nor the Orchowski findings are sufficient. The latter in particular speak to the position of that person and the conditions which he endured during his periods of imprisonment. It does not follow in my view that those conclusions can avail other persons who are sought for surrender to Poland.

This Court must be forward-looking in its considerations, and in that regard it is worth repeating that it is not known at this stage even which prison or other detention centre the respondent may be required to spend time if surrendered. Speculation as to what conditions he may have to experience in some prison somewhere in Poland, even if supported by the criticisms and shortcomings which have been identified in various reports and even cases before the European Court of Human Rights, is insufficient to enable the respondent's objection to surrender to succeed."

16–105   The respondent found himself in the somewhat impossible position of having shown that the situation that previously pertained in relation to Polish prisons was unacceptable, but being unable to prove on a prospective basis what would definitively happen to him on his return. In effect the principle of mutual trust presented itself as an almost irrebuttable presumption against any allegation of prospective misconduct.

16–106   The High Court, however, certified an appeal on a point of law of exceptional public importance specifically in relation to the appropriate standard and burden of proof to be applied on such applications. The Supreme Court[90] concluded that the test applied by the High Court had not been the appropriate test and that it was not

---

[90] [2010] IESC 45.

necessary for the respondent to show on the balance of probability that he would be subject to mistreatment:

> "The High Court and this Court on appeal has been invited by the appellant to prohibit his surrender pursuant to section 37 of the Act of 2003. The High Court may not make an order for surrender which would *"be incompatible with the State's obligations...under the Convention..."* More specifically and though the section does not expressly refer to the Convention from which the words are taken, it must not take place if *"there are reasonable grounds for believing that... were the person to be surrendered to the issuing state...... he or she would be tortured or subjected to other inhuman or degrading treatment."* The Oireachtas here gives precise statutory effect to part of the wording of Article 3 of the Convention, which provides:
>
> > *"No one shall be subjected to torture or to inhuman or degrading treatment or punishment."*
>
> The Oireachtas here legislated so as to give effect to the objectives of the Convention. An Irish Court must not surrender to another Member State a person who can show that there are reasonable grounds for believing that he will be subjected to inhuman or degrading treatment. The section requires no more than that there be reasonable grounds. It does not require proof on the balance of probability."[91]

Fennelly J went on to consider the various other authorities which had made **16–107** reference to a "heavy onus" resting on the respondent in such matters and concluded in light of the decision of the European Court of Human Rights in *Saadi v Italy*[92] that it was not appropriate to impose such an evidential burden due to the absolute nature of the prohibition of inhuman or degrading treatment. In *Saadi* the United Kingdom had intervened and argued that a different approach might be taken in relation to persons convicted or suspected of terrorist offences. The court rejected such an approach citing the absolute obligation imposed by Art 3. Fennelly J considered that such an approach did not conflict with the underlying principles of the Framework Decision:

> "The inevitable consequence of the principle of absoluteness is that the objectives of the system of surrender pursuant to the Council Framework Decision on the European Arrest Warrant cannot be invoked to defeat an established real risk of ill-treatment contrary to Article 3. This does not mean that there is any underlying conflict between the Convention and the Framework Decision. As is stated in recital 10, *"[t]he mechanism of the European arrest warrant is based on a high level of confidence between member states."* The normal presumption is, as I said in my judgment in *Stapleton*, cited above at page 689, that the courts, *"when deciding whether to make an order for surrender must proceed on the assumption that the courts of the issuing member state will, as is required by Article 6.1 of the Treaty on European Union 'respect human rights and fundamental rights and fundamental freedoms.'"*

---

[91] As per Fennelly J.
[92] Application No. 37201/06, 28 February 2008.

A partial answer to these questions can be found in the very wording of section 37(1)(c) of the Act of 2003. According to the section, it is sufficient to establish that *"there are reasonable grounds for believing that"* the person would be *"subjected to ......inhuman or degrading treatment."* The European Court in *Soering* spoke of *"substantial grounds for believing that the person concerned, if extradited, would face a real risk of being subjected to torture or to inhuman or degrading treatment..."* Each test focuses, firstly, on the quality of the evidence or *"grounds"* and, secondly, on the level of risk. In practice, the two elements are closely connected and will, in many cases, merge into a single test. The subject matter of the enquiry is the level of danger to which the person is exposed. There is no discernible difference between *"reasonable grounds"* and *"substantial grounds."* It is equally clear that it is not necessary to prove that the person will *probably* suffer inhuman or degrading treatment. It is enough to establish that there is a *"real risk."* The 13th recital to the Framework Decision speaks of *"serious risk;"* the term *"real risk"* is consistently used by the European Court in its case law, including *Soering* and *Saadi*. It is appropriate to the seriousness of the subject matter. It would be absurd to require a person threatened with expulsion to a state where he may be exposed to inhuman or degrading treatment, not to mention torture, to prove that he would *probably* suffer such treatment. It must be sufficient to establish *"real risk."* "

16-108 A concurring judgment was also given by Denham J in which she helpfully summarised the approach to be taken by the High Court and the material which might be considered on such an application:

"27. Thus I would apply the following principles:-

(i) A court should consider all the material before it, and if necessary material obtained of its own motion.

(ii) A court should examine whether there is a real risk, in a rigorous examination.

(iii) The burden rests upon an applicant, such as the appellant in this case, to adduce evidence capable of proving that there are substantial grounds for believing that if he (or she) were returned to the requesting country he, or she, would be exposed to a real risk of being subjected to treatment contrary to Article 3 of the ECHR.

(iv) It is open to a requesting State to dispel any doubts by evidence. This does not mean that the burden has shifted. Thus, if there is information from an applicant as to conditions in the prisons of a requesting State with no replying information, a court may have sufficient evidence to find that there are substantial grounds for believing that if the applicant were returned to the requesting state he would be exposed to a real risk of being subjected to treatment contrary to Article 3 of the ECHR. On the other hand, the requesting State may present evidence which would, or would not, dispel the view of the court.

(v) The court should examine the foreseeable consequences of sending a person to the requesting State.

(vi)   The court may attach importance to reports of independent international human rights organisations, such as Amnesty International, and to governmental sources, such as the U.S. State Department.

(vii)   The mere possibility of ill treatment is not sufficient to establish an applicant's case.

(viii)   The relevant time to consider the conditions in the requesting state is at the time of the hearing in the High Court. Although, of course, on an appeal to this Court an application could be made, under the rules of court, seeking to admit additional evidence, if necessary.

28. The above test should be applied in an application such as this."

Undoubtedly the judgment of the Supreme Court in *Rettinger* changes matters **16–109** significantly. The principle of mutual trust no longer can be regarded as trumping Art 3 concerns particularly where there is a cogent evidential basis underlying them. Moreover, in practical terms at least, in such cases an evidential burden may well rest on the State and the issuing State to refute such concerns.

SURRENDER OF REFUGEES

Although there is no specific provision in either the Framework Decision or the **16–110** 2003 Act which prohibits the surrender of a recognised refugee to his country of nationality, it seems clear that to so surrender would amount to a breach of the principle of non-*refoulement*, as provided for by Art 33(1) of the *UN Convention Relating to the Status of Refugees,* which states:

"No Contracting State shall expel or return ("refouler") a refugee in any manner whatsoever to the frontiers of territories where his life or freedom would be threatened on account of his race, religion, nationality, member-ship of a particular social group or political opinion".

This principle is given effect in Irish law through s 5(1) of the Refugee Act 1996. **16–111** The respondent in *Minister for Justice, Equality and Law Reform v Pollak*[93] was a national of the Czech Republic and had been granted a declaration of refugee status by the applicant in 2001, having fled persecution in his home country arising from his membership of the Roma community. When his surrender was some years later sought by the Czech Republic by way of a European arrest warrant, he objected on the basis that his surrender would be in breach of s 37 of the 2003 Act and would amount to an abuse of process. The High Court rejected the argument that the application for surrender was an abuse of process, as there was no evidence of *mala fides* on the part of either the issuing judicial authority or the applicant, particularly in circumstances where the applicant had a statutory duty to apply for an order for surrender on receipt of a European arrest warrant.

However, the court concluded that the surrender of the respondent was **16–112** prohibited by s 37 of the 2003 Act as it would amount to a breach of the State's obligations under Art 3 of the European Convention on Human Rights to guarantee

---

[93]   [2010] IEHC 209.

the respondent's right not to be subjected to "torture or to inhuman or degrading treatment or punishment", and also possibly its obligations under Art 5 of the Convention relating to the right to liberty and security of the person. The court found that where any conflict arises between the obligation to surrender under the 2003 Act and the principle of non-*refoulement*, the former must yield. It was further held that there was no question of the court in proceedings under the 2003 Act engaging in an examination of whether there was a continuing risk of persecution in the requesting State as there were specific procedures in place for the revocation of refugee status where such a risk had ceased to exist, and the applicant had chosen not to invoke these procedures in the respondent's case.

APPENDIX 1

THE EUROPEAN ARREST WARRANT ACT 2003

(AS AMENDED)

ARRANGEMENT OF SECTIONS

PART 1

Preliminary and General

Section

PART 2

European Arrest Warrant

Chapter 1

European Arrest Warrant Received in State

SCHEDULE

PART A

Text in the Irish language of Council Framework Decision of
13 June 2002 on the European arrest warrant and the
surrender procedures between Member States.

PART B

Text in the English language of Council Framework Decision
of 13 June 2002 on the European arrest warrant and the
surrender procedures between Member States.

APPENDIX 1

Acts Referred to

Criminal Justice (Administration) Act 1924

Criminal Justice Act 1960

European Communities Act 1972

Extradition Act 1965

Extradition Acts 1965 to 2001

Extradition (European Convention on the Suppression of Terrorism) Act 1987

Extradition (European Union Conventions) Act 2001

EUROPEAN ARREST WARRANT ACT, 2003

AN ACT TO GIVE EFFECT TO COUNCIL FRAMEWORK DECISION OF 13 JUNE 2002 ON THE EUROPEAN ARREST WARRANT AND THE SURRENDER PROCEDURES BETWEEN MEMBER STATES; TO AMEND THE EXTRADITION ACT 1965 AND CERTAIN OTHER ENACTMENTS; AND TO PROVIDE FOR MATTERS CONNECTED THEREWITH. [28*th December*, 2003] BE IT ENACTED BY THE OIREACHTAS AS FOLLOWS:

PART 1

Preliminary and General

Short title and commencement

    1.— (1) This Act may be cited as the European Arrest Warrant Act 2003.

    (2) This Act comes into operation on 1 January 2004.

Interpretation

    2.—(1) In this Act, except where the context otherwise requires—

"Act of 1965" means the Extradition Act 1965;

"Act of 2001" means the Extradition (European Union Conventions) Act 2001;

'alert' means an alert entered in the SIS for the arrest and surrender, on foot of a European arrest warrant, of the person named therein;

"Central Authority in the State" shall be read in accordance with *section 6*;

'Council Decision' means Council Decision 2007/533/JHA of 12 June 2007 on the establishment, operation and use of the second generation Schengen Information System;

"Eurojust" means the body established by Council Decision of 28 February 2002 setting up Eurojust with a view to reinforcing the fight against serious crime;

"European arrest warrant" means a warrant, order or decision of a judicial authority of a Member State, issued under such laws as give effect to the Framework Decision in that Member State, for the arrest and surrender by the State to that Member State of a person in respect of an offence committed or alleged to have been committed by him or her under the law of that Member State;

"European Communities" has the same meaning as it has in the European Communities Act 1972;

"Framework Decision" means Council Framework Decision of 13 June 2002 on the European arrest warrant and the surrender procedures between Member States, the text of which—

(a) in the Irish language, is set out in *Part A* of the *Schedule*, and

(b) in the English language, is set out in *Part B* of the *Schedule*;

"functions" includes powers and duties, and references to the performance of functions include, as respects powers and duties, references to the exercise of the powers and the carrying out of the duties;

"issuing judicial authority" means, in relation to a European arrest warrant, the judicial authority in the issuing state that issued the European arrest warrant concerned;

"issuing state" means, in relation to a European arrest warrant, a Member State designated under *section 3*, a judicial authority of which has issued that European arrest warrant;

"judicial authority" means the judge, magistrate or other person authorised under the law of the Member State concerned to perform functions the same as or similar to those performed under *section 33* by a court in the State;

"Member State" means a Member State of the European Communities (other than the State) or Gibraltar;

"Minister" means the Minister for Justice, Equality and Law Reform;

'Schengen Convention' means the Convention implementing the Schengen Agreement of 14 June 1985 between the Governments of the States of the Benelux Economic Union, the Federal Republic of Germany and the French Republic on the gradual abolition of checks at their common borders done at Schengen on 19 June 1990 and includes any amendment to or modification of that Convention whether before or after the passing of this Act but does not include the Council Decision;

'SIS' means the system referred to in Title IV of the Schengen Convention or, as appropriate, the system established under Chapter 1 of the Council Decision;

"third country" means a country other than the State or a Member State;

"true copy" shall be read in accordance with *section 12(7)*.

(2) In this Act—

    (a) a reference to a section, Part or Schedule is a reference to a section or Part of, or a Schedule to, this Act, unless it is indicated that a reference to some other enactment is intended,

    (b) a reference to a subsection, paragraph or subparagraph is a reference to a subsection, paragraph or subparagraph of the provision in which the reference occurs, unless it is indicated that a reference to some other provision is intended, and

    (c) a reference to any enactment is a reference to that enactment as amended, extended or adapted, whether before or after the passing of this Act, by or under any subsequent enactment.

Designated States

3.—(1) For the purposes of this Act, the Minister for Foreign Affairs may, by order, designate a Member State that has, under its national law, given effect to the Framework Decision.

(2) The Minister for Foreign Affairs may, by order, amend or revoke an order under this section, including an order under this subsection.

Application of Act

4.—This Act shall apply in relation to an offence, whether committed or alleged to have been committed before or after the commencement of this Act.

Issuing State Presumed to comply with Framework Decision

4A.—It shall be presumed that an issuing state will comply with the requirements of the Framework Decision, unless the contrary is shown.

Corresponding Offences

5.— For the purposes of this Act, an offence specified in a European arrest warrant corresponds to an offence under the law of the State, where the act or omission that constitutes the offence so specified would, if committed in the State on the date on which the European arrest warrant is issued, constitute an offence under the law of the State.

Central Authority in the State

6.—(1) The Minister shall be the Central Authority in the State for the purposes of this Act.

(2) The Minister may, by order, designate such persons as he or she considers appropriate to perform such functions of the Central Authority in the State as are specified in the order and different persons may be so designated to perform different functions of the Central Authority in the State.

(3) For so long as an order under *subsection (2)* remains in force, a reference in this Act to the Central Authority in the State shall, insofar as it relates to the performance of a function specified in the order, be construed as a reference to the person designated by the order to perform the function concerned.

(4) The Minister shall, by notice in writing, inform the General Secretariat of the Council of the European Union of the making of an order under this section and of the names of the persons designated under the order.

(5) The Minister may, by order, amend or revoke an order under this section (including an order under this subsection).

(6) The Central Authority in the State shall, in each year, prepare a report on the operation, in the preceding year, of *Part 2*, and shall cause copies of each such report to be laid before both Houses of the Oireachtas as soon as may be after it is so prepared.

Orders and Regulations

7.—Every order and regulation under this Act shall be laid before each House of the Oireachtas as soon as may be after it is made and, if a resolution annulling the order or regulation is passed by either such House within the next 21 days on which that House sits after the order or regulation is laid before it, the order or regulation shall be annulled accordingly, but without prejudice to anything previously done thereunder.

Expenses

8.—The expenses incurred by the Minister in the administration of this Act shall, to such extent as may be sanctioned by the Minister for Finance, be paid out of moneys provided by the Oireachtas.

PART 2

European Arrest Warrant

Chapter 1

European Arrest Warrant Received in State

Executing judicial authority in the State

9.—For the purposes of the Framework Decision, the High Court shall be the executing judicial authority in the State.

Obligation to surrender

10.—Where a judicial authority in an issuing state issues a European arrest warrant in respect of a person—

(a) against whom that state intends to bring proceedings for an offence to which the European arrest warrant relates,

(b) who is the subject of proceedings in that state for an offence to which the European arrest warrant relates,

(c) who has been convicted of, but not yet sentenced in respect of, an offence in that state to which the European arrest warrant relates, or

(d) on whom a sentence of imprisonment or detention has been imposed in that state in respect of an offence to which the European arrest warrant relates,

that person shall, subject to and in accordance with the provisions of this Act and the Framework Decision, be arrested and surrendered to the issuing state.

European arrest warrant

11.—(1) A European arrest warrant shall, in so far as is practicable, be in the form set out in the Annex to the Framework Decision.

(1A) Subject to subsection (2A), a European arrest warrant shall specify—

(a) the name and the nationality of the person in respect of whom it is issued,

(b) the name of the judicial authority that issued the European arrest warrant, and the address of its principal office,

(c) the telephone number, fax number and email address (if any) of that judicial authority,

(d) the offence to which the European arrest warrant relates, including the nature and classification under the law of the issuing state of the offence concerned,

(e) that a conviction, sentence or detention order is immediately enforceable against the person, or that a warrant for his or her arrest, or other order of a judicial authority in the issuing state having the same effect, has been issued in respect of one of the offences to which the European arrest warrant relates,

(f) the circumstances in which the offence was committed or is alleged to have been committed, including the time and place of its commission or alleged commission, and the degree of involvement or alleged degree of involvement of the person in the commission of the offence, and

(g) (i) the penalties to which that person would, if convicted of the offence specified in the European arrest warrant, be liable,

(ii) where that person has been convicted of the offence specified in the European arrest warrant but has not yet been
sentenced, the penalties to which he or she is liable in
respect of the offence, or

(iii) where that person has been convicted of the offence specified in the European arrest warrant and a sentence has
been imposed in respect thereof, the penalties of which
that sentence consists.

(2) Where it is not practicable for the European arrest warrant to be in
the form referred to in *subsection (1)*, it shall include such information,
additional to the information specified in *subsection (1A)*, as would be
required to be provided were it in that form.

(2A) If any of the information to which subsection (1A) (inserted by
section 72(*a*) of the Criminal Justice (Terrorist Offences) Act 2005)
refers is not specified in the European arrest warrant, it may be specified in a separate document.

(4) For the avoidance of doubt, a European arrest warrant may be
issued in respect of one or more than one offence.

Transmission of European arrest warrant

12.—(1) A European arrest warrant shall be transmitted by, or on
behalf of, the issuing judicial authority to the Central Authority in the
State and, where the European arrest warrant is in a language other
than the Irish language, the English language or such other languages
as the Minister may by order prescribe, a translation of the European
arrest warrant into the Irish language or the English language shall be
so transmitted with the European arrest warrant.

(2) Such undertakings as are required to be given under this Act shall
be transmitted by, or on behalf of, the issuing judicial authority or the
issuing state, as may be appropriate to the Central Authority in the
State, and where any such undertaking is in a language other than the
Irish language, the English language or such other languages as the
Minister may by order prescribe, a translation of that undertaking into
the Irish language or the English language shall be so transmitted with
the undertaking.

(3) A European arrest warrant, or an undertaking required to be given
under this Act, or any other document to be transmitted for the purposes of this Act, may be transmitted to the Central Authority in the
State by—

(a) delivering it to the Central Authority in the State, or

(b) any means capable of producing a written record under conditions allowing the Central Authority in the State to establish its
authenticity.

(3A) An undertaking required under this Act may be set out in the European arrest warrant or in a separate document.

(7) For the purposes of this Act, a document shall be deemed to be a true copy of an original document if it has been certified as a true copy of the original document by

    (a) the issuing judicial authority, or

    (b) an officer of the central authority of the issuing state.

(8) In proceedings to which this Act applies, a document that purports to be—

    (a) a European arrest warrant issued by a judicial authority in the issuing state,

    (b) an undertaking required under this Act of an issuing judicial authority or the issuing state, as may be appropriate,

    (c) a translation of a European arrest warrant or undertaking under this Act, or

    (d) a document referred to in section 11(2A) (inserted by *section 72(b)* of the *Criminal Justice (Terrorist Offences) Act 2005*),[1]

    (e) a true copy of such a document,

    shall be received in evidence without further proof.

(9) In proceedings to which this Act applies, a document that purports to be a true copy of a European arrest warrant, undertaking or translation referred to in *subsection (8)* shall, unless the contrary is shown, be evidence of the European arrest warrant, undertaking or translation concerned, as the case may be.

(10) The Minister may, for the purposes of ensuring the accuracy of documents transmitted in accordance with this section, make regulations prescribing—

    (a) the procedures that shall be followed in connection with the transmission of documents in accordance with this section, and

    (b) that such features as are specified in the regulations shall be present in any equipment being used in that connection.

(11) In this section 'European arrest warrant' includes a document referred to in section 11(2A) (inserted by *section 72(b)* of the *Criminal Justice (Terrorist Offences) Act 2005*).

---

[1] There appears to be a minor formatting error in the amendment effected by Section 73(g) of the Criminal Justice (Terrorist Offences) Act, 2005 which purports to insert a "new paragraph" rather than substitute the existing Section 11(8)(c) resulting in the creation of two Section 11(8)(c)'s.

Application to High Court for endorsement to execute European arrest warrant

13.—(1) The Central Authority in the State shall, as soon as may be after it receives a European arrest warrant transmitted to it in accordance with *section 12*, apply, or cause an application to be made, to the High Court for the endorsement by it of the European arrest warrant, or a true copy thereof, for execution of the European arrest warrant concerned.

(2) If, upon an application under *subsection (1)*, the High Court is satisfied that, in relation to a European arrest warrant, there has been compliance with the provisions of this Act, it may endorse—

(a) the European arrest warrant for execution, or *[sic]*

(3) A European arrest warrant may, upon there being compliance with *subsection (2)*, be executed by any member of the Garda Síochána in any part of the State and may be so executed notwithstanding that it is not in the possession of the member when he or she executes the European arrest warrant, and the warrant, the true copy of the warrant, as the case may be, endorsed in accordance with *subsection (2)*, shall be shown to and a copy thereof given to, the person arrested at the time of his or her arrest or, if the warrant, or true copy, as the case may be, is not then in the possession of the member, not later than 24 hours after the person's arrest.

(4) A person arrested under a European arrest warrant shall, upon his or her arrest, be informed of his or her right to—

(a) consent to his or her being surrendered to the issuing state under *section 15*,

(b) obtain, or be provided with, professional legal advice and representation, and

(c) where appropriate, obtain, or be provided with, the services of an interpreter.

(5) A person arrested under a European arrest warrant shall, as soon as may be after his or her arrest, be brought before the High Court, and the High Court shall, if satisfied that that person is the person in respect of whom the European arrest warrant was issued—

(a) remand the person in custody or on bail (and, for that purpose, the High Court shall have the same powers in relation to remand as it would have if the person were brought before it charged with an indictable offence),

(b) fix a date for the purpose of *section 16* (being a date that falls not later than 21 days after the date of the person's arrest), and

(c) inform the person that he or she has the right to—

   (i) consent to his or her surrender to the issuing state under *section 15*,

   (ii) obtain, or be provided with, professional legal advice and representation, and

   (iii) where appropriate, obtain, or be provided with, the services of an interpreter.

Arrest without warrant for surrender purposes

14.—(1) A member of the Garda Síochána may arrest any person without a warrant that the member believes, on reasonable grounds, to be a person named in an alert.

(2) A person arrested under this section shall, upon his or her arrest, be informed, in ordinary language, of the reason for the arrest and of his or her right to—

   (a) obtain or be provided with professional legal advice and representation, and

   (b) where appropriate, obtain or be provided with the services of an interpreter.

(3) A person arrested under this section shall, as soon as may be after his or her arrest—

   (a) be furnished with a copy of the alert, and

   (b) be brought before the High Court, which court shall, if satisfied that he or she is the person named in the alert—

      (i) inform the person of his or her right to—

         (I) obtain or be provided with professional legal advice and representation, and

         (II) where appropriate, obtain or be provided with the services of an interpreter, and

      (ii) remand the person in custody or, at its discretion, on bail for a period not exceeding 14 days (and for that purpose the High Court shall have the same powers in relation to remand as it would have if the person were brought before it charged with an indictable offence) for production to the High Court of the European arrest warrant on foot of which the alert was entered.

(4) Where, in respect of a person remanded in custody or on bail under subsection (3), a European arrest warrant is transmitted to the Central Authority in the State pursuant to section 12—

   (a) that person shall be brought before the High Court as soon as may be,

(b) the European arrest warrant shall be produced to the High Court,

(c) a copy shall be given to that person, and

(d) the High Court, if satisfied that the provisions of this Act have been complied with and that the person before it is the person in respect of whom the European arrest warrant was issued, shall—

    (i) inform the person of his or her right to consent to being surrendered to the issuing state under section 15, and

    (ii) if the person does not exercise his or her right to consent under paragraph (i)—

        (I) remand the person in custody or on bail (and for that purpose the High Court shall have the same powers in relation to remand as it would have if the person were brought before it charged with an indictable offence), and

        (II) fix a date for the purposes of section 16 within the period of 21 days next following.

(5) Where, in respect of a person remanded in custody or on bail under subsection (3), the European arrest warrant is not produced on the date fixed by the Court for the purpose under that subsection the person shall be released from custody.

Consent to surrender

15— (1) Where a person is brought before the High Court under section 13, he or she may consent to his or her being surrendered to the issuing state and, if he or she so consents, the High Court shall—

(a) if the European arrest warrant, or a true copy thereof, has been endorsed in accordance with section 13 for execution of the warrant,

(b) if it is satisfied that—

    (i) the person voluntarily consents to his or her being surrendered to the issuing state concerned and is aware of the consequences of his or her so consenting, and

    (ii) the person has obtained, or has been afforded the opportunity of obtaining or being provided with professional legal advice before consenting to his or her surrender,

(c) if it is not required, under section 21A, 22, 23 or 24 (inserted by *sections 79, 80, 81* and *82* of the *Criminal Justice (Terrorist Offences) Act 2005*), to refuse to surrender the person under this Act, and

(d) if the surrender of the person is not prohibited by Part 3 or the Framework Decision (including the recitals thereto),

make an order directing that the person be surrendered to such other person as is duly authorised by the issuing state to receive him or her.

(2) Where a person is brought before the High Court under section 14, he or she may consent to his or her being surrendered to the issuing state and, if he or she so consents, the High Court shall—

(a) upon production to the High Court of the European arrest warrant or a true copy thereof,

(b) if it is satisfied that—

    (i) the person voluntarily consents to his or her being surrendered to the issuing state concerned and is aware of the consequences of his or her so consenting, and

    (ii) the person has obtained, or has been afforded the opportunity of obtaining or being provided with, professional legal advice and representation before consenting to his or her surrender,

(c) if it is not required, under section 21A, 22, 23 or 24 (inserted by *sections 79, 80, 81* and *82* of the *Criminal Justice (Terrorist Offences) Act 2005*), to refuse to surrender the person under this Act, and

(d) if the surrender of the person is not prohibited by Part 3 or the Framework Decision (including the recitals thereto),

make an order directing that the person be surrendered to such other person as is duly authorised by the issuing state to receive him or her.

(3) An order under this section shall take effect upon the expiration of 10 days beginning on the date of the making of the order or such earlier date as the High Court, upon the request of the person to whom the order applies, directs.

(3A) An appeal against an order under this section or a decision not to make such an order may be brought in the Supreme Court if, and only if, the High Court certifies that the order or decision involves a point of law of exceptional public importance and that it is desirable in the public interest that an appeal should be taken to the Supreme Court.

(4) Where the High Court makes an order under this section, it shall—

(a) inform the person to whom the order relates of his or her right to make a complaint under Article 40.4.2 of the Constitution at any time before his or her surrender to the issuing state,

(b) record in writing that the person concerned has consented to his or her being surrendered to the issuing state concerned, and

(c) commit the person to a prison (or, if the person is not more than 21 years of age, to a remand institution) pending the carrying out of the terms of the order.

(5) Subject to *subsection (6)* , subsection (7) and *section 18*, a person to whom an order for the time being in force under this section applies shall be surrendered to the issuing state concerned not later than 10 days after—

(a) the order takes effect in accordance with subsection (3) (inserted by *section 75(b)* of the *Criminal Justice (Terrorist Offences) Act 2005*), or

(b) such date (being a date that falls after the expiration of that period) as may be agreed by the Central Authority in the State and the issuing state.

(6) Where a person—

(a) appeals an order made under this section, or

(b) makes a complaint under Article 40.4.2 of the Constitution,

he or she shall not be surrendered to the issuing state while proceedings relating to the appeal or complaint are pending.

(7) Where a person (to whom an order for the time being in force under this section applies) is not surrendered to the issuing state within the relevant period specified in subsection (5) and the surrender is not prohibited by reason of subsection (6) the High Court may remand the person in custody or on bail for such further period as is necessary to effect the surrender unless it considers it would be unjust or oppressive to do so.

(8) *Subsection (7)* shall not apply if—

(a) (i) the person has been sentenced to a term of imprisonment for an offence of which he or she was convicted in the State,

(ii) on the date on which he or she would, but for this subsection, be entitled to be released from custody under *subsection (7)*, all or part of that term of imprisonment remains unexpired, and

(iii) the person is required to serve all or part of the remainder of that term of imprisonment, or

(b) (i) the person has been charged with or convicted of an offence in the State, and

(ii) on the date on which he or she would, but for this paragraph, be entitled to be released from custody under *subsection (7)*, he or she is required to be in custody by virtue of having been remanded in custody pending his or her being tried, or the imposition of sentence, in respect of that offence.

(9) Where a person lodges an appeal pursuant to subsection (3A), the High Court may remand the person in custody or on bail pending the hearing of the appeal and, for that purpose, the High Court shall have the same powers in relation to remand as it would have if the person were brought before it charged with an indictable offence.

Committal of person named in European arrest warrant

16.—(1) Where a person does not consent to his or her surrender to the issuing state the High Court may, upon such date as is fixed under section 13 or such later date as it considers appropriate, make an order directing that the person be surrendered to such other person as is duly authorised by the issuing state to receive him or her, provided that—

(a) the High Court is satisfied that the person before it is the person in respect of whom the European arrest warrant was issued,

(b) the European arrest warrant, or a true copy thereof, has been endorsed in accordance with section 13 for execution of the warrant,

(c) where appropriate, an undertaking under section 45 or a true copy thereof is provided to the court,

(d) the High Court is not required, under section 21A, 22, 23 or 24 (inserted by *sections 79, 80, 81* and *82* of the *Criminal Justice (Terrorist Offences) Act 2005*), to refuse to surrender the person under this Act, and

(e) the surrender of the person is not prohibited by Part 3 or the Framework Decision (including the recitals thereto).

(2) Where a person does not consent to his or her surrender to the issuing state, the High Court may, upon such date as is fixed under section 14 or such later date as it considers appropriate, make an order directing that the person be surrendered to such other person as is duly authorised by the issuing state to receive him or her, provided that—

(a) the European arrest warrant and, where appropriate, an undertaking under section 45, or true copies thereof are provided to the court,

(b) the High Court is satisfied that the person before it is the person in respect of whom the European arrest warrant was issued,

(c) the High Court is not required, under section 21A, 22, 23 or 24 (inserted by *sections 79, 80, 81* and *82* of the *Criminal Justice (Terrorist Offences) Act 2005*), to refuse to surrender the person under this Act, and

(d) the surrender of the person is not prohibited by Part 3 or the Framework Decision (including the recitals thereto).

(2A) Where the High Court does not—

(a) make an order under subsection (1) on the date fixed under section 13, or

(b) make an order under subsection (2) on the date fixed under section 14,

it may remand the person before it in custody or on bail and, for those purposes, the High Court shall have the same powers in relation to remand as it would have if the person were brought before it charged with an indictable offence.

(3) An order under this section shall take effect upon the expiration of 15 days beginning on the date of the making of the order or such earlier date as the High Court, upon the request of the person to whom the order applies, directs.

(4) When making an order under this section the High Court shall also make an order committing the person to a prison (or if he or she is not more than 21 years of age, to a remand institution) there to remain pending his or her surrender in accordance with the order under this section, and shall inform the person—

(a) that he or she will not, without his or her consent, be surrendered to the issuing state, before the expiration of the period of 15 days specified in *subsection (3)*, and

(b) of his or her right to make a complaint under Article 40.4.2 of the Constitution at any time before his or her surrender to the issuing state.

(5) Subject to *subsection (6)*, *subsection (7)* and *section 18*, a person to whom an order for the time being in force under this section applies shall be surrendered to the issuing state not later than 10 days after—

(a) the order takes effect in accordance with subsection (3) (inserted by *section 76(d)* of the *Criminal Justice (Terrorist Offences) Act 2005*), or

(b) such date (being a date that falls after the expiration of that period) as may be agreed by the Central Authority in the State and the issuing state.

(6) Where a person—

(a) appeals an order made under this section, or

(b) makes a complaint under Article 40.4.2 of the Constitution,

he or she shall not be surrendered to the issuing state while proceedings relating to the appeal or complaint are pending.

(7) Where a person (to whom an order for the time being in force under this section applies) is not surrendered to the issuing state within the relevant period specified in subsection (5) and the surrender is not prohibited by reason of subsection (6) the High Court may remand the person in custody or on bail for such further period as is necessary to effect the surrender unless it considers it would be unjust or oppressive to do so.

(8) Where the High Court decides not to make an order under this section—

    (a) it shall give reasons for its decision, and

    (b) the person shall, subject to *subsection (9)*, be released from custody.

(9) *Subsections (7) and (8)* shall not apply if—

    (a) (i)   the person has been sentenced to a term of imprisonment for an offence of which he or she was convicted in the State,

         (ii) on the date on which he or she would, but for this subsection, be entitled to be released under *subsection (7) or (8)*, all or part of the term of imprisonment remains unexpired, and

         (iii) the person is required to serve all or part of the remainder of that term of imprisonment,

    or

    (b) (i)   the person has been charged with or convicted of an offence in the State, and

         (ii) on the date on which he or she would, but for this paragraph, be entitled to be released from custody under *subsection (7) or (8)*, he or she is required to be in custody by virtue of having been remanded in custody pending his or her being tried, or the imposition of sentence, in respect of that offence.

(10) If the High Court has not, after the expiration of 60 days from the arrest of the person concerned under *section 13 or 14*, made an order under this section or *section 15*, or has decided not to make an order under this section, it shall direct the Central Authority in the State to inform the issuing judicial authority and, where appropriate, Eurojust in relation thereto and of the reasons therefor specified in the direction, and the Central Authority in the State shall comply with such direction.

(11) If the High Court has not, after the expiration of 90 days from the arrest of the person concerned under *section 13 or 14*, made an order under this section or *section 15*, or has decided not to make an order

under this section, it shall direct the Central Authority in the State to inform the issuing judicial authority and, where appropriate, Eurojust in relation thereto and of the reasons therefor specified in the direction, and the Central Authority in the State shall comply with such direction.

(12) An appeal against an order under this section or a decision not to make such an order may be brought in the Supreme Court if, and only if, the High Court certifies that the order or decision involves a point of law of exceptional public importance and that it is desirable in the public interest that an appeal should be taken to the Supreme Court.

(13) Where a person lodges an appeal pursuant to subsection (12), the High Court may remand the person in custody or on bail pending the hearing of the appeal and, for that purpose, the High Court shall have the same powers in relation to remand as it would have if the person were brought before it charged with an indictable offence.

European arrest warrant relating to more than one offence

17.—Where, in relation to an offence specified in a European arrest warrant, the High Court decides not to make an order under *section 15* or *16*, it shall not be necessary for the issuing judicial authority to issue another European arrest warrant in respect of such other offences as are specified in that warrant, and, where such other offences are specified in the European arrest warrant, that warrant shall be treated as having been issued in respect of those other offences only.

Postponement of surrender

18.—(1) The High Court may, if satisfied that circumstances exist that would warrant the postponement, on humanitarian grounds, of the surrender to the issuing state of a person to whom an order under *section 15* or *16* applies, direct that the person's surrender be postponed until such date as the High Court states that, in its opinion, those circumstances no longer exist.

(2) Without prejudice to the generality of *subsection (1)*, circumstances to which that paragraph applies include a manifest danger to the life or health of the person concerned likely to be occasioned by his or her surrender to the issuing state in accordance with *section 15(5)* or *16(5)*.

(2A) Where the High Court decides to postpone a person's surrender under this section, it may remand the person in custody or on bail and, for that purpose, the High Court shall have the same powers in relation to remand as it would have if the person were brought before it charged with an indictable offence.

(3) Subject to *section 19*, where a person to whom an order under *section 15* or *16* applies—

    (a) is being proceeded against for an offence in the State, or

    (b) (i) has been sentenced to a term of imprisonment for an offence of which he or she was convicted in the State, and

       (ii) is required to serve all or part of that term of imprisonment,

the High Court may direct the postponement of that person's surrender to the issuing state until—

        (I) in the case of a person who is being proceeded against for an offence, the date of the final determination of those proceedings (where he or she is not required to serve a term of imprisonment), or

        (II) in the case of a person who is required to serve all or part of a term of imprisonment, the date on which he or she is no longer required to serve any part of that term of imprisonment.

(4) Subject to *subsection (5)*, a person to whom this section applies shall be surrendered to the issuing state not later than 10 days after such date (being a date that falls after the date specified in *subsection (1)* or subsection (3)(*b*)(I) or (II), as the case may be) as may be agreed by the Central Authority in the State and the issuing state.

(5) Where a person makes a complaint under Article 40.4.2 of the Constitution, he or she shall not be surrendered to the issuing state while proceedings relating to the complaint are pending.

Conditional surrender

19.—(1) Where a person to whom an order under *section 15* or *16* applies—

    (a) has been sentenced to a term of imprisonment for an offence of which he or she was convicted in the State, and

    (b) is, at the time of the making of the order, required to serve all or part of that term of imprisonment,

the High Court may, subject to such conditions as it shall specify, direct that the person be surrendered to the issuing state for the purpose of his or her being tried for the offence to which the European arrest warrant concerned relates.

(2) Where a person is surrendered to the issuing state under this section, then any term of imprisonment or part of a term of imprisonment that the person is required to serve in the State shall be reduced by an amount equal to any period of time spent by that person in custody or detention in the issuing state consequent upon his or her being so surrendered, or pending trial.

Additional documentation and information

20.—(1) In proceedings to which this Act applies the High Court may, if of the opinion that the documentation or information provided to it is not sufficient to enable it to perform its functions under this Act, require the issuing judicial authority or the issuing state, as may be appropriate, to provide it with such additional documentation or information as it may specify, within such period as it may specify.

(2) The Central Authority in the State may, if of the opinion that the documentation or information provided to it under this Act is not sufficient to enable it or the High Court to perform functions under this Act, require the issuing judicial authority or the issuing state, as may be appropriate, to provide it with such additional documentation or information as it may specify, within such period as it may specify.

(3) In proceedings under this Act, evidence as to any matter to which such proceedings relate may be given by affidavit, declaration, affirmation, attestation or by a statement in writing that purports to have been sworn—

    (a) by the deponent in a place other than the State, and

    (b) in the presence of a person duly authorised under the law of the place concerned to attest to the swearing of such a statement by a deponent, howsoever such a statement is described under the law of that place.

(4) In proceedings referred to in *subsection (3)*, the High Court may, if it considers that the interests of justice so require, direct that oral evidence of the matters described in the affidavit or statement concerned be given, and the court may, for the purpose of receiving oral evidence, adjourn the proceedings to a later date.

Movement of persons detained under this Act

21.—(1) The Minister may direct that a person remanded in custody under this Act or committed to a prison or remand institution under *section 15* or *16* be removed to a hospital or any other place if the Minister considers that in the interests of the person's health, it is necessary that he or she be so removed, and the person shall, while detained in a hospital or other place pursuant to a direction under this subsection be deemed to be in lawful custody.

(2) Sections 10 and 11 of the Criminal Justice Act 1960 shall apply to a person who is not less than 16, nor more than 21, years of age remanded in custody under this Act or committed to a prison or remand institution under *section 15* or *16*, subject to the following modifications:

    (a) in section 10(1), the reference to "a person detained under section 9 of this Act or this section" shall be construed as a reference to "a person remanded in custody or committed to a prison or remand institution under the *European Arrest Warrant Act 2003*";

(b) in section 11(1), the reference to "a person who is detained in a remand institution pursuant to section 9 of this Act" shall be construed as a reference to "a person remanded in custody or committed to a prison or remand institution under the *European Arrest Warrant Act 2003*"; and

(c) in section 11(3), the reference to "section 9" shall be construed as a reference to "the *European Arrest Warrant Act 2003*".

Refusal of surrender where no decision to prosecute

21A.—(1) Where a European arrest warrant is issued in the issuing state in respect of a person who has not been convicted of an offence specified therein, the High Court shall refuse to surrender the person if it is satisfied that a decision has not been made to charge the person with, and try him or her for, that offence in the issuing state.

(2) Where a European arrest warrant is issued in respect of a person who has not been convicted of an offence specified therein, it shall be presumed that a decision has been made to charge the person with, and try him or her for, that offence in the issuing state, unless the contrary is proved.

Rule of specialty

22.—(1) In this section, except where the context otherwise requires, 'offence' means, in relation to a person to whom a European arrest warrant applies, an offence (other than an offence specified in the European arrest warrant in respect of which the person's surrender is ordered under this Act) under the law of the issuing state committed before the person's surrender, but shall not include an offence consisting, in whole, of acts or omissions of which the offence specified in the European arrest warrant consists in whole or in part.

(2) Subject to this section, the High Court shall refuse to surrender a person under this Act if it is satisfied that—

(a) the law of the issuing state does not provide that a person who is surrendered to it pursuant to a European arrest warrant shall not be proceeded against, sentenced or detained for the purposes of executing a sentence or detention order, or otherwise restricted in his or her personal liberty, in respect of an offence, and

(b) the person will be proceeded against, sentenced, or detained for the purposes of executing a sentence or detention order, or otherwise restricted in his or her personal liberty, in respect of an offence.

(3) It shall be presumed that, in relation to a person to whom a European arrest warrant applies, the issuing state does not intend to—

(a) proceed against him or her,

(b) sentence or detain him or her for a purpose referred to in subsection (2)(*a*), or

(c) otherwise restrict him or her in his or her personal liberty,

in respect of an offence, unless the contrary is proved.

(4) The surrender of a person under this Act shall not be refused under subsection (2) if—

(a) upon conviction in respect of the offence concerned he or she is not liable to a term of imprisonment or detention, or

(b) the High Court is satisfied that, where upon such conviction he or she is liable to a term of imprisonment or detention and such other penalty as does not involve a restriction of his or her personal liberty, the said other penalty only will be imposed if he or she is convicted of the offence.

(5) The surrender of a person under this Act shall not be refused under subsection (2) if it is intended to impose in the issuing state a penalty (other than a penalty consisting of a restriction of the person's liberty) including a financial penalty in respect of an offence of which the person claimed has been convicted, notwithstanding that where such person fails or refuses to pay the penalty concerned (or, in the case of a penalty that is not a financial penalty, fails or refuses to submit to any measure or comply with any requirements of which the penalty consists) he or she may, under the law of the issuing state be detained or otherwise deprived of his or her personal liberty.

(6) The surrender of a person under this Act shall not be refused under subsection (2) if the High Court—

(a) is satisfied that—

(i) proceedings will not be brought against the person in respect of an offence,

(ii) a penalty will not be imposed on the person in respect of an offence, and

(iii) the person will not be detained or otherwise restricted in his or her personal liberty for the purposes of an offence,

without the issuing judicial authority first obtaining the consent thereto of the High Court,

(b) is satisfied that—

(i) the person consents to being surrendered under section 15,

    (ii) at the time of so consenting he or she consented to being so proceeded against, to such a penalty being imposed, or being so detained or restricted in his or her personal liberty, and was aware of the consequences of his or her so consenting, and

    (iii) the person obtained or was afforded the opportunity of obtaining, or being provided with, professional legal advice in relation to the matters to which this section relates,

(c) is satisfied that—

    (i) such proceedings will not be brought, such penalty will not be imposed and the person will not be so detained or otherwise restricted in his or her personal liberty before the expiration of a period of 45 days from the date of the person's final discharge in respect of the offence for which he or she is surrendered, and

    (ii) during that period he or she will be free to leave the issuing state,

except where having been so discharged he or she leaves the issuing state and later returns thereto (whether during that period or later), or

(d) is satisfied that such proceedings will not be brought, such penalty will not be imposed and the person will not be so detained or restricted in his or her personal liberty unless—

    (i) the person voluntarily gives his or her consent to being so proceeded against, such a penalty being imposed, or being so detained or restricted in his or her personal liberty, and is fully aware of the consequences of so doing,

    (ii) that consent is given before the competent judicial authority in the issuing state, and

    (iii) the person obtains or is afforded the opportunity of obtaining, or being provided with, professional legal advice in the issuing state in relation to the matters to which this section relates before he or she gives that consent.

(7) The High Court may, in relation to a person who has been surrendered to an issuing state under this Act, consent to—

(a) proceedings being brought against the person in the issuing state for an offence,

(b) the imposition in the issuing state of a penalty, including a penalty consisting of a restriction of the person's liberty, in respect of an offence, or

(c) proceedings being brought against, or the detention of, the person in the issuing state for the purpose of executing a sentence or order of detention in respect of an offence,

upon receiving a request in writing from the issuing state in that behalf.

(8) The High Court shall not give its consent under subsection (7) if the offence concerned is an offence for which a person could not by virtue of Part 3 or the Framework Decision (including the recitals thereto) be surrendered under this Act.

Surrender of person by issuing state to other Member State

23.—(1) In this section, except where the context otherwise requires—

'offence' means, in relation to a person to whom a European arrest warrant applies, an offence under the law of a Member State (other than the issuing state) committed before the person's surrender to the issuing state under this Act; and

'Member State' means a Member State other than the issuing state.

(2) Subject to this section, the High Court shall refuse to surrender a person under this Act if it is satisfied that—

(a) the law of the issuing state does not provide that a person who is surrendered to it pursuant to a European arrest warrant shall not be surrendered to a Member State pursuant to a European arrest warrant issued by a judicial authority in that Member State in respect of an offence, and

(b) the person will be surrendered to a Member State pursuant to a European arrest warrant issued by a judicial authority in that Member State in respect of an offence.

(3) It shall be presumed that, in relation to a person to whom a European arrest warrant applies, the issuing state does not intend to surrender him or her to a Member State pursuant to a European arrest warrant issued by a judicial authority in that Member State in respect of an offence, unless the contrary is proved.

(4) The surrender of a person under this Act shall not be refused under subsection (2) if the High Court—

(a) is satisfied that the issuing judicial authority will not surrender the person to a Member State pursuant to a European arrest warrant issued by a judicial authority in that Member State, without first obtaining the consent thereto of the High Court,

(b) is satisfied that—

    (i) the person consents to being surrendered under section 15,

    (ii) at the time of so consenting he or she consented to being surrendered by the issuing state to a Member State pursuant to a European arrest warrant issued by a judicial authority in that Member State, and was aware of the consequences of his or her so consenting, and

    (iii) the person obtained or was afforded the opportunity of obtaining, or being provided with, professional legal advice in relation to the matters to which this section relates,

(c) is satisfied that—

    (i) the person will not be surrendered by the issuing state to a Member State pursuant to a European arrest warrant issued by a judicial authority in that Member State, before the expiration of a period of 45 days from the date of the person's final discharge in respect of the offence for which he or she is surrendered under this Act, and

    (ii) during that period he or she will be free to leave the issuing state,

except where having been so discharged he or she leaves the issuing state and later returns thereto (whether during that period or later), or

(d) is satisfied that the person will not be surrendered to a Member State pursuant to a European arrest warrant issued by a judicial authority in that Member State unless—

    (i) the person voluntarily gives his or her consent to being so surrendered and is fully aware of the consequences of his or her so doing,

    (ii) that consent is given before the competent judicial authority in the issuing state, and

    (iii) the person obtains or is afforded the opportunity of obtaining, or being provided with, professional legal advice in the issuing state in relation to the matters to which this section relates before he or she gives that consent.

(5) The High Court may, in relation to a person who has been surrendered to an issuing state under this Act, consent to the person being surrendered by the issuing state to a Member State pursuant to a European arrest warrant issued by a judicial authority in that Member State, upon receiving a request in writing from the issuing state in that behalf.

(6) The High Court shall not give its consent under subsection (5) if the offence concerned is an offence for which a person could not by virtue

of Part 3 or the Framework Decision (including the recitals thereto) be surrendered under this Act.

Extradition of person by issuing state to third state

24.—(1) The High Court shall refuse to surrender a person under this Act if it is satisfied that—

(a) the law of the issuing state does not provide that a person who is surrendered to it pursuant to a European arrest warrant shall not be extradited to a third country without the consent of the High Court and the Minister first being obtained, and

(b) the person will be extradited to a third country without such consent first being obtained.

(2) It shall be presumed that, in relation to a person to whom a European arrest warrant applies, the issuing state does not intend to extradite him or her to a third country, unless the contrary is proved.

(3) The issuing state may request, in writing, the High Court to consent to the extradition to a third country by the issuing state of a person surrendered to the issuing state under this Act.

(4) The High Court shall give its consent to a request under subsection (3) if it is satisfied that—

(a) were the person concerned in the State, and

(b) were a request for his or her extradition received in the State from the third country concerned,

his or her extradition pursuant to such a request would not be prohibited under the Extradition Acts 1965 to 2001.

Searches for purposes of European arrest warrant

25.—(1) A member of the Garda Síochána, may, for the purposes of performing functions under *section 13* or *14*, enter any place (if necessary by the use of reasonable force) and search that place, if he or she has reasonable grounds for believing that a person in respect of whom a European arrest warrant has been issued is to be found at that place.

(2) Where a member of the Garda Síochána enters a place under *subsection (1)*, he or she may search that place and any person found at that place, and may seize anything found at that place or anything found in the possession of a person present at that place at the time of the search that the said member believes to be evidence of, or relating to, an offence specified in a European arrest warrant, or to be property obtained or received at any time (whether before or after the passing of this Act) as a result of or in connection with the commission of that offence.

(3) Subject to *subsection (4)*, a member of the Garda Síochána, who has reasonable grounds for believing that evidence of, or relating to,

an offence specified in a European arrest warrant, or property obtained or received at any time (whether before or after the passing of this Act) as a result of, or in connection with, the commission of that offence is to be found at any place, may enter that place (if necessary by the use of reasonable force) and search that place and any person found at that place, and may seize anything found at that place or anything found in the possession of a person present at that place at the time of the search that the member believes to be such evidence or property.

(4) (a) A member of the Garda Síochána shall not enter a dwelling under *subsection (3)*, other than—

    (i)   with the consent of the occupier, or

    (ii) in accordance with a warrant issued under *paragraph (b)*.

(b) On the application of a member of the Garda Síochána, a judge of the District Court may, if satisfied that there are reasonable grounds for believing that—

    (i)   evidence of, or relating to, an offence specified in a European arrest warrant, or

    (ii) property obtained or received at any time (whether before or after the passing of this Act) as a result of or in connection with the commission of that offence,

is to be found in any dwelling, issue a warrant authorising a named member of the Garda Síochána accompanied by such other members of the Garda Síochána as may be necessary, at any time or times, within one month of the date of the issue of the warrant, to enter the dwelling (if necessary by the use of reasonable force) and search the dwelling and any person found at the dwelling, and a member of the Garda Síochána who enters a dwelling pursuant to such a warrant may seize anything found at the dwelling or anything found in the possession of a person present at the dwelling at the time of the search that the member believes to be such evidence or property.

(5) A member of the Garda Síochána who is performing functions under this section may—

    (a) require any person present at the place where the search is carried out to give to the member his or her name and address, and

    (b) arrest otherwise than pursuant to a warrant any person who—

        (i)   obstructs or attempts to obstruct that member in the performance of his or her functions,

        (ii) fails to comply with a requirement under *paragraph (a)*, or

        (iii) gives a name or address which the member has reasonable cause for believing is false or misleading.

(6) A person who—

(a) obstructs or attempts to obstruct a member of the Garda Síochána in the performance of his or her functions under this section,

(b) fails to comply with a requirement under *paragraph (a)* of *subsection (5)*, or

(c) gives a false name or address to a member of the Garda Síochána,

shall be guilty of an offence and shall be liable on summary conviction to a fine not exceeding €3,000, or to imprisonment for a period not exceeding 6 months, or to both.

(7) In this section "place" includes a ship or other vessel, an aircraft, a railway wagon or other vehicle, and a container used for the transporting of goods.

Handing over property

26.—(1) Subject to the provisions of this section, any property seized under *section 25* shall, if a person is surrendered under this Act, be handed over to any person duly authorised by the issuing state to receive it, as soon as may be after the surrender of the person, and the said property shall be so handed over notwithstanding that the surrender of the person cannot be carried out by reason of the death or escape from custody of the person claimed.

(2) Any property seized under *section 25* may, if any criminal proceedings to which the property relates are pending in the State, be retained in the State for the purposes of those proceedings or may, if the Central Authority in the State, after consultation with the Director of Public Prosecutions, so directs, be handed over to the issuing state subject to the issuing state agreeing to return the property.

(3) This section shall not operate to abrogate any rights lawfully vested in the State, or any person, in any property to which this section applies and, where any such rights exist, the property shall not be handed over unless an undertaking is given by the issuing state that it will return the property as soon as may be after the trial of the person surrendered and without charge to the State or person in whom such rights vest.

Remand

27.—(1) A person remanded in custody under this Act may be detained in a prison (or, if he or she is not more than 21 years of age, in a remand institution) or, for a period not exceeding 48 hours, in a Garda Síochána station.

(2) A person shall not be remanded on bail or otherwise released from custody under this Act if—

    (a) (i) the person has been sentenced to a term of imprisonment for an offence of which he or she was convicted in the State,

        (ii) on the date of his or her being remanded or on which he or she would, but for this paragraph, be entitled to be released, all or part of the term of imprisonment remains unexpired, and

        (iii) the person is required to serve all or part of the remainder of that term of imprisonment,

    or

    (b) (i) the person has been charged with or convicted of an offence in the State, and

        (ii) on the date of his or her being remanded or on which he or she would, but for this paragraph, be entitled to be released, he or she is required to be in custody by virtue of having been remanded in custody pending trial for that offence or the imposition of sentence in respect of that offence.

Transit

28.—(1) Transit through the State of a person being conveyed from an executing state to an issuing state, upon his or her surrender pursuant to a European arrest warrant, shall be permitted where the Central Authority in the State receives a request in that behalf from the issuing state and where the issuing state provides the Central Authority in the State with the following information:

    (a) the nationality of the person and such other information as will enable the person to be identified by the Central Authority in the State;

    (b) information showing that a European arrest warrant has been issued by the issuing state in respect of the person;

    (c) the nature and classification under the law of the issuing state of the offence to which the European arrest warrant relates;

    (d) the circumstances in which the offence specified in the European arrest warrant was committed or is alleged to have been committed, including the date and place of its commission.

(2) The transit of a person through the State shall be supervised by members of the Garda Síochána if the Central Authority in the State considers it appropriate, and where a person's transit is so supervised the person shall be deemed to be in the custody of any member of the Garda Síochána who accompanies him or her.

(3) (a) This subsection applies to an aircraft that has taken off from a place (other than the State) and that is scheduled to land in a place (other than the State) and on board which there is a person who is being conveyed to an issuing state upon his or her surrender pursuant to a European arrest warrant.

(b) Where an aircraft to which this subsection applies lands (for whatever reason) in the State, the issuing state shall, upon its landing or as soon as may be after it lands, provide the Central Authority in the State with the information referred to in *subsection (1)*.

(c) While an aircraft to which this subsection applies is in the State, a person referred to in *paragraph (a)* who is on board that aircraft shall be deemed to be in transit through the State and *subsection (2)* shall apply accordingly.

(4) Where a person has been extradited by a third country to a Member State this section shall apply subject to the modifications that—

(a) the reference to an executing state shall be construed as a reference to a third state,

(b) references to a European arrest warrant shall be construed as references to an extradition request, and

(c) references to an issuing state shall be construed as references to a Member State.

(5) In this section ''executing state'' means, in relation to a European arrest warrant, a Member State (a judicial authority of which has ordered the arrest and surrender to the issuing state, pursuant to the European arrest warrant, of a person in respect of whom that warrant was issued).

Multiple European arrest warrants

29.—(1) Where the Central Authority in the State receives two or more European arrest warrants in respect of a person, the Central Authority in the State shall, where the High Court has not yet made an order under *section 15*, or *subsection (1)* or *(2)* of *section 16*, in relation to the person, inform the High Court as soon as may be of the receipt by it of those warrants and the High Court shall, having regard to all the circumstances, decide, in relation to which of those European arrest warrants it shall—

(a) perform functions under *section 13*, or

(b) where it has already performed such functions in relation to one of those European arrest warrants, perform functions under *section 15* or *16*, as may be appropriate.

(2) Without prejudice to the generality of *subsection (1)*, the High Court shall in making a decision under *subsection (1)* have regard to—

    (a) the seriousness of the offences specified in the European arrest warrants concerned,

    (b) the places where the offences were committed or are alleged to have been committed,

    (c) the dates on which the European arrest warrants were issued, and

    (d) whether the European arrest warrants concerned were issued for the purposes of bringing proceedings for an offence against the person named in the warrants or for the purposes of executing a sentence or detention order in respect of the person.

European arrest warrants and requests for extradition

30.—(1) If the Central Authority in the State receives a European arrest warrant in respect of a person and a request from a third country for the extradition of that person, the Central Authority in the State shall, where the High Court has not yet made an order under *section 15*, or *subsection (1)* or *(2)* of *section 16*, in relation to the person, inform the High Court as soon as may be of the receipt by it of the European arrest warrant and the request for extradition, and the High Court shall, having regard to all the circumstances, decide whether it shall perform functions—

    (a) in relation to the European arrest warrant, under this Act, or

    (b) in relation to the request for extradition, under the Extradition Acts 1965 to 2001.

(2) Without prejudice to the generality of *subsection (1)*, the High Court shall in making a decision under *subsection (1)* have regard to—

    (a) the seriousness of—

        (i) the offence specified in the European arrest warrant, and

        (ii) the offence to which the request for extradition relates,

    (b) the places where the offences concerned were committed or are alleged to have been committed,

    (c) the date on which the European arrest warrant was issued and the date on which the request for extradition was made,

    (d) whether the European arrest warrant was issued, or the request for extradition was made, for the purposes of bringing proceedings for an offence against the person concerned or for the purposes of executing a sentence or detention order in respect of the person, and

    (e) the relevant extradition provisions.

(3) If the Central Authority in the State receives a European arrest warrant in respect of a person and the State receives a request from the International Criminal Court for the arrest and surrender of the same person, the Central Authority in the State shall, where an order has not yet been made under *section 15*, or *subsection (1)* or *(2)* of *section 16*, in relation to that person, so inform the High Court, and the High Court shall not perform functions under this Act in relation to the European arrest warrant, unless the arrest and surrender of that person pursuant to such a request is prohibited, or not provided for, under the law of the State.

(4) In this section ''extradition provisions'' has the same meaning as it has in the Act of 1965.

Chapter 2

Issue of European Arrest Warrant by State

Definition

31.—In this Chapter—

''domestic warrant'' means a warrant (other than a European arrest warrant) issued, for the arrest of a person, by a court in the State;

''European arrest warrant'' means a warrant to which the Framework Decision applies issued by a court, in accordance with this Chapter and for the purposes of—

(a) the arrest, in a Member State, of that person, and

(b) the surrender of that person to the State by the Member State concerned.

Offences to which Article 2.2 of Framework Decision applies

32.—(1) For the purposes of paragraph 2 of Article 2 of the Framework Decision, the Minister may, by order, specify the offences under the law of the State to which that paragraph applies.

(2) The Minister may, by order, amend or revoke an order under this section (including an order under this subsection).

(3) This section shall not operate to require that an order under this section be in force before a court may issue a European arrest warrant under *section 33*.

Issue of European arrest warrant issued in State

33.—(1) A court may, upon an application made by or on behalf of the Director of Public Prosecutions, issue a European arrest warrant in respect of a person where it is satisfied that—

    (a) a domestic warrant has been issued for the arrest of that person but has not been executed, and

    (b) the person may not be in the State, and

(b^2) where—

       (i) the person would, if convicted of the offence concerned, be liable to a term of imprisonment or detention of 12 months or more than 12 months, or

       (ii) a term of imprisonment or detention of not less than 4 months has been imposed on the person in respect of the offence concerned and the person is required to serve all or part of that term of imprisonment or detention.

(1A) Where a court issues a European arrest warrant in respect of a person under this section, such issue shall be deemed to constitute a request by the court for entry of an alert and of a copy of the European arrest warrant in respect of that person.

(1B) For the purposes of subsection (1), where a member of the Garda Síochána not below the rank of Sergeant states that he or she believes that a person may not be in the State, the statement is admissible as evidence that the person may not be in the State.

(2) A European arrest warrant shall, in so far as is practicable, be in the form set out in the Annex to the Framework Decision and shall specify—

    (a) the name and the nationality of the person to whom it relates,

    (b) the name, address, fax number and e-mail address of—

       (i) the District Court Office for the district in which the District Court was sitting when it issued the European arrest warrant,

       (ii) the Circuit Court Office of the county in which the Circuit Criminal Court was sitting when it issued the European arrest warrant,

      (iii) the Central Office of the High Court, or

      (iv) the Registrar of the Special Criminal Court,

    as may be appropriate,

    (c) the offence to which the European arrest warrant relates including a description thereof,

---

[2] There appears to be a slight formatting error in the amending provision (Section 16 of the Criminal Justice (Miscellaneous Provisions) Act, 2009) which results in the creation of two subsection 33(1)(b)'s.

(d) that a conviction, sentence or detention order is immediately enforceable against the person, or that a domestic warrant for his or her arrest has been issued in respect of that offence,

(e) the circumstances in which the offence was committed or is alleged to have been committed, including the time and place of its commission or alleged commission, and the degree of involvement or alleged degree of involvement of the person in the commission of the offence, and

(f) (i) the penalties to which the person named in the European arrest warrant would, if convicted of the offence to which the European arrest warrant relates, be liable,

(ii) where the person named in the European arrest warrant has been convicted of the offence specified therein and a sentence has been imposed in respect thereof, the penalties of which that sentence consists, and

(iii) where the person named in the European arrest warrant has been convicted of the offence specified therein but has not yet been sentenced, the penalties to which he or she is liable in respect of the offence.

(3) Where it is not practicable for the European arrest warrant to be in the form set out in the Annex to the Framework Decision, the European arrest warrant shall, in addition to containing the information specified in *subsection (2)*, include such other information as would be required to be provided were it in that form.

(4) For the avoidance of doubt, a European arrest warrant may be issued in respect of one or more than one offence.

(5) In this section ''court'' means—

(a) the court that issued the domestic warrant to which *subparagraph (i)* of *section 33(1)(a)* applies, or

(b) the High Court.

Transmission of European arrest warrant issued in State

34.—A European arrest warrant issued under *section 33* may be transmitted to a Member State by the Central Authority in the State.

Arrest of person surrendered to State

35.—(1) Where a person is surrendered to the State pursuant to a European arrest warrant—

(a) the domestic warrant issued for his or her arrest and referred to in *subparagraph (i)* of *section 33(1)(a)*,

(b) subject to *paragraph (c)*, where more than one such domestic warrant was issued, those domestic warrants, or

(c) where—

    (i) more than one such domestic warrant was issued, and

    (ii) the executing judicial authority ordered the surrender of the person in respect of one or more but not all of the offences specified in the European arrest warrant,

the domestic warrants issued in respect of the offences for which the person was surrendered,

may be executed by any member of the Garda Síochána in any part of the State and may be so executed notwithstanding that the domestic warrant concerned is not in the possession of the member when he or she executes the warrant, and the domestic warrant concerned shall be shown to and a copy thereof given to the person arrested at the time of his or her arrest or, if the domestic warrant or copy thereof is not then in the possession of the member, not later than 24 hours after the person's arrest.

(2) Where a person is surrendered to the State pursuant to a European arrest warrant issued by the High Court (whether or not sitting as the Central Criminal Court), the Central Authority in the State shall inform the Central Office of the High Court, in writing, of the person's surrender.

Deduction of period of detention in executing state from sentence

36.—(1) Where a person is surrendered to the State pursuant to a European arrest warrant, then any term of imprisonment that the person is required to serve by virtue of the imposition of a sentence by a court in the State (whether before or after the person's surrender) in respect of the offence specified in that European arrest warrant shall be reduced by an amount equal to any period of time spent by that person in custody or detention in the executing state in contemplation, or in consequence, of the execution of the European arrest warrant.

(2) In this section ''executing state'' means, in relation to a European arrest warrant, a Member State (a judicial authority of which has ordered the arrest and surrender to the State, pursuant to the European arrest warrant, of a person in respect of whom that warrant was issued).

PART 3

Prohibition on Surrender

Fundamental rights

37.—(1) A person shall not be surrendered under this Act if—

(a) his or her surrender would be incompatible with the State's obligations under—

(i)   the Convention, or

(ii) the Protocols to the Convention,

(b) his or her surrender would constitute a contravention of any provision of the Constitution (other than for the reason that the offence specified in the European arrest warrant is an offence to which *section 38(1)(b)* applies),

(c) there are reasonable grounds for believing that—

(i)   the European arrest warrant was issued in respect of the person for the purposes of facilitating his or her prosecution or punishment in the issuing state for reasons connected with his or her sex, race, religion, ethnic origin, nationality, language, political opinion or sexual orientation, or

(ii) in the prosecution or punishment of the person in the issuing state, he or she will be treated less favourably than a person who—

(I)   is not of his or her sex, race, religion, nationality or ethnic origin,

(II) does not hold the same political opinions as him or her,

(III) speaks a different language than he or she does, or

(IV) does not have the same sexual orientation as he or she does, or

(iii) were the person to be surrendered to the issuing state—

(I)   he or she would be sentenced to death, or a death sentence imposed on him or her would be carried out, or

(II) he or she would be tortured or subjected to other inhuman or degrading treatment.

(2) In this section—

"Convention" means the Convention for the Protection of Human Rights and Fundamental Freedoms done at Rome on the 4th day of

November, 1950, as amended by Protocol No. 11 done at Strasbourg on the 11th day of May, 1994; and

"Protocols to the Convention" means the following protocols to the Convention, construed in accordance with Articles 16 to 18 of the Convention:

(a) the Protocol to the Convention done at Paris on the 20th day of March, 1952;

(b) Protocol No. 4 to the Convention securing certain rights and freedoms other than those already included in the Convention and in the First Protocol thereto done at Strasbourg on the 16th day of September, 1963;

(c) Protocol No. 6 to the Convention concerning the abolition of the death penalty done at Strasbourg on the 28th day of April, 1983;

(d) Protocol No. 7 to the Convention done at Strasbourg on the 22nd day of November, 1984.

Offence in respect of which a person shall not be surrendered

38.—(1) Subject to *subsection (2)*, a person shall not be surrendered to an issuing state under this Act in respect of an offence unless—

(a) the offence corresponds to an offence under the law of the State, and—

(i) under the law of the issuing state the offence is punishable by imprisonment or detention for a maximum period of not less than 12 months, or

(ii) a term of imprisonment or detention of not less than 4 months has been imposed on the person in respect of the offence in the issuing state, and the person is required under the law of the issuing state to serve all or part of that term of imprisonment,

or

(b) the offence is an offence to which paragraph 2 of Article 2 of the Framework Decision applies and under the law of the issuing state the offence is punishable by imprisonment for a maximum period of not less than 3 years.

(2) The surrender of a person to an issuing state under this Act shall not be refused on the ground that, in relation to a revenue offence—

(a) no tax or duty of the kind to which the offence relates is imposed in the State, or

(b) the rules relating to taxes, duties, customs or exchange control that apply in the issuing state differ in nature from the rules that apply in the State to taxes, duties, customs or exchange control.

(3) In this section "revenue offence" means, in relation to an issuing state, an offence in connection with taxes, duties, customs or exchange control.

Pardon or amnesty

39.—(1) A person shall not be surrendered under this Act where he or she has been granted a pardon, under Article 13.6 of the Constitution, in respect of an offence consisting of an act or omission that constitutes in whole or in part the offence specified in the European arrest warrant issued in respect of him or her.

(2) A person shall not be surrendered under this Act where he or she has, in accordance with the law of the issuing state, become immune, by virtue of any amnesty or pardon, from prosecution or punishment in the issuing state for the offence specified in the European arrest warrant issued in respect of him or her.

(3) A person shall not be surrendered under this Act where he or she has, by virtue of any Act of the Oireachtas, become immune from prosecution or punishment for an offence consisting of an act or omission that constitutes in whole or in part the offence specified in the European arrest warrant issued in respect of him or her.

Double jeopardy

41.—(1) A person shall not be surrendered under this Act for the purpose of his or her being proceeded against in the issuing state for an offence consisting of an act or omission that constitutes in whole or in part an offence in respect of which final judgment has been given in the State or a Member State.

(2) A person shall not be surrendered under this Act for the purpose of his or her being proceeded against in the issuing state for an offence consisting of the act or omission that constitutes an offence in respect of which final judgment has been given in a third country, provided that where a sentence of imprisonment or detention was imposed on the person in the third country in respect of the second-mentioned offence—

   (a) the person has completed serving the sentence, or

   (b) the person is otherwise no longer liable under the law of the third country to serve any period of imprisonment or detention in respect of the offence.

Proceedings in the State

42.—A person shall not be surrendered under this Act if—

(a) the Director of Public Prosecutions or the Attorney General is considering, but has not yet decided, whether to bring proceedings against the person for an offence, or

(b) proceedings have been brought in the State against the person for an offence consisting of an act or omission of which the offence specified in the European arrest warrant issued in respect of him or her consists in whole or in part.

Age

43.—A person shall not be surrendered under this Act if the offence specified in the European arrest warrant issued in respect of him or her corresponds to an offence under the law of the State in respect of which a person of the same age as the person in respect of whom the European arrest warrant was issued could not be proceeded against by reason of his or her age.

Commission of offence outside issuing state

44.—A person shall not be surrendered under this Act if the offence specified in the European arrest warrant issued in respect of him or her was committed or is alleged to have been committed in a place other than the issuing state and the act or omission of which the offence consists does not, by virtue of having been committed in a place other than the State, constitute an offence under the law of the State.

Persons convicted in absentia

45.—A person shall not be surrendered under this Act if—

(a) he or she was not present when he or she was tried for and convicted of the offence specified in the European arrest warrant, and

(b) (i) he or she was not notified of the time when, and place at which, he or she would be tried for the offence, or

(ii) he or she was not permitted to attend the trial in respect of the offence concerned,

unless the issuing judicial authority gives an undertaking in writing that the person will, upon being surrendered—

(I) be retried for that offence or be given the opportunity of a retrial in respect of that offence,

(II) be notified of the time when, and place at which any retrial in respect of the offence concerned will take place, and

(III) be permitted to be present when any such retrial takes place.

Identification Procedures

45A.—(1) Where a member of the Garda Síochána arrests a person under any power conferred by this Act, the member of the Garda Síochána may, in order to assist in verifying or ascertaining his or her identity for the purpose of proceedings under this Act and for no other purpose—

(a) take, or cause to be taken, his or her fingerprint,

(b) take, or cause to be taken, his or her palm print,

(c) photograph him or her or cause him or her to be photographed.

(2) Where a fingerprint, palm print or photograph taken pursuant to subsection (1) is lost or damaged, or is otherwise unsuitable for use for the purpose referred to in that subsection, it may be taken on a second or any further occasion.

(3) The powers conferred by subsection (1) shall not be exercised except on the authority of a member of the Garda Síochána not below the rank of inspector.

(4) A member of the Garda Síochána may, where a person fails or refuses to allow his or her fingerprint, palm print or photograph to be taken pursuant to subsection (1), use such force as he or she reasonably considers necessary to take the fingerprint, palm print or photograph or to cause the photograph to be taken.

(5) (a) The powers conferred by subsection (4) shall not be exercised except on the authority of a member of the Garda Síochána not below the rank of superintendent.

(b) An authorization pursuant to paragraph (*a*) may be given orally or in writing and if given orally shall be confirmed in writing as soon as practicable.

(6) Where a member of the Garda Síochána intends to exercise a power conferred by subsection (4), he or she shall inform the person—

(a) of that intention, and

(b) that an authorization to do so has been given pursuant to subsection (5)(*a*).

(7) Every fingerprint, palm print or photograph taken pursuant to subsection (4) shall be taken in the presence of a member of the Garda Síochána not below the rank of inspector.

(8) The taking of every fingerprint, palm print or photograph pursuant to subsection (4) shall be video-recorded.

(9) Every fingerprint, palm print or photograph of a person taken in pursuance of a power conferred by this section and every copy and record thereof shall be destroyed within the period of 12 months from

the date of the taking of the fingerprint, palm print or photograph, as the case may be, or on the conclusion of proceedings under this Act in relation to the person, whichever occurs later.

(10) A person who obstructs a member of the Garda Síochána in exercise of the powers under this section shall be guilty of an offence and shall, on summary conviction, be liable to a fine not exceeding €5,000 or to imprisonment for a term not exceeding 12 months or to both.

(11) Where a fingerprint, palm print or photograph of a person to whom a European arrest warrant relates is transmitted by or on behalf of an issuing judicial authority, such fingerprint, palm print or photograph shall be received in evidence without further proof.

Transfer of persons to state from which surrendered

45B.—(1) Where a national or resident of another state from which he or she is surrendered—

(a) is surrendered to the State pursuant to a European arrest warrant with a view to being prosecuted in the State, and

(b) whose surrender is subject to the condition that he or she, after being so prosecuted, is returned if he or she so consents to that other state in order to serve any custodial sentence or detention order imposed upon him or her in the State,

the Minister shall, following the final determination of the proceedings and if the person consents, issue a warrant for the transfer of the person from the State to that other state in order to serve there any custodial sentence or detention order so imposed.

(2) A warrant issued under subsection 45 (1) shall authorise—

(a) the taking of the person to a place in any part of the State and his or her delivery at a place of departure from the State into the custody of a person authorized by the other state to receive the person, for conveyance to the other state concerned, and the keeping of the person in custody until the delivery is effected, and

(b) the removal of the person concerned, by the person to whom he or she is delivered, from the State.

(3) Where a warrant has been issued in respect of a person under this section, the person shall be deemed to be in legal custody at any time when he or she is being taken under the warrant to or from any place or being kept in custody under the warrant and, if the person escapes or is unlawfully at large, he or she shall be liable to be retaken in the same manner as any person who escapes from lawful custody.

(4) The Minister may designate any person as a person who is for the time being authorised to take the person concerned to or from any

place under the warrant or to keep the person in custody under the warrant.

(5) A person authorized pursuant to subsection (4) to take the person concerned to or from any place or to keep the person in custody shall, while so taking or keeping the person, have all the powers, authority, protection and privileges of a member of the Garda Síochána.

(6) The order by virtue of which a person is required to be detained at the time a warrant is issued in respect of him or her under this section shall continue to have effect after his or her removal from the State so as to apply to him or her if he or she is again in the State at any time when under that order he or she is to be or may be detained.

Technical flaws in applications for surrender

45C.—(1) Subject to subsection (2), an application for surrender under section 16 shall not be refused on the grounds of—

(a) a defect in substance or in form or an omission of non-substantial detail in the European arrest warrant or any accompanying document grounding the application,

(b) any variance between any such document and the evidence adduced on the part of the applicant at the hearing of the application, or

(c) failure to comply with any provision of this Act where the Court is satisfied that such failure is of a technical nature and does not impinge on the merits of the application.

(2) Subsection (1) shall not apply where the Court is satisfied that an injustice would thereby be caused to the respondent.

Immunity from prosecution

46.—A person who, by virtue of his or her holding any office or other position, is under the law of the State immune from prosecution for any offence, shall not while he or she holds such office or position be surrendered under this Act.

PART 4

Miscellaneous

Section 47, 48, 49, 50, 51 and 52 are omitted. These provide for various amendments to other Acts.

APPENDIX 2

FRAMEWORK DECISION

COUNCIL FRAMEWORK DECISION

of 13 June 2002

on the European arrest warrant and the surrender procedures between Member States

(2002/584/JHA)

THE COUNCIL OF THE EUROPEAN UNION,

Having regard to the Treaty on European Union, and in particular Article 31(a) and (b) and Article 34(2)(b) thereof,

Having regard to the proposal from the Commission [Footnote 1: OJ C 332 E, 27.11.2001, p. 305.],

Having regard to the opinion of the European Parliament [Footnote 2: Opinion delivered on 9 January 2002 (not yet published in the Official Journal).],

Whereas:

(1) According to the Conclusions of the Tampere European Council of 15 and 16 October 1999, and in particular point 35 thereof, the formal extradition procedure should be abolished among the Member States in respect of persons who are fleeing from justice after having been finally sentenced and extradition procedures should be speeded up in respect of persons suspected of having committed an offence.

(2) The programme of measures to implement the principle of mutual recognition of criminal decisions envisaged in point 37 of the Tampere European Council Conclusions and adopted by the Council on 30 November 2000 [Footnote 3: OJ C 12 E, 15.1.2001, p. 10.], addresses the matter of mutual enforcement of arrest warrants.

(3) All or some Member States are parties to a number of conventions in the field of extradition, including the European Convention on extradition of 13 December 1957 and the European Convention on the suppression of terrorism of 27 January 1977. The Nordic States have extradition laws with identical wording.

(4) In addition, the following three Conventions dealing in whole or in part with extradition have been agreed upon among Member States and form part of the Union acquis: the Convention of 19 June 1990 implementing the Schengen Agreement of 14 June 1985 on the gradual abolition of checks at their common borders [Footnote 4: OJ L 239, 22.9.2000, p.19.] (regarding relations between the Member States which are parties to that Convention), the Convention of 10 March 1995 on simplified extradition procedure between the Member States of the European Union [Footnote 5: OJ C 78, 30.3.1995, p. 2.] and the Convention of 27 September 1996 relating to extradition between the Member States of the European Union [Footnote 6: OJ C 313, 13.10.1996, p. 12.].

(5) The objective set for the Union to become an area of freedom, security and justice leads to abolishing extradition between Member States and replacing it by a system of surrender between judicial authorities. Further, the introduction of a new simplified system of surrender of sentenced or suspected persons for the purposes of execution or prosecution of criminal sentences makes it possible to remove the complexity and potential for delay inherent in the present extradition procedures. Traditional cooperation relations which have prevailed up till now between Member States should be replaced by a system of free movement of judicial decisions in criminal matters, covering both pre-sentence and final decisions, within an area of freedom, security and justice.

(6) The European arrest warrant provided for in this Framework Decision is the first concrete measure in the field of criminal law implementing the principle of mutual recognition which the European Council referred to as the 'cornerstone' of judicial cooperation.

(7) Since the aim of replacing the system of multilateral extradition built upon the European Convention on Extradition of 13 December 1957 cannot be sufficiently achieved by the Member States acting unilaterally and can therefore, by reason of its scale and effects, be better achieved at Union level, the Council may adopt measures in accordance with the principle of subsidiarity as referred to in Article 2 of the Treaty on European Union and Article 5 of the Treaty establishing the European Community. In accordance with the principle of proportionality, as set out in the latter Article, this Framework Decision does not go beyond what is necessary in order to achieve that objective.

(8) Decisions on the execution of the European arrest warrant must be subject to sufficient controls, which means that a judicial authority of the Member State where the requested person has been arrested will have to take the decision on his or her surrender.

(9) The role of central authorities in the execution of a European arrest warrant must be limited to practical and administrative assistance.

(10) The mechanism of the European arrest warrant is based on a high level of confidence between Member States. Its implementation may be suspended only in the event of a serious and persistent breach by one of the Member States of the principles set out in Article 6(1) of the Treaty on European Union, determined by the Council pursuant to Article 7(1) of the said Treaty with the consequences set out in Article 7(2) thereof.

(11) In relations between Member States, the European arrest warrant should replace all the previous instruments concerning extradition, including the provisions of Title III of the Convention implementing the Schengen Agreement which concern extradition.

(12) This Framework Decision respects fundamental rights and observes the principles recognised by Article 6 of the Treaty on European Union and reflected in the Charter of Fundamental Rights of the European Union [Footnote 1: OJ C 364, 18.12.2000, p. 1.], in particular Chapter VI thereof. Nothing in this Framework Decision may be interpreted as prohibiting refusal to surrender a person for whom a European arrest warrant has been issued when there are reasons to believe, on the basis of objective elements, that the said arrest warrant has been issued for the purpose of prosecuting or punishing a person on the grounds of his or her sex, race, religion, ethnic origin, nationality, language, political opinions or sexual orientation, or that that person's position may be prejudiced for any of these reasons.

This Framework Decision does not prevent a Member State from applying its constitutional rules relating to due process, freedom of association, freedom of the press and freedom of expression in other media.

(13) No person should be removed, expelled or extradited to a State where there is a serious risk that he or she would be subjected to the death penalty, torture or other inhuman or degrading treatment or punishment.

(14) Since all Member States have ratified the Council of Europe Convention of 28 January 1981 for the protection of individuals with regard to automatic processing of personal data, the personal data processed in the context of the implementation of this Framework Decision should be protected in accordance with the principles of the said Convention

HAS ADOPTED THIS FRAMEWORK DECISION:

Chapter 1

General Principles

Article 1

Definition of the European arrest warrant and obligation to execute it

1. The European arrest warrant is a judicial decision issued by a Member State with a view to the arrest and surrender by another Member State of a requested person, for the purposes of conducting a criminal prosecution or executing a custodial sentence or detention order.

2. Member States shall execute any European arrest warrant on the basis of the principle of mutual recognition and in accordance with the provisions of this Framework Decision.

3. This Framework Decision shall not have the effect of modifying the obligation to respect fundamental rights and fundamental legal

principles as enshrined in Article 6 of the Treaty on European Union.

Article 2

Scope of the European arrest warrant

1. A European arrest warrant may be issued for acts punishable by the law of the issuing Member State by a custodial sentence or a detention order for a maximum period of at least 12 months or, where a sentence has been passed or a detention order has been made, for sentences of at least four months.

2. The following offences, if they are punishable in the issuing Member State by a custodial sentence or a detention order for a maximum period of at least three years and as they are defined by the law of the issuing Member State, shall, under the terms of this Framework Decision and without verification of the double criminality of the act, give rise to surrender pursuant to a European arrest warrant:

   —participation in a criminal organisation,

   —terrorism,

   —trafficking in human beings,

   —sexual exploitation of children and child pornography,

   —illicit trafficking in narcotic drugs and psychotropic substances,

   —illicit trafficking in weapons, munitions and explosives,

   —corruption,

   —fraud, including that affecting the financial interests of the European Communities within the meaning of the Convention of 26 July 1995 on the protection of the European Communities' financial interests,

   —laundering of the proceeds of crime,

   —counterfeiting currency, including of the euro,

   —computer-related crime,

   —environmental crime, including illicit trafficking in endangered animal species and in endangered plant species and varieties,

   —facilitation of unauthorised entry and residence,

   —murder, grievous bodily injury,

   —illicit trade in human organs and tissue,

   —kidnapping, illegal restraint and hostage-taking,

   —racism and xenophobia,

— organised or armed robbery,

— illicit trafficking in cultural goods, including antiques and works of art,

— swindling,

— racketeering and extortion,

— counterfeiting and piracy of products,

— forgery of administrative documents and trafficking therein,

— forgery of means of payment,

— illicit trafficking in hormonal substances and other growth promoters,

— illicit trafficking in nuclear or radioactive materials,

— trafficking in stolen vehicles,

— rape,

— arson,

— crimes within the jurisdiction of the International Criminal Court,

— unlawful seizure of aircraft/ships,

— sabotage.

3. The Council may decide at any time, acting unanimously after consultation of the European Parliament under the conditions laid down in Article 39(1) of the Treaty on European Union (TEU), to add other categories of offence to the list contained in paragraph 2. The Council shall examine, in the light of the report submitted by the Commission pursuant to Article 34(3), whether the list should be extended or amended.

4. For offences other than those covered by paragraph 2, surrender may be subject to the condition that the acts for which the European arrest warrant has been issued constitute an offence under the law of the executing Member State, whatever the constituent elements or however it is described.

Article 3

Grounds for mandatory non-execution of the European arrest warrant

The judicial authority of the Member State of execution (hereinafter 'executing judicial authority') shall refuse to execute the European arrest warrant in the following cases:

1. if the offence on which the arrest warrant is based is covered by amnesty in the executing Member State, where that State had jurisdiction to prosecute the offence under its own criminal law;

2. if the executing judicial authority is informed that the requested person has been finally judged by a Member State in respect of the same acts provided that, where there has been sentence, the sentence has been served or is currently being served or may no longer be executed under the law of the sentencing Member State;

3. if the person who is the subject of the European arrest warrant may not, owing to his age, be held criminally responsible for the acts on which the arrest warrant is based under the law of the executing State.

Article 4

Grounds for optional non-execution of the European arrest warrant

The executing judicial authority may refuse to execute the European arrest warrant:

1. if, in one of the cases referred to in Article 2(4), the act on which the European arrest warrant is based does not constitute an offence under the law of the executing Member State; however, in relation to taxes or duties, customs and exchange, execution of the European arrest warrant shall not be refused on the ground that the law of the executing Member State does not impose the same kind of tax or duty or does not contain the same type of rules as regards taxes, duties and customs and exchange regulations as the law of the issuing Member State;

2. where the person who is the subject of the European arrest warrant is being prosecuted in the executing Member State for the same act as that on which the European arrest warrant is based;

3. where the judicial authorities of the executing Member State have decided either not to prosecute for the offence on which the European arrest warrant is based or to halt proceedings, or where a final judgment has been passed upon the requested person in a Member State, in respect of the same acts, which prevents further proceedings;

4. where the criminal prosecution or punishment of the requested person is statute-barred according to the law of the executing Member State and the acts fall within the jurisdiction of that Member State under its own criminal law;

5. if the executing judicial authority is informed that the requested person has been finally judged by a third State in respect of the same acts provided that, where there has been sentence, the sentence has been served or is currently being served or may no longer be executed under the law of the sentencing country;

6. if the European arrest warrant has been issued for the purposes of execution of a custodial sentence or detention order, where

the requested person is staying in, or is a national or a resident of the executing Member State and that State undertakes to execute the sentence or detention order in accordance with its domestic law;

7. where the European arrest warrant relates to offences which:

   (a) are regarded by the law of the executing Member State as having been committed in whole or in part in the territory of the executing Member State or in a place treated as such; or

   (b) have been committed outside the territory of the issuing Member State and the law of the executing Member State does not allow prosecution for the same offences when committed outside its territory.

Article 5

Guarantees to be given by the issuing Member State in particular cases

The execution of the European arrest warrant by the executing judicial authority may, by the law of the executing Member State, be subject to the following conditions:

1. where the European arrest warrant has been issued for the purposes of executing a sentence or a detention order imposed by a decision rendered and if the person concerned has not been summoned in person or otherwise informed of the date and place of the hearing which led to the decision rendered in absentia, surrender may be subject to the condition that the issuing judicial authority gives an assurance deemed adequate to guarantee the person who is the subject of the European arrest warrant that he or she will have an opportunity to apply for a retrial of the case in the issuing Member State and to be present at the judgment;

2. if the offence on the basis of which the European arrest warrant has been issued is punishable by custodial life sentence or lifetime detention order, the execution of the said arrest warrant may be subject to the condition that the issuing Member State has provisions in its legal system for a review of the penalty or measure imposed, on request or at the latest after 20 years, or for the application of measures of clemency to which the person is entitled to apply for under the law or practice of the issuing Member State, aiming at a non-execution of such penalty or measure;

3. where a person who is the subject of a European arrest warrant for the purposes of prosecution is a national or resident of the executing Member State, surrender may be subject to the condition that the person, after being heard, is returned to the executing Member State in order to serve there the custodial sentence or detention order passed against him in the issuing Member State.

Article 6

Determination of the competent judicial authorities

1. The issuing judicial authority shall be the judicial authority of the issuing Member State which is competent to issue a European arrest warrant by virtue of the law of that State.

2. The executing judicial authority shall be the judicial authority of the executing Member State which is competent to execute the European arrest warrant by virtue of the law of that State.

3. Each Member State shall inform the General Secretariat of the Council of the competent judicial authority under its law.

Article 7

Recourse to the central authority

1. Each Member State may designate a central authority or, when its legal system so provides, more than one central authority to assist the competent judicial authorities.

2. A Member State may, if it is necessary as a result of the organisation of its internal judicial system, make its central authority(ies) responsible for the administrative transmission and reception of European arrest warrants as well as for all other official correspondence relating thereto.

Member State wishing to make use of the possibilities referred to in this Article shall communicate to the General Secretariat of the Council information relating to the designated central authority or central authorities. These indications shall be binding upon all the authorities of the issuing Member State.

Article 8

Content and form of the European arrest warrant

1. The European arrest warrant shall contain the following information set out in accordance with the form contained in the Annex:

    (a) the identity and nationality of the requested person;

    (b) the name, address, telephone and fax numbers and e-mail address of the issuing judicial authority;

    (c) evidence of an enforceable judgment, an arrest warrant or any other enforceable judicial decision having the same effect, coming within the scope of Articles 1 and 2;

    (d) the nature and legal classification of the offence, particularly in respect of Article 2;

    (e) a description of the circumstances in which the offence was committed, including the time, place and degree of participation in the offence by the requested person;

    (f) the penalty imposed, if there is a final judgment, or the prescribed scale of penalties for the offence under the law of the issuing Member State;

    (g) if possible, other consequences of the offence.

2.   The European arrest warrant must be translated into the official language or one of the official languages of the executing Member State. Any Member State may, when this Framework Decision is adopted or at a later date, state in a declaration deposited with the General Secretariat of the Council that it will accept a translation in one or more other official languages of the Institutions of the European Communities.

Chapter 2

Surrender Procedure

Article 9

Transmission of a European arrest warrant

1.   When the location of the requested person is known, the issuing judicial authority may transmit the European arrest warrant directly to the executing judicial authority.

2.   The issuing judicial authority may, in any event, decide to issue an alert for the requested person in the Schengen Information System (SIS).

3.   Such an alert shall be effected in accordance with the provisions of Article 95 of the Convention of 19 June 1990 implementing the Schengen Agreement of 14 June 1985 on the gradual abolition of controls at common borders. An alert in the Schengen Information System shall be equivalent to a European arrest warrant accompanied by the information set out in Article 8(1).

For a transitional period, until the SIS is capable of transmitting all the information described in Article 8, the alert shall be equivalent to a European arrest warrant pending the receipt of the original in due and proper form by the executing judicial authority.

Article 10

Detailed procedures for transmitting a European arrest warrant

1.   If the issuing judicial authority does not know the competent executing judicial authority, it shall make the requisite enquiries, including through the contact points of the European Judicial Network [Footnote 1: Council Joint Action 98/428/JHA of 29 June 1998 on the creation of a European Judicial Network (OJ L 191, 7.7.1998, p. 4).], in order to obtain that information from the executing Member State.

2. If the issuing judicial authority so wishes, transmission may be effected via the secure telecommunications system of the European Judicial Network.

3. If it is not possible to call on the services of the SIS, the issuing judicial authority may call on Interpol to transmit a European arrest warrant.

4. The issuing judicial authority may forward the European arrest warrant by any secure means capable of producing written records under conditions allowing the executing Member State to establish its authenticity.

5. All difficulties concerning the transmission or the authenticity of any document needed for the execution of the European arrest warrant shall be dealt with by direct contacts between the judicial authorities involved, or, where appropriate, with the involvement of the central authorities of the Member States.

6. If the authority which receives a European arrest warrant is not competent to act upon it, it shall automatically forward the European arrest warrant to the competent authority in its Member State and shall inform the issuing judicial authority accordingly.

Article 11

Rights of a requested person

1. When a requested person is arrested, the executing competent judicial authority shall, in accordance with its national law, inform that person of the European arrest warrant and of its contents, and also of the possibility of consenting to surrender to the issuing judicial authority.

2. A requested person who is arrested for the purpose of the execution of a European arrest warrant shall have a right to be assisted by a legal counsel and by an interpreter in accordance with the national law of the executing Member State.

Article 12

Keeping the person in detention

When a person is arrested on the basis of a European arrest warrant, the executing judicial authority shall take a decision on whether the requested person should remain in detention, in accordance with the law of the executing Member State. The person may be released provisionally at any time in conformity with the domestic law of the executing Member State, provided that the competent authority of the said Member State takes all the measures it deems necessary to prevent the person absconding.

Article 13

Consent to surrender

1. If the arrested person indicates that he or she consents to surrender, that consent and, if appropriate, express renunciation of entitlement to the 'speciality rule', referred to in Article 27(2), shall be given before the executing judicial authority, in accordance with the domestic law of the executing Member State.

2. Each Member State shall adopt the measures necessary to ensure that consent and, where appropriate, renunciation, as referred to in paragraph 1, are established in such a way as to show that the person concerned has expressed them voluntarily and in full awareness of the consequences. To that end, the requested person shall have the right to legal counsel.

3. The consent and, where appropriate, renunciation, as referred to in paragraph 1, shall be formally recorded in accordance with the procedure laid down by the domestic law of the executing Member State.

4. In principle, consent may not be revoked. Each Member State may provide that consent and, if appropriate, renunciation may be revoked, in accordance with the rules applicable under its domestic law. In this case, the period between the date of consent and that of its revocation shall not be taken into consideration in establishing the time limits laid down in Article 17. A Member State which wishes to have recourse to this possibility shall inform the General Secretariat of the Council accordingly when this Framework Decision is adopted and shall specify the procedures whereby revocation of consent shall be possible and any amendment to them.

Article 14

Hearing of the requested person

Where the arrested person does not consent to his or her surrender as referred to in Article 13, he or she shall be entitled to be heard by the executing judicial authority, in accordance with the law of the executing Member State.

Article 15

Surrender decision

1. The executing judicial authority shall decide, within the timelimits and under the conditions defined in this Framework Decision, whether the person is to be surrendered.

2. If the executing judicial authority finds the information communicated by the issuing Member State to be insufficient to allow it to decide on surrender, it shall request that the necessary supplementary information, in particular with respect to Articles 3 to 5 and

Article 8, be furnished as a matter of urgency and may fix a time limit for the receipt thereof, taking into account the need to observe the time limits set in Article 17.

3. The issuing judicial authority may at any time forward any additional useful information to the executing judicial authority.

Article 16

Decision in the event of multiple requests

1. If two or more Member States have issued European arrest warrants for the same person, the decision on which of the European arrest warrants shall be executed shall be taken by the executing judicial authority with due consideration of all the circumstances and especially the relative seriousness and place of the offences, the respective dates of the European arrest warrants and whether the warrant has been issued for the purposes of prosecution or for execution of a custodial sentence or detention order.

2. The executing judicial authority may seek the advice of Eurojust [Footnote 1: Council Decision 2002/187/JHA of 28 February 2002 setting up Eurojust with a view to reinforcing the fight against serious crime (OJ L 63, 6.3.2002, p.1).] when making the choice referred to in paragraph 1.

3. In the event of a conflict between a European arrest warrant and a request for extradition presented by a third country, the decision on whether the European arrest warrant or the extradition request takes precedence shall be taken by the competent authority of the executing Member State with due consideration of all the circumstances, in particular those referred to in paragraph 1 and those mentioned in the applicable convention.

4. This Article shall be without prejudice to Member States' obligations under the Statute of the International Criminal Court.

Article 17

Time limits and procedures for the decision to execute the European arrest warrant

1. A European arrest warrant shall be dealt with and executed as a matter of urgency.

2. In cases where the requested person consents to his surrender, the final decision on the execution of the European arrest warrant should be taken within a period of 10 days after consent has been given.

3. In other cases, the final decision on the execution of the European arrest warrant should be taken within a period of 60 days after the arrest of the requested person.

4. Where in specific cases the European arrest warrant cannot be executed within the time limits laid down in paragraphs 2 or 3, the executing judicial authority shall immediately inform the issuing judicial authority thereof, giving the reasons for the delay. In such case, the time limits may be extended by a further 30 days.

5. As long as the executing judicial authority has not taken a final decision on the European arrest warrant, it shall ensure that the material conditions necessary for effective surrender of the person remain fulfilled.

6. Reasons must be given for any refusal to execute a European arrest warrant.

7. Where in exceptional circumstances a Member State cannot observe the time limits provided for in this Article, it shall inform Eurojust, giving the reasons for the delay. In addition, a Member State which has experienced repeated delays on the part of another Member State in the execution of European arrest warrants shall inform the Council with a view to evaluating the implementation of this Framework Decision at Member State level.

Article 18

Situation pending the decision

1. Where the European arrest warrant has been issued for the purpose of conducting a criminal prosecution, the executing judicial authority must:

    (a) either agree that the requested person should be heard according to Article 19;

    (b) or agree to the temporary transfer of the requested person.

2. The conditions and the duration of the temporary transfer shall be determined by mutual agreement between the issuing and executing judicial authorities.

3. In the case of temporary transfer, the person must be able to return to the executing Member State to attend hearings concerning him or her as part of the surrender procedure.

Article 19

Hearing the person pending the decision

1. The requested person shall be heard by a judicial authority, assisted by another person designated in accordance with the law of the Member State of the requesting court.

2. The requested person shall be heard in accordance with the law of the executing Member State and with the conditions determined by

mutual agreement between the issuing and executing judicial authorities.

3. The competent executing judicial authority may assign another judicial authority of its Member State to take part in the hearing of the requested person in order to ensure the proper application of this Article and of the conditions laid down.

Article 20

Privileges and immunities

1. Where the requested person enjoys a privilege or immunity regarding jurisdiction or execution in the executing Member State, the time limits referred to in Article 17 shall not start running unless, and counting from the day when, the executing judicial authority is informed of the fact that the privilege or immunity has been waived. The executing Member State shall ensure that the material conditions necessary for effective surrender are fulfilled when the person no longer enjoys such privilege or immunity.

2. Where power to waive the privilege or immunity lies with an authority of the executing Member State, the executing judicial authority shall request it to exercise that power forthwith. Where power to waive the privilege or immunity lies with an authority of another State or international organisation, it shall be for the issuing judicial authority to request it to exercise that power.

Article 21

Competing international obligations

This Framework Decision shall not prejudice the obligations of the executing Member State where the requested person has been extradited to that Member State from a third State and where that person is protected by provisions of the arrangement under which he or she was extradited concerning speciality. The executing Member State shall take all necessary measures for requesting forthwith the consent of the State from which the requested person was extradited so that he or she can be surrendered to the Member State which issued the European arrest warrant. The time limits referred to in Article 17 shall not start running until the day on which these speciality rules cease to apply. Pending the decision of the State from which the requested person was extradited, the executing Member State will ensure that the material conditions necessary for effective surrender remain fulfilled.

Article 22

Notification of the decision

The executing judicial authority shall notify the issuing judicial authority immediately of the decision on the action to be taken on the European arrest warrant.

Article 23

Time limits for surrender of the person

1. The person requested shall be surrendered as soon as possible on a date agreed between the authorities concerned.

2. He or she shall be surrendered no later than 10 days after the final decision on the execution of the European arrest warrant.

3. If the surrender of the requested person within the period laid down in paragraph 2 is prevented by circumstances beyond the control of any of the Member States, the executing and issuing judicial authorities shall immediately contact each other and agree on a new surrender date. In that event, the surrender shall take place within 10 days of the new date thus agreed.

4. The surrender may exceptionally be temporarily postponed for serious humanitarian reasons, for example if there are substantial grounds for believing that it would manifestly endanger the requested person's life or health. The execution of the European arrest warrant shall take place as soon as these grounds have ceased to exist. The executing judicial authority shall immediately inform the issuing judicial authority and agree on a new surrender date. In that event, the surrender shall take place within 10 days of the new date thus agreed.

5. Upon expiry of the time limits referred to in paragraphs 2 to 4, if the person is still being held in custody he shall be released.

Article 24

Postponed or conditional surrender

1. The executing judicial authority may, after deciding to execute the European arrest warrant, postpone the surrender of the requested person so that he or she may be prosecuted in the executing Member State or, if he or she has already been sentenced, so that he or she may serve, in its territory, a sentence passed for an act other than that referred to in the European arrest warrant.

2. Instead of postponing the surrender, the executing judicial authority may temporarily surrender the requested person to the issuing Member State under conditions to be determined by mutual agreement between the executing and the issuing judicial authorities. The agreement shall be made in writing and the conditions shall be binding on all the authorities in the issuing Member State.

Article 25

Transit

1. Each Member State shall, except when it avails itself of the possibility of refusal when the transit of a national or a resident is

requested for the purpose of the execution of a custodial sentence or detention order, permit the transit through its territory of a requested person who is being surrendered provided that it has been given information on:

(a) the identity and nationality of the person subject to the European arrest warrant;

(b) the existence of a European arrest warrant;

(c) the nature and legal classification of the offence;

(d) the description of the circumstances of the offence, including the date and place.

Where a person who is the subject of a European arrest warrant for the purposes of prosecution is a national or resident of the Member State of transit, transit may be subject to the condition that the person, after being heard, is returned to the transit Member State to serve the custodial sentence or detention order passed against him in the issuing Member State.

2. Each Member State shall designate an authority responsible for receiving transit requests and the necessary documents, as well as any other official correspondence relating to transit requests. Member States shall communicate this designation to the General Secretariat of the Council.

3. The transit request and the information set out in paragraph 1 may be addressed to the authority designated pursuant to paragraph 2 by any means capable of producing a written record. The Member State of transit shall notify its decision by the same procedure.

4. This Framework Decision does not apply in the case of transport by air without a scheduled stopover. However, if an unscheduled landing occurs, the issuing Member State shall provide the authority designated pursuant to paragraph 2 with the information provided for in paragraph 1.

5. Where a transit concerns a person who is to be extradited from a third State to a Member State this Article will apply mutatis mutandis. In particular the expression 'European arrest warrant' shall be deemed to be replaced by 'extradition request'.

Chapter 3

Effects of the Surrender

Article 26

Deduction of the period of detention served in the executing Member State

1. The issuing Member State shall deduct all periods of detention arising from the execution of a European arrest warrant from the

total period of detention to be served in the issuing Member State as a result of a custodial sentence or detention order being passed.

2. To that end, all information concerning the duration of the detention of the requested person on the basis of the European arrest warrant shall be transmitted by the executing judicial authority or the central authority designated under Article 7 to the issuing judicial authority at the time of the surrender.

Article 27

Possible prosecution for other offences

1. Each Member State may notify the General Secretariat of the Council that, in its relations with other Member States that have given the same notification, consent is presumed to have been given for the prosecution, sentencing or detention with a view to the carrying out of a custodial sentence or detention order for an offence committed prior to his or her surrender, other than that for which he or she was surrendered, unless in a particular case the executing judicial authority states otherwise in its decision on surrender.

2. Except in the cases referred to in paragraphs 1 and 3, a person surrendered may not be prosecuted, sentenced or otherwise deprived of his or her liberty for an offence committed prior to his or her surrender other than that for which he or she was surrendered.

3. Paragraph 2 does not apply in the following cases:

    (a) when the person having had an opportunity to leave the territory of the Member State to which he or she has been surrendered has not done so within 45 days of his or her final discharge, or has returned to that territory after leaving it;

    (b) the offence is not punishable by a custodial sentence or detention order;

    (c) the criminal proceedings do not give rise to the application of a measure restricting personal liberty;

    (d) when the person could be liable to a penalty or a measure not involving the deprivation of liberty, in particular a financial penalty or a measure in lieu thereof, even if the penalty or measure may give rise to a restriction of his or her personal liberty;

    (e) when the person consented to be surrendered, where appropriate at the same time as he or she renounced the speciality rule, in accordance with Article 13;

    (f) when the person, after his/her surrender, has expressly renounced entitlement to the speciality rule with regard to specific offences preceding his/her surrender. Renunciation shall be given before the competent judicial authorities of the issuing Member State and shall be recorded in accordance with that State's domestic law. The renunciation shall be drawn up in such a way as to make clear that the person has given it voluntarily and in full awareness of the consequences. To that end, the person shall have the right to legal counsel;

(g) where the executing judicial authority which surrendered the person gives its consent in accordance with paragraph 4.

4. A request for consent shall be submitted to the executing judicial authority, accompanied by the information mentioned in Article 8(1) and a translation as referred to in Article 8(2). Consent shall be given when the offence for which it is requested is itself subject to surrender in accordance with the provisions of this Framework Decision. Consent shall be refused on the grounds referred to in Article 3 and otherwise may be refused only on the grounds referred to in Article 4. The decision shall be taken no later than 30 days after receipt of the request.

For the situations mentioned in Article 5 the issuing Member State must give the guarantees provided for therein.

Article 28

Surrender or subsequent extradition

1. Each Member State may notify the General Secretariat of the Council that, in its relations with other Member States which have given the same notification, the consent for the surrender of a person to a Member State other than the executing Member State pursuant to a European arrest warrant issued for an offence committed prior to his or her surrender is presumed to have been given, unless in a particular case the executing judicial authority states otherwise in its decision on surrender.

2. In any case, a person who has been surrendered to the issuing Member State pursuant to a European arrest warrant may, without the consent of the executing Member State, be surrendered to a Member State other than the executing Member State pursuant to a European arrest warrant issued for any offence committed prior to his or her surrender in the following cases:

(a) where the requested person, having had an opportunity to leave the territory of the Member State to which he or she has been surrendered, has not done so within 45 days of his final discharge, or has returned to that territory after leaving it;

(b) where the requested person consents to be surrendered to a Member State other than the executing Member State pursuant to a European arrest warrant. Consent shall be given before the competent judicial authorities of the issuing Member State and shall be recorded in accordance with that State's national law. It shall be drawn up in such a way as to make clear that the person concerned has given it voluntarily and in full awareness of the consequences. To that end, the requested person shall have the right to legal counsel;

(c) where the requested person is not subject to the speciality rule, in accordance with Article 27(3)(a), (e), (f) and (g).

3. The executing judicial authority consents to the surrender to another Member State according to the following rules:

(a) the request for consent shall be submitted in accordance with Article 9, accompanied by the information mentioned in Article 8(1) and a translation as stated in Article 8(2);

(b) consent shall be given when the offence for which it is requested is itself subject to surrender in accordance with the provisions of this Framework Decision;

(c) the decision shall be taken no later than 30 days after receipt of the request;

(d) consent shall be refused on the grounds referred to in Article 3 and otherwise may be refused only on the grounds referred to in Article 4.

For the situations referred to in Article 5, the issuing Member State must give the guarantees provided for therein.

4. Notwithstanding paragraph 1, a person who has been surrendered pursuant to a European arrest warrant shall not be extradited to a third State without the consent of the competent authority of the Member State which surrendered the person. Such consent shall be given in accordance with the Conventions by which that Member State is bound, as well as with its domestic law.

Article 29

Handing over of property

1. At the request of the issuing judicial authority or on its own initiative, the executing judicial authority shall, in accordance with its national law, seize and hand over property which:

(a) may be required as evidence, or

(b) has been acquired by the requested person as a result of the offence.

2. The property referred to in paragraph 1 shall be handed over even if the European arrest warrant cannot be carried out owing to the death or escape of the requested person.

3. If the property referred to in paragraph 1 is liable to seizure or confiscation in the territory of the executing Member State, the latter may, if the property is needed in connection with pending criminal proceedings, temporarily retain it or hand it over to the issuing Member State, on condition that it is returned.

4. Any rights which the executing Member State or third parties may have acquired in the property referred to in paragraph 1 shall be preserved. Where such rights exist, the issuing Member State shall return the property without charge to the executing Member State as soon as the criminal proceedings have been terminated.

Article 30

Expenses

1. Expenses incurred in the territory of the executing Member State for the execution of a European arrest warrant shall be borne by that Member State.

2. All other expenses shall be borne by the issuing Member State.

Chapter 4

General And Final Provisions

Article 31

Relation to other legal instruments

1. Without prejudice to their application in relations between Member States and third States, this Framework Decision shall, from 1 January 2004, replace the corresponding provisions of the following conventions applicable in the field of extradition in relations between the Member States:

   (a) the European Convention on Extradition of 13 December 1957, its additional protocol of 15 October 1975, its second additional protocol of 17 March 1978, and the European Convention on the suppression of terrorism of 27 January 1977 as far as extradition is concerned;

   (b) the Agreement between the 12 Member States of the European Communities on the simplification and modernisation of methods of transmitting extradition requests of 26 May 1989;

   (c) the Convention of 10 March 1995 on simplified extradition procedure between the Member States of the European Union;

   (d) the Convention of 27 September 1996 relating to extradition between the Member States of the European Union;

(e) Title III, Chapter 4 of the Convention of 19 June 1990 implementing the Schengen Agreement of 14 June 1985 on the gradual abolition of checks at common borders.

2. Member States may continue to apply bilateral or multilateral agreements or arrangements in force when this Framework Decision is adopted in so far as such agreements or arrangements allow the objectives of this Framework Decision to be extended or enlarged and help to simplify or facilitate further the procedures for surrender of persons who are the subject of European arrest warrants.

Member States may conclude bilateral or multilateral agreements or arrangements after this Framework Decision has come into force in so far as such agreements or arrangements allow the prescriptions of this Framework Decision to be extended or enlarged and help to simplify or facilitate further the procedures for surrender of persons who are the subject of European arrest warrants, in particular by fixing time limits shorter than those fixed in Article 17, by extending the list of offences laid down in Article 2(2), by further limiting the grounds for refusal set out in Articles 3 and 4, or by lowering the threshold provided for in Article 2(1) or (2).

The agreements and arrangements referred to in the second subparagraph may in no case affect relations with Member States which are not parties to them.

Member States shall, within three months from the entry into force of this Framework Decision, notify the Council and the Commission of the existing agreements and arrangements referred to in the first subparagraph which they wish to continue applying.

Member States shall also notify the Council and the Commission of any new agreement or arrangement as referred to in the second subparagraph, within three months of signing it.

3. Where the conventions or agreements referred to in paragraph 1 apply to the territories of Member States or to territories for whose external relations a Member State is responsible to which this Framework Decision does not apply, these instruments shall continue to govern the relations existing between those territories and the other Members States.

Article 32

Transitional provision

1. Extradition requests received before 1 January 2004 will continue to be governed by existing instruments relating to extradition. Requests received after that date will be governed by the rules adopted by Member States pursuant to this Framework Decision. However, any Member State may, at the time of the adoption of this Framework Decision by the Council, make a statement indicating that as executing Member State it will continue to deal with requests relating to acts committed before a date which it specifies in accordance with the extradition system applicable before 1 January 2004.

The date in question may not be later than 7 August 2002. The said statement will be published in the Official Journal of the European Communities. It may be withdrawn at any time.

Article 33

Provisions concerning Austria and Gibraltar

1. As long as Austria has not modified Article 12(1) of the 'Ausliefer-ungs- und Rechtshilfegesetz' and, at the latest, until 31 December 2008, it may allow its executing judicial authorities to refuse the enforcement of a European arrest warrant if the requested person is an Austrian citizen and if the act for which the European arrest warrant has been issued is not punishable under Austrian law.

2. This Framework Decision shall apply to Gibraltar.

Article 34

Implementation

1. Member States shall take the necessary measures to comply with the provisions of this Framework Decision by 31 December 2003.

2. Member States shall transmit to the General Secretariat of the Council and to the Commission the text of the provisions transposing into their national law the obligations imposed on them under this Framework Decision. When doing so, each Member State may indicate that it will apply immediately this Framework Decision in its relations with those Member States which have given the same notification.

The General Secretariat of the Council shall communicate to the Member States and to the Commission the information received pursuant to Article 7(2), Article 8(2), Article 13(4) and Article 25(2). It shall also have the information published in the Official Journal of the European Communities.

3. On the basis of the information communicated by the General Secretariat of the Council, the Commission shall, by 31 December 2004 at the latest, submit a report to the European Parliament and to the Council on the operation of this Framework Decision, accompanied, where necessary, by legislative proposals.

4. The Council shall in the second half of 2003 conduct a review, in particular of the practical application, of the provisions of this Framework Decision by the Member States as well as the functioning of the Schengen Information System.

Article 35

Entry into force

This Framework Decision shall enter into force on the twentieth day following that of its publication in the Official Journal of the European Communities.

Done at Luxembourg, 13 June 2002.

For the Council

The President

M. RAJOY BREY

ANNEX

EUROPEAN ARREST WARRANT[*]

This warrant has been issued by a competent judicial authority. I request that the person mentioned below be arrested and surrendered for the purposes of conducting a criminal prosecution or executing a custodial sentence or detention order.

(a) Information regarding the identity of the requested person: .....

Name: ....

Forename(s): ....

Maiden name, where applicable: ....

Aliases, where applicable: ....

Sex: ..

Nationality: ....

Date of birth: ....

Place of birth: ....

Residence and/or known address: ....

Language(s) which the requested person understands (if known): ......

....

Distinctive marks/description of the requested person: ....

....

Photo and fingerprints of the requested person, if they are available and can be transmitted, or contact details of the person to be contacted in order to obtain such information or a DNA profile (where this evidence can be supplied but has not been included)

---

[*] This warrant must be written in, or translated into, one of the official languages of the executing Member State, when that State is known, or any other language accepted by that State.

    (b) Decision on which the warrant is based:

1. Arrest warrant or judicial decision having the same effect: ....

....

Type:

2. Enforceable judgement:

....

....

Reference..

    (c) Indications on the length of the sentence:

1. Maximum length of the custodial sentence or detention order which
   may be imposed for the offence(s):

....

....

2. Length of the custodial sentence or detention order imposed:

....

Remaining sentence to be served: ....

....

....

    (d) Decision rendered in absentia and:

— the person concerned has been summoned in person or otherwise
  informed of the date and place of the hearing which led to the decision rendered in absentia,

or

— the person concerned has not been summoned in person or otherwise informed of the date and place of the hearing which led to the
  decision rendered in absentia but has the following legal guarantees after surrender (such guarantees can be given in advance)

Specify the legal guarantees

....

....

....

(e) Offences:

This warrant relates to in total: .... offences.

Description of the circumstances in which the offence(s) was (were) committed, including the time, place and degree of participation in the offence(s) by the requested person:

....

....

....

Nature and legal classification of the offence(s) and the applicable statutory provision/code: ....
....

I.   If applicable, tick one or more of the following offences punishable in the issuing Member State by a custodial sentence or detention order of a maximum of at least 3 years as defined by the laws of the issuing Member State:

☐   participation in a criminal organisation;

☐   terrorism;

☐   trafficking in human beings;

☐   sexual exploitation of children and child pornography;

☐   illicit trafficking in narcotic drugs and psychotropic substances;

☐   illicit trafficking in weapons, munitions and explosives;

☐   corruption;

☐   fraud, including that affecting the financial interests of the European Communities within the meaning of the Convention of 26 July 1995 on the protection of European Communities' financial interests;

☐   laundering of the proceeds of crime;

☐   counterfeiting of currency, including the euro;

☐   computer-related crime;

☐   environmental crime, including illicit trafficking in endangered animal species and in endangered plant species and varieties;

☐   facilitation of unauthorised entry and residence;

☐   murder, grievous bodily injury;

- ☐ illicit trade in human organs and tissue;

- ☐ kidnapping, illegal restraint and hostage-taking;

- ☐ racism and xenophobia;

- ☐ organised or armed robbery;

- ☐ illicit trafficking in cultural goods, including antiques and works of art;

- ☐ swindling;

- ☐ racketeering and extortion;

- ☐ counterfeiting and piracy of products;

- ☐ forgery of administrative documents and trafficking therein;

- ☐ forgery of means of payment;

- ☐ illicit trafficking in hormonal substances and other growth promoters;

- ☐ illicit trafficking in nuclear or radioactive materials;

- ☐ trafficking in stolen vehicles;

- ☐ rape;

- ☐ arson;

- ☐ crimes within the jurisdiction of the International Criminal Court;

- ☐ unlawful seizure of aircraft/ships;

- ☐ sabotage.

II. Full descriptions of offence(s) not covered by section I above:

....

....

(f) Other circumstances relevant to the case (optional information):

(NB: This could cover remarks on extraterritoriality, interruption of periods of time limitation and other consequences of the offence)

....

....

(g) This warrant pertains also to the seizure and handing over of property which may be required as evidence:

This warrant pertains also to the seizure and handing over of property acquired by the requested person as a result of the offence:

Description of the property (and location) (if known):

....

....

....

(h) The offence(s) on the basis of which this warrant has been issued is(are) punishable by/has(have) led to a custodial life sentence or lifetime detention order:

— the legal system of the issuing Member State allows for a review of the penalty or measure imposed — on request or at least after 20 years — aiming at a nonexecution of such penalty or measure,

and/or

— the legal system of the issuing Member State allows for the application of measures of clemency to which the person is entitled under the law or practice of the issuing Member State, aiming at non-execution of such penalty or measure.

(i) The judicial authority which issued the warrant:

Official name:

Name of its representative*: ....

....

Post held (title/grade): ....

....

File reference: ....

Address: ....

....

Tel: (country code) (area/city code) (...) ....

Fax: (country code) (area/city code) (...) ....

---

* In the different language versions a reference to the "holder" of the judicial authority will be included.

E-mail: ....

Contact details of the person to contact to make necessary practical arrangements for the surrender: ....

....

_____

Where a central authority has been made responsible for the transmission and administrative reception of European arrest warrants:

Name of the central authority:

....

Contact person, if applicable (title/grade and name):

....

Address: ....

....

Tel: (country code) (area/city code) (...) ....

Fax: (country code) (area/city code) (...) ....

E-mail: ....

_____

Signature of the issuing judicial authority and/or its representative:

....

Name: ...

Post held (title/grade):

....

Date: .....

Official stamp (if available)

_____

STATEMENTS MADE BY CERTAIN MEMBER STATES ON THE ADOPTION OF THE FRAMEWORK DECISION

Statement provided for in Article 32

Statement made by France:

Pursuant to Article 32 of the framework decision on the European arrest warrant and the surrender procedures between Member States, France states that as executing Member State it will continue to deal with requests relating to acts committed before 1 November 1993, the date of entry into force of the Treaty on European Union signed in Maastricht on 7 February 1992, in accordance with the extradition system applicable before 1 January 2004.

Statement by Italy:

Italy will continue to deal in accordance with the extradition rules in force with all request relating to acts committed before the date of entry into force of the framework decision on the European arrest warrant, as provided for in Article 32 thereof.

Statement by Austria:

Pursuant to Article 32 of the framework decision on the European arrest warrant and the surrender procedures between Member States, Austria states that as executing Member State it will continue to deal with requests relating to punishable acts committed before the date of entry into force of the framework decision in accordance with the extradition system applicable before that date.

Statements provided for in Article 13(4)

Statement by Belgium:

The consent of the person concerned to his or her surrender may be revoked until the time of surrender.

Statement by Denmark:

Consent to surrender and express renunciation of entitlement to the 'specialty rule' may be revoked in accordance with the relevant rules applicable at any time under Danish law.

Statement by Ireland:

In Ireland, consent to surrender and, where appropriate, express renunciation of the entitlement to the 'specialty rule' referred to in Article 27(2) may be revoked. Consent may be revoked in accordance with domestic law until surrender has been executed.

Statement by Finland:

In Finland, consent to surrender and, where appropriate, express renunciation of entitlement to the 'specialty rule' referred to in Article 27(2) may be revoked. Consent may be revoked in accordance with domestic law until surrender has been executed.

Statement by Sweden:

Consent or renunciation within the meaning of Article 13(1) may be revoked by the party whose surrender has been requested. Revocation must take place before the decision on surrender is executed.

INDEX

A

Absconding test [5–32]
Air Navigation and Transport Act 1973 [12–32]
"Alert"
    definition [5–46]
    in SIS system [5–47]
    use of [5–48], [5–49]
Appeals
    see also Bail; McKechnie J
    case-law [9–06]
    certification [9–03], [9–04]
        effects of [9–12], [9–13]
        in Supreme Court [9–14]
        without [9–15], [9–16], [9–17]
    requirements [9–09], [9–10], [9–11]
    restrictions on [9–05], [9–08]
    scope of [9–02]
    stay pending [9–18], [9–20], [9–21]
        case-law [9–19]
Area of freedom and security
    creating [1–14], [1–17]
Arrest [5–01], [5–50]
    see also Bail; Post-Arrest Procedure; Voluntary surrender
    delay in [5–13]
        state's [5–14]
    due process [5–04]
    execution application [5–12]
    High Court [5–18]
        custody/bail [5–28], [5–29]
        identified before [5–19], [5–20]
            case-law [5–23]
            dis/satisfied [5–24]
            fingerprints/photographs [5–20], [5–21]
            without prejudice [5–22]
    rights of respondent [5–26], [5–27]
    strict procedure [5–02], [5–03]
    upon arrest [5–16], [5–17]
    warrant endorsed [5–06]
        respondents' entitlements [5–08], [5–09]
            difficulties [5–10], [5–11]
        to be shown [5–07]
Art 40 *see* Constitution, the
Article 2.2 offence *see* Correspondence

Criminal Justice Act 1984 [10–95], [10–96]
Criminal Justice Act 1991 [12–47]
Criminal Justice (Public Order) Act 1994 [10–123], [10–124]
Criminal Justice (Theft and Fraud Offences) Act 2001 [10–44], [10–45], [10–47], [10–51], [10–52], [10–97], [10–98], [10–99]
Criminal Justice (Terrorist Offences) Act 2005 [1–38], [3–07], [3–15], [6–01], [7–10], [7–14], [8–12], [10–26]
Criminal Justice (Miscellaneous Provisions) Act 2009 [1–39], [3–11], [3–36], [5–42], [6–08], [7–14], [9–01], [9–18], [9–24]
Criminal Law (Jurisdiction) Act 1976 [12–33]
Criminal Law Act 1997 [12–26], [12–47]
Czech Republic [1–66]
    Code of Criminal Procedure of the [13–33]

D

Denham, J [1–46], [1–56], [1–57]
    Article 2.2 offence [10–19]
    bad faith prosecution [16–63]
    bail pending appeal [9–23]
    blameworthy prosecutorial delay [16–52]
    evidential burden [16–108]
    lawful arrest [5–16]
    nature of hearing [7–01]
    surrender time limits [8–04]
    undertakings [7–35]
Denmark
    judicial authorities [2–13]
Designated State [2–04]
Detention
    see also Peart, J
    credit against sentencing [8–50]
    reducing time spent [8–48], [8–49]
Detention Orders [1–55]
    definition [1–56]
        broad [3–17], [3–18], [3–19]
Discovery [6–16]
    see also Peart, J
    case-law [6–17], [6–18]
    no presumption [6–23]
Domestic warrant [2–03]
    production ordered [6–21], [6–22], [6–25]
Double construction test [1–51]
Double/dual criminality [1–27], [10–02]
    versus principle of reciprocity [12–14]
"Duly issued" *see* European Arrest Warrant Act 2003
Dutch Narcotics Act [2–41]
Dyson, LJ
    minor offences [11–23]

E

L

Lateran Council, 4th [12–02]
Latham, LJ [2–31]
Latvia
    "First Instance Riga Vidzeme Suburb Court of the Republic of Latvia" [8–20],
        [8–21], [8–22], [8–23]
    surrender time limits [8–18], [8–19]
"Legal counsel" [6–02]
Lithuania
    criticisms of [2–12]
    "Lithuanian Minister for Justice" [2–10]
    Lithuanian Penal Code [3–28], [3–29], [13–30]
    prison conditions [16–91], [16–92], [16–93]
        improving [16–94], [16–95]
    "Prosecutor General of the Republic of Lithuania" [2–08], [2–09], [2–72]
London Underground Bombings [12–20]

M

Macken, J [6–13]
    legitimate expectation [16–68], [16–69], [16–70]
    minimum gravity [11–03], [11–16]
Maritime Security Act 2004 [12–30]
McKechie, J [1–14], [1–24]
    right of appeal [9–06], [9–07]
        without certification [9–16]
McMenamin, J [1–52]
    judicial authorities [2–08], [2–09]
Member States
    diverse criminal processes [3–31]
Minimum gravity [11–01]
    see also Principle of proportionality
    aggravated offences [11–12]
    Article 2.2 offences [11–06]
    composite sentences [11–13], [11–14], [11–15]
        case-law [11–16], [11–17], [11–18], [11–20]
            in House of Lords [11–19]
    corresponding Irish offence [11–10], [11–11]
    pre-conviction [11–07], [11–08], [11–09]
    requirements [11–02]
        in Framework Decision [11–03]
        prison sentence [11–04], [11–05]
Misuse of Drugs Act 1977 [10–91]
Morris, LJ
    ne bis in idem [15–32], [15–33]
Multiple offences *see* European Arrest Warrant; Murray, CJ
Murray, CJ [6–17]
    bail pending surrender [8–41]

T

U